Diderot

AND THE ART OF
THINKING FREELY

ANDREW S. CURRAN

 Other Press New York

Production editor: Yvonne E. Cárdenas
This book was set in Californian with Didot.

10 9 8 7 6 5 4 3 2 1

Library of Congress Cataloging-in-Publication Data
Names: Curran, Andrew S., author.
Title: Diderot and the art of thinking freely / Andrew S. Curran.
Description: New York : Other Press, [2019] | Includes bibliographical
    references and index.
Identifiers: LCCN 2018019273 (print) | LCCN 2018046590 (ebook) |
    ISBN 9781590516720 (ebook) | ISBN 9781590516706 (hardcover)
Subjects: LCSH: Diderot, Denis, 1713–1784. | Philosophers — France —
    Biography.
Classification: LCC B2016 (ebook) | LCC B2016 .C87 2019 (print) |
    DDC 194 — dc23
LC record available at https://lccn.loc.gov/2018019273

For Jen

Contents

Prologue

UNBURYING DIDEROT

Sometime during the snowy winter of 1793, under cover of night, a small group of thieves pried open a wooden door leading into the Church of Saint-Roch. Forced entry into the Paris sanctuary was nearly a weekly occurrence during this time of revolution. In the early 1790s, anticlerical vandals had pulled enormous religious paintings off the walls and slashed the canvases. Other trespassers had made off with more portable works of art, including an exquisite statue sculpted by Étienne-Maurice Falconet. On this particular night, however, the intruders came to steal whatever copper, silver, or lead they could find in the crypt located underneath the Chapel of the Virgin. Setting to work in front of the chapel's altar, the grave robbers used long iron bars to lever aside the mattress-sized marble slab in the center of the floor. Though they surely had no idea who was buried in the vault, the most loutish of the group, assuming he could read, would still have recognized the name of the writer Denis Diderot inscribed on one of the caskets. Dead for nine years, the notorious atheist had been the driving force behind the most controversial book project of the eighteenth century, the *Encyclopédie*.

This massive dictionary had not only dragged sacrilege and free-thinking out into the open, but triggered a decades-long scandal that involved the Sorbonne, the Paris Parlement, the Jesuits, the Jansenists, the king, and the pope.

None of this old history mattered to the burglars. After removing Diderot's lead coffin from the vault, the men simply shook his decomposing body onto the church's marble floor. The following day, Denis Diderot's remains (along with the other desecrated cadavers from the crypt) were presumably gathered up and transferred without ceremony to a mass grave about a mile to the east.[1] Nobody noticed; nobody reported it in the press. Assuming the church's few remaining parish priests had realized that Diderot had been buried in the church, they were undoubtedly relieved to be rid of the scandalous unbeliever.

Some twenty years before his remains were carted out of Saint-Roch, Diderot had prophetically remarked that whether "you rot beneath marble or under the ground, you still rot."[2] Yet being discarded and forgotten among a mound of recently guillotined aristocratic corpses would not have been his preference. Atheist or not, Diderot had long expressed a keen interest in being remembered and, if all things worked out, celebrated by future generations. "Posterity is to the philosophe," he once stated, as "heaven is to the man of religion."[3]

Diderot's interest in speaking to future generations from beyond the grave had come about out of necessity. In 1749, shortly after the then thirty-four-year-old writer had published a work of intemperate atheism entitled the *Lettre sur les aveugles* (*Letter on the Blind*), two gendarmes showed up at his house, arrested him, and dragged him off to Vincennes prison. Three months later, shortly before he was released, the lieutenant-général de police made a special trip to the prison to warn the writer that any further immoral or irreligious publications would bring about a jail sentence measured in decades, not months.

Diderot took this threat seriously. For the next thirty-three years, he avoided publishing the kind of inflammatory books that he had authored as a young man. Much of the energy that he might have devoted to such endeavors was redirected toward the all-consuming *Encyclopédie*. When he finally completed the last volume of illustrations, in 1772, the now-elderly writer was well aware that he was a celebrity throughout Europe and even in parts of North America, but he was not really considered a literary great. His fate, as he admitted quite openly, was perhaps to "survive" long after his reputation as an *Encyclopedist* had faded, growing ever older and vanishing without leaving a significant work behind.[4] This, in fact, seemed to be the case when he died in 1784. Although several obituaries credited him for being the leader of the generation of thinkers that had utterly changed the country, they also hinted that he had not lived up to his indisputable genius.[5] Even his friends reluctantly agreed. Jacques-Henri Meister, who revered the man, wistfully acknowledged that Diderot never produced a book that would have placed him among the first tier of "our philosophes or our poets."[6]

Charitable friends blamed the writer's supposedly limited literary production on the burden of the *Encyclopédie*. Others privately ascribed this failing to his famously whirligig brain. As was often the case, the sharp-tongued Voltaire, who both admired and distrusted Diderot, came up with the cleverest remark on the subject; he apparently joked that the Encyclopedist's mind "was an oven that burns everything that it cooks."[7]

What Voltaire and virtually everybody else did not know was

that Diderot had actually written an astonishing range of improbably modern books and essays *for the drawer*, as the French like to say. Holed up in his sixth-floor garret office on the rue Taranne for the last third of his life, Diderot produced this cache of writing with the hope that it might one day explode like a bomb. This moment was prepared for carefully. When the author reached his sixties — borrowed time during the eighteenth century — he hired copyists to produce three separate collections of manuscripts. The first and most complete set was entrusted to his daughter, Angélique, whom we know as Madame de Vandeul; a second, less complete group of writings was transferred to his designated literary heir and devotee, Jacques-André Naigeon. And six months after his death, thirty-two bound volumes of manuscripts along with Diderot's entire library of three thousand books traveled by ship to Catherine the Great in Saint Petersburg.

Diderot's unedited books, essays, and criticism far surpassed what he had published during his lifetime. Among these writings were two very dissimilar, but equally brilliant novels. The first of these, *La religieuse* (*The Nun*), is a gripping pseudo-memoir of a nun who suffers unspeakably cruel abuse after she announces that she wants to leave her convent. The second, *Jacques le fataliste*, is an open-ended antinovel where Diderot used fiction to take up the problem of free will. But there were also thick notebooks of revolutionary art criticism, a godless science-fiction-like chronicle of the human race, a secret political treatise written for Catherine the Great, a humorous satire on the absurdity of Christian sexual mores set in Tahiti, as well as some of the most moving love letters in the history of French literature. To become familiar with the range of Diderot's work is to be stupefied: among other things, the philosophe dreamed of natural selection before Darwin, the Oedipus complex before Freud, and genetic manipulation two hundred years before Dolly the Sheep was engineered.

These hidden works did not appear in the months after Diderot died; they trickled out over the course of decades. Several of his lost books were published during the waning years of the French Revolution; others appeared during the course of the Bourbon Restoration (1814–30), while still more of his writing emerged during the Second Empire (1852–70). Perhaps the most significant addition to Diderot's corpus came in 1890 when a librarian discovered a complete manuscript version of Diderot's masterpiece, *Le neveu de Rameau* (*Rameau's Nephew*), in a *bouquiniste*'s stand on the banks of the Seine. In this riotous philosophical dialogue, the writer courageously gave life to an unforgettable antihero who extolled the virtues of evil and social parasitism while preaching the right to unbridled pleasure.

To say that the arrival of these lost books had an effect on subsequent generations would be putting it mildly. Diderot's effusive art criticism inspired Stendhal, Balzac, and Baudelaire. Émile Zola credited Diderot's "vivisections" of society as the foundation of the naturalism that characterized his and Balzac's novels.[8] Social theorists, too, were spellbound by Diderot's prescient thought. Karl Marx, who borrowed deeply from Diderot's musings on class struggle, listed the writer as his favorite author.[9] And Sigmund Freud credited the ancien régime thinker for recognizing the unconscious psychosexual desires of childhood in *Rameau's Nephew* long before he or his fellow psychoanalysts had.[10] If many critics continued to disdain the writer as too atheistic, too paradoxical, and too unrestrained, Diderot was nonetheless becoming the preferred writer of the nineteenth-century avant-garde.[11]

The full extent of Diderot's influence was not truly known, however, until a young German-American academic, Herbert Dieckmann, located the final lost cache of Diderot's writings. Having heard rumors that Diderot's conservative descendants continued to possess some of the lost manuscripts originally given to the writer's daughter, the Harvard professor finally obtained permission to visit the family château in Normandy in 1948. After overcoming the postwar suspicions of the caretaker, who was initially put off by his German-accented French, Dieckmann was ultimately directed to some armoires on the château's second floor. Entering a room that contained several large freestanding closets, he sidled over to the first one and peeled back the door panel. Hoping, perhaps, to find a lost work or two, he was confronted with an enormous stockpile of Diderot's bound manuscripts. So stunned was Dieckmann that he simply dropped to the floor. Diderot's final cache, the lost collection of manuscripts he had given to his daughter, had at last been found.

What are now known as the Vandeul archives—labeled as such since they came from Diderot's daughter—have become the most important source for what we know about Diderot and his works. Most astonishing, perhaps, was the discovery of several manuscripts annotated in his hand that revealed that he had been the primary ghostwriter for abbé Raynal's *Histoire philosophique et politique des deux Indes* (*Philosophical and Political History of the Two Indies*), the best-selling critical examination of European colonization. It had been Diderot, as it turned out, who had penned the most influential and best-known anticolonial sections of this multivolume book, including an imagined exchange between an enslaved African who not only claimed the right to be free, but who predicted a day when Caribbean slaves would justifiably put their masters to the sword. Composed in 1779, a decade before the events in Saint-Domingue (Haiti) would prove him right, this is perhaps the most telling example of the writer's radical politics, not to mention his ability to see into the future.

Some three hundred years after he was born, Diderot has now become the most relevant of Enlightenment philosophers. That he refrained from publishing (or taking credit for) his most forward-looking ideas during his lifetime was not simply a matter of avoiding persecution; he intentionally chose to forgo a conversation with his contemporaries in order to have a more fruitful dialogue with later generations — us, in short. His heartfelt hope was that we, the sympathetic and enlightened interlocutors of the future, might finally be capable of sitting in judgment of his hidden writings, writings that not only question the moral, aesthetic, political, and philosophical conventions of the ancien régime, but our own as well.

PORTRAYING DIDEROT

Despite repeated allusions to the importance of posterity, Diderot has not made life easy for his biographers. A more cooperative subject would have left behind a trail of uninterrupted correspondence, the raw material for a tidy account of the author's acts, words, and interior world. What Diderot handed down to us, especially from his early years, is a comparative wasteland. Of the hundreds of letters that he presumably sent before the age of thirty, only thirteen remain. This dearth of primary sources is compounded by the philosophe's relative silence about his youth. In contrast to Jean-Jacques Rousseau, who plunged deeply into his earliest memories in a quest to identify his own inner truth,

Diderot studiously refused to look back in any substantive way at the years he spent growing up in his small citadel-like hometown of Langres. The writer is similarly unhelpful regarding his later adolescence and young adulthood, sharing precious little information about his studies at the collège d'Harcourt and the Sorbonne, and never detailing the precise reasons why he, an aspiring ecclesiastic, grew into the most prominent atheist of his era.

What we lack in terms of early correspondence is perhaps compensated by the multiple, overlapping descriptions of Diderot provided by his friends and associates. By the 1750s, people began calling him *le philosophe* (*the* philosopher as opposed to *a* philosopher). Some of this had to do with his legendary appetite for learning. The man was a *pantophile*, according to Voltaire: the type of thinker who falls desperately in love with every subject he studies, be it mathematics, sciences, medicine, philosophy, politics, classical antiquity, drama, literature, musicology, or the fine arts. This passion for learning made him seem like an ancient truth-seeker, a simple and "honest soul" who was "born without ambition."[12] But his friends also dubbed him *le philosophe* because he had become the greatest advocate for the emancipatory power of philosophy. Far more than Voltaire, Diderot was the face of an increasingly vocal and skeptical opposition to all received ideas: the embodiment of an era that was subjecting religion, politics, contemporary mores, and a whole host of other notions to withering interrogation. His *Encyclopédie* summed up this mission quite succinctly when it said that the role of the philosophe is to "trample underfoot prejudice, tradition, antiquity, shared covenants, authority—in a word, everything that controls the mind of the common herd."[13]

Much of Diderot's celebrity came from his status as a prominent man of letters. The rest stemmed from his abilities as a conversationalist or, perhaps more accurately, as a man who excelled at the art of talking. Spending time with Diderot—a thinker who not only wrote seven thousand wildly divergent articles for the *Encyclopédie*, but had an accompanying ability to bring together the most disparate realms of knowledge—was apparently an overwhelming and often exhausting experience. Goethe and Madame de Staël, neither of whom ever met the philosophe, knew that, by reputation, no one's conversation ever surpassed Diderot's in liveliness, strength, wit, variety, and grace.[14] Rousseau called him an "astonishing, universal, perhaps singular genius."[15] Friedrich Melchior Grimm, Diderot's most cherished friend and colleague, marveled at the "force and violent leaps of his imagination."[16] And the same Jacques Henri Meister who lamented Diderot's inability to produce a great stand-alone work of literature, also stood in awe at the way that his friend's brain worked. Diderot, according to Meister, actually had little influence over his extravagant mind; it was, rather, the philosophe's own thoughts that led him around without his "being able to either stop or control their movement."[17] Once he began chasing his own ideas, Diderot was a man possessed, flitting about rapidly and lightly from one extravagant notion to the next, like a goldfinch in a tree.

The anecdote most illustrative of Diderot's intellectual exuberance comes from Catherine the Great. In a now-lost letter that apparently circulated in Paris in the 1770s, the Russian monarch recounted that when Diderot came to the Hermitage, she ordered that a table be put between them during their meetings because the philosophe, who often went into fevered monologues, had gotten in the habit of grabbing her knees and slapping her thighs to make a point.[18]

Various stories and anecdotes have left us with a complex, mosaiclike image of the philosophe. But we have also inherited the writer's own comments about how he might best be remembered. Diderot generated most of these autobiographical insights, as it turns out, when he discussed the portraits, drawings, and marble busts that the century's artists created in his likeness. That he took the time to speak about his personality, psychology, and even physical size while contemplating these artworks is hardly a surprise: on numerous occasions he affirmed that such portraits absolutely "needed to be well painted in the interest of posterity."[19] These were the images, he assumed correctly, around which his legacy would crystallize.

DENIS DIDEROT, ENGRAVING
BY PIERRE CHENU AFTER GARAND

The most accurate likeness of the writer, in Diderot's own opinion, was painted in September 1760 by a wandering, virtually unknown artist named Jean-Baptiste Garand, who chanced to meet the philosophe at the Château de la Chevrette, the picturesque country estate outside of Paris belonging to his friend and fellow writer, Louise d'Épinay. The forty-seven-year-old Diderot had been an ideal model for Garand, having been confined to a chair after running into a shin-level metal bar while chasing swans around the château's fountain.[20] Garand's oil portrait, which is now lost, depicted Diderot serenely holding his head in his right hand. "Whoever sees [this] portrait," wrote Diderot, "sees me."[21]

Diderot's most recognized portrait was executed by one of his friends, Louis-Michel van Loo. As one of the better-known portrait painters of Louis XV, van Loo had an indisputable talent for conveying political power, authority, and luxury.[22] In many ways, the wigless Diderot, who preferred his well-worn black suit to either silks or velvets, was hardly a worthy subject. Van Loo nonetheless accepted this artistic challenge, and attempted to imbue his friend's image with the same nobility he attributed to his more stately subjects. Posing the philosophe behind what was presumably a paint-spattered table in his studio in the Louvre, the artist placed a quill in the writer's right hand, and asked his subject to imagine himself deep in thought.

Diderot came face-to-face with the final version of the canvas in the summer of 1767, when he attended the Royal Academy of Painting and Sculpture's biennial Salon, which took place at the Louvre. The portrait, hung at eye level along with the images of dozens of other notables, was received as a triumph of virtuosity. Van Loo's Diderot sits serenely on a caned chair in front of an inkwell and a small pile of folded manuscripts. In contrast to the timeworn and ink-streaked *robe de chambre* (dressing gown) that the writer actually wore in his office on the rue Taranne, van Loo painted his friend wearing a luxurious, iridescent blue-gray banyan of shot silk that falls softly over a matching waistcoat. As the philosophe looks off to the right, a gentle light lands softly on his compassionate, heavy-lidded brown eyes and protruding forehead. Van Loo clearly sought not only to capture a moment in the busy workday of the philosophe, but to canonize the man and his career.

DENIS DIDEROT, PAINTING BY LOUIS-MICHEL VAN LOO

When the Salon concluded in September, van Loo very generously gave the portrait to Diderot. He was moved. The writer acknowledged that it certainly looked like him and lost no time hanging it over his daughter Angélique's harpsichord in the family apartment. Yet the art critic in him was also secretly disappointed that van Loo did not convey his heft, his height, and the fact that, as he wrote elsewhere, he was built like a porter. Working himself into a tizzy as he contemplated the portrait, Diderot declares that van Loo's static and formulaic composition failed to capture his defining characteristic, his profound mutability. He then cautions his descendants — and us — that he is a difficult subject to grasp. This charming rant culminates with him speaking directly to his own likeness, whom he calls his "pretty philosopher":

> My pretty philosopher, you will always serve me as precious testimony to the friendship of an artist, an excellent artist, and a more excellent man. But what will my grandchildren say, when they compare my sad works to this smiling, affected, effeminate old flirt? My children, I warn you that this is not me. In the course of a single day I assumed a hundred different expressions, in accordance with the things that affected me. I was serene, sad, pensive, tender, violent, passionate, enthusiastic. But I was never such as you see me here.[23]

Throughout his career, Diderot often emphasized how quickly his volatile mood and mind shifted. On one occasion, he famously compared his spirit to a weathercock that moves with the prevailing wind.[24] On another, he equated his thoughts with the passing harlots that young rogues might pursue, willy-nilly, through the Palais Royal pleasure gardens.[25] This is not evidence

of capriciousness or flightiness, as some people have said about
Diderot, but his bloodhoundlike eagerness to pursue any idea,
wherever it went.

Years of reading, thinking, and writing about this dazzling
intellect have convinced me that our era can learn a lot from
Diderot. Yet doing justice to a man who might write on ancient
Chinese and Greek music first thing in the morning, study the
mechanics of a cotton mill until noon, help purchase some paintings for Catherine the Great in the afternoon, and then return
home and compose a play and a twenty-page letter to his mistress
in the evening, is as challenging as it is enchanting. To render
this complex and busy life understandable, particularly for those
people who do not know Diderot well, this book begins with
a chronicle of the successive stages in the future philosophe's
existence: the aspiring ecclesiastic in the small city of Langres,
the student and increasingly skeptical freethinker in Paris, the
atheist and prisoner of the state, and, finally, the century's most
famous Encyclopedist. The second half of the book is more thematic, and corresponds more or less to the period in Diderot's
life during which he censored himself, creating a series of unpublished masterpieces (c. 1760–84) that ultimately sowed the seeds
for the greatest late harvest of the Enlightenment era. Here I focus
on the compelling questions that preoccupied Diderot during his
lifetime. What is the incentive to be moral in a world without
God? How should we appreciate art? What does it mean to be
human, and where do we come from? What is sex? What is love?
And how might a writer or philosophe effectively intervene in
political affairs? These chapters tend to coincide with some of the
many roles that the writer played in life: that of the playwright,

the art critic, the science fiction writer, the sexologist, the moralist, the father, the lover, and the political theorist and commentator. They also remind us why Diderot was the most creative and noteworthy thinker of his era, even though he chose primarily to speak to those who came after it.

PART ONE

FORBIDDEN FRUITS

I forbade you from eating this fruit to prevent your ruin.
What excuse do you have for being disobedient?
—SAINT JEAN CHRYSOSTOME,
Homelies or Sermons on Genesis, c. 388

If you forbid me to write about religion or the government,
I have nothing more to say.
—DIDEROT, *The Skeptic's Walk,* 1748

VIEW OF THE CITY OF LANGRES, 1700

I

THE ABBOT FROM LANGRES

Perched between Franche-Comté, Lorraine, and Burgundy, the mile-square city of Langres is concealed by stone ramparts that rise 550 meters from the valley below. For more than two thousand years, pedestrians, horse-drawn coaches, and now cars have reached this fortresslike burg by climbing steep roads toward one of the city's stone gates. Within minutes of passing through any of these posterns, one arrives at a triangular plaza that used to be called the place Chambeau. It was here that Denis Diderot was born to his parents, Didier and Angélique, on October 5, 1713.

Langres's central square retains much of the feel of the eighteenth century. Virtually all of the city's two-, three-, and four-story limestone houses are seemingly unchanged, though now some sag at the beams with age.[1] As is often the case in old French cities, the most noteworthy shifts in this neighborhood have been symbolic. In 1789, the Revolutionary government redubbed the place Chambeau the "place de la Révolution," a name it maintained until the restoration of the Bourbon monarchy in 1814. The next emblematic change took place seventy years later, on August 3, 1884, when

Jean-Ernest Darbot, mayor of Langres, rebaptized the square as the "place Diderot" in honor of the city's most famous son.

THE PLACE CHAMBEAU, LANGRES, c. 1840

The ceremony organized in the writer's honor garnered more international press coverage than Langres has ever received, either before or since. According to numerous reports, Darbot had the city festooned with paper lanterns and streamers.[2] He and the city council also arranged for gymnastics demonstrations, shooting contests, and a marching band that played throughout the day, its fanfares melding with the din of twenty thousand celebrators.[3] The highlight of the day, however, was the unveiling of the bronze statue of Denis Diderot designed by the celebrated creator of the Statue of Liberty, Frédéric Auguste Bartholdi. The sculptor depicted Diderot in a dressing gown and an insouciantly buttoned waistcoat. Looking out over the square from atop a marble pedestal, Diderot turns his head to his right, as if in the middle of a thought. Like Bartholdi's massive Lady Liberty, which was under construction at that very moment back in Paris, Diderot clutches a book in his left hand.[4]

Journalists reported that the crush of people on the newly christened place Diderot called out a jubilant *"Vive la république!"* when they first spied the statue. A smaller group of observant Catholics looked on glumly from the edges of the crowd. What an outrage the whole event had been from their point of view: in addition to the fact that Darbot and the other republican politicians of Langres had scheduled the event on a Sunday, the city's workers had also positioned the statue so that Diderot was conspicuously turning his back on Langres's most famous religious icon, the nearby Saint-Mammès Cathedral.

STATUE OF DIDEROT IN LANGRES

Some 135 years after Darbot unveiled Bartholdi's statue, the
city's atmosphere remains thick with memories of the writer.
The place Diderot leads to the rue Diderot, which, in turn, leads
to the collège Diderot, the city's junior high school. Every third or
fourth shop within the walled city also seems to display the name
of its most famous son. In addition to a beautifully executed new
museum dedicated to the philosophe, there is a Diderot café, a
Diderot coffee bean shop, a boulangerie Diderot, a Diderot cigarette
and cigar store, a Diderot motorcycle dealership, and a Diderot
driving school. The town's Freemasons, according to someone I met
at a café in Langres, attend monthly meetings at the Diderot Lodge.

THE HOUSE WHERE DIDEROT WAS BORN

More important, however, are the early-modern buildings,
houses, and churches that Diderot knew during his lifetime.
Today, one can still stand in front of the chalky, limestone facade
of Diderot's grandparents' house and look up into the windows
of its second floor where he came into this world. On the same

square, a hundred feet to the west, stands another landmark, the narrow four-story stone house that Didier Diderot purchased in early 1714 (several months after Denis's birth) to accommodate what was destined to be a large household.

DIDIER DIDEROT

Angélique and Didier Diderot would ultimately have nine children while living on the place Chambeau, many of whom did not make it through the perilous first years of life. In addition to the baby boy who died before Denis was born, four girls succumbed to various ailments. One died when Denis was two, another when he was five, another when he was six. Yet another perished at an unknown date. The four surviving children, two girls and two boys, had dispositions that split down the middle. The older two siblings, the firstborn Denis and his sister Denise (1715–97) — Diderot once described her as a female Diogenes — had powerful personalities with ironic senses of humor. The younger children grew into far more somber and devout adults. Angélique (1720 – c. 1749), about whom we know virtually nothing, insisted

on joining the Ursulines' convent at age nineteen. The youngest
child in the family, Didier-Pierre (1722–87), also dedicated his life
to God. Nine years younger than his brother, Didier-Pierre seems
to have crafted his entire life as a response to his older sibling's
freethinking iconoclasm. He became disciplined where Denis was
rebellious, pious where Denis was irreverent, abstemious where
Denis was self-indulgent, and a doctrinaire priest where Denis
was a skeptic. By the end of his career, Didier-Pierre had not only
become a particularly unyielding member of the Langres clergy,
but the archdeacon of the Saint-Mammès Cathedral.

Denis and his three younger siblings grew up in a bourgeois
milieu where girls would ideally enter into strategic and suitable
marriages and boys would become cutlers, tanners, or perhaps
priests. Diderot's mother, née Angélique Vigneron, had come from
a family that typically earned its living through the "odoriferous
trade" of tanning and selling animal hides. Denis's father, Didier
Diderot, had also followed long-standing family tradition and
embraced the profession of his father and grandfather as a fabrica-
tor of knives and surgical tools.[5] Expanding the business inherited
from his father, Didier became known throughout eastern France
as the manufacturer of some of the finest surgical instruments in
the region — including a type of lancet that he had invented.

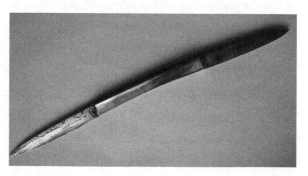

KNIFE MADE BY DIDIER DIDEROT, MASTER CUTLER

Life in and around the place Chambeau revolved around the cutlery business. Six days a week, Diderot *père* came downstairs from his family's living quarters to the ground floor workshop, where he toiled alongside several workers. The household was constantly filled with the sounds and smells of knife making: the smolder and respiration of the bellows, the incessant pings of the tack hammer, and the screech of the grinding wheel, which was operated by a worker lying on a plank, his nose quite literally to the grindstone.

WORKSHOP OF A CUTLER

Though Diderot ultimately had little affinity for the trade of cutler, he admired his father tremendously. Until his dying day, he praised the civic and moral values associated with Didier Diderot's patriarchal, bourgeois world, even "staging" some of these values in his plays. The few written descriptions or anecdotes related to the elder Diderot all portray him as a hard worker, a profoundly religious man, and a devoted subject of the king. Didier Diderot's granddaughter, Madame de Vandeul, also stresses his fairness and severity, describing him as the type of man who once took the three-year-old Denis to witness the public execution of a criminal outside the city walls. This horrific spectacle, she adds parenthetically, made the small boy violently ill.[6]

At some point during Denis's childhood, his parents decided that he was not destined to become either a cutler or a tanner. Perhaps witnessing his startling intellect, they began to groom him for the priesthood, which had also been a career choice for a dozen or so blood relatives on both sides of the family. Diderot surely met many of these pious family members, among them the vicar in neighboring Chassigny, the two great-uncles and two second cousins serving as country priests outside the city walls, and another uncle who was a Dominican friar.[7] The most important and prominent ecclesiastic in his life, however, was his mother's older brother, Didier Vigneron, who occupied the coveted position of *chanoine*, or canon, in Langres's cathedral.

For a number of years, Didier and Angélique Diderot not only hoped that their son would become a priest, but succeed his uncle as canon at the cathedral. Had Diderot replaced the aging Vigneron, he would have become an influential member of the cathedral's Chapter, the group of clerics who controlled the Langres bishopric.[8] In addition to garnering immense prestige for the family, the young canon would also have received a generous portion of the revenues—called a prebend—from a diocese whose reach extended to some six hundred parishes and seventeen hundred priests outside the city's ramparts.[9] In an era where a typical worker might earn two hundred livres a year, a canon's basic annual income was a more than respectable one thousand to two thousand livres.

The young Denis took the initial, small step toward becoming a man of the cloth on his seventh birthday. This was seen as the dawn of the "age of responsibility" for young boys.[10] From this point forward, the Sunday morning clangor of church bells called Denis to a day of worship and study at the neighboring Church of Saint-Martin. For the first few years that he attended church, the Latin liturgy washed over him ineffectually. After mass, however, Denis moved on to catechism, which was offered in French. This weekly obligation, which was conducted simultaneously in hundreds of churches throughout the Langres diocese, consisted of a particularly monotonous routine. Once the children were settled, the local *curé* or his representative read a series of scripted questions pertaining to matters of faith, religious practice, and God.[11] The older children in attendance, who had memorized the answers over the years, responded in unison. The younger ones stammered out the answers as best they could.

In October 1723, at age ten, Diderot was admitted to Langres's Jesuit *collège*, which was on the other side of the place Chambeau. Diderot was eligible for such an advanced education because he had the good fortune of being born into a family that could afford tutoring or ad hoc schooling in French and Latin, the languages required for admission. Once he had begun attending the *collège*, he (and his two hundred classmates) took classes that were largely based on the *Ratio Studiorum*, the formal "plan of education" created at the end of the sixteenth century by an international group of Jesuit scholars. In addition to deepening Diderot's understanding of the foundational aspects of the Catholic faith, this program introduced the young boy to what we would now consider traditional humanities disciplines, such as ancient Greek, Latin, literature, poetry, philosophy, and rhetoric.[12]

As the twelve-year-old Diderot was finishing his third year at the *collège*, he or his family decided that he should take the next step to joining the priesthood, by becoming an *abbé*, or abbot. This ceremony, which took place at the nearby Saint-Mammès Cathedral on August 22, 1726, followed a strict script. Diderot was called up from a pew and told to kneel before his diocese's bishop, the doughy-faced Pierre de Pardaillan de Gondrin. The prelate then began the tonsuring ceremony, cutting several tufts of the boy's blondish hair from the front, back, sides, and top of his head—forming a cross—and, after taking off his miter, prayed over the young Diderot. In the final part of the ceremony, the prelate helped the newly tonsured abbot don a white surplice, proclaiming that the Lord was reclothing him.[13]

TONSURING OF AN ABBOT

Diderot had entered into the minor orders, but the plan to have him succeed Vigneron as canon was doomed to fail. In the early spring of 1728—less than two years after he had become abbé Diderot—the cathedral's Chapter voted resoundingly against his uncle's nepotistic succession plan. Furious, Vigneron decided to circumvent his own diocese and took the audacious step of writing directly to Pope Benedict XIII, asking him to push this promotion through. Unfortunately for the *chanoine* (and for his nephew's budding career as a Langres ecclesiastic), Vigneron died while this letter was en route to the Vatican, thereby rendering his request null and void. Shortly thereafter, the Chapter voted to offer the position of canon to someone else. As a nineteenth-century historian of the Langrois diocese wistfully wrote, "If the death of Diderot's cousin had only been delayed by a few days, the boy would have undoubtedly become canon in Langres…While Diderot might not have been an ideal canon, he would not have become a nonbeliever."[14]

PARIS

After learning that he would not be replacing his uncle within the Saint-Mammès Chapter, the fourteen-year-old Diderot resigned himself to completing his final year at the *collège*. During his last months in school, he continued to distinguish himself as a brilliant and, at times, troublesome student. This began with the baiting of his teachers. By his own admission, Diderot apparently took a perverse pleasure in undertaking translations of Latin or Greek into which he slipped arcane, but grammatically accurate, syntax so that his teachers would correct him. He would then enjoy pointing out to his instructors where they were mistaken.

In addition to engaging in such erudite mischief, the young Diderot also had a tendency to get into scraps. On one occasion, after being sent home from school for fighting, he realized that he was missing out on the annual prize day, a day when his teachers were identifying their strongest pupils through a series of exams and competitions. Refusing to be shut out of the contest, he attempted to sneak back into the school by rushing in with the other students, but was singled out by the *collège*'s guard. While the sentinel was unable to prevent Diderot from slipping by, he nonetheless managed to stab the boy with his halberd. Bleeding from a wound that his family only found out about a week later, Diderot nonetheless prevailed over all of his classmates, winning prizes in essay writing, poetry, and Latin translation. In one of the few moments when he looked back at his days at the Jesuit *collège* in Langres, Diderot luxuriated in the memory of his triumphal return after the contest:

> I remember this moment as if it were yesterday; I arrived home from school, my arms filled with prizes that I had won, and my shoulders covered with crowns that had been bestowed on me and that, because they were too big for my brow, had slipped over my head. My father saw me from afar, stopped work, walked into the doorway, and began to cry. It is a beautiful thing to see an honest, austere man cry.[15]

Two of Diderot's most deep-rooted tendencies are present in this telling story: his eternal struggle against various forms of authority and the deep respect and admiration that he felt for his father.

Accolades and parental tears notwithstanding, by the time Diderot completed his studies at the *collège* in 1728, he was well aware that his career options in Langres had narrowed considerably. Rejected as canon — and having scorned the family occupation of cutler as unsuitably mind-numbing — the young Denis fell back on the possibility of a different ecclesiastical career, one that would involve further study of philosophy in Paris. It was at this time, it seems, that the young Diderot fell under the influence of a Jesuit priest who gave him the idea to run off to Paris to join the Society of Jesus. Diderot apparently told no one in his immediate family about these plans, though he did alert an indiscreet cousin who immediately informed Diderot's father. On the night that Diderot was supposed to leave for the capital, his father caught him at the door. "Where are you going?" the elder Diderot apparently asked, to which Diderot replied, "To Paris where I'm supposed to join the Jesuits." "Your desire to do so will be satisfied, but not tonight," his father countered.[16] Soon thereafter, Didier Diderot granted his son permission to study in Paris, but under conditions that he, as paterfamilias, would determine.

In late 1728 or early 1729, Didier Diderot booked two seats on the *diligence* coach that passed through Langres and Troyes on its way to the capital. The route to Paris crossed gently undulating plains and large expanses of farmland. Each night, after fifty or so miles of rutted, root-covered roads, the coach would stop at roadside taverns where the father and son would eat typical hostelry fare, most often mutton stew. After four or five days, they arrived in Paris, a city fifty times bigger than Langres.

As was inevitably the case for first-time provincial travelers coming into the capital, Denis and his father were presumably shocked by the tremendous concentration of soot-caked buildings, constricted, mud-filled streets, and foul neighborhoods teeming with starving, half-naked children. As they moved from the city's outlying quarters to the heart of the capital, they must also have marveled at the scale of the royal and ecclesiastical architecture.

Their final destination in Paris was the young abbot's new school, the collège d'Harcourt, which was located in the Latin

Quarter, on the rue de la Harpe, about a five-minute walk from Notre Dame.[17] Harcourt, a Jansenist-leaning institution within the University of Paris, was composed of a hodgepodge of contiguous buildings, some dating from the thirteenth century. Didier Diderot enrolled Denis in the school on a provisional basis, and rented a room in a nearby inn for two weeks. According to Madame de Vandeul, the young Denis nearly got expelled during this trial period because he helped a fellow pupil with Latin homework. The assignment, ironically enough, was an exercise on temptation, whose subject was "What the serpent said to Eve." Despite the severe reprimand that Denis surely received for aiding his schoolmate, the would-be ecclesiastic ultimately announced to his father at the end of two weeks that he wished to remain at the *collège*. Once this decision was made, Diderot *père* and *fils* said their goodbyes. And soon thereafter, Didier Diderot made his way across the Seine to the rue de Braque to board the Langres coach. As he set off on this four-to-five-mile-an-hour journey back toward the southeast, the master cutler probably thought he would see his son a year or two later. Thirteen years would pass, however, before the two Diderots would meet again.

HARCOURT AND THE SORBONNE

Life at the collège d'Harcourt was far from gratifying for Diderot. Much like the collège des Jésuites that he had attended in Langres, the structure of the school mirrored the social stratification of the ancien régime itself. Among the 150 or so boarders, the better-off students often had servants and fireplaces, while the students of more modest means, such as the son of a cutler, endured lesser quarters.

The daily routine was grueling. Students were called to prayer at 6:00 a.m. and spent the rest of the day in class and study sessions, during which they painstakingly copied their rhetoric and physics lessons into notebooks.[18] The few interruptions in this routine included a very short recess after *dîner* (lunch) and, of course, various religious obligations, including an evening prayer at 8:45 p.m.[19] The day of reckoning for each pupil came every Saturday. After mass, the school's teachers went over the week's work one final time before doling out rewards and punishments according to each student's particular merit. While Diderot did not write about such rituals at Harcourt, later in life he often maligned the repetitive and reclusive world of the religious *collèges* into which, as he put it, some of his best years had vanished.[20]

THE COLLÈGE D'HARCOURT, ENGRAVING

After three years of study at Harcourt, on September 2, 1732, the nineteen-year-old Diderot earned the most common degree dispensed by the school, the *maîtrise ès arts*, which is roughly the equivalent of a bachelor's degree today.[21] Shortly thereafter, he entered the Sorbonne, the designated college of theology within the University of Paris.[22] As was the case for all first-year students, Diderot began by studying philosophy here. During his second year, he went on to physics, theology, and, with far less enthusiasm, scholasticism. Like many of his fellow philosophes, Diderot harbored a great deal of scorn for the "frivolities" of the scholastic method, which involved the often tortured application of Aristotelian ideas to Church dogma. While details of these years are scant, it is quite easy to imagine how this increasingly skeptical thinker would have become exasperated among a sea of aspiring ecclesiastics, all engaged in scholasticism's impenetrable debates on the distinctness of substantial forms, the different types of matter, the immateriality of the soul, and the final causes of all bodies. Voltaire best summed up these maddening abstractions when he quipped that the "sectarians of Aristotle use words that no one understands to explain things that are inconceivable."[23]

VIEW OF THE SORBONNE, AQUATINT

Diderot never documented the precise reasons why he abandoned his plan to be a priest. What we do know, however, is that by 1735 the twenty-two-year-old had reached the point in his studies where he had the option of committing to an ecclesiastical career. Having completed five years of study—the quinquennium—in Paris, he was now eligible to apply for a respectable *benefice* or pension of perhaps four hundred or six hundred livres a year.[24] In October 1735, he even seems to have flirted with this idea, going as far as taking the initial steps of registering such a request with the bishop of Langres, Gilbert Gaspard de Montmorin de Saint-Hérem. As would often be the case at such points in his life, however, Diderot never finished the application process, and simply let this opportunity pass.[25]

Diderot's ambivalence toward the Church and further religious training intersected with his larger disinclination to commit to any real profession. From 1736 to around 1738, he worked halfheartedly for a solicitor named Clément le Ris, reportedly spending most of his time at the law office reading mathematics, Latin, and Greek, and teaching himself two new languages: Italian and English. Diderot's obvious lack of interest in a legal career ultimately prompted the solicitor to write to Didier Diderot to let him know that his son was not working out. The elder Diderot reportedly asked le Ris to inform his reluctant employee that the time had come for him to choose among three professions: doctor, solicitor, or lawyer. Madame de Vandeul relates her father's waggish reaction with a smile:

> My father requested some time to think it over, and was granted this wish. After several months, the question was put to him again. He replied that the profession of doctor did not appeal because he

did not want to kill anyone; that the profession of solicitor was too difficult to perform scrupulously; that he would gladly choose the profession of lawyer, except that he had an indomitable distaste for taking care of others' affairs.[26]

Madame de Vandeul then recounts that her father was asked what he wanted to do with his life. He replied: "*My gosh*, nothing, nothing at all. I like to study; I am very happy, very content; I don't ask for anything else."[27] Diderot's relationship with the law and le Ris ended shortly thereafter.

To make ends meet, Diderot next found a well-paid position as a tutor to the children of a wealthy banker by the name of Élie Randon de Massanes. After three months of watching over and instructing the financier's children — this task began at breakfast and ended with their bedtime — Diderot informed his employer that he could no longer stand being cooped up: "Monsieur," he supposedly said, "[t]ake a look at me. A lemon is less yellow than my face. I am making men of your children, but with every day I am becoming a child with them. I am a thousand times *too* rich and *too* well-off in your house, but I have to leave it."[28]

On the few occasions where Diderot referred to this unpredictable period in his life, he tended to downplay its difficulties and conjure up its joys, joys which included the occasional wooing of courtesans or actresses, long strolls in the Luxembourg Gardens, extended conversations with friends at cafés such as the Procope, and, if his purse allowed it, a place within the crowded, standing-only parterre at the Comédie-Française.[29] How to pay for this self-indulgent existence soon became a problem, however. Although Diderot's obstinacy and independence would serve him well later in life, in the second half of the 1730s these traits exasperated his father, who ultimately cut off his pension. His mother was apparently of a softer heart. On at least one occasion, she sent him some money via a servant who, incredibly enough, walked the 238 kilometers from Langres to Paris (and back) to deliver it to him.

Despite this occasional bit of help, Diderot had nonetheless sentenced himself to a hardscrabble life spent in a succession of Latin Quarter fleapits. This was an era of threadbare stockings, cold and empty fireplaces, and precious little food in the larder. His most consistent source of income in the late 1730s and early 1740s came from tutoring students in mathematics. There were other gambits as well. On one occasion, he reportedly drew on his theological training in order to produce a series of sermons for a missionary setting off for the Portuguese colonies.

Diderot's most remarkable moneymaking scheme, however, involved swindling a Carmelite monk by the name of Brother Ange.[30] Brother Ange had grown up in Langres and was either a friend or distant relative of the Diderot family. Like the other members of his monastic order, he resided in the Carmelite monastery situated just south of the Luxembourg Gardens. Diderot first got in contact with the friar under the pretense of touring the monastery's library, which held over fifteen thousand volumes and manuscripts. As Madame de Vandeul joyfully recounts, her father let it be known during his initial visit that he had tired of the "stormy" existence he was leading outside the monastery's walls and was now drawn to the peaceful and studious life of a monk.[31] Brother Ange immediately realized that the erudite Diderot would be an excellent prospect for his order. After several more visits, Diderot announced that he had decided to become a postulant, but first needed to pay off his worldly debts.

In particular, he informed Brother Ange that he needed to work for perhaps one more year to earn enough money to do right by a young woman whom he had dragged into sin. Fearing that this delay might slow things down, Brother Ange advanced Diderot 1,200 livres, a considerable sum. Shortly thereafter, Diderot returned to the monastery and informed the monk that he was now far closer to taking his vows but that he also needed to pay off his neighborhood's public cook and his tailor. The good friar once again lent him another eight hundred or nine hundred livres. During his final visit to meet with Brother Ange, Diderot used the same line: he was very much ready to join the order, but he needed a last advance to purchase the necessary books, linens, and furniture for his new life. The monk assured him that none of this would be necessary and that all would be provided for him once he arrived. At this point, Diderot then decreed angrily that if the monk did not want to advance him any more money, then he no longer wanted to become a monk, and stormed off.[32] Hoodwinked and humiliated, Brother Ange wrote to Didier Diderot, complaining that his son had defrauded him for over two thousand livres. The elder Diderot, who had already been obliged to repay similar debts, reimbursed the Carmelite, but not before deriding the monk for being so gullible.[33]

JEAN-JACQUES AND ANNE-ANTOINETTE

Diderot's career as dilettante and occasional scoundrel came to a close, more or less, by the early 1740s. Now in his late twenties, he was not only reading deeply in mathematics, physics, and natural history, but had also taught himself both Italian and English, the latter language, improbably enough, by using a Latin–English

dictionary. Mastering written English had an immediately positive effect on Diderot's life. By early 1742 he was able to secure his
first real gainful employment as a translator of Temple Stanyon's
The Grecian History.

It was during this same era that Diderot met some of the most
important people in his life. In September 1742, while drinking
coffee and watching games of chess at the Café de la Régence,
Diderot was introduced to a fine-boned, thirty-year-old Genevan named Jean-Jacques Rousseau. Rousseau and Diderot realized straightaway that they had a remarkable store of things in
common. In addition to their passions for chess, reading, music,
theater, philosophy, and literature, they had also both rejected
professions that would have provided settled, secure lives in favor
of far more precarious careers. Even their relationship to their
families had significant similarities: Rousseau, like Diderot, had
grown up in a household in which the father was a skilled crafts-
man (a watchmaker in Rousseau's case); what was more, both of
these Parisian transplants were now alienated from their families.

The fundamental difference between the two men was one
of temperament. Diderot was intensely optimistic, a powerful
conversationalist, and far more effusive and confident than the
introverted Rousseau. Some of this surely had to do with their
respective familial histories. Diderot had chosen to leave his family, while Rousseau had felt orphaned or abandoned from his first
moments on earth. Referring, in *The Confessions*, to the fact that his
mother had died nine days after he was born, Rousseau famously
proclaimed that "I cost my mother her life. So my birth was the
first of my misfortunes."[34] Raised by his aunt and his father and
lacking the formal education enjoyed by Diderot, the boy learned
to read and write by poring over long adventure novels produced

by the likes of Honoré d'Urfé. This comparatively peaceful time
in his life came to an end shortly after his tenth birthday in 1722,
when his father, Isaac Rousseau, was apprehended for trespass-
ing on a noble's property. Fearful of being condemned in court, he
deserted his family and fled to Bern.

JEAN-JACQUES ROUSSEAU BY LA TOUR

Handed off to yet another aunt along with his brother, Rousseau was soon dispatched to live with a Calvinist minister in the
neighboring village of Bossey. Two years later, at age thirteen,
Rousseau began preparing himself for his adult life by appren-
ticing with a notary and then a brutish engraver named Monsieur Ducommun, who would sometimes beat him mercilessly.
At sixteen, Rousseau left Geneva and made his way to the city
of Annecy, some forty miles to the west. It was here that he met
a handsome, cow-eyed aristocrat named Françoise-Louise de
Warens (née de la Tour du Pil), a woman who would function

for the young philosophe as both surrogate mother and object of desire.

For the next ten years or so, Rousseau wandered from city to city, living in Turin — where he converted to Catholicism — as well as in Lyon, Montpellier, Neuchâtel, and Chambéry. Despite his many travels, he always returned to Annecy and Madame de Warens for extended stays. When he reached nineteen or twenty, his onetime mother figure took him as her lover. This curious arrangement lasted until the summer of 1742, when Madame de Warens replaced Rousseau with another young and lost Calvinist. It was at this point that the thirty-year-old Rousseau decided to move to Paris, where he quickly inserted himself into the group of writers and philosophes who would ultimately be responsible for the *Encyclopédie*.

During the same months that Rousseau was settling into life in the capital, Diderot was busy courting the woman whom he considered to be the love of his life: the alluring, statuesque, and very pious Anne-Antoinette Champion.[35] At thirty-one years old, this hardworking laundress, whom Diderot called Toinette or Nanette, should have been leading the life of a provincial noble in her hometown of Le Mans, married to someone befitting her rank and beauty. A series of financial disasters, however, had struck her family. The hard luck had begun with her grandfather who, like many military-oriented aristocrats, ruined himself by playing at war.[36] His daughter (Anne-Antoinette's mother) was nonetheless able to leverage her noble birth and marry decently, to Ambroise Champion, a wealthy bourgeois whose fortunes were heavily tied to the fur trade. This marriage also ended in financial disaster. Much like his aristocratic father-in-law, Champion went bankrupt, his investments disappearing in the snowy

forests of Canada. To make matters worse, he fell ill soon thereafter and died in 1713, leaving his young wife and three-year-old
daughter alone and destitute. Faced with few prospects, the widowed Madame Champion subsequently traveled to Paris with her
daughter, where she set up a small business as a laundress, a profession far below her station. With the little money that she had
either kept from Le Mans or earned in the capital, she soon dispatched Anne-Antoinette to the Miramiones convent. The young
girl emerged from her seclusion at age thirteen or so, barely able
to read.[37]

Diderot had started cozying up to Mademoiselle Champion
in 1741, when he happened to move into the same building where
she and her mother were living, on the rue Boutebrie. After initially running afoul of Madame Champion, he realized that to
have any success with the beautiful thirty-one-year-old laundress, he would need to overcome her mother's qualms with a bit
of deception. Announcing that he was on the verge of entering the
priesthood — in this particular instance, at the Saint-Nicolas-du-
Chardonnet seminary on rue Saint-Victor — Diderot reintroduced
himself to the Champion household as an unthreatening future
ecclesiastic who, as it happened, often needed the services of
the two laundresses. As Madame de Vandeul recounts this story,
this ploy allowed her professionless father to overcome Madame
Champion's well-placed skepticism and spend more time with
Toinette. Eventually, Diderot was not only able to declare his love,
but let Toinette know that he had concocted the entire scheme
because he had wanted to marry her in the first place. Sometime
later, when Diderot finally announced his intentions to Madame
Champion, the older widow recoiled at the idea that her daughter would "marry a man with such a flashy mind, a man who did

nothing, a man whose sole quality was…the silver tongue with which he had so completely seduced her daughter." But this hesitancy, according to Diderot's daughter, soon gave way.[38] Once Diderot had received Madame Champion's blessing to marry Toinette, he decided that he should ask his parents' permission as well. Stitching together the money for the Langres coach, the young man returned home in December 1742 for the first time since leaving for Paris more than a decade before.[39]

Diderot's short stay in Langres began as well as could be expected; it would end, however, in incarceration. The first thing that he did upon arriving was to explain what he had been doing in the capital. Over the years, news trickling back from Paris had given him the reputation of a ne'er-do-well, a loafer, and a possible freethinker who was seemingly incapable of finding a proper career for himself. By 1742, however, he was able to present himself to his parents and friends as one of the new "men of letters" taking Paris by storm. This image was spectacularly confirmed in Langres thanks to Antoine-Claude Briasson, the publisher who had commissioned Diderot's translation of Temple Stanyon's *The Grecian History*.[40] Having reached the point in the project where the book was going to print, Diderot had made arrangements before he left to have the book's proofs sent to him via the coach. These periodic dispatches from Paris to Langres apparently impressed Diderot's family no end. How amazing, indeed, that an important Parisian publisher was going to the trouble of sending printed pages by carriage to the young man in Langres! Diderot's family once again had reason to brag about their son, the ecclesiastic-turned-important-translator.

Diderot's self-presentation as the prodigal son—once lost, now found and redeemed—came to an abrupt end when he finally

revealed the primary motive behind his trip: asking his parents'
permission to marry a laundress with no father, no dowry, and
who, despite her birth, was obviously a less-than-ideal match for
their firstborn son. To add insult to injury, Diderot also requested
a stipend of twenty-five pistoles (2,500 livres) per year to support
his new household.[41] Didier Diderot reacted to this proposition
with disdain. The sacrament of matrimony, everyone knew, was
not merely about love and tenderness: marriage was a yoke that
parents placed over their children's necks. Until the age of thirty,
in fact, Diderot did not have the right to legally marry without
their consent.

After a ferocious dispute during which Diderot *fils* threatened
his father with legal action, the elder Diderot had his son locked
up behind the walls of what many historians now assume was the
neighboring Carmelite monastery. Once this was accomplished,
Didier dashed off an unfeeling letter to Toinette's mother, hoping
to drive a wedge between the irresponsible lovers once and for
all: "If your daughter is [really] of noble birth and loves [my son]
as much as he claims, she will convince him to forsake her. This is
the only way that my son will be released. With the help of a few
friends who were as outraged by his audacity as I was, I have had
him locked away in a safe place, and it is within our ability to keep
him there until he changes his mind [about your daughter]."[42]

While this letter traveled to Paris, the Carmelite monks who
held Diderot were only too happy to teach the reckless lover a lesson. According to Diderot's own account of this episode, the friars
not only delighted in taunting and manhandling him, but also cut
off half of his hair, ostensibly so that he would be easy to identify
if he escaped. While such punishment was perhaps sanctioned
by Diderot's father, it is also possible that the order's members

delighted in evening the score with the young man who had made a fool of one of their own, the aforementioned Brother Ange.

Diderot's shearing at the hands of the Carmelites turned out to be his second and last tonsure in Langres. After several days of captivity, he managed to climb through an open window sometime after midnight. He then presumably made his way to the *porte du marché*, the closest gate within the walled city. Passing through the stone gateway, the fugitive then walked 120 kilometers to Troyes, fearing, quite reasonably, that his father would dispatch men to bring him back. Once he had arrived at this midway point between Langres and Paris, Diderot found an inn and penned a dramatic note to Toinette, before boarding the Paris coach: "I have walked thirty leagues in atrocious weather…My father is in such a fury that I am sure that he will now disinherit me, as he threatened. If I lose you again, is there anything that could convince me to remain in this world?"[43] Toinette must have been devastated. Diderot had gone to Langres with promises of obtaining both an allowance and parental consent to marry; he was now returning to Paris a reprobate and an escapee.

The next months were emotionally distressing. Rejected by his family and anxious that he might be arrested and dragged back to Langres in irons, Diderot was forced to abandon his former apartment and take up squalid quarters on rue des Deux-Ponts on the Île de la Cité. Worse yet, he discovered upon his return that Toinette had been deeply affected by the letter that his father had sent to her mother; she informed him in no uncertain terms that she had no intention of marrying into a family "where she was not regarded favorably" and broke off the engagement.[44]

According to Madame de Vandeul, Toinette apparently did not waver in her resolve until early 1743, when she was informed that her erstwhile lover had fallen gravely ill in his small room on the Île de la Cité. She (and her mother) ultimately flew to her ex-fiancé's sickbed, where they discovered the young man in a pitiful and emaciated state.[45] The two women then took it upon themselves to nurse the malnourished and ailing Diderot back to health. Sometime during or shortly after this stint of caregiving, Toinette broke her previous vow and once again agreed to marry Diderot. The couple were wed on November 6, 1743, at the nearby Church of Saint-Pierre-aux-Bœufs, one of the few Parisian parishes where young couples could be married without parental consent. Though Diderot had turned thirty in October and was thus able to wed Toinette legally, he nonetheless arranged an inconspicuous ceremony that took place at the stroke of midnight.

Other than several sentimental love letters that he sent to Toinette, Diderot preserved very little correspondence from this era. He wrote about these early years, curiously enough, while commenting on a painting by Nicolas-Guy Brenet exhibited at the Salon of 1767. Twenty-five years after he had first met his future wife, he summed up this tumultuous time in his life in his characteristically flippant style:

> I arrive in Paris. I was going to adopt academic garb [robe with a fur collar worn by the professors of theology] and install myself among the doctors of the Sorbonne. I encounter a woman beautiful as an angel; I want to sleep with her, and I do; I have four children with her and find myself obliged to abandon the mathematics I loved, the Homer and Virgil that I always carried in my pocket, and the theater I enjoyed.[46]

What Diderot leaves unsaid here speaks volumes. Writing about his own life as if he were the victim of unavoidable circumstances, Diderot passes over the painful fact that his father had actually been right about Toinette; her upbringing and social standing ultimately made her a poor match. Missing as well from this account is the immense guilt that Diderot felt (and sometimes admitted) about this time in his life, an era during which he let down his father, did not visit his mother before she died, and created a terrible rift in the Diderot clan. But there is also a good deal of psychological truth present in this cursory assessment of his early years. Despite the fact that Diderot takes little responsibility for his own actions, he nonetheless acknowledges the legitimacy of his own longing, as well as his lifelong tendency to embrace existence fully, completely, and audaciously, with little regard for the potential consequences. It was this precise aspect of his temperament that would soon lead him to write a series of books challenging the religious foundations of the ancien régime itself.

II

LEAVING GOD

In the years after Diderot escaped from the Carmelite monastery and returned to Paris, his parents became increasingly aware that he had fallen in with the capital's freethinkers and doubters. The guilt and disappointment must have been excruciating. How distressing that their firstborn son was daring to substitute personal belief for revealed truth. How utterly shortsighted, as well, that he was forgoing an eternity of happiness in exchange for the fleeting pleasures of sacrilege. Angélique Diderot grieved for her boy; as she put it, he had gone "blind" during his years in Paris.[1]

Diderot saw his slide into apostasy from an entirely different point of view. Extricating himself from the comfort of Christianity was anything but a thoughtless or self-interested act; it was serious-minded, transformative, and more illumination than blindness. Perhaps the most critical insight that he had had by the time he left the Sorbonne was that reasonable people had the right to subject religion to the same scrutiny as any other human tradition or practice. Seen from this critical angle, the Catholic faith itself could be rationalized, improved, and perhaps even discarded.

Diderot's susceptibility to such blasphemous thinking had several sources. To begin with, the future philosophe obviously had an ingrained tendency both to chafe at authority and to question the ideas upon which authority is founded. But there were also other more concrete reasons that explain his increasingly skeptical relationship with Catholicism. As a young man, the former abbot had become preoccupied by what he believed to be a series of major inconsistencies in Christian dogma, the most famous being the age-old problem of evil. How could it be, he wondered, that the Christian deity was both a benevolent father who loved and protected his flock as well as an implacable magistrate who indignantly condemned the unrighteous to a never-ending gnashing of teeth in a sea of fire and torment?

The murkiness of God's intentions was only one of Diderot's qualms. As an aspiring ecclesiastic living in a neighborhood teeming with religious schools, parish churches, abbeys, and dozens of monasteries and convents, he also had ample opportunity to observe and criticize the people who acted as the interpreters of God's will. This aversion had started with the Sorbonne's doctors of theology, but it soon ballooned into a far more generalized exasperation with the Church in general.

Diderot ultimately created his most far-reaching satire of religion and religious life in The Nun, a biting novel that featured hypocritical monks, manipulative confessors, do-nothing priests, and, most memorably, legions of cloistered women whose repressed sexual energy expressed itself through violence or sexual deviancy.[2] Earlier in his career, however, he sometimes voiced his frustration with a lighter touch. One of his favorite objects of ridicule was the order of Cistercian monks known as Bernardins, supposed ascetics whom Diderot invariably described as pleasure-loving epicureans with bellies as distended as those of any of the city's bankers. Far more seriously, the former student of theology also puzzled over the diverging doctrinal views expressed by the exponents of the "one true faith"; over the years, he had met Cartesians who maintained that God was perfect and therefore could not deceive humankind, Socinianists who rejected both the Trinity and the divinity of Jesus Christ, and Quietists who claimed that the only way to achieve union with the Divinity was through spiritual passivity and mysticism. As editor of the *Encyclopédie*, Diderot would later amuse himself by writing (or commissioning) tongue-in-cheek articles that mocked Catholicism's various subcultures for squabbling about arcane and unsolvable metaphysical questions.

One such dispute — the particularly destructive debate that split Jesuits and Jansenists — was not a laughing matter. This fissure had begun in the 1640s, when a combative group of French Catholic ecclesiastics began disseminating the beliefs of Cornelius Jansen, the bishop of Ypres. At a time when France still suffered enormously from the consequences of the Protestant Reformation, the Jansenists challenged the foundation of the Gallic Church from within. Condemning the supposed moral laxity and worldliness of the powerful Jesuit order, they advocated for a return to a far more austere view of existence, one where original sin and depravity defined the human condition. Most shocking from the Jesuits' point of view, Jansen's followers (who came to include Blaise Pascal) emphasized the predestination of a limited group of people blessed with God's grace. Jesuit theologians, with their emphasis on education and human perfectibility, obviously had a far more conciliatory position. Echoing prevailing Church dogma, and embracing their role as traditional defenders of the faith, they claimed that the world was a proving ground for God's chosen creatures, and that humankind could attain salvation by exercising its free will.[3] They also declared the Jansenists to be heretics.

As a student of both the Jesuits in Langres and the Jansenist-leaning collège d'Harcourt in Paris, Diderot was intimately familiar with this theological and political infighting. The events that especially preoccupied Diderot's generation had begun with Louis XIV's decision, in 1709, to dissolve and then raze Port-Royal des Champs, the stronghold of the Jansenist movement. This violent attempt to crush the Jansenists was seconded four years later by Pope Clement IX, who issued the highest level of papal decree — an apostolic constitution — that condemned the fundamental tenets of the movement as false, scandalous, rash, and detrimental to the well-being of the Church. Various forms of both royal and papal persecution had continued during Louis XV's reign, which, in turn, had triggered an unending stream of Jansenist pamplets. Versailles responded by exiling or imprisoning numerous Jansenist leaders. It was a vicious circle.

Such a conflict was anything but unusual from Diderot's point of view; it was emblematic of how religion functioned more generally in the world. Far from bringing people together, it seemed that each religious faction saw their adversaries as either spiritual infidels or political foes that needed to be crushed. Diderot later explained this phenomenon in the plainest of terms: "I have seen the deist arm himself ... against the atheist; the deist and the atheist attack the Jew; the atheist, the deist, and the Jew band together against the Christian; the Christian, the deist, the atheist, and the Jew oppose the Muslim; the atheist, the deist, the Jew, the Muslim, and a multitude of Christian sects attack the Christian."[4]

Differences in dogma, Diderot knew all too well, had a long and bloody history in France. During the sixteenth century, Catholic bishops and kings had expelled, hanged, burned, and slaughtered thousands of Protestants, bringing about an era during which, as he put it, "half the nation was piously bathing in the blood of the other half."[5] Such persecution and intolerance was not only ancient history. Less than twenty years before Diderot was born, Louis XIV had issued the 1685 Edict of Fontainebleau, which put an end to the era of comparative tolerance that had been guaranteed by the 1598 Edict of Nantes. In the days after this proclamation was signed, Versailles ordered a two-pronged assault on the country's Protestants; the French army crossed the country, laying waste to Huguenot churches and sanctuaries, while, at the same time, organized bands of dragoons burst into Protestant households with explicit instructions to terrorize, convert, or exile France's supposed heretics. More than two hundred thousand were driven from the country, fleeing to England, Germany, Holland, and America. Where, Diderot wondered, was God's will in all this religious infighting and persecution?

AN ENGLISH APPRENTICESHIP

By the time that Diderot had begun actively questioning what he perceived to be the inconsistencies and failings of Catholicism, he was surely familiar with (or had heard about) the long tradition of freethinking and clandestine books that served to introduce "irreligion" and even atheism into the capital's cultural fabric. The oldest of these works came from a long line of Epicurean philosophers, the most famous of them Titus Lucretius, author of *De rerum natura* (*On the Nature of Things*, c. 50 BCE).[6]

The sole remaining copy of Lucretius's six-book poem was discovered in a German monastery in 1417 and first printed in 1473.
Written in heroic hexameter—the grand style of epic verse—
De rerum natura rejected the existence of immaterial gods, asserted
that the soul was both material and mortal, and explained the
world, universe, and all life solely in terms of material and atomic
particles. What was more, the Roman poet took great pains to
describe the nefarious effects of religion and superstition in a
series of memorable aphorisms, the most famous being *Tantum reli-
gio potuit suadere malorum* (So great the evils to which men are driven
by religion).[7] This prominent, comprehensive, and delightful elegy
to godlessness remained a touchstone during Diderot's era.[8]

More modern treatments of heterodoxy were available as
well, especially if one knew the right bookseller or had the right
friends. The most influential treatise was Baruch Spinoza's *Tractatus theologico-politicus* (*Theologico-Political Treatise*, 1670). In addition
to providing an unflinchingly skeptical analysis of Scripture, this
Dutch philosopher of Jewish-Portuguese descent rejected revelation and denied the possibility that a God could exist outside the
boundaries of nature and philosophy.[9] To the extent that Spinoza
allowed for the existence of a divine being at all, his deity was
entirely different from the Christian God. In addition to occupying the same plane of existence as everything else in the universe,
this god had no "psychology," no goals, and certainly no interest
in humankind.[10] Eighteenth-century ecclesiastics did not bother
debating the subtleties of Spinoza's worldview, however; they
simply castigated him as the "leader and master of the atheists."[11]

The *Tractatus*'s heirs were many during the eighteenth century. The Dutch philosopher's most remarkable spiritual descen-
dent in France was a country priest from the obscure parish of

Étrépigny named Jean Meslier who, while taking care of his flock, had produced an atheist "testament" that was discovered shortly after his death in 1729. Manuscript copies of the *Mémoires des pensées et sentiments de Jean Meslier* (*Memoirs of the Thoughts and Sentiments of Jean Meslier*) soon started circulating among freethinkers. Borrowing deeply from Spinoza, Meslier's testament maintains that the entire Catholic religion was nothing more than a human invention; that faith is the foundation of error; that the revelation, prophecies, and miracles are fabrications; and that any reasonable person should conclude that the world's gods, including the Christian God, simply do not exist.[12] If the Roman Catholic Church was supposed to be "mother and teacher," Meslier's testament amounted to matricide.

Though Paris was awash in such impious manuscripts and books when Diderot was coming of age, scholars have no idea if he actually read Spinoza or, even more unlikely, Meslier, in the years right after he left the Sorbonne. What is indisputable is that, if Diderot did peruse any such works, they did not lead him headlong into atheism. His conversion to unbeliever began far more slowly, with a series of seemingly more benign books, most of them English.

Like many philosophically minded thinkers of his generation, Diderot knew that the intellectual contributions of the English nation paralleled their increasing mastery of the sea. If most Europeans recognized (rightly or wrongly) that the French had a virtual monopoly on the highest expressions of theater, painting, and poetry in the 1730s, they also conceded that England had originated many of the ideas and methods associated with what would, in retrospect, be called the Enlightenment.[13] Diderot's first real exposure to a body of English ideas occurred, perhaps not coincidentally, several months before he dropped his theology studies at the Sorbonne. This was in 1734, when Voltaire's *Lettres philosophiques* (*Letters Concerning the English Nation*) appeared in Parisian bookshops.

VOLTAIRE, STUDY BY LA TOUR

Almost twenty years older than Diderot, the gifted playwright Voltaire (born François-Marie Arouet in 1694) had always been drawn to theatrical gestures, even in philosophy.[14] This was certainly the case in the *Lettres* as well. In this short work of twenty-four essaylike letters, Voltaire provides a blueprint for a fundamental realignment of the French mind. Moving quickly from subject to subject, he lauds England's (comparative) tolerance of different religious faiths, praising, along the way, the country's seemingly reasonable Quakers. He commends the country's forward-thinking mercantilism, stock exchange, and new inoculation program. He also has good things to say about the English constitution and political situation, which provided more political freedom to its citizens than France did. The most forceful and influential portion of the *Lettres*, however, comes in Voltaire's short introduction of England's renowned savants and philosophers, among them Francis Bacon, John Locke, and Isaac Newton. These men, as Voltaire makes quite clear, had changed the world by redefining the long-standing relationship between philosophy, science, and religion.

Voltaire's praise of the "new philosophy" coming out of England did not go over well with the authorities. Accusing France of suffering from a backward scientific practice and a superstition-infused religion, the *Lettres* set off a firestorm. Although the Paris Parlement ordered the *Lettres* to be burnt, citing them as "scandalous and against religion,"[15] an estimated twenty-five thousand copies—including several pirated editions—made their way into French and European libraries.[16] This was a watershed moment in the history of Enlightenment thought. In addition to asking his countrymen to come out of their intellectual infancy, Voltaire had single-handedly created a new and communal public space for unvarnished discussion of religion and science. He had, in essence, redefined the role of the philosophe, of the public intellectual. And he had passed this idea on to younger writers like Diderot as well.

Sometime in the late 1730s, after teaching himself English, Diderot followed Voltaire's lead and began reading Bacon, Locke, and Newton.[17] Each of these thinkers provided the up-and-coming philosopher with specific foundational lessons. From Bacon, Diderot learned that science need not bow down before a Bible-based view of the world; it should be based on induction and experimentation, and, ideally, used to further humankind's mastery of nature. Locke delivered two related concepts. The first was a theory of mind that rejected the long-standing belief that humans were born with *innate* ideas (and, therefore, with an inborn understanding of the divine). In Locke's view, the mind is a blank slate at birth, and our understanding of the exterior world comes about solely through sensation and reflection. This entirely nonspiritual view of cognition set up a second critical lesson. Since, according to the English philosopher, true knowledge is limited to what we can learn through our senses, anyone involved in seeking out nature's secrets must rely on observation and experiment — on a so-called empirical approach — and avoid building huge systems based on fantasy. Like Bacon before him, Locke called for an entirely new relationship to both scientific and philosophical truth.

Of the three English luminaries that Diderot read about in Voltaire's *Lettres*, Isaac Newton arguably had the greatest impact on the budding philosophe in the 1740s. To begin with, Newton had overthrown the reigning understanding of the cosmos and planetary motion, which had been put forward by René Descartes in 1633. Gone in an instant was Descartes's wildly speculative assertion that corpuscles and planets churned away in massive cosmic whirlpools; in its place, Newton had conclusively demonstrated the theory of universal laws of motion and universal gravitation (the French called it *attraction*), using broad mathematical tools, including infinitesimal calculus. One still gets gooseflesh when reading Newton's announcement of what he had accomplished in his first edition of the *Philosophiæ Naturalis Principia Mathematica* (*Mathematical Principles of Natural Philosophy*, 1687): "I derive from the celestial phenomena the forces of gravity with which bodies tend to the sun and the several planets. Then from these forces, by other propositions which are also mathematical, I deduce the motions of the planets, the comets, the moon, and the sea."[18]

Perhaps as important as the discovery itself, however, was the fact that Newton summarized his findings with a recommendation that launched a thousand experiments: "I wish we could derive the rest of the phenomena of Nature by the same kind of reasoning from mechanical principles."[19]

Newton's effect on Diderot's generation cannot be overestimated; over the course of two decades, the English physicist convinced an entire scientific culture that a mathematical, mechanical philosophy of nature could illuminate the secrets of the physical world.[20] Yet the natural philosopher's most profound influence on Diderot in the 1740s was not related to the physical sciences per se, but to Newton's belief that one could also reconcile religious faith with the mathematically perfect functioning of the universe.[21] This had been one of the ancillary goals in the *Principia* from the beginning: highlighting the fact that the "most elegant system of the sun, planets, and comets could not have arisen without the design and dominion of an intelligent and powerful being."[22] Newton, in short, had used calculus to find traces of God's handiwork.

Various forms of the argument from design (or the teleological argument for God's existence) had existed well before Newton published his *Principia*. To begin with, most people accepted as indisputable fact that the stars, the mountains, animals, and man himself all pointed to a divine intent. The Church fathers, too, had formally cited creation as one of the sanctioned proofs of God's "invisible qualities—his eternal power and divine nature."[23] Yet the status of the argument shifted considerably in the decades after Newton's theories appeared. Long considered a supplement to the word of God, the design argument progressively displaced the importance of Scripture in certain circles.

By the end of the seventeenth century, a new generation of English-language writers began to put forward a more "reasonable" and Bible-free understanding of the deity's existence.[24] Partisans of this natural theology included the Irishman John Toland, who, in his 1696 *Christianity Not Mysterious*, asserted not only that God's existence was best extrapolated through the experimental method preached by Locke, but that there was a need to demythologize the faith, to make it *natural*.[25] Matthew Tindal developed similar ideas in his 1730 *Christianity as Old as the Creation*, claiming that the "external revelation" was the best way to commune with the reality of the deity.[26]

Several works of natural theology and deism, all of which suggested that organized religion had confused our relationship to God, fell into Diderot's hands in the 1740s.[27] At a time when he was plagued with doubts and uncertainties about God's existence, these texts provided a longed-for compromise between the emptiness of atheism and the absurdity of Church doctrine. Not only did the English deists implicitly and explicitly invite attempts at a far more "scientific" understanding of the deity, but they invited people to forge a relationship with God based on their capacity to *think*, not obey. This was a revelation to Diderot: according to the deists, God gave us the tools necessary to believe in Him, and to live a simple and moral life, but He had not given us organized religion; we had inflicted that problem on ourselves.[28]

À MON FRÈRE (1745)

As intrigued as Diderot was by natural religion or deism, he initially held back from publishing anything related to this dangerous way of thinking. During the short time that he had been employed as a translator of the English language, he restricted his activities to two straightforward commissions: the aforementioned *Grecian History* and Robert James's six-volume *Medicinal Dictionary*, which he undertook with two colleagues, François-Vincent Toussaint and Marc-Antoine Eidous. Neither of these works was polemical.

By late 1744, however, Diderot decided to approach the printer Laurent Durand with a proposal to translate a work of English deism: the Earl of Shaftesbury's *An Inquiry Concerning Virtue or Merit*.[29] Despite the risks involved in disseminating this nontraditional understanding of God, Durand was either convinced or cajoled into financing the translation. Several months later, he paid Diderot the sum of fifty louis (1,200 livres, or approximately three times a manual worker's annual salary) for the completed manuscript. As Durand would often do when publishing the young writer's books in subsequent years, he circumvented royal approval and published the book anonymously and illegally. He also added two other layers of protection: in addition to delegating the actual printing to another Paris shop, he indicated that the book had been edited in Amsterdam, which did away with the need for the censor's approval.

Translating Shaftesbury allowed Diderot to begin a career as a public intellectual, but it also let him explain his views on God and religion to his family, particularly to his brother, Didier-Pierre. Of all the Langrois who condemned Diderot for his irreligious thinking during the 1740s — and there were surely many — it was Didier-Pierre who took the most aggressive stand against him. Nine years younger than Denis, Didier-Pierre had really only met his sibling for the first time when Diderot returned home from Paris in December 1742. At the time, the twenty-year-old

Didier-Pierre had still been a student at the collège Jésuite in Langres. Undoubtedly vexed by the suffering that Denis was causing his parents at home, he plainly decided to compensate for his brother's sins by beginning an uninterrupted march toward the priesthood, disparaging his wayward sibling the whole way.[30]

Two years later, Diderot responded to Didier-Pierre's ongoing criticism by dedicating his translation of Shaftesbury to him. This was as much a provocation as an attempt at reconciliation. In the sermonlike speech that he published alongside this homage, Diderot vacillated between brotherly love and brutal condescension. After informing his brother that he was providing him with this translation as a "present" and "sign of fraternal friendship,"[31] he hints that his overly pious younger sibling might want to become a bit more broad-minded himself. The message was clear: censorious extremists like Didier-Pierre were doing more damage to the appeal of religion than anyone else.

Diderot sent a copy of his translation off to his brother shortly after it appeared. Didier-Pierre was incensed.[32] While God leaps from each and every page of Shaftesbury's text, the English author had obviously done away with the deity that Didier-Pierre knew and worshipped. Instead of the vengeful celestial judge who examines, adjudicates, and punishes his flock, Shaftesbury (and Diderot) describe a far more benevolent being who has supposedly fashioned the best of all possible worlds "with intelligence and goodness."[33] The most scandalous aspect of this book was that Shaftesbury's perfectly engineered universe had no need for the revealed morality taught and enforced by the Catholic Church. From Shaftesbury's point of view, God had engineered humankind with a moral sense that allowed people to recognize true virtue, and that impelled them to commit virtuous acts because doing so produced pleasure and happiness. Not surprisingly, Didier-Pierre found this anti-Christian way of thinking to be a "horrible doctrine" and an outrage.[34]

Diderot had had the opposite reaction. Shaftesbury's theory of natural morality heralded the birth of an optimistic new trinity, one where truth, beauty, and doing good functioned as an integrated whole. The advantages of this non-Scriptural relationship to morality were manifest. The English philosopher had not only broken the Church's monopoly on ethics, he had also done away with the need for threats of hell and eternal suffering. Perhaps most importantly, Shaftesbury had rehabilitated human pleasure, one of the bugbears of Christian moralists. This was immensely appealing to Diderot. How satisfying it was to discover a philosophical system that not only allowed a skeptic like himself to feel virtuous, but did so by inviting him to listen to the pleasure-seeking body that God had given him.[35]

PHILOSOPHICAL THOUGHTS:
LET MAN BE FREE

By the time Diderot's translation of Shaftesbury appeared in 1745, the thirty-one-year-old writer had been estranged from his family for two years. Still wary of being hauled back to Langres in irons, he had continued to keep a low profile. In addition to asking Toinette to go by her maiden name, he had moved his small family to an apartment on the rue Traversière in the fall of 1744. This was an unusual address to say the least. Not only was this neighborhood on the other side of the river from where the city's printers were located, but it was fully a mile outside the city limits, past the Bastille. While Diderot never revealed precisely why they left the center of Paris, it was perhaps related to the fact that his judgmental younger brother had moved to the Latin Quarter to finish his studies.

The months that the couple spent exiled in the Faubourg Saint-Antoine were not easy on Toinette and Diderot. Though there is no correspondence from this time, one suspects that their relationship began to fall apart sometime after they had moved to the area. Six weeks after the couple had settled into their new lodgings, their firstborn child, Angélique, succumbed to one of the many diseases that claimed babies in the first three months of their lives. The bereaved parents buried her in the Sainte-Marguerite de Paris Church cemetery on September 29, 1744. To add to Toinette's misery, her mother died soon thereafter.

Life became even more complicated several months later when Diderot met the woman who would become his first mistress, the writer Madeleine d'Arsant de Puisieux. Madeleine, to whom we will return in greater detail, had a significant effect on the early years of Diderot's career. Diderot fell in love with her as he had fallen in love with Toinette: suddenly, wholeheartedly, and with little regard for the pain or problems that such a relationship would cause.

Madeleine and Diderot were more than just lovers; they were collaborators who exchanged their writing, and even worked as partners on at least one short story, the orientalist "Oiseau blanc: conte bleu" ("White Bird: Blue Tale," 1748).[36] More importantly, it was apparently Madeleine who encouraged Diderot to produce his first single-authored book, *Pensées philosophiques* (*Philosophical Thoughts*). Diderot's daughter, to whom we owe this biographical detail, understandably does not paint Diderot's first mistress in a terribly positive light. Instead of presenting her as a fellow writer and *femme de lettres*, she depicts Madeleine as covetous and financially insatiable, supposedly encouraging her father to produce this book so that she could pocket the entire fifty louis he received for the manuscript.

PHILOSOPHY RIPPING THE MASK OFF SUPERSTITION;
FRONTISPIECE FROM THE *PENSÉES PHILOSOPHIQUES*

Diderot allegedly wrote the sixty-two short essays on God, deism, skepticism, and atheism that constitute the *Philosophical*

Thoughts in a fortnight, around Easter 1746. Well before it began appearing in bookshops in May, he knew that the book was destined to provoke an uproar. To give prospective readers a hint at what was contained within its pages, he asked his printer Laurent Durand to add a Latin inscription to the title page. This warning reads *"Piscis hic non est omnium,"* or "This fish is not for everybody."

Most eighteenth-century readers who saw this anonymously published work would have been on alert even before opening up its cover. By labeling his book *Philosophical Thoughts*, Diderot was alluding to two famous but diametrically opposed works of philosophy. The first was Voltaire's aforementioned *Lettres philosophiques*, a book whose sneering criticism of the Catholic Church had sent its author into exile when it appeared in 1734. The second title was one of the great Christian spiritual texts of the seventeenth century, Blaise Pascal's *Pensées* (*Thoughts*, 1669). What Diderot's short book promised, it appeared, was a philosophical analysis of Pascal's pessimistic views on the horror of the human condition.[37]

Pascal, for philosophes like Diderot, was Hobbes in a hair shirt. To the already gloomy idea that life is short, nasty, and brutish, Pascal had added a layer of thick metaphysical dread that continued to hover over France seventy-five years after his book was first published. Crafting his arguments in clever and often biting prose, the mathematician and philosopher implores his readers to focus on the fundamental desperation of human life. Not only has our fall from God's grace tragically separated us from the divinity, he argues, but we are deceived by our wicked passions and the misleading lure of the material world.[38] Humanity's only recourse, he suggests, is to turn inward and contemplate the full extent of our misery. This is our sole redeeming quality; we have the ability to study our fundamental wretchedness, whereas "a tree does not."[39]

Combating this cheerless view of the human condition was far more difficult for Diderot than it might appear. The notion that humans were debased creatures who carried the burden of original sin was, for most people, a foundational reality of existence, not only endorsed by Saint Augustine and the Jansenists, but inculcated in most Christians from a tender age in church, during catechism and confession.

The efficacy of Diderot's case against this bleak cosmology did not come from a direct attack against Pascal, Saint Augustine, or any other Christian theologian. Though he had more training in theology than most philosophes of his generation, his ploy was to confront the supposed misery of the human condition with the reality of everyday living, often by weaving his own experiences and opinions into his beguiling arguments. That he had stumbled upon a new and successful method of subverting long-standing religious ideas was not lost on his more perceptive readers, including Anne-Robert-Jacques Turgot, the soon-to-be-famous economist and future controller-general of finances of France: "Erudition bores people. Metaphysics repels them. A bon mot is remembered and moves from mouth to mouth; its poison [is] more volatile, and insinuates itself through breathing. [Diderot's toxin] is even more dangerous in that it produces the most mirthful pleasures of the imagination and the most refined gratifications of the mind."[40]

Turgot understood better than most people what Diderot's intention was in these philosophical thoughts: creating a knowable and likable persona who could appeal to people's common sense and aesthetic sensibility with irony, pithy aphorisms, and, as it turned out, intoxicating tidbits of sacrilege.

This is precisely what Diderot attempted to do when taking up the very serious subject of Catholicism's obsession with death and the afterlife. Of particular concern was the fact that Jansenist-leaning ecclesiastics and spiritual directors were teaching their most susceptible believers to turn away from their earthly existence, to "desire nothing, love nothing, feel nothing."[41] Diderot presumably saw some of the effects of this asceticism firsthand in the spring of 1746. Having recently moved to an apartment on the rue Mouffetard, only steps away from the Jansenist-oriented Church of Saint-Médard, Diderot had settled in the quarter of the so-called *convulsionnaires* (convulsionaries), a fringe group of Jansenist-leaning disciples of God who believed that their highest goal was to achieve spiritual purity through the mortification of the flesh.

The "convulsionary" phenomenon had begun almost twenty years earlier, in 1727, when a group of particularly fervent Jansenists began coming to the Church of Saint-Médard to observe or participate in the miracles that supposedly took place at the grave of a famous Jansenist hermit (and deacon) named François de Pâris. By all accounts, Pâris had been a kindhearted man of indefatigable generosity. Dedicating himself to the destitute inhabitants of the tawdry Saint-Marcel quarter, the deeply abstemious deacon rarely took communion, had no shoes, wore a hair shirt, slept on rusty nails, and effectively starved himself. While Pâris had certainly been well-known while he was alive, this likely candidate for canonization became a sensation after he died at the age of thirty-six. At his wake, which took place in the Saint-Médard chapel, numerous mourners, including members of the clergy, reportedly removed fingernails and locks of hair from the deacon's remains for use (and perhaps sale) as relics.[42] But most spectacularly, during the next day's well-attended funeral, an old woman boisterously interrupted the service and declared that she had suddenly regained use of her formerly paralyzed arm.[43] Overnight, Pâris's tomb was transformed from a place of memorial to a site of pilgrimage that drew the sick and infirm hoping for similar cures.[44]

FRANÇOIS DE PÂRIS, ENGRAVING

The Saint-Médard cemetery and its environs soon took on something of a carnival feel. Every day, from dawn to dusk, a mass of ailing and dying people—irrespective of class but generally Jansenist in orientation—draped themselves over Pâris's black marble tomb. Those fortunate enough to receive the cure went into convulsions, accompanied by vociferous grunting, shaking, and shrieking.[45] During a five-year span, over one hundred people claimed to have experienced the healing powers of

God in the Saint-Médard cemetery.[46] Thousands more came to watch the spectacle; enterprising merchants rented chairs to the curious.

BELIEVERS AND *CONVULSIONNAIRES*
AT FRANÇOIS DE PÂRIS'S TOMB, ENGRAVING

By the early 1730s, Louis XV tired of this state of affairs and ordered the cemetery gates locked. Although the *convulsionnaires* were not known for their humor, one of their supporters apparently had a highly developed sense of irony, and posted a sign on the metal gate that read BY ORDER OF THE KING IT IS FORBIDDEN FOR GOD TO MAKE MIRACLES IN THIS PLACE.[47] Royal interdiction did not put an end to the movement, however; instead, it drove them underground and inspired more violent practices that would demonstrate their unworthiness and devotion to God.[48] In addition to driving nails into their own flesh, women — it was always women — were subjected to horrifying suffering, including having full-grown men stand on their throats.

Diderot describes just such a disturbing example of holy violence in *Philosophical Thoughts*. Though this famous *pensée* begins without introduction or context, his readers knew exactly what he was talking about: bloodcurdling screams of women tearing their bodies apart in the service of God:[49] "What voices! What cries! What whimpering! Who has locked away these plaintive bodies in the dungeons? What crimes have these unfortunate people committed? Some are hitting their chests with stones; others are ripping their bodies apart with iron claws; all have regrets, pain, and death in their eyes."[50]

Reacting to this appalling tableau, Diderot then asks a series of penetrating questions. How could a caring God have condemned these people to such torment? Why would He find pleasure in this suffering? The next *pensée* amplifies these accusations. Lashing out at the implacable deity who supposedly inspired these acts, Diderot then wonders aloud why this all-powerful being only intervenes in the interest of his immediate worshippers, and lets thousands die on a daily basis: "Regarding the portrait of the deity that [some] have painted, regarding His tendency to anger, regarding the severity of His revenge, regarding the disparity between those whom He lets perish and those to whom He deigns to lend a hand... [bearing all this in mind], the most decent soul would be tempted to wish that this God did not exist."[51]

While writing these sentences, Diderot may have been thinking about his own daughter, who had died the year before. Whatever the source of this outburst, this moment is among the most moving in the *Philosophical Thoughts*. In addition to rejecting the Christian-inspired belief that suffering on earth is our highest calling, Diderot claims the right to free himself (and us) from the supposed caprices of the deity.

_____

TOWARD GODLESSNESS

At age thirty-two, the author of *Philosophical Thoughts* no longer had any need for Roman Catholicism and its spiteful trickster of a God. Yet the writer remained wary of the emptiness of atheism. While it may be hard to understand now, the most frightening aspect of a godless world was not godlessness itself; it was what remained after God was gone: soulless humans who seemed little more than machines living in a world that was potentially determinist, where all future events were preordained, not by an omniscient deity, but by a set of mechanistic rules.[52] Such was the dark side of the joyous impiety that Diderot preached.

Part of this threat may explain why *Philosophical Thoughts* is not a work of straightforward atheism. Reflecting Diderot's own hesitation in 1746, the book is a staccato succession of essays that gives the floor to the deist, the atheist, the skeptic, and the author himself, the latter vowing to die practicing the religion of his "fathers."[53] This is the genius of the book. Rather than pummeling us with an unrelenting and straightforward assault on the Catholic faith — something of which the author was more than capable — Diderot shares his own insecurities and hesitations about God's existence. This strategy made the *Philosophical Thoughts* more seductive, and arguably more dangerous, than a book of straightforward materialism.

The *Philosophical Thoughts* does not deliver an unequivocal message. And yet, if there is a dominant voice in the book, it unsurprisingly belongs to the skeptic. The skeptic, from Diderot's own point of view, is not an ignoramus who blindly asserts that he knows nothing, but a person who engages in profound and disinterested study of a question before admitting his inability to decide.[54] It is he who, while seeking out proof, finds only "difficulties."[55]

Overlapping to a large degree with how Diderot himself felt in 1746, the skeptic's voice comes across most effectively in a series of aphorisms emblematic of the Enlightenment movement as a whole. The first became Diderot's mantra: "Skepticism is the first step toward truth."[56] The second is a logical clarification of this point: "What has never been called into question has never been proven."[57] And the third is a forceful declaration of the right to think freely: "One can demand of me that I seek truth, but not that I must find it."[58]

Readers reacted vociferously to this deep and probing challenge to religion. One month after the book appeared, in June 1746, the Paris Parlement condemned Diderot's book to be burned on the place de Grève. In subsequent months, numerous religious writers also took it upon themselves to publish lengthy refutations of the book with titles such as the *Pensées raisonnables* (*Reasonable Thoughts*), *Pensées chrétiennes* (*Christian Thoughts*), and *Pensées anti-philosophiques* (*Antiphilosophical Thoughts*). One could not have asked for better publicity. Diderot's *Philosophical Thoughts* sold briskly: six editions of the authorless book appeared within three years.[59] His dangerous game of cat-and-mouse with the powers of the ancien régime had begun.

III

A PHILOSOPHE IN PRISON

Diderot's first brush with the Paris authorities came not long after *Philosophical Thoughts* appeared in 1746. At the time, he and his small family were still living on the rue Mouffetard in a first-floor apartment (or room) belonging to a friend named François-Jacques Guillotte.[1] A military officer who later contributed an article on bridges to the *Encyclopédie*, Guillotte presumably tolerated or even enjoyed Diderot's animated conversation and freethinking. Guillotte's wife, on the other hand, was appalled by the blasphemous ideas that she heard under her roof.[2] Only a year after standing as godmother to the Diderots' second child—the ill-fated François-Jacques— Madame Guillotte marched down to the neighboring Church of Saint-Médard to denounce her lodger. On the receiving end of this complaint was the recently ordained *curé* Pierre Hardy de Levaré.[3] Convinced that it was his duty to protect his flock from subversive thought, the priest passed on Guillotte's allegation to a royal gendarme named Perrault, who then contacted the all-seeing lieutenant-général de police, Nicolas-René Berryer, comte de La Ferrière.

In his capacity as a royally appointed magistrate, Berryer had power and responsibilities far in excess of what we now associate with law enforcement. In addition to policing trade standards, criminal activity, thousands of prostitutes, the servant class, the poor and the indigent, as well as Paris's chronic sewage and mud situation, Berryer also supervised the French publishing industry. To keep tabs on this powerful guild — along with the pack of writers who made their home in the capital — Berryer ran a massive intelligence-gathering operation with hundreds of spies.[4] These informants, referred to as his *mouchards* (flies or snitches), reported to him on a range of misdeeds, including seditious thinking, violations of public morality, and written challenges to religious orthodoxy.[5]

NICOLAS-RENÉ BERRYER, PAINTING

Madame Guillotte's tip was the first such accusation against Diderot to arrive on Berryer's desk. As he did for hundreds of other novelists, playwrights, poets, and journalists, Berryer would eventually create a file on "*sieur Didrot* [*sic*]." The first documents came to include Perrault's assessment that "Diderot is a dangerous man who speaks of the sacred mysteries of our religion with scorn."[6] He also inserted a follow-up note by Father de Levaré that castigated Diderot for marrying without his father's permission and being a "libertine," a "blasphemer," and a "deist, at the very least."[7] Such information, in Berryer's opinion, clearly merited an interview and a warning. As early as 1747, he dispatched the police inspector in charge of the book trade, Joseph d'Hémery, to advise Diderot to keep his sacrilegious views to himself.[8] D'Hémery not only passed on this message, but also confiscated a manuscript version of *La promenade du sceptique* (*The Skeptic's Walk*), which the writer had presumably hoped to sell to his publisher, Laurent Durand, at some point.

The Skeptic's Walk disappeared into the police archives and Diderot never saw it again during his lifetime. (It was finally rediscovered and published in 1830.) Though Diderot lamented this loss, critics generally agree that this early text — which was perhaps even written before *Philosophical Thoughts* — is not nearly as interesting as the other works he wrote in the 1740s. Lacking the dialogical verve that he infused into his later writings on God, *The Skeptic's Walk* is a somewhat plodding allegory that describes three paths one might take in life: the path of thorns (Christianity), the path of chestnut trees (philosophy), and the path of flowers (carnal pleasure). The most thought-provoking portions of the text come among the chestnut trees, where Diderot conjures up an Athens-like academy of philosophy where skeptics,

Spinozists, atheists, and deists have at it.[9] Diderot inserted his more anticlerical positions during the discussion of the Christian-inspired path of thorns, where an illogical "prince" rules over his blindfolded soldiers as they tramp ignorantly through life.

Despite d'Hémery's discovery that Diderot had produced yet another unorthodox text, the author was let off with a warning. The lieutenant-général de police most likely wanted to avoid transforming the writer into a persecuted and celebrated martyr. For a time, Louis XV himself played a role in encouraging this policy of relative clemency. Often positioning himself against the far more volatile Parlement and Church, the king and his royally appointed officers sought to find a balance between creating scandals, supporting the hugely profitable book trade, and maintaining the kingdom's orthodoxy.

Diderot surely benefited as well from the fact that he was increasingly seen as a thoughtful man of letters. While Berryer and those responsible for overseeing the book trade were perfectly aware that he had published the impious *Philosophical Thoughts*, they also recognized that he was also one of the translators of Robert James's *A Medicinal Dictionary* (1746–48) and was currently working on *Memoirs on Different Mathematical Subjects* (1748), a short work which demonstrated how math could elucidate problems related to the physical world, including harmonic theory. Most importantly, however, Diderot had been hired by the eminent printer André-François Le Breton to contribute to the forthcoming *Encyclopédie* project, which was being referred to as a matter of national pride.

Yet neither his "worthwhile" ventures nor the warning he received from d'Hémery dissuaded Diderot from further testing the limits of the ancien régime's patience. Not long after receiving his visit from the police inspector, the writer anonymously published his first novel, an erotic tale entitled *Les bijoux indiscrets* (*The Indiscreet Jewels*, 1748). This story of an African sultan whose magic ring could compel women's genitals to recount their erotic adventures — a book to which we will return — was followed by an even more dangerous work.[10] The following summer, while he was busy laying the groundwork for the first volume of the *Encyclopédie*, Diderot published his *Letter on the Blind*. This polished and complex work of free-flowing philosophy aimed to refute the existence of God in a way that *The Skeptic's Walk* and *Philosophical Thoughts* had not.

LEADING THE BLIND

In early June 1749, Diderot received some of the first copies of the *Letter on the Blind* to come off the press. In addition to keeping an edition or two for himself, he likely reserved copies for Jean-Jacques Rousseau and for his then-mistress, Madeleine de Puisieux. More strategically, he dispatched a copy to the most famous philosophe of his generation, the fifty-four-year-old Voltaire, whom he had never met.[11] Voltaire was not only flattered, but obviously very keen to see what the young and impudent philosophe had concocted in this meandering two-hundred-page "letter." Three years earlier, the famous philosophe had carefully read and annotated Diderot's *Philosophical Thoughts*, sometimes exalting in the young writer's enthusiasm, other times taking him to task for his atheistic leanings.

Diderot had doubtless thought that Voltaire — the most celebrated French champion of Locke — would find his discussion of perception and sightlessness to be a stimulating read. The book, after all, was filled with a fascinating examination of how the congenitally blind reacted to regaining their sight after a cataract operation, how they envisioned and adapted to a dark world, and, more generally, how sensation itself is relative. Voltaire read the *Letter* as soon as he received it — he was in Paris at the time — and wrote back to Diderot a day or so later, praising the author for his "ingenious and profound book."[12] After dispensing with these pleasantries, however, Voltaire made plain that he had serious qualms over the climax of the work, a scene where one of the book's characters forcefully denies the existence of the deity "because he was born blind."[13]

NICHOLAS SAUNDERSON,
ENGRAVING

The "character" to which Voltaire refers was a real person named Nicholas Saunderson (1682–1739), the most famous blind man to have lived during the eighteenth century. This prodigy had been a distinguished professor at Cambridge, the author of the influential ten-volume *The Elements of Algebra*, and a student of Newton's. Much of Diderot's account praises the unseeing man's astonishing abilities: his exquisite sense of touch, his uncommon capacity to relate abstract ideas, and the system of "palpable" arithmetic he had created for himself. Toward the end of this discussion, however, the narrator of Diderot's text interrupts himself and announces that he will now share the true story of the last moments of the blind man's life. This portion of the *Letter*, supposedly based on unpublished manuscript "fragments," was entirely fabricated by Diderot himself.[14]

The staging of Saunderson's deathbed scene initially hints at a triumphal religious conversion, one where a man of science finally humbles himself before the truth of Christianity. But what follows is far from a return to the faith; instead, Diderot's version of Saunderson launches into an impassioned debate on the existence of God with Gervais Holmes, a Protestant minister who is there to give the blind man his last rites.[15] In contrast to Diderot's *Philosophical Thoughts*—where deist, atheist, and skeptical viewpoints spar without clear resolution—Saunderson's godlessness here overpowers Holmes's deistlike presentation of Christianity. Among other things, the blind man ridicules the minister for explaining the wonders of nature with pathetic fairy tales: "If we think a phenomenon is beyond man, we immediately say it's God's work; our vanity will accept nothing less, but couldn't we be a bit less vain and a bit more philosophical in what we say? If nature presents us with a problem that is difficult to unravel, let's leave it as it is and not try to undo it with the help of a being who then offers us a new problem, more insoluble than the first."[16]

Saunderson then reframes this same idea with a much more mordant parable:

> Ask an Indian [from India] how the world stays up in the air, and he'll tell you that an elephant is carrying it on its back; and the elephant, what's he standing on? "A tortoise," [says the Indian]. And that tortoise, what's keeping him up? ... To you, Mr. Holmes, that Indian is pitiful, yet one could say the same thing of you as you say of him. So, my friend, you should perhaps start by confessing your ignorance, and let's do without the elephant and the tortoise.[17]

These two paragraphs are as much about humanity's conceit and bigheadedness as they are about atheism. Through his blind oracle, Diderot asks us why we continue to look beyond nature in order to explain nature. He then supplies the answer: we have created this illusory myth so that we may flatter our own supposed self-importance.

Treating believers as bumptious fools—imploring them to do away with their "tortoise"—was not Saunderson's last word. Shortly before he dies, he enters into a delirium during which he invites us to consider how the universe might have come into being. This poetic vision of the primordial soup is among the most daring passages ever published during Diderot's lifetime:

> [W]hen the universe was hatched from fermenting matter, my fellow men [blind men] were very common. Yet could not [this] belief about animals also hold for worlds? How many lopsided, failed worlds are there that have been dissolved and are perhaps being remade and redissolved every minute in faraway spaces, beyond the reach of my hands and your eyes, where movement is still going on and will keep going until the bits of matter arrange themselves in a combination that is sustainable? Oh philosophers!

Come with me to the edge of this universe, beyond the point where I can feel and you can see organized beings; wander across that new ocean with its irregular and turbulent movements and see if you can find in them any trace of that intelligent being whose wisdom you admire here.[18]

For the eighteenth-century reader, Saunderson's dreamlike vision of failed worlds and monstrous human prototypes would have recalled Lucretius's *De rerum natura*. What is innovative about this part of the *Letter*, however, is how Diderot makes use of this vision of chance and godlessness. Rather than fold this into a pedantic account of the earth's origins, Diderot lets Saunderson's visionary ideas emerge from his agitated, delusional state. This atheistic fever is supposed to be contagious, infecting us with the idea that we are little more than the fleeting result of happenstance.[19]

VINCENNES

Sometime during July 1749, the second-most powerful man in France, the Comte d'Argenson—his administrative titles included royal minister of the press, minister of censorship, minister of war, and supervisor of the Department of Paris—received a complaint about an irreverent book published by an upstart philosophe named Denis Diderot. This time the grievance did not originate from a *mouchard*, censorious priest, or attentive censor; it had come from one of the minister's friends, Madame Dupré de Saint-Maur, who had philosophic ambitions of her own.

Dupré de Saint-Maur had been disparaged. In the first paragraphs of the *Letter on the Blind*, Diderot (or, more precisely, his narrator) had complained that he was not invited to observe one of the first cataract operations in France, which had been presided over by René-Antoine Ferchault de Réaumur. The narrator went on to ridicule those who attended the procedure as dim-witted "eyes without consequence." Dupré, who had been present at the event, felt personally attacked and presumably asked d'Argenson to teach the disrespectful philosophe a lesson about criticizing his betters.[20]

Had the Letter appeared at any other time, the minister of censorship might have ignored his lady friend's grousing. But Diderot's past brazenness, heretical ideas, and police file came to d'Argenson's attention during a tumultuous moment in French history. Economic troubles, widespread starvation among the urban poor, and an almost universal disappointment with the terms of the peace treaty of Aix-la-Chapelle—which required France to return most of present-day Belgium to Austria—had led to widespread unrest and disenchantment.[21] Paris had been on edge for months.

Some of the turmoil of 1749 had come from decommissioned soldiers who were wreaking havoc in the capital, including abducting and killing a number of women during a "celebration of the peace" ceremony near the Hôtel de Ville. A flurry of antigovernment poems and songs were also crisscrossing the city.[22] What was perhaps most galling to Louis XV was the pervasive rumor that he had supposedly ordered the police to kidnap the capital's children and take them to Versailles, where he was supposedly having them slaughtered so that he might bathe in their blood, thereby purifying himself of his sins. Not surprisingly, the king called on d'Argenson to reassert control over both the population and this circulation of unseemly ideas. This he did. By the spring of 1749, all fifty cells in the Bastille were full with tax protesters, "*philosophes*, Jansenists, and people who simply spoke ill of the regime."[23]

It was in this anxious climate that d'Argenson decided to make an example of Diderot. On July 22, he ordered Berryer, the lieutenant-général de police, to arrest the writer and take him to the Château de Vincennes, a former royal palace that had been converted into a prison. Two days later, Agnan Philippe Miché de Rochebrune, a lawyer at Parlement and commissioner of police, and Joseph d'Hémery, the inspector of the book trade, arrived at Diderot's apartment on the ruc de la Vieille Estrapade at 7:30 a.m. to take the writer into custody. After gaining entrance into his second-story flat, they interrogated the writer and searched for any papers or works that attacked morality or religion.[24]

Based on Berryer's file on the writer, which included the testimony of a printer who had divulged the exact list of Diderot's publications, Commissioner Rochebrune hoped to unearth a treasure trove of impious treatises or pornographic short stories. (In later years, it was discovered that Rochebrune had actually gathered a substantial collection of forbidden works for his own edification.)[25] Yet the commissioner found nothing akin to the talking vaginas of Diderot's *The Indiscreet Jewels* or any discernibly materialist treatises. What he reported in his inventory was twenty-one wooden boxes of manuscripts related to the as yet unpublished *Encyclopédie* and a manuscript version of the already published *Letter on the Blind*.

Rochebrune nevertheless informed Diderot that he was the object of a royal lettre de cachet, a writ of incarceration signed by Louis XV himself at his royal residence in Compiègne. This legal document, one of the most hated expressions of arbitrary power associated with the ancien régime, could send prisoners to jail without a trial, in certain cases for life. According to Madame de Vandeul's account of this episode, her mother, Toinette, was in a back bedroom getting François-Jacques dressed when Berryer's men arrived. Once Diderot realized that he was being taken to prison, he asked and received permission to let his wife know that he was leaving. For fear of worrying her, however, he simply said that he needed to take care of some business related to the *Encyclopédie* and that he would see her later that evening. A few minutes later, perhaps feeling like something was not quite right, Toinette stuck her head out of the window and saw one of the guards shoving her husband toward the waiting coach. Finally realizing what had transpired, she collapsed.

Diderot's eight-kilometer trip from the rue de la Vieille Estrapade to the Château de Vincennes—just east of Paris—took about an hour. D'Argenson had specified that Diderot be taken to Vincennes because the Bastille's cells continued to be full of political prisoners, among them a significant number of purveyors and aficionados of antigovernment poetry.[26]

THE CHÂTEAU DE VINCENNES

Upon his arrival at Vincennes, Diderot was once again interrogated and then shepherded to a cheerless cell within the château's massive dungeon tower. Today it is possible to visit this imposing 165-foot-tall fortification, including the rooms that served as prison cells. Contemporary craftsmen and stonemasons, however, have restored much of the dungeon tower to its former glory as a royal manor used by French kings from the fourteenth to the seventeenth century. This was hardly what the tower looked and felt like in 1749. As Diderot described it, the part of the dungeon he inhabited had become a foul-smelling and (as he would claim) disease-producing hideaway where the monarchy locked up its undesirables.[27]

SOLITARY

Incarcerated life under the ancien régime could vary widely. While all prisons had their share of lice, mice, rats, and rampant contagions, prisoners at Vincennes received different treatment based on their presumed wrongdoings, notoriety, or social class. Aristocratic or wealthy internees, with the right bribes or relations, could readily arrange for a comfortable internment. When the Marquis de Sade was arrested and taken to the prison in the late 1770s, he quickly made the best of his situation by paying to have his cell furnished with Turkish carpets, his own furniture, and a library with hundreds of volumes. The contrast with political prisoners such as Jean-Henri Latude, could not have been more stark. Unlike Sade, Latude had incurred the full wrath of the state by sending a box of poison to Louis XV's cherished mistress, the Marquise de Pompadour, in 1749. The intention of this struggling writer had not been to do her harm, however. On the contrary, the misguided man had actually hoped to become a national hero by informing Pompadour of the conspiracy shortly before she ingested any of the toxin. This gambit backfired spectacularly. Not long after the deadly package arrived, Latude was quickly identified as the culprit and ended up spending the next thirty-five years locked up in both Vincennes and the Bastille, often consigned to dungeon cells with little more to eat than stale bread and bouillon.[28]

Police documents indicate that Diderot's treatment fell somewhere between Sade's and Latude's. While the philosophe was confined to an insalubrious room in the dungeon tower, Berryer instructed the château's warden to treat him decently, exactly like "Boyer and Ronchères," two Jansenist priests who were spending the rest of their lives in prison for publishing anti-Jesuit tracts.[29] This meant that Diderot was to receive his food at the king's expense, generally a bowl of pot roast or, occasionally, liver or tripe, along with a bottle of wine and a large serving of bread.[30] On Fridays, the prison served cheap fish—herring or stingray—along with some boiled vegetables.[31]

Diderot had settled into this routine for a week before Berryer finally reached out to him about his case. On Thursday, July 31, the chief of police himself made the trip from Paris to Vincennes to interrogate the philosophe about his activities. The transcript from their encounter not only contains the specifics of the debriefing, but Diderot's continued attempts to deceive his interrogator:

> Interrogation...of Mr. Diderot, prisoner by order of the King in the Dungeon of Vincennes...on the 31st of July, 1749, in the afternoon, in the counsel room of the aforementioned keep, after the prisoner swore to tell and respond truthfully.

Interrogated regarding his names, surnames, age, class, country, address, profession, and religion:

[Prisoner] replied that his name was Denis Diderot, native of Langres, 36 years old, from Paris, when he was arrested on rue de la Vieille Estrapade, in the Parish of Saint-Étienne du Mont, and of the catholic, apostolic and Roman faith.

Asked if he had authored a work entitled: *Letter on the Blind for the Benefit of Those Who See*:

He replied no.

Interrogated by whom he printed the same work:

He replied that it was not he who published the book.

Asked if he had sold or given the manuscript to someone:

He replied no.

Asked if he knew the name of the author of the work:

He replied he had no idea...

Asked if he composed a work, that appeared two years before, and that was titled *The Indiscreet Jewels*:

He said no, etc. [32]

In the remainder of the document, Berryer asks about each of the works that Diderot had been accused of writing. Each time, Diderot denied having anything to do with the manuscripts, the publishers, or the distribution of said books. At the end of the interview, the philosophe read through the questions and answers, attested to their validity, and signed his name.

Diderot's fraudulent defense did not sit well with Berryer. Irritated by the philosophe's stonewalling, the police chief returned to Paris and immediately ordered the interrogation of Diderot's publisher, the thirty-seven-year-old Laurent Durand. Brought before Berryer the very next day, Durand was far more cooperative than Diderot, quickly revealing the history of clandestine arrangements into which he had entered in order to publish the author's proscribed books. Proof in hand, Berryer now had very little incentive to free the unrepentant philosophe. His next move, which turned out to be quite effective, was to simply cease communication with his prisoner.

Eight days after Berryer interrogated Diderot — and approximately three weeks after Diderot had been taken to Vincennes — the philosophe understood that the deafening silence coming from Paris meant his time in prison would not be measured in weeks, but in months or years. This became painfully clear one day when a guard came by his cell to provide him with his weekly allotment of candles, which amounted to two per day. According to Madame de Vandeul, Diderot informed the jailer that he did not need any at this point, for he had plenty in reserve. The guard replied curtly that he might not need them now, but that he would be glad to have them in the winter, when the sun came up shortly before nine and set well before five p.m.[33]

Diderot's stubbornness began to waiver by the middle of his fourth week in the isolated cell. Requesting paper, he sent carefully worded letters to both Count d'Argenson and Berryer. In his letter to d'Argenson, he employed a dual strategy. At times, he apologized somewhat vaguely for his indiscretions; more effectively, perhaps, he laced his missive with flattery and a thinly disguised inducement. After commending the count for being a great supporter of the era's literature, Diderot let slip that he (as editor of the *Encyclopédie*) had been on the cusp of announcing that the entire project was going to be dedicated to d'Argenson himself. The message was crystal clear: release me and the dedication page of the forthcoming *Encyclopédie* is yours. Two years later, this tribute appeared in the first volume of the great dictionary.[34]

At the same time that he was enticing d'Argenson, Diderot threw himself on the mercy of Berryer in a longer and more doleful letter. After conjuring up the possibility of dying an agonizing death in his cell, he spilled a great deal of ink playing up his career as a diligent intellectual engaged in disseminating math and "letters." No mention was made, however, of why he had been imprisoned in the first place.

This absence did not escape Berryer's notice, and once again the police chief did not respond to Diderot's letter. Increasingly desperate, Diderot sent another note to Berryer in which he not only admitted to being the author of *Philosophical Thoughts*, *The Indiscreet Jewels*, and *Letter on the Blind*, but also apologized for sharing these "self-indulgences of the mind" with the French public. A week after receiving this confession, Berryer traveled personally to the prison to speak to Diderot, and told him that he would soon be liberated from solitary confinement and given a proper room and bed, provided that he promise in writing not to do anything in the future that would be in any way contrary to religion and good morals.[35]

While carrying on these negotiations with both Berryer and d'Argenson, Diderot also managed to write two letters to his father in Langres.[36] Though the two men had been estranged for more than six years, the thirty-four-year-old Denis had obviously dreaded the moment that his father (and the rest of Langres) would hear of his imprisonment. To temper the effect that this news might have in his home city, he hinted in at least one of his letters that he had been the victim of slander and that the police were accusing him of publishing books that he had not authored. While this was technically true—Berryer had accused him of being the author of François-Vincent Toussaint's outlawed *Les mœurs* (*The Manners*, 1748), for example—Diderot hid or downplayed the full extent of his anonymous publications. One imagines how hard it would have been to admit to being the author of a disgraceful work of libertine fiction like *The Indiscreet Jewels*.

Didier Diderot was no dupe, however. In the letter he sent back to Denis, he signaled that he knew full well why his son had found himself locked up in a "stone box" at Vincennes. He then coolly informed the prisoner that he should take advantage of his time in jail to reflect on his life. From the elder Diderot's point of view, his son's downfall had come from a poor use of both his education and his mind. If "God has given you talents," he wrote pointedly, "it is not for weakening the dogma of our sainted religion."[37]

But the most significant aspect of the letter was not this gentle scolding, but rather the sentiment that it was time for the errant son to come back to the family. Some of this change of heart may have stemmed from the fact that prison had, quite paradoxically, opened lines of communication that had been closed for years. Perhaps as importantly, Didier Diderot also saw his life and family slipping away in 1749. His wife of thirty-six years, Angélique, had died the previous October, at seventy-one years of age; his twenty-seven-year-old daughter, also named Angélique, had gone mad and died behind the thick limestone walls of the Ursuline convent the same year. Faced with the prospect of a far smaller family, and surely touched that his son had reached out to him despite his own pitiful circumstances, Didier Diderot extended an olive branch. Though his letter was full of admonitions, the patriarch announced that he was now happy to approve of Denis's marriage to Toinette, assuming that he was in fact married in the eyes of the Church. He then added that he was counting on his son to allow him to meet his grandchildren.

PRISON TALES

Didier Diderot's letter presumably reached his son in mid-September, two months into his stay at Vincennes. By this time, the prisoner's conditions and mood had both improved markedly. Released from his cell in the château's keep, he now had access to the garden and courtyard and had moved to more comfortable quarters. Berryer had also granted him the right to receive visits from both family members and associates working on the *Encyclopédie*.

Toinette traveled to Vincennes on the first day that Diderot was granted visitation rights. The four printers, who had dispatched several letters to both Berryer and d'Argenson pleading for his release, also came to discuss how best to proceed on the stalled dictionary. In the following days and weeks, Diderot also received visits from his coeditor, Jean le Rond d'Alembert, and from the artist Louis-Jacques Goussier, who had been hired to begin work on the *Encyclopédie*'s illustrations. What remained of his stay at Vincennes became a working jail term.

As is the case with the imprisonment of any famous person, there are stories and family folklore associated with Diderot's time in Vincennes. Madame de Vandeul recounts how, during her father's days in solitary confinement, he took a slate shingle off the roof, ground it up to make his own ink, fashioned a toothpick into a quill, all in order to write in the margins of Milton's *Paradise Lost*. This example of prison ingenuity is entirely plausible compared with Madame de Vandeul's account of how her father escaped from Vincennes in order to spy on his mistress of four years, Madame de Puisieux. Madeleine was apparently as concerned as anyone else about Diderot's incarceration; shortly after he was able to receive visitors, she joined the list of pilgrims making their way to Vincennes. Hoping for a warm reunion, she was instead greeted with a jealous interrogation after Diderot noticed she was dressed far too elegantly for a prison visit. After forcing his lover to admit that she was continuing on to nearby Champigny to attend a party, Diderot was apparently so convinced that she had replaced him with another lover that, after her coach left, he supposedly slipped out of the prison and made the seven-kilometer trek on foot to Champigny to keep an eye on her. This jaunt — through the woods of Vincennes and across the Marne River — does not seem terribly likely; nor does the supposed denouement of the story, where Diderot allegedly returned to the château and confessed his temporary breakout to the Marquis du Châtelet, the governor of the prison. Regardless of his warm relationship with his genteel host, Diderot rarely came clean so readily.

Whether or not Diderot made this trip to Champigny matters very little within the overall history of his stay at Vincennes. Far more consequential were Jean-Jacques Rousseau's trips to the prison during the fall of 1749. In *The Confessions*, Rousseau relates that his friend's incarceration distressed him immensely and that, when he was able to tear himself from his work, he made the long journey on foot from Paris to Vincennes on several occasions to see Diderot. The first time that Rousseau arrived at the prison, as he tells it, he found the jailed philosophe engaged in conversation with a priest and Diderot's coeditor, d'Alembert.[38] Describing Diderot as "much affected by his imprisonment," Rousseau writes that he was moved to tears by this reunion: "I saw only him as I entered; I made one bound, uttered one cry, pressed my face to his, and embraced him tightly, speaking to him only with my tears and sighs, for my joy and affection choked me."[39]

Rousseau's description of his emotional reunification with his friend is followed by his mythical account of how he — a budding philosophe — was struck with the idea of turning his back on the corrupting influences of knowledge and civilization, the very cornerstones of the Enlightenment project. This story begins on a hot summer afternoon when Rousseau is making his way on foot to the Vincennes prison. Exhausted and sweaty, he decides to take shelter under a tree on the side of the road, where he pulls out the *Mercure de France*, the era's premier magazine for high literary and philosophical exchange. It is in the pages of this monthly periodical that Rousseau fatefully stumbles upon an essay contest proposed by the Academy of Dijon, soliciting responses to the following question: "Has the revival of the arts and sciences contributed more to the corruption or the purification of morals?"[40]

This was more than a question of technical progress and moral decline. The Dijon academicians were tacitly recognizing that something drastic was happening in France. While this massive country of twenty-five million people continued to be held back (compared with England) by its entrenched guilds, a rigid social system, and problems related to a crippling debt, its scientists and philosophes had nonetheless dragged the country into a stimulating phase of intellectual fervor that risked being far more radical than the more genteel forms of Enlightenment taking place across the Channel or in Holland. These intellectual and "philosophical" advances, in many people's view, had come at a cost: philosophes including Voltaire and Diderot had not only encouraged people to separate the spheres of religion and science, but were asking them to rethink basic moral questions — such as human happiness — that had been the purview of the Church. In a world of profound change, where the "revival of the arts and sciences" had been accompanied by a tremendous amount of freethinking, the Dijon Academy's contest seemed to cry out for a careful survey of recent achievements in painting, sculpture, music, and the sciences — alongside a few pointed remarks regarding excesses of certain misguided souls.

Rousseau had something else in mind. Describing his reaction after he discovered the Academy's contest, Rousseau explains that "the moment I read this I beheld another universe and became another man." By the time he arrived at the prison, he continues, "I was in a state of agitation bordering on delirium."[41] Rousseau then recounts how he and Diderot reportedly discussed this question at length during their visit and how Diderot not only encouraged him to compete for this prize, but to go forward with the contrarian "truth" that he had received while on the road to the prison, namely, that the arts and sciences had done more harm than good to humankind.[42] Of this conversation, Diderot writes,

> I was at this time at the Château de Vincennes. Rousseau came to see me, and while he was there, he consulted me on how to respond to the question [proposed by the Academy of Dijon]. "There is no hesitating," I told him, "you will take the side that no one else will take." "You are right," Rousseau responded to me; and he set to work transforming this *jeu d'esprit* into a "philosophical system."[43]

In the final form of his *Discours sur les sciences et les arts* (*Discourse on Sciences and Arts*, 1750), which he completed with Diderot's help a few months later, Rousseau put forward a genealogy of ruin which traces the scientific and technical disciplines back to the vices human beings acquired when they left the state of nature: our greed, he argues, gave rise to mathematics; our unbridled ambition spawned mechanics; and our idle curiosity produced physics. Rousseau's message was simple and compelling: the more we advance technically and intellectually, the more we regress morally. Progress is not only a mirage that humankind is foolishly chasing, it is our downfall.

Rousseau's essay not only won the Academy of Dijon prize, but led him to produce a second and more powerful account of humankind's fall, which he entitled the *Discours sur l'origine et les fondements de l'inégalité parmi les hommes* (*Discourse on the Origin and Basis of Inequality Among Men*, 1755). Also known as the *Second Discourse*, this profoundly influential piece of speculative anthropology chronicles humankind's unfortunate transition from the state of nature—where humans were solitary, savage, and without reason or rationality—to the time when they began to cohabitate, develop reason and language, compare themselves to others, and enter the realm of social competition and rank. From there, Rousseau demonstrates, it was only a small step to private property and social inequality, both of which could only arise in man's newly civilized state. Diderot once again served as Rousseau's primary reader before he published the *Second Discourse*. Little did he know, however, that this stunningly pessimistic understanding of history was far more than a provocative argument; it reflected a fundamental realignment in the way that Rousseau understood the "social system," his friendships, and the way that he would henceforth relate to Diderot and the rest of the philosophes.

THE RETURN

Diderot was finally released from Vincennes on November 3, 1749, 102 days after his arrest. One of the few possessions that he brought back with him was a small edition of Plato's *Apology of Socrates* (399 BCE) that he had managed to keep with him during his stay. According to Madame de Vandeul, the prison's guards had decided not to confiscate this particular book because they could not imagine that he could read the ancient Greek. Diderot reportedly made good use of the text, translating extensive portions of the *Apology* during his imprisonment.

That he was able to keep Plato's *Apology* must have seemed appropriate. In this book Plato recounts the trial of his mentor and his speech of self-defense; he also details how Socrates had been accused, among other things, of being an unbeliever. Later in his career, Diderot often referred to the Greek philosopher as a kindred spirit who, like himself, was ill-suited to his own bullying era. As he put it in 1762, "When Socrates died, he was seen in Athens as we [philosophes] are seen in Paris. His morals were attacked; his life slandered." He was "a mind who dared speak freely about the Gods."[44]

Despite such similarities, aspects of Socrates' captivity diverge significantly from the account of Diderot's stay in Vincennes. Unlike the French philosophe, Socrates remained famously resigned in the face of persecution, calmly and knowingly drinking the hemlock that ended his life. Diderot, on the other hand, was ready to do anything to gain his freedom, deliberately putting on a series of masks designed to deceive his captors. When he first arrived at the prison, he played the defiant philosophe; soon thereafter he became the suffering prisoner; by the end of his stay, he was the remorseful sycophant. Some years later, he famously justified such moral shilly-shallying as the direct result of unequal power relations. Humans, he suggested, actually have very little agency most of the time, and must strike poses depending on who has influence over them; life, in short, demands moral compromises. In *Rameau's Nephew*, Diderot labeled these ethical slippages "vocational idioms." Each occupation, in his view, tends to accept certain repeated moral lapses as established practice, and thus ethically tolerable, much in the same way that linguistic idioms — curious turns of phrase — also become commonly accepted over time. If there was one "vocational idiom" employed by the persecuted philosophe while he was in prison, it was undoubtedly duplicity, especially vis-à-vis the police.

Shortly before he was finally released from Vincennes, Diderot had his last meeting with Berryer, the lieutenant-général de police. During this encounter, the prisoner signed a statement promising to never again publish the type of heretical works that had led to his humiliating imprisonment. For the next thirty-three years, he would essentially keep his word. Part of this had to do with the fact that Diderot knew that, for the rest of his life, each time he talked in a café, met strangers in a salon, or sent a letter, he might well be under the surveillance of the city's *mouchards*. And yet, if the state effectively put an end to his public career as a writer of audacious, single-authored books, Diderot nonetheless intended to disseminate the joys of freethinking even more boldly upon his release from Vincennes. The labyrinthine *Encyclopédie*, as it turned out, would provide just the right venue.

IV

THE ENLIGHTENMENT BIBLE

Diderot's incarceration at Vincennes took place exactly halfway through his seventy years on earth. An unwelcome caesura, prison became the dramatic pause that gave shape and meaning to both sides of his life. Before prison, Diderot had been a journeyman translator, the editor of an unpublished encyclopedia, and a relatively unknown author of clandestine works of heterodoxy; on the day that he walked out of Vincennes, he was forever branded as one of the most dangerous evangelists of freethinking and atheism in the country.

During Diderot's three-month imprisonment, the Count d'Argenson and his brother the marquis had looked on with amusement while this "insolent" philosophe had bowed and scraped before the authority of the state. In a diary entry from October 1749, the marquis related with glee how his brother the count had supposedly broken Diderot's will. Solitary confinement and the prospect of a cold winter had succeeded where the police's warnings had failed; in the end, the once-cheeky writer had not only begged for forgiveness, but his "weak mind," "damaged imagination," and "senseless brilliance" had been subdued. Diderot's days as a writer of "entertaining but amoral books," it seemed, were over.[1]

The marquis was only half right. When Diderot was finally released from Vincennes in November 1749, he certainly returned to Paris with his tail between his legs. Entirely silenced, however, he was not. Two years after he left prison, the first volume of the *Encyclopédie* that he and Jean le Rond d'Alembert were editing together appeared in print. Its extended and self-important title, which indicated a *systematic* and critical treatment of the era's knowledge *and* its trades, promised something far beyond a normal reference work:

> *Encyclopédie, ou Dictionnaire raisonné des sciences, des arts et des métiers,* par une société de gens de lettres. Mis en ordre par M. Diderot, de l'Académie royale des Sciences et des Belles-Lettres de Prusse; et quant à la partie mathématique, par M. D'Alembert, de l'Académie royale de Prusse, et de la Société royale de Londres.

> *Encyclopédie, or a Systematic Dictionary of the Sciences, Arts, and Crafts,* by a Society of Men of Letters. Edited by Mr. Diderot, of the Royal Academy of Sciences and Belles-Lettres of Prussia; and, regarding the mathematical parts, by Mr. D'Alembert, of the Royal Academy of Prussia and the Royal Society of London.

Far more influential and prominent than the short single-authored works that Diderot had produced up to this point in his life, the *Encyclopédie* was expressly designed to pass on the temptation and method of intellectual freedom to a huge audience in Europe and, to a lesser extent, in faraway lands like Saint Petersburg and Philadelphia. Ultimately carried to term through ruse, obfuscation, and sometimes cooperation with the authorities, the *Encyclopédie* (and its various translations, republications, and pirated excerpts and editions) is now considered the supreme achievement of the French Enlightenment: a triumph of secularism, freedom of thought, and eighteenth-century commerce. On a personal level, however, Diderot considered this dictionary to be the most thankless chore of his life.

PARIS, 1745: THE GROUNDWORK

Though the *Encyclopédie* is now synonymous with Diderot, the project did not begin as his brainchild. The original idea came from a hapless immigrant from Danzig (Gdańsk) named Gottfried Sellius. Sometime in January 1745, this tall, bone thin academic contacted the printer-bookseller André-François Le Breton to propose a potentially lucrative venture: a French translation of one of the first "universal" encyclopedias of both the arts and the sciences to be published, Ephraim Chambers's two-volume *Cyclopaedia* (1728). The printer was intrigued. English-to-French translations, which could be done without paying a livre to the foreign author or printer, had become big business for his guild. Two years before, in fact, he had hired the then unknown Diderot to help translate another English reference work, Robert James's *Medicinal Dictionary* (1743–45).

Le Breton agreed to meet on a subsequent occasion with Sellius and his partner, an ostensibly well-to-do English gentleman named John Mills. Mills must have initially seemed like a valuable contributor: in addition to bringing a native understanding of English to the proposed translation, he also hinted that he had the means to bankroll part of the project. Two months later, Le Breton signed an agreement with Mills that called for an augmented four-volume translation of the English dictionary, along with a fifth volume containing 120 plates.[2]

Preparations for the new *Encyclopédie* commenced immediately. Le Breton reportedly ordered reams of high-grade paper as well as a shipment of metal *fonte* — an alloy of lead, pewter, and antimony — for a new set of movable type.[3] Working with Sellius and Mills, he also printed and distributed a grandiloquent pamphlet that solicited subscribers for the book project. To his delight, several journals, including the Jesuit *Mémoires de Trévoux*, quoted the leaflet's buoyant prose verbatim: "There is nothing more useful, more fecund, better analyzed, better linked, in a word more perfect and beautiful than this dictionary. This is the present that Mr. Mills has bestowed upon France, his adopted country."[4]

Mills's gift to the French nation hardly lived up to this rhetoric. When Le Breton received examples of the work, he was furious to discover that the translation was riddled with inaccuracies and mistakes. Mills also revealed himself to be anything but a wealthy aristocrat when he began pressuring Le Breton to sign over a portion of the project's future proceeds. The hard-nosed printer, while smallish in stature, responded with his fists and cane, beating his business partner so badly on a Saturday night in 1745 that Mills brought criminal charges.[5] Le Breton answered this accusation with his own suit against Mills, whom he besmirched as a cheat and an imposter in a publicly circulated *mémoire*. The well-publicized *Encyclopédie*, it seemed, was going nowhere.[6]

Despite this debacle, Le Breton continued to believe in both the feasibility and profitability of the proposed *Encyclopédie* project. After waiting several months for the air to clear, he once again began preparations for soliciting another royal privilege. More cognizant this time of the substantial logistics and financial risks involved in producing this multivolume work, Le Breton entered into partnership with three printers — Antoine-Claude Briasson, Michel-Antoine David, and Laurent Durand — the same men who had collaborated on the publication of the multivolume *Medicinal Dictionary*. He also sought out a different type of general editor to replace Mills, someone who was not only French, but seasoned, and with sterling credentials. This turned out to be Jean-Paul de Gua de Malves.[7] An accomplished mathematician and fellow of the Royal Society of London, the Académie Royale des Sciences in Paris, and the Collège de France, the lanky and seemingly undernourished Gua de Malves signed a contract with the consortium on June 27, 1746, in front of two witnesses, the twenty-nine-year-old Jean le Rond d'Alembert and the thirty-two-year-old Denis Diderot, both of whom had been brought on to the project to edit and, in Diderot's case, translate some of the articles.[8]

Gua de Malves's involvement in the project lasted for no more than a year.[9] This time the *Encyclopédie* was undone by the new chief editor's irascible personality and shameful organizational skills. Like Mills before him, he, too, entered into a series of bitter disagreements with Le Breton and the other printers and ultimately left the project in the summer of 1747.[10] The departure of the short-tempered geometrician would change Diderot's life: after two months of indecision, Le Breton and the small consortium of printers officially named Diderot and d'Alembert to be the new coeditors of the *Encyclopédie*.

From the point of view of the four printers, d'Alembert and Diderot were as different as chalk and cheese. The celebrated d'Alembert — who had published a groundbreaking work on fluid dynamics in 1744 — could recruit among his colleagues at the

Berlin Academy of Sciences, oversee articles having to do with the sciences and mathematics, and, like Gua de Malves, provide an air of institutional respectability to the project. Although he had only just celebrated his thirtieth birthday, this handsome man had already established himself as the most famous geometer in Europe. An undisputed genius who was in contact with the greatest mathematical minds of his era, d'Alembert had been chosen to become the most famous face of the *Encyclopédie*. The printers saw Diderot in an entirely different light. On the one hand, all of these men knew that Diderot was a workhorse. While penning his own clandestine books, Diderot had also been the lead translator of James's substantial *Medicinal Dictionary*. On the other hand, Le Breton and his associates were well aware that this up-and-coming translator and writer — the former abbé Diderot — had a potentially dangerous tendency to challenge accepted religious ideas in print.[11]

PLANNING AT THE "FLOWER BASKET"

That someone of André-François Le Breton's stature entrusted the biggest investment of his career to a writer with Diderot's doubtful reputation may now seem quite odd. Unlike some of the other more daring printers operating in the 1740s — in particular, Le Breton's partner in the *Encyclopédie* enterprise, Laurent Durand — Le Breton had carefully avoided controversial publication projects. This was smart business practice. Named one of the six official printers of the king in 1740, Le Breton benefited from a number of privileges, including tax breaks and a steady stream of easy-to-print royal commissions.[12]

Most importantly, however, Le Breton was the designated

printer of the *Almanach Royal*, a calendar that Louis XIV had asked Le Breton's grandfather, Laurent-Charles Houry, to begin printing in 1683. This extremely profitable reference work, which had swollen to six hundred pages under Le Breton's editorship, included an impressive range of useful information: astronomical occurrences, saints' days, religious obligations, and even coach departures (arrivals were less easy to predict). But most of the *Almanach* was dedicated to a roster of the monarchic, aristocratic, religious, and administrative notables who ruled over twenty-five million Frenchmen. As Louis-Sebastien Mercier put it, Le Breton's little book anointed the "gods of the earth."[13] With the exception of the royal printworks located in the Louvre, one would have been hard pressed to find a bookseller or printer more thoroughly associated with the power structure of the ancien régime. Bearing this in mind, when Le Breton brought on d'Alembert and Diderot to the *Encyclopédie* project, he had no intention of commissioning one of the most provocative works of the century. Some of his lack of concern surely had to do with the genre of the dictionary or encyclopedia itself. While it was true that the Huguenot Pierre Bayle had printed a contentious, four-volume dictionary in 1697 that engaged very critically with Christian dogma and history, he had done so from the relative safety of Holland. The most prominent French Catholic dictionary makers (who were effectively at war with their Protestant counterparts) tended, on the contrary, to corroborate and even strengthen the era's most traditional ideas on a given subject.[14] If the *Encyclopédie*'s direct French antecedents — Furetière's *Dictionnaire universel*, the Jesuits' so-called *Dictionnaire de Trévoux*, and the *Dictionnaire de l'Académie française* — had been any predictor, Diderot's and d'Alembert's *Encyclopédie* should have been an uncontroversial, although much larger, compendium of knowledge defining the arts and sciences.[15] This, of course, was not the editors' intention at all; the kind of dictionary that they were envisioning meant completely rethinking the way that dictionaries functioned.

JEAN LE ROND D'ALEMBERT,
ENGRAVING FROM LA TOUR'S PASTEL

Much of the planning for the third attempt at producing the *Encyclopédie* took place about a half mile from Le Breton's print shop, at a Left Bank "eating house" called the Panier fleuri (Flower Basket) on the rue des Grands-Augustins. Well before Diderot began work on the *Encyclopédie*, he had often come to this teeming quarter near the Pont Neuf—which had several boarding-houses, taverns, and cook-caterers—to meet up with Rousseau.[16] At the time, both men were leading modest, if not marginal, lives. Rousseau had been living in a series of small flats across the river, near the Palais Royal, earning enough money to feed himself by copying music; Diderot, who seemingly moved from apartment to apartment every six months, was also struggling to find his way in Paris. During these days of zealous companionship, the two men even made plans to create a waggish literary magazine called *Le Persifleur* (*The Scoffer*). Twenty years later, when Rousseau looked back sentimentally at this happy time in his life, he joked sarcastically that these gatherings must have been the highlight of the week for a man who "always failed to keep his appointments," because he never "missed a date at the Panier fleuri."[17]

After Diderot became coeditor of the *Encyclopédie* in late 1747, d'Alembert too joined these regular meetings at the eatery. Rousseau, who had volunteered to write articles on music for the dictionary, also introduced a soft-chinned priest by the name of abbé Étienne Bonnot de Condillac into the group.

ABBÉ ÉTIENNE BONNOT DE CONDILLAC

Unlike the three other men who congregated at the Panier fleuri, Condillac would not contribute a single article to the *Encyclopédie*. And yet, his philosophical orientation and interests had a decisive effect on the theoretical underpinnings of the project.

This became particularly true after Condillac shared a manuscript version of his *Essai sur l'origine des connaissances humaines* (*Essay on the Origin of Human Knowledge*) with the group in 1746.[18] Building on Locke's rejection of innate ideas, Condillac put forward a sweeping empiricist understanding of cognition that maintained that our senses are more than the source of the "raw material" for cognition; they also inform the way that our mind works, "teaching" us how to remember, desire, think, judge, and reason.[19] Condillac's contribution came at a critical point in the project's prehistory. Though the Catholic priest preferred as a matter of policy to give a wide berth to the *Encyclopédie*'s heterodoxy, he had nonetheless focused his friends' gaze on the critical relationship between theories of mind and a proper scientific approach to the study of the exterior world. This would turn out to be one of the foundations of the *Encyclopédie* project: replacing a theologically compatible theory of cognition with one that had little room for either the soul or an innate awareness of God's existence.[20]

PROMOTING THE *ENCYCLOPÉDIE*

During these anxious years before the first volume of the *Encyclopédie* finally appeared, Diderot and d'Alembert spent much of their time poring over the era's dictionaries and reference works. In addition to identifying the headwords for which they would need to commission articles, the coeditors needed to sketch out what they believed to be the myriad relationships between tens of thousands of possible entries. Thinking through the entire project before delegating their first article, for fear of missing a cross-reference, may have been the most punishing aspect of the *Encyclopédie* in the early days.

In addition to determining the scope and content of the project, and how exactly to proceed, the coeditors participated in
an equally critical venture — attracting subscribers. In the early
months of 1750, shortly after his return from Vincennes, Diderot
penned a nine-page "Prospectus" in which he announced tri-
umphantly that this book would be far more than a straightforward compendium of the era's facts and learning; in contrast to
earlier dictionaries, the forthcoming *Encyclopédie* was described
as a living, breathing text that would highlight the obvious and
obscure relationships between diverse spheres of learning. This
was evident in the way that Diderot defined the term "encyclopedia." Far more than a simple *circle* or *compass of learning* — the
literal meaning of the Greek *enkuklios paideia* — this new form of
reasoned dictionary would actively examine and restructure the
era's understanding of knowledge.

At the same time that Diderot emphasized the project's innovative qualities, he also let slip several white lies. Such were the
conventions of the prospectus genre. The first of these was that
the book, which simply did not exist at this point, was nearly
completed: "The work that we are announcing is no longer a work
to be accomplished. The manuscript and the drawings are complete. We can guarantee that there will be no fewer than eight
volumes and six hundred plates, and that the volumes will appear
without interruption."[21]

This bit of creative marketing dovetailed with Diderot's
romantic account of how the *Encyclopédie* had come into being. In
contrast to previous dictionaries or compendiums, he explained,
he and d'Alembert had selected an international team of specialists who were experts in their field. The era of the dabbler and the
dilettante, he implied, was over:

> We realized that to bear a burden as great as the one [d'Alembert
> and I] had to carry, we needed to share the load; and we immedi-
> ately looked to a significant number of savants…; we distributed
> the appropriate piece to each; mathematics to the mathematician;
> fortifications to the engineer; chemistry to the chemist; ancient
> and modern history to a man well versed in both; grammar to an
> author known for the philosophical spirit that reigns in his works;
> music, maritime subjects, architecture, painting, medicine, natu-
> ral history, surgery, gardening, the liberal arts, and the principles
> of the applied arts to men who have proved themselves in these
> areas; as such each person only [wrote on] what he understood.[22]

To be fair, not all of what Diderot asserts in this 1750 "Prospectus" was untrue. As the project gained momentum, d'Alembert
and Diderot convinced more than 150 so-called *Encyclopédistes* to
provide articles. Forty came from the fields of natural history,
chemistry, mathematics, and geography; another twenty-two
were doctors and surgeons; and twenty-five more were poets,
playwrights, philosophers, grammarians, or linguists. Diderot
and d'Alembert also commissioned fourteen artists, a group
which included engravers, draftsmen, architects, and painters.[23]
Some of these specialists ultimately produced large portions of
the *Encyclopédie*. Louis-Jean-Marie Daubenton, the keeper of the
king's natural history cabinet, provided almost one thousand
articles on the world's botanical specimens, minerals, and animal life. The famous Montpellier doctor Gabriel-François Venel
illuminated over seven hundred topics, ranging from constipation
to the forced evacuation of the stomach. Guillaume Le Blond, a
military historian and tutor to the king's children, wrote some
750 articles, among them dissertations on battlefield strategies,

military tribunals, and the various rituals associated with a victory. The renowned legal expert Antoine-Gaspard Boucher d'Argis would ultimately produce four thousand articles ranging from one documenting a plaintiff's legal recourse after a dog bite to the definition of and punishments for committing sodomy.

And yet, during the first years of *Encyclopédie* production, Diderot was the motor of the project. Although the title page of the first volume of the work proudly proclaims that the book was being produced by a "Society of Men of Letters" (with eighteen named contributors), he was ultimately obliged to write two thousand articles for this first tome on subjects as varied as geography, childbirth, botany, natural history, mythology, carpentry, gardening, architecture, geography, and literature.[24] He found himself similarly burdened for the second.

MIND AND METHOD

While Diderot was furiously writing articles for the first two volumes of the *Encyclopédie*, d'Alembert was engaged in producing one of the most celebrated texts of the French Enlightenment, the "Discours préliminaire" ("Preliminary Discourse," 1751). Serving as the primary introduction to the *Encyclopédie*, this manifesto signaled a dramatic shift in Europe's cultural and intellectual landscape.

In the first section of the "Discourse," d'Alembert explains how he and Diderot planned to categorize the tens of thousands of articles that the dictionary would ultimately contain. Implicitly rejecting any a priori categories or authorities, d'Alembert proposes what we might now call a mind-based organization of human knowledge. Beginning with the basic Lockean notion that our ideas arise solely through sensory contact with the exterior world, the mathematician then associates three forms of human cognition with their corresponding branches of learning. Borrowing this idea directly from the English philosopher, statesman, and scientist Francis Bacon and his 1605 *Advancement of Learning*, d'Alembert asserts that our Memory gives rise to the discipline of History; our Imagination corresponds to the category of Poetry (or artistic creativity); and our ability to Reason relates to the discipline of Philosophy.[25] In addition to creating the three major rubrics under which all the book's articles would supposedly be organized, this tripartite breakdown established an entirely secular foundation for the web of knowledge presented in the dictionary.

The second part of the "Discourse" situates the *Encyclopédie* project within a much larger chronicle of humankind's scientific and intellectual achievements. After lambasting the medieval era as a millennium of scholarly and scientific darkness, d'Alembert goes on to laud the intellectual heroes of the previous three hundred years, among them Bacon, Leibniz, Descartes, Locke, Newton, Buffon, Fontenelle, and Voltaire. These leading lights, according to the mathematician, had not only combated obscurantism and superstition, but they also gave rise to a new generation of scholars and savants that was now intent on ushering in a more rational and secular era. While d'Alembert's view of history does not advocate political upheaval by any stretch of the imagination, he was promoting what one might call an Enlightenment version of manifest destiny.

Diderot republished two companion pieces alongside d'Alembert's "Preliminary Discourse." The first was the aforementioned "Prospectus," which not only specifies how the various disciplines would be treated, but provides a useful history of dictionaries. (It is also here that Diderot states, somewhat pessimistically, that, in times of despair or revolution, the *Encyclopédie* might serve as a "sanctuary" of preserved knowledge, akin to a massive time capsule.)[26] The second document was a large foldout road map for the project, a slightly modified version of the "Système des connaissances humaines" (System of Human Knowledge) that had appeared with the "Prospectus" a year before. Graphically rendering the same breakdown of human understanding that d'Alembert described in the "Preliminary Discourse," Diderot's "System" paired Memory with History, Reason with Philosophy, and Imagination with Poetry. And under these cognitively based categories, Diderot spelled out the long list of subjects to be treated.

At first glance, this large map of topics, which ranged from comets to epic poetry, seems quite inoffensive. Indeed, the *Encyclopédie*'s earliest critic, the Jesuit priest Guillaume-François Berthier, did not quibble with how Diderot had organized the "System"; he simply accused Diderot of stealing this aspect of Bacon's work without proper acknowledgment. Diderot's real transgression, however, was not following the English philosopher more closely. For, while it was true that Diderot freely borrowed the overall structure of his tree of knowledge from Bacon, he had actually made two significant changes to the Englishman's conception of human understanding. First, he had broken down and subverted the traditional hierarchical relationship between liberal arts (painting, architecture, and sculpture) and "mechanical arts" or trades (i.e., manual labor). Second, and more subversively, he had shifted the category of religion squarely under humankind's ability to reason. Whereas Bacon had carefully and sagely preserved a second and separate level of knowledge

for theology outside the purview of the three human faculties,
Diderot made religion subservient to philosophy, essentially giving his readers the authority to critique the divine.

It is now somewhat difficult to pick up on the subtle yet substantial examples of heterodoxy that Diderot embedded in his
"System." To do so, one needs to do what an eighteenth-century
censor would do: scan the least prominent parts of the chart in
search of the most outrageous ideas. Let us look, for example, at
how Diderot further mocked the notion of religion in the subsec-
tion of the tree of knowledge dedicated to the so-called Science
of God.

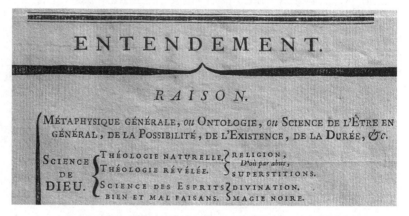

DIDEROT'S "SYSTEM OF HUMAN KNOWLEDGE,"
FROM VOLUME 1 OF THE *ENCYCLOPÉDIE* (DETAIL)

Already subjected to human reason, the "Science of God"
breaks down into two smaller categories: the first is natural theology (belief in God as deduced from the order of creation) and
the second is "revealed" theology (belief based on Holy Scripture
and the supposed demonstration of divine will). Both of these
rubrics are then reduced more generally to "religion." Diderot

buried his first somewhat irreverent notion underneath this
rubric, indicating that religion was ultimately indistinguishable
from superstition. This insulting idea—that religion and superstition were contiguous practices, not distinct categories—also
appears under the second major subcategory, the "Science of
Good and Evil Spirits," where religious practice seems to bleed
imperceptibly into divination and black magic. Close readers
got the joke: the more one studies the so-called Science of God,
the more it becomes clear that religion leads inevitably to occult
and irrational practices. Indeed, within the *Encyclopédie*'s overall
breakdown of human knowledge, the so-called Science of God
could have just as easily been classified under humankind's ability to "imagine" as its capacity to "reason."[77]

THE ACCESSIBLE LABYRINTH

In their correspondence, Diderot and d'Alembert often described
the *Encyclopédie* project as a theater of war where Enlightenment
intellectuals intent on ushering in an era of social change strug-
gled against the constant scrutiny and interference of the French
Church and state. The result, from d'Alembert's point of view, was
a book that suffered from a fundamental inability to say precisely
what it needed to say, especially in matters having to do with religion. Diderot was even more categorical. As he finally completed
work on the last volume, he blamed the radically uneven quality of
the articles on the unending compromises he was obliged to make
to satisfy the censors. And yet one of the many ironies associated
with the *Encyclopédie* is that the same conservative constituencies
that succeeded in censoring and shutting down the publication
of the *Encyclopédie* on two occasions—a story to which we will

return — were partially responsible for the genius and texture of this huge dictionary. After all, it was the most repressive elements of the ancien régime that spawned the book's brilliant feints, satire, and irony, not to mention its overall methodological apparatus and structure.

Even the most noncontroversial and seemingly benign aspect of the *Encyclopédie* — its alphabetical order — was chosen with this in mind.[28] By organizing the book's 74,000 articles alphabetically (as opposed to thematically), d'Alembert and Diderot implicitly rejected the long-standing separation of monarchic, aristocratic, and religious values from those associated with bourgeois culture and the country's trades.[29] In their *Encyclopédie*, they decided, an article on the most sacred subject of Catholicism could find itself next to an involved discussion of how brass was made. Furthermore, the arbitrary nature of alphabetical order authorized them to "orient" their reader as they saw fit, through a highly developed and subtle system of linking and cross-references.[30]

Through the power of the digital humanities, we now know much more than Diderot himself ever did about the network of cross-references or *renvois* that he and d'Alembert sprinkled throughout the *Encyclopédie*. In all, approximately 23,000 articles, or about one-third, had at least one cross-reference. The total number of links — some articles had five or six — reached almost 62,000.[31] Early on, Diderot and d'Alembert were quite coy about the function of their cross-references in both the "Preliminary Discourse" and the "Prospectus." But by the time that Diderot wrote his famous self-referential article on the project — the entry for "*Encyclopédie*" that appeared in the fifth volume in November 1755 — he had allowed himself to be more forthright about how this system of cross-references functioned.

The *Encyclopédie*, Diderot explains, contains two kinds of *renvois*: material and verbal. The material references are akin to contemporary hyperlinks: discipline- or subject-based recommendations for further study that "indicate the subject's closest connections to others immediately related to it, and its distant connections with others that might have seemed remote from it."[32] Designed to produce a dynamic relationship between and among subjects, the material *renvoi* echoes the vibrant and forceful way that Diderot himself tended to think. As he put it, "at any time, Grammar can refer [us] to Dialectics; Dialectics to Metaphysics; Metaphysics to Theology; Theology to Jurisprudence; Jurisprudence to History; History to Geography and Chronology; Chronology to Astronomy; Astronomy to Geometry; Geometry to Algebra, and Algebra to Arithmetic, etc."[33] Earlier dictionaries, with the exception, once again, of Bayle's *Dictionnaire historique et critique* (*Historical and Critical Dictionary*), generally sought to communicate a linear and singular vision of truth. This new interdynamic presentation of knowledge and cross-references had a different function: it not only highlighted unobserved relationships among various disciplines, but intentionally and blatantly put contradictory articles into dialogue, thereby underscoring the massive incongruities and fissures that existed within the era's knowledge. Readers who followed d'Alembert and Diderot on this intellectual journey could not help but question a number of the era's traditional convictions related to religion, morality, and politics.

In addition to these potentially thought-provoking cross-references, the *Encyclopédie*'s articles were interspersed with what Diderot called "verbal" links that guilefully satirized some of the era's sacred cows, or "national prejudices." He writes: "Whenever [an absurd preconception] commands respect, [the corresponding]

article ought to treat it respectfully, and with a retinue of plausibil-
ity and persuasion; but at the same time, this same article should
also dispel such rubbish and muck, by referring to articles in which
more solid principles form a basis for contrary truths."[34]

Some of these satirical *renvois* functioned quite bluntly. The
article on "Freedom of Thought," for example, pointed to Diderot's
biting entry on ecclesiastical "Intolerance," inviting its reader to
cultivate a critical viewpoint. Other references were more playful, including the *renvoi* that Diderot embedded in the article
"Cordeliers" or "Franciscans." This humorless entry begins with
the history of the religious order before arriving at an in-depth
description of the Cordeliers' vestments, particularly their hoods;
it then concludes by praising the religious order for its sobriety,
piety, morals, and the great men it has produced in the service of
God. The cross-reference, however, sends the reader to the article
"Hood," a comical entry where Diderot explains that a number of
religious orders, including the Cordeliers, have hotly debated the
type and shape of hood that their order should wear. This "fact" is
followed by a fabricated story detailing how a century-long war
broke out between the two factions of the Cordelier sect: "The
first [faction of Cordeliers] wanted a narrow hood, the others
wanted it wider. The dispute lasted for more than a century with
much intensity and animosity, and was just barely put to an end
by the papal bulls of four popes."[35]

As satire goes, the linking of *"Cordeliers"* and "Hood"—which
drew an implicit comparison between this ridiculous anecdote
and the far more serious and insoluble debate between Jansenists and Jesuits—was comparatively mild. Less so were some
of the other subject couplings that Diderot did not mention in
his article *"Encyclopédie."* The most famous example is the entry

on "*Anthropophages*" or "Cannibals": its cross-references directed readers to the entries for "Altar," "Communion," and "Eucharist."

The possibility of finding such scandalous satire incited the *Encyclopédie*'s audience to read the book more comprehensively than one did a typical dictionary. Yet Diderot and d'Alembert were very careful not to insert such patently irreligious ideas in the most obvious places. Indeed, for potentially touchy subjects such as "Adam," "Atheist," "Angels," "Baptism," "Christ," "Deists," and "Testament," the editors tended to commission orthodox articles. For the most incendiary topics, including materialism, Diderot decided to forgo commissioning or writing an article altogether.

"THE VEGETABLE LAMB PLANT,"
A LEGENDARY PLANT
DESCRIBED IN THE *ENCYCLOPÉDIE*

Yet Diderot and d'Alembert certainly amused themselves by sprinkling the dictionary with irreligious notions, often within the most arcane of articles. Consider, for example, Diderot's treatment of the Central Asian "Vegetable Lamb Plant" ("*Agnus scythicus*"). Commenting on claims that this massive flower sup-posedly produces a goatlike animal with head and hooves on its tall central stem, Diderot reminds his readers that the more extraordinary an asserted "fact" may be, the more one must seek out witnesses to confirm it. Few readers would have misunder-stood what Diderot was talking about when he concluded that all such miracles, which always seem to be witnessed by only a few people, "hardly deserve to be believed."[36]

Diderot and d'Alembert also encouraged another form of sat-ire, commissioning articles whose stodgy and earnest conformism provided their own form of mockery. Such was the case for abbé Mallet's plodding, five-thousand-word assessment of "Noah's Ark," a creationist account of the world that enters into absurdly laborious detail about the amount of wood used for the great ship, the number of animals saved (and those to be slaughtered for meat), and the system of manure disposal needed for the thou-sands of creatures aboard. Whether Mallet realized it or not, his explications of traditional Church doctrine not only bog down under the weight of their own improbable and contradictory assertions, but raise far more questions than they resolve.

Not all articles employed such oblique irony. Sometime in 1750, Diderot wrote a provocative entry on the subject of the human *âme* (soul) that he appended to a much longer article on the same subject, written by the Christian philosopher abbé Claude Yvon. Yvon's article, which Diderot himself had commis-sioned, gives a massive, 17,000-word history of the concept of the soul that includes frequent attacks against Spinoza, Hobbes, and the threat of materialism. From Yvon's Cartesian point of view, the soul is linked to God and, like the deity, is immaterial and immortal; and only humans, as opposed to animals, are blessed with this incorporeal essence. One suspects that, against his better judgment, Diderot simply could not let this lengthy dissertation stand without some sort of rebuttal.[37]

In his supplementary article, which the Jesuits attacked immediately upon its publication, Diderot did not get bogged down in abstruse theological questions. Instead, he asked a far simpler question: if the immaterial soul is supposedly the seat of consciousness and emotion, where does it connect to the body? In the pineal gland, as Descartes had asserted? In the brain? In the nerves? The heart? The blood?[38] Drawing attention to theology's inability to answer this question, he then went on to demonstrate that the supposed immateriality of consciousness — and the soul — was more tied to the physical world than many people believed. If someone is delivered poorly at birth by a midwife, has a stroke, or is hit violently on the head, says Diderot, "bid adieu to one's judgment and reason" and "say goodbye" to the supposed transcendence of the soul.[39] Diderot's critics understood perfectly well what the philosophe was saying in this article: the true location of the soul is in the imagination.[40]

The only other subject more problematic than religion was politics. In a country without political parties, where sedition was punished by sentencing to a galley ship or death, d'Alembert and Diderot never overtly questioned the spiritual and political authority of the monarchy. Yet the *Encyclopédie* nonetheless succeeded in advancing liberal principles, including freedom of thought and a more rational exercise of political power. As tepid as some of these writings may seem when compared with the political discourse of the Revolutionary era, the *Encyclopédie* played a significant role in destabilizing the key assumptions of absolutism.

Diderot's most direct and dangerous entry in this vein was his unsigned article on "Political Authority" (*"Autorité politique"*), which also appeared in the first volume of the *Encyclopédie*. Readers who chanced upon this article immediately noticed that it does not begin with a definition of political authority itself; instead, it opens powerfully with an unblemished assertion that neither God nor nature has given any one person the indisputable author- ity to reign.[41]

> POLITICAL AUTHORITY: No man has received from nature the
> right to command other men. Freedom is a gift from the heavens,
> and each individual of the same species has the right to enjoy it as
> soon as he is able to reason.[42]

"Autorité politique" did more than simply challenge the idea that a monarch derives his political legitimacy from the will of God. Anticipating what Rousseau would write several years later in the much more famous *Discourse on Inequality* (1755), Diderot goes on to recount the origins of political power and social inequality as arising from one of two possible sources, either "the force or vio- lence" of the person who absconded with people's freedom, which was Hobbes's view, or the consent of the subjugated group through established contract, which came from Locke. While Diderot does not contradict the right of the French kings to rule directly—he later goes on to praise Louis XV—he also puts forward the perilous idea that the real origin of political authority stems from the peo- ple, and that this political body not only has the inalienable right to delegate this power, but to take it back as well. Forty years later, during the Revolution, the most incendiary elements of *"Autorité*

politique" would provide the skeleton for the thirty-fifth and last article of the 1793 Declaration of the Rights of Man and of the Citizen, which asserted not only the sovereignty of the people, but the right to resist oppression and the duty to revolt.

THE VISUAL *ENCYCLOPÉDIE*

The most intriguing facet of the *Encyclopédie* is the artful ways in which its editors engineered the dissemination of subversive ideas—be it in a self-imploding article on theology or a satirical cross-reference. Yet the vast majority of its entries lacked even a trace of irony. At the heart of the *Encyclopédie* are tens of thousands of straightforward articles in fields including anatomy, architecture, astronomy, clock making, colonial practice, gardening, hydraulics, medicine, mineralogy, music, natural history, painting, pharmacology, physics, and surgery. Much of what is contained in this collective inventory of the era's learning is politically neutral compared to the *Encyclopédie*'s anticlerical or political commentary. And yet this massive flood of information reflects what is perhaps the *Encyclopédie*'s ultimate political act: the overturning of established orders of knowledge.

Nowhere was this truer than in the representation of the era's major trades and occupations, which are sumptuously depicted within the *Encyclopédie*'s eleven volumes of *planches*, or illustrated plates. These illustrations begin, in volume 1, with several bucolic scenes of domestic agriculture; they conclude, almost three thousand images later, with a stunning series of schematic drawings of the silk loom. This far-reaching inventory of craftsmanship and technical knowledge—which includes trades as varied as pin making, boot making, and ship construction—not only elevated the era's occupations and crafts to new heights, but helped redefine the scope of what encyclopedias could and should endeavor to accomplish.[43]

As originally conceived, the illustrated portion of the *Encyclopédie* was supposed to be something of a supplement, a visual compendium of several hundred images.[44] In its final form, however, the plates became as crucial to the overall project as the text itself. The lore associated with the production of these engravings conjures up Diderot at his most dynamic and polymathic, flitting about Paris from workshop to workshop, interviewing tradesmen, translating their technological knowledge into high French, and creating models of their machines. Diderot himself gave this impression in the "Prospectus": "We took pains to go into their workshops, to ask them questions, to take down what they said and develop their thoughts, to use the terms specific to their professions, to lay out the tables and diagrams...and to clarify, through long and frequent interviews, what others had imperfectly, obscurely, and sometimes unreliably explained."[45]

While it is certainly true that this Langres-born son of a master cutler took an active interest in certain trades — he was apparently fascinated by a stocking machine model that he kept at his desk — it seems that Diderot played up his involvement with the tradesmen. His later correspondence indicates that he spent most of his time during the 1750s and 1760s in editorial mode, while the real work on the plates was delegated to a series of illustrators, chief among them Jean-Jacques Goussier.

Goussier, who is among the greatest unsung heroes of the *Encyclopédie*, signed onto the project in 1747. Acting under Diderot's supervision, the illustrator toiled alongside a relatively small team of draftsmen for twenty-five years, producing well over 900 of the 2,885 illustrations.⁴⁶ The labor involved in this process is, by contemporary standards, inconceivable. To begin with, many of the subjects treated in the plates necessitated an enormous amount of preliminary research before the first proper sketch was made. Goussier himself reportedly spent six weeks studying paper making in Montargis, a month studying how anchors were made in Cosne-sur-Loire, and six months in Champagne and Burgundy studying ironworks and the complicated manufacture of mirrors.

Once Goussier and his fellow illustrators (who included Benoît-Louis Prévost, A. J. de Fert, and Jacques-Raymond Lucotte) had produced refined drawings, they turned them over to Diderot, who signed off on each illustration with a short note indicating that they were ready to be engraved (*bon à tirer*).⁴⁷ Approved drawings then moved on to the engravers, who were responsible for transposing the sketches onto folio-sized copper plates.

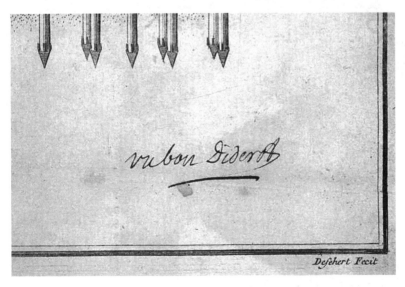

DIDEROT'S SIGNED APPROVAL TO PUBLISH

The illustrations in the *Encyclopédie* devoted to the process of engraving conjure up an orderly workplace.

ENGRAVER'S STUDIO

LETTERPRESS PRINT SHOP

Le Breton's print shop on the rue de la Harpe was surely more frenzied and filthy. While the *Encyclopédie*'s images of printing technology certainly allow us to envision the basic steps involved in creating an engraving — heating the plate on a grill, applying the ink to the plate's small grooves, wiping the plate so that the oily ink remains only in the incised parts, applying the paper on the plate, and finally, pressing and rolling the paper through the press — they do not reflect the scale of the *Encyclopédie* production itself. To produce over four thousand copies of each illustration, Le Breton's operation often had fifty workers laboring full-time on the project — a far cry from a clinically organized room with three workers hanging sheets of paper on a line to dry.[48]

Whatever the working conditions of Le Breton's workshop may have been, the illustrations that his workers produced were as beautiful as they were revelatory. Presumably acting on Diderot's deep-seated belief that we are often deceived by exterior forms, Goussier and his team deconstructed the objects they were drawing. Thus the illustrators drew the working parts of hundreds of machines and contraptions, including windmills, sugarcane "factories," grandfather clocks, various naval vessels, coal mines, and artillery canons, among other things. Perhaps the most revealing "demystification" was that of the fantastic theatrical machines of the Paris Opéra, whose cunning mechanical elevators and moving stages were depicted in painstaking detail.

The goal of the *Encyclopédie*'s plates was to pull back the world's curtain. This tendency carried over to the presentation of the human body as well. Taking a page from Vesalius (and contemporary books of anatomy), Goussier's illustrators produced stomach-churning renderings of the splayed, dissected, and dismembered human body. In addition to featuring images of severed and ligatured penises and full abdomenal cavity dissections, the book's anatomical plates also highlighted recently pioneered surgical procedures such as cataract removal. These illustrations, which sometimes include the type of restraints necessary to hold down the patient, effectively convey both the wonders of surgical technique and the corresponding fear of medical treatment.

SURGICAL TOOLS

In addition to depicting the inner workings of both machines and bodies, the illustrators grouped various objects and animals according to type, size, and other similar criteria. Sets of insects, seashells, printing typefaces, marine standards, coats of arms, and even architectural columns appear in neatly arranged progressions. If the designers of these compositions were seeking to bring order to the various objects being represented, the illustrations now appear to us, paradoxically, to have lost their initial simple rationality.[49] This is particularly true for the thousands of pages dedicated to long-forgotten tools, all of which are arranged with compulsive precision. Often drifting in space with little or no obvious scale or reference points, these unrecognizable instruments have outlived their original context.

Just as important as what was featured in the plates is, of course, that which does not appear. The greatest visual absence among the "trades" is one of the most lucrative of them all: the business of selling and buying enslaved Africans. Although some of the plates dedicated to colonial agriculture do feature small, bucolic vignettes of African slaves working in the French cotton and indigo industries, Diderot did not commission images of cargo ship conversions, human stowage plans, or the various forms of imprisonment that made the trade possible.[50]

AFRICAN SLAVES WORKING IN A SUGAR MILL

To be fair, Diderot seemed equally uninterested in portraying the often brutal conditions under which the French working class labored. If the occasional plate inadvertently conjures up the reality of the era's laborers—in the image on page 128, for example, one can see a young boy holding a pitcher into which an engraver is pouring acid—the intent of the editors and the artists was hardly to raise consciousness about the plight of either slaves or the workhands who made the country function. On the contrary, the *Encyclopédie*'s objective was to portray an idealized and aestheticized view of human ingenuity, effort, and industry, especially when it resided among the lower classes. The point of view reflected in the *Encyclopédie*'s plate volumes is, in many ways, that of the proud son of a master cutler. As "political" documents go, this inventory of trades and occupations is certainly subtler than what is contained in the *Encyclopédie*'s letterpress volumes. Yet the seemingly unthreatening and informative nature of the illustrations, like the whole of the dictionary itself, nonetheless hints at the latent political aspirations of the Third Estate, several decades before the Revolution.

V

THE *ENCYCLOPÉDIE*

HAIR SHIRT

In late August 1772, more than a quarter century after he had begun his career as a freelance translator for the *Encyclopédie*, Diderot brought the greatest publishing project in history to a close. The toll on him had been enormous. Among the 150 or so writers, naturalists, historians, philosophes, doctors, geographers, and artists who had contributed to the enterprise, only he had suffered through the entire process. His coeditor, Jean le Rond d'Alembert, left the project in 1758; the vast majority of contributors followed suit. Diderot, however, stubbornly finished what he had begun by taking the enterprise underground, neglecting his family, his health, and his literary ambitions in the process.[1]

In retrospect, some of the difficulties and obstacles that Diderot confronted must not have been unexpected. Although Le Breton and his partners had obtained a royal privilege to publish the work in 1746, everybody involved in the project was well aware that Chancellor Henri François d'Aguesseau's signature provided

nothing akin to carte blanche. Indeed, the go-ahead from the
chief censor was not only contingent upon, but also theoretically superseded by, a larger network of both formal and informal surveillance. This began with two men who had been key
players in Diderot's incarceration in 1749: the book trade's chief
inspector, Joseph d'Hémery, and the lieutenant-general de police,
Nicolas René Berryer.[2] Other would-be faultfinders included the
Sorbonne's theologians, some of whom provided counsel to the
state censor regarding the morality of proposed publications.[3]
Further oversight came from the Jansenist-leaning Paris Parlement. A far cry from what we now associate with the legislative
branch of representative government, this formidable and hered-
itary class of magistrates not only "registered" and approved the
edicts and laws issued by the king, but acted as yet another regu-
lator of dangerous beliefs. The Parlement knew Diderot well; they
had already voted to burn his *Philosophical Thoughts* on the place de
Grève in 1746.

The biggest threat to the *Encyclopédie* did not stem, however,
from either the Sorbonne or the Parlement; instead, it came from
the powerful Jesuit order. Much like the varied faces of the Society of Jesus itself, the Jesuits' antipathy to the dictionary project
took several forms. There were, first and foremost, the conservative Jesuit priests living at Versailles who railed against the
Encyclopédie's irreligion and corrosive influence on the country.
This group included not only Louis XV's confessor, the Reverend
Father Desmarets, but the influential tutor of the dauphin, Jean-
François Boyer.

In addition to the more reactionary Jesuits at court, there
was also an important network of academic priests who had
a different bone to pick with Diderot and d'Alembert. Far from

anti-intellectual or rearguard, some of these erudite "priests of letters" had assumed that they, too, would be invited to participate in the project. While some historians who have written on the "battle of the *Encyclopédie*" tend to assign the Jesuits to an "anti-Enlightenment" group, the truth was that this Roman Catholic order of priests had long considered themselves key players in the scholarly arena.[4] This was, after all, a religious order that prided itself not only on its remarkably influential network of schools, but on publications including the best lexical dictionary of the day, the *Dictionnaire de Trévoux*, and the similarly titled *Mémoires de Trévoux*, an important monthly journal that featured book reviews and academic papers on a variety of literary and scientific subjects.[5]

Small wonder, then, that the Jesuits—chief among them the editor of the *Mémoires de Trévoux*, Guillaume-François Berthier—were agitated when the Encyclopedists consciously excluded them from the early organization of the project. This resentment only increased when the first volumes of the *Encyclopédie* began to appear in 1751. In particular, d'Alembert's article "*Collège*" not only disparaged the religious order's schooling as backward, obsolete, superficial, and inadequate, but implied that the Jesuits were producing students who were so poorly trained that they became unbelievers after their "first impious conversation or dangerous book."[6] For a significant number of Jesuits, the greatest threat posed by the Encyclopedists was not the book's anthropocentrism or even its anticlericalism, but the unmistakable tendency to define the Enlightenment project as diametrically opposed to traditional religion in general.

Between the powerful Jesuit network, the Paris Parlement, the Sorbonne, and the conservative clergy in orbit around Louis

XV, it would have been difficult to find a less favorable climate for publishing such a work. And yet, while many forces conspired against the *Encyclopédie*, the project also had advocates at all levels of society, even at Versailles. Chief among the *Encyclopédie* apologists at court was Louis XV's mistress, Madame de Pompadour. A sworn enemy of the Jesuits, Pompadour had presumably met Diderot sometime when the philosophe was paying a visit to her personal physician, the physiocrat François Quesnay.[7] During the next few years, and particularly in 1752, when backlash reached its peak, Pompadour would help counter the Jesuit cabal at court. Though she ultimately pulled back her support when the pressure became politically dangerous, her early feelings toward these pioneering men of letters were nonetheless memorialized in a telling pastel executed by Maurice Quentin de La Tour that featured her at her desk, with the third volume of the *Encyclopédie* at her fingertips.[8]

MADAME DE POMPADOUR, PASTEL BY LA TOUR (DETAIL)

GUILLAUME-CHRÉTIEN DE LAMOIGNON
DE CHIEBES DE MALESHERBES

Improbably enough, Diderot and the Encyclopedists also found another critical ally in the royal censor and director of the book trade, Guillaume-Chrétien de Lamoignon de Chiebes de Malesherbes. Named by his father to this elevated post during the winter of 1750 when he was only thirty years old, Malesherbes was a member of the new generation of enlightened aristocrats at the highest levels of society, not to mention a great admirer of and advocate for the philosophes.[9] But even the support provided by both Malesherbes and Pompadour could not fully protect Diderot, d'Alembert, and the *Encyclopédie* from what would be a seemingly unending series of unforeseen crises.

THE ABBÉ DE PRADES

Only four months after the first volume of the *Encyclopédie* appeared in 1751, an unrelated event threw the entire enterprise into jeopardy. This episode occurred a few days after an obscure ecclesiastic by the name of abbé Jean-Martin de Prades—a friend of Diderot and contributor of the contentious *Encyclopédie* article *"Certitude"*—defended his Latin doctoral thesis in front of an examining committee of theologians at the Sorbonne. The title of this thesis, "Who is he upon whose face God has breathed the breath of life?," came from Genesis and suggested an orthodox contemplation of the fate of Adam or perhaps a meditation on the intentions of God.[10]

Prades had carefully fulfilled all the requisite steps before his public examination. He had obtained the required permission to print his thesis from the appropriate doctors at the Sorbonne.[11] He had arranged for 450 copies of his unusually long eight-thousand-word dissertation to be typeset, per tradition, on single sheets of thick elephant folio paper, which was almost two feet tall. He had also posted the thesis for several days before his defense.

This seven-hour public examination, which took place on November 18, 1751, went exceptionally well: all accounts affirm that the young abbé received accolades for his discussion of what turned out to be a synthesis of natural philosophy and Christianity. The problems began when someone actually read the thesis. Like Spinoza and Hobbes, Prades had pointed out problems with the internal chronology found in the Pentateuch.[12] Like Locke, he had intimated that there was no such thing as innate ideas (including the notion of God) and that all knowledge came from sensation. Prades had even advanced a somewhat Hobbesian understanding of political power that not only rejected the divine right of kings, but located the origin of political authority in the will of the governed. Although all these ideas had been circulating in various forms for decades, this was the first time that the most celebrated theological institution in the country had sanctioned such blasphemy. Word soon spread across Paris that the Sorbonne had conferred the title of doctor of theology on a heretic. Not surprisingly, the faculty soon regretted their decision. To escape punishment, some of the faculty claimed that the type had been too small to read; this excuse was found unpersuasive when coming from Prades's dissertation supervisor, the Irishman Luke Joseph Hooke, who soon lost his enviable perch within the Sorbonne faculty.[13]

Opponents of the dictionary project immediately saw Prades's thesis as an excuse to indict the *Encyclopédie* and the liberal atmosphere it was creating. Early in 1752, only days after the second volume of the *Encyclopédie* appeared, the Paris Parlement denounced Prades's thesis, claiming that it was emblematic of "a new science that substituted itself for the dogma of the faith and the natural notions of our reason."[14] Other religious authorities issued similar decrees. On January 27, the Sorbonne itself chimed in, taking the unprecedented and humiliating step of condemning one of its own dissertations, declaring that its sacred faculty shuddered with revulsion — *horruit sacra Facultas.*[15] Two days later, one of the greatest opponents of the *Encyclopédie*, the archbishop of Paris, produced a similar indictment. The final authority to come out against Prades was Pope Benedict XIV himself, who issued a bull proclaiming that the thesis was an abomination.

By early February 1752, pressure to move beyond simple condemnations increased on a daily basis. Reacting to the ire of various religious entities, the group of high-placed ministers at Versailles known as the king's council lashed out at the *Encyclopédie* itself, issuing an *arrêt* that accused the Encyclopedists of "destroying royal authority and encouraging a spirit of independence and revolt."[16] This stop order also prohibited the distribution of any remaining copies of the second volume of the *Encyclopédie*.

Tasting victory, members of Parlement next sought to punish Prades himself. On February 11, the country's chief judicial body ordered that the abbé de Prades be taken to the medieval prison on the Île de la Cité—the Conciergerie—to answer for his crimes.[17] Fearing that the fury of the entire conservative faction in both Paris and Versailles would soon turn on him, Prades shrewdly left France, first for Holland and then for Frederick the Great's court in Berlin, where the enlightened despot had sought to attract other beleaguered members of the *parti des philosophes*, including Voltaire.[18]

Diderot looked on Prades's situation with dread. The basic message that Berryer had delivered to him before he left prison in 1749—the next time you find yourself here for such an offense, you will never leave—must have rung in his ears. The easiest thing would have been to follow Prades's example, fleeing to more hospitable lands and appreciative royal patrons.[19] Some Paris gossipmongers spread the word that Diderot's departure was imminent. Others whispered that the king had signed another lettre de cachet with Diderot's name on it that would soon send him to the Bastille. Neither of these rumors was true. Yet there was one report that crisscrossed Paris at this time that was entirely accurate. The Jesuits were lobbying to take over the entire *Enyclopédie* project once the two editors had been pushed aside or, even better, imprisoned.[20]

Louis XV ultimately decided not to lock up the editors in the Bastille. Instead, he issued a lettre de cachet that ordered the remaining *Encyclopédie* manuscripts to be impounded. Malesherbes, in his capacity as director of the book trade, was forced to carry out his duty or, at least, to pretend to do so. While there is a great deal of uncertainty about what transpired during these tense days, historians now assume that Malesherbes himself secretly warned Diderot that the king had commanded him to seize the *Encyclopédie*. Whatever the case may have been, when Malesherbes and his entourage solemnly arrived at Le Breton's print shop to confiscate the remaining papers on February 21, they found nothing. This bit of high theater served several purposes. In addition to reassuring Versailles, the Jesuits, and the Jansenists that they had little to fear, Malesherbes had eliminated the need for a more sweeping interdiction of the project by the Parlement.

Diderot's strategy during this stressful time was to keep a low profile, while furtively working on the dictionary's third volume.[21] D'Alembert, on the other hand, threatened to abandon the project. On March 1, he wrote to the secretary of the Berlin Academy of Sciences, Johann Heinrich Samuel Formey, proclaiming, "I don't know if this project will be continued, but what I can assure you is that it won't be done by me."[22]

Malesherbes, meanwhile, was working diligently at Versailles to find a compromise that would allow the remaining volumes of the *Encyclopédie* project to appear. With the support of Madame de Pompadour, who willingly positioned herself against religious conservatives at court, the censor ultimately brokered a bewildering deal that reflected the conflicted atmosphere at court. Henceforth, the first two volumes of the *Encyclopédie* would remain illegal, whereas work on the subsequent volumes was tacitly allowed to continue, albeit with yet another level of censorship. As part of this arrangement, Malesherbes allowed Boyer, the *Encyclopédie*'s most vocal and powerful ecclesiastic critic at court, to choose three more censors who would pore over every article looking for traces of "irreligion" or heterodoxy before it was approved for publication.[23] Although the dictionary's editors complained loudly about the difficulty of working under such conditions, both Diderot and d'Alembert ultimately accepted these terms. Their strategy, which they surely discussed in private, was to overwhelm the three men with articles until their scrutiny would begin to wane.[24]

THE EYE OF THE STORM

Banning and then reauthorizing the *Encyclopédie* only further whetted the public's appetite for the dictionary. This translated into a windfall for Le Breton and his fellow publishers. Once word spread that new volumes of the *Encyclopédie* would again begin appearing, new subscribers flocked to sign on. By late 1752, subscriptions had increased by 50 percent to three thousand. Two years later, the editors had taken another 1,200 orders, which brought the final print run to 4,200 copies.

During the mid-1750s, the Encyclopedists passed through what can only be described as the eye of the storm. Despite the fact that d'Alembert had informed various parties in March 1752 that his relationship with the *Encyclopédie* had come to an end, by July he had reluctantly agreed to continue work on the mathematical portions of the book. Two years later, he had even moved back into more of an editorial mode when he authored the preface to the fourth volume, proudly recording the long list of distinguished contributors associated with the project while proclaiming the triumph of the dictionary over the era's backward forces.[25]

The philosophes had clearly picked up a tailwind. Even the Académie française, once filled with high-ranking bishops who wrote very little and published even less, was increasingly can-onizing members of the movement. Seven years after Voltaire was elected to the Académie in 1746, the august association inducted Georges Louis Leclerc, Comte de Buffon, who was not only the keeper of the king's garden, but also the author of one of the most important books of the century, his *Histoire naturelle* (*Natural History*, 1749–88). The following year, the Académie also welcomed d'Alem-bert to its ranks on December 19, 1754. As had been the case for Vol-taire and Buffon, the mathematician took over a chair that had been held by a high-ranking ecclesiastic. The implications of this shift in orientation were not lost on the philosophes or the clergy.[26]

The mid-1750s were also a better era for Diderot. For the ten years that Diderot and Toinette had been married, their lives had seemingly been interrupted by a series of heartbreaks. Indeed, despite the fact that Toinette had given birth three times, the cou-ple had never had two children alive at the same time. Their infant daughter, Angélique, had died in September 1744 at one month of age; six years later, in 1750, the four-year-old François-Jacques Denis succumbed to illness. The final calamity came later that same year, in June 1750. On the very day that their third child, Denis-Laurent, was baptized, his godmother dropped him on his head on the stone steps of the Church of Saint-Étienne-du-Mont. The boy died not long thereafter, in December 1750. Diderot and Toinette finally had more luck with their fourth child. Born on the second floor of their rue de la Vieille Estrapade apartment in September 1753, Marie-Angélique (the future Madame de Vandeul) was the only Diderot offspring to escape the treacherous first years of childhood. She would soon become the joy of her father's life.

This milestone was also accompanied by other significant developments. By 1754, the associated editors had understood

that Diderot—more so than the famous but short-tempered
d'Alembert—had established himself as the heart and soul of the
project. Diderot must have realized this too, for he renegotiated a
much more favorable contract for himself during the course of the
year. In addition to becoming the sole owner of the many books
he had purchased with the printers' money, he could now count
on being paid 2,500 livres each time a new volume appeared. This
income stream was accompanied by an even greater incentive: the
printers had agreed to pay Diderot the substantial sum of 20,000
livres upon the publication of the final volume.[27]

THE RUE TARANNE, LOWER RIGHT
ON TURGOT'S MAP OF PARIS, 1734–39

Relatively prosperous for the first time in his life, Diderot also
decided to move his family from their cramped flat on the rue de

la Vieille Estrapade to a fifth-floor apartment on the rue Taranne, in the far more bourgeois Faubourg Saint-Germain. These new lodgings, for which the writer would pay an annual rent of six hundred livres, had six rooms and four fireplaces, including a cooking area in the back of the apartment. The real advantage of the rue Taranne, however, was the separate study located on the sixth floor, just under the building's mansard roof. It was here that Diderot spent most of the next thirty years, bent over his desk, surrounded by his library, and dressed in his *robe de chambre* and slippers.

BACKLASH

This period of relative calm did not last long; by the second half of the 1750s, the *Encyclopédie*'s critics had rallied their forces and began attacking with renewed vigor. As far away as Lyon, a new and influential group of Jesuits began to militate vociferously and effectively against the project, writing libels and holding conferences on the spiritual quicksand of the era's "encyclopedism."[28] New types of criticism began to appear on the Paris front as well. The most effective anti-*Encyclopédie* voice to join the fray in the mid-1750s was that of Élie Catherine Fréron, the brilliant conservative critic and protégé of the queen. In 1754, he began publishing the first true literary periodical in France, the *Année littéraire* (*Literary Year*). Appearing every ten days, this hugely influential and well-distributed journal soon became the most strident voice within an ever-expanding chorus directed against the philosophes and the *Encyclopédie*. Among other things, Fréron enjoyed scrutinizing every new volume of the *Encyclopédie*, meticulously mocking its authors for supposed plagiarism, and castigating them for their irreligion.[29]

Yet it was not allegations of intellectual piracy or the crime of impiety that ultimately had the greatest effect on the *Encyclopédie*; instead, it was the act of a would-be political assassin.

ROBERT-FRANÇOIS DAMIENS, ENGRAVING

On January 5, 1757, Robert-François Damiens—a tall, broad-shouldered, and presumably disturbed man who believed that he was acting with God's approval—gained entrance to the palace grounds at Versailles with the intention of killing, or, as he later maintained, injuring, Louis XV. Once inside, Damiens ascertained that the king would be leaving his quarters to visit his ailing daughter, Madame Victoire, that same evening. He then joined up with a small group of onlookers and guards who were lingering near the monarch's coach in a passageway between the North Parterre and royal courtyard.

At 5:45 p.m., the forty-six-year-old monarch emerged from his small suite of rooms in the main palace and began to descend the stairway that led to his waiting carriage.[30] Damiens, who delayed his attack until Louis was just about to step into the horse-drawn vehicle, surged from the dark winter night, grabbed the king by his left shoulder, and thrust a pocketknife between the king's fourth and fifth ribs. Although the king was protected by his thick winter overcoat, he bled profusely. Whisked off to his bedchamber by the guards, Louis thought that he had been mortally wounded. Despite the fact that everyone in the room reassured him that Damiens's weapon had not inflicted a life-threatening injury, the French king nonetheless asked for his confessor and apologized to his wife for any distress he could have caused her. In a week's time, however, Louis had almost completely recovered from the wound; the only irreparable damage had been to his psyche and his stature as monarch.

In the days and weeks after the attack, Louis's attention turned from his recovery to the unsettling idea that there was a potentially larger conspiracy behind Damiens's actions. To ascertain if this were true, the country's most expert torturers spent two and a half months interrogating the prisoner, both in Versailles and, later, in Damiens's prison cell in the Conciergerie in Paris. His gruesome execution, which took place on the day after Easter—March 28, 1757—accurately reflected how the country had changed after this traumatic attempt on the king's life.

Shortly before three p.m., Damiens's guards dragged him from his cell in the Conciergerie. He was quickly stripped naked, tied to a cart, and taken across the Seine to the place de Grève, where sixteen executioners had planned a spectacle of unspeakable agony for him. Adopting the same methods that had been used to execute François Ravaillac—the Catholic zealot who had slain the beloved Henry IV in 1610 — the executioners began by tearing open the hand that had sought to kill the king; into this wound, they poured a mixture of boiling sulfur, lead, oil, and wax, before inflicting the same torture to other parts of the body. Shortly thereafter, the executioners prepared the prisoner to be drawn and quartered. This did not go as planned. Four horsemen (and their horses) tried some thirty times to dismember Damiens, yet his joints held firm. By six p.m., Damiens's executioners decided to slice partially through their prisoner's limbs and to set the horses to work again; this time, his arms and legs snapped free, and the would-be regicide expired. As a final symbolic act, the men responsible for this spectacle gathered Damiens's remains and threw them on a raging fire.

THE EXECUTION OF DAMIENS, ENGRAVING

Damiens's execution was designed, quite literally, to destroy any evidence of his body and his unthinkable act. Yet the madman's attack had succeeded in casting a pall over Louis XV's reign, ushering in a particularly morose and increasingly conservative period in the monarchy's history. Though philosophes and Encyclopedists had spent years condemning the kind of religious fanaticism that gave rise to Damiens's crime, the *Encyclopédie*, which certain ecclesiastics had already associated with the threat of potential revolution, had once again entered a perilous era.

As the editors prepared to publish the seventh volume in late 1757, the usual band of critics—conservative writers and outraged members of the clergy—were joined by a new generation of literary satirists who turned their pens loose on the philosophe movement and the *Encyclopédie*.[31] In October 1757, Jacob-Nicolas Moreau, a journeyman columnist and government propagandist writing for the *Mercure de France*, published some "Useful Advice" for the country's philosophes, in the process coining the pseudo-ethnographic term *Cacouac* to describe the freethinking "tribe." Allegedly derived from Greek (from kakos, "bad, mean") and designed to recall the senseless quacking of ducks, the term implicitly accused the philosophes of being a race of "strange," "malevolent," and "corrupted" creatures, whose venom was derived from their perverted ideas.[32] Encouraged by the success of his first satire, Moreau published his *Nouveau mémoire pour servir à l'histoire des Cacouacs* (*New Memoir to Serve as the History of the Cacouacs*), which described in detail the habits of these odd humans and the means by which to vanquish them: whistling (the equivalent of booing).[33] The book sold well.

Moreau's satirical bent was rivaled only by the opportunistic writer and dramatist Charles Palissot de Montenoy, who, like Moreau, had realized that there was now a significant market for antiphilosophe writing. In 1757, Palissot published his *Petites lettres sur les grands philosophes* (*Little Letters on the Great Philosophers*), a book in which Diderot and d'Alembert were accused of intellectual piracy, mocked for their presumption and arrogance, ridiculed for the inconsistency of their opinions, and chided for their sensitivity to criticism.[34] These assaults on the *Encyclopédie* project overlapped with more serious denunciations as well. Most ominously, the king signed a new declaration regulating sedition and freethinking, warning the public that, henceforth, anyone found guilty of "composing, having someone else compose, or printing writings that tend to attack religion, to incite minds, to undermine our authority, and trouble the order and tranquillity of our State, will be sentenced to death."[35]

Such was the sulfurous climate in which the ill-fated seventh volume of the *Encyclopédie* finally appeared in November 1757. Among the articles to incite criticism in this tome, d'Alembert's imprudent entry on "Geneva" drew the most fire. Penned in part during the previous year, while the mathematician was visiting Voltaire in Geneva, d'Alembert's traveloguelike entry was perhaps the only *Encyclopédie* article to create an international incident.[36]

D'Alembert began his article by extolling many of the virtues of Geneva; he waxed poetic about the city's ideal geographic situation on Lac Léman, its wealth, and its industrious people. But he also slipped a number of offensive opinions into this disproportionally long entry. To begin with, he criticized the Calvinist city-state for its prohibition on theatrical productions, while simultaneously maligning the quality of the singing in Protestant churches. Far more provocatively, d'Alembert attributed theological beliefs to the city's Protestant clergy that they simply did not hold. A significant percentage of Swiss ministry, according to his article, had become wary of superstition and unnecessary abstractions, and had even rejected the notion of the divinity of Jesus Christ and various other Christian mysteries (e.g., hell) as absurd and unneeded. What a welcome contrast, he implied, to the superstitious Catholic clergy on the other side of the border.[37]

D'Alembert's article enraged religious communities on both sides of the French-Swiss border. The Swiss, who had effectively been accused of heresy, demanded a retraction. French Catholics, who were being cast as credulous and religiously backward, lashed out at d'Alembert as well. To make matters worse, Versailles (along with the theological censors appointed to go over every article published after 1752) realized that neither Diderot nor d'Alembert had sought approval for this provocative and heretical entry, or it would never have appeared.[38] The resulting brouhaha quickly jeopardized the entire enterprise. The mulish d'Alembert did not help the situation. Refusing to apologize, recant, or back down in any way, he simply complained about the inquisitionlike atmosphere in France, the reactionary religious parasites at Versailles, and the literary critics who were now drowning him in "satires and brochures."[39]

THE PECULIAR CITIZEN

The aftershock of d'Alembert's ill-timed article contributed to a long line of sleepless nights for Diderot. In addition to providing yet more fodder for the *Encyclopédie*'s enemies, it also played a decisive role in bringing about the final rupture between Diderot and his oldest and dearest friend, Jean-Jacques Rousseau.

The first real conflict that erupted between Diderot and Rousseau had occurred several years earlier, in October 1752. At the time, Diderot was deeply absorbed by his work and the ongoing scandal of abbé de Prades's thesis; Rousseau, meanwhile, was enjoying what turned out to be a short-lived but very successful musical career. Only two years after his *Discourse on the Arts and Sciences* had appeared to great acclaim, the musician-philosophe succeeded in having his one-act opera, *Le devin du village* (*The Village Soothsayer*), staged in Fontainebleau for the court. Louis XV was so charmed by the performance that he not only sought to arrange an audience with the eccentric librettist and composer, but also let Rousseau know through one of his agents that he wanted to offer him a royal pension. Much to Diderot's consternation, Rousseau declined both offers.

Diderot did not blame his friend for turning down an opportunity to speak with the king: he knew that Rousseau's chronically weak bladder might lead to a humiliating accident in front of the the monarch. What had vexed him was Rousseau's high-minded decision not to accept the royal pension. As Rousseau recounts this story in *The Confessions*, Diderot not only tried to force him to agree to the stipend, but accused Rousseau of neglecting the financial well-being of his longtime companion, Thérèse Levasseur, and her mother. Rousseau reportedly explained to Diderot that he could not become a protégé of the king because he needed to preserve his all-important relationship to truth, liberty, and courage. This rationalization, according to Rousseau, did not satisfy Diderot, who reportedly stormed off in a huff.[40]

Future squabbles between the two men tended to follow a similar pattern. Often precipitated by seemingly insignificant events, these disputes raised bigger philosophical questions related to how we should conduct our lives; what company we should keep; and how we should maintain our integrity and purity in a corrupted world.[41]

Many of these same strains in their relationship had worsened in the months before d'Alembert's "Geneva" appeared. By 1756, Rousseau had already expressed his distaste for Paris society and, to a certain degree, what he believed to be the insincerity and artifice of the philosophes who gathered at the Baron d'Holbach's freethinking bacchanals on Thursday and Sunday afternoons. This "coterie," as Rousseau called them, had initially assumed that the Genevan's diatribes against civilization were simply part of a clever philosophical stance. This turned out to be a serious miscalculation: by the mid-1750s his indictment of society and the supposed benefits of progress had become a deep-seated belief.

By April 1756, Rousseau had somewhat theatrically left the capital, retreating to a charming cottage in Montmorency — aptly named the Hermitage — located about ten miles north of Paris. This house had been lovingly renovated and prepared for him by his wealthy aristocratic friend of many years, Louise d'Épinay. Living on the grounds of the Château de La Chevrette was hardly a clean break from the philosophe circle, however. D'Épinay, who was a famous *salonnière* and deep-thinking *femme de lettres* in her own right, had important ties with this same group. Most notably, by 1755, she had become the lover of one of Rousseau's and Diderot's best friends, the literary critic, Encyclopedist, and philosophe Friedrich Melchior Grimm.

Grimm, like d'Épinay, came to play an important role in what became the split between Rousseau and his Parisian friends. Well before any harsh words were exchanged between Rousseau and d'Épinay, Grimm had counseled his mistress to be wary of her new lodger: "If you refuse one single time to be at his command," he warned, Rousseau "will accuse you of having begged him to live near you and of preventing him from living in his native land."[42] Madame d'Épinay related her own (embellished) version of Grimm's cautionary letter in the epistolary roman à clef she wrote some years later, *L'histoire de Madame de Montbrillant* (*The History of Madame de Montbrillant*). Grimm's character in this book, writing to d'Épinay's alter ego, puts his feelings in even stronger words: "You are not helping him by offering him the Hermitage. Solitude will further sully his imagination; he will soon see all his friends as unjust and ungrateful, and this will befall you before anyone else."[43]

MADAME D'ÉPINAY,
PASTEL BY LIOTARD

In addition to warning d'Épinay about Rousseau's unreasonableness and paranoia, Grimm also disparaged the reclusive writer throughout Paris society. The most accusatory anecdote he told revolved around Rousseau's callous treatment of Madame d'Épinay. D'Épinay, who was suffering from a stomach ulcer and a series of unpleasant symptoms related to syphilis, had invited her lodger to accompany her to Geneva, where she was going to consult the famous Swiss doctor Théodore Tronchin. Rousseau not only refused, which was certainly his prerogative, but sent d'Épinay a churlish letter in which he accused her of making him her "slave."[44] After d'Épinay shared this note with Grimm, he became so angry that he took it upon himself to show Rousseau's letter to anyone who would read it, accusing the freeloading hermit of being a sanctimonious hypocrite in the process. Grimm also wrote Rousseau directly to break off their relationship: "I will never see you again as long as I live," he wrote, "and I will think myself happy if I succeed in erasing all memory of your actions from my mind."[45]

F. M. GRIMM, ENGRAVING

Although not as well known as the rupture between Diderot and Rousseau, Grimm's split from his former friend was perhaps as painful. The two men had met in 1749, when Grimm had just arrived in Paris in the service of the Count of Schomberg. During the first months that they knew each other, Rousseau and Grimm quickly discovered that they were both enthusiastic aficionados of music. According to Rousseau, the two men were joined at the hip, and spent many evenings in Grimm's flat, playing the harpsichord and "singing Italian airs and barcarolles, without pause or intermission from morning till evening, or rather from evening till morning."[46]

By the mid-1750s, however, Grimm's and Rousseau's dispositions and worldviews had diverged significantly. Rousseau had abandoned Paris, powdered wigs, and the white stockings of the courtier for a life of relative solitude in the country. Grimm, who had begun his days as the son of a modest Lutheran pastor in Regensburg, chose an entirely opposite path. By 1753, he had taken over as the editor of the *Correspondance littéraire* (*Literary Correspondence*), a secret manuscript-only journal of literature and criticism distributed by diplomatic courier to a number of monarchs throughout Europe. In frequent contact with Frederick the Great, a number of German princes and princesses, the king of Sweden, the queen of Poland, and, in later years, Catherine the Great, Grimm quickly became one the most important cosmopolitan figures of the second half of the eighteenth century. He had also acquired a taste for the latest sartorial fashions and perfumed white face powder. Some of his friends jokingly called him the White Tyrant, not only due to his ghostly, albinolike mien, but for his somewhat officious demeanor.[47]

Grimm embraced the kind of life that Rousseau had so resolutely rejected; more importantly, he supplanted him among the philosophes. It had been through Rousseau, ironically, that Grimm had first come to attend d'Holbach's salons. Rousseau had also introduced the young Prussian to d'Alembert and, far more significantly, to Diderot, who would grow to view Grimm as his soul mate. The irony and misery of this situation was not lost on Rousseau, who later lamented, "[Grimm] never introduced me to any of his friends. I introduced him to all of mine, and finally he took them all away from me."[48]

Even Rousseau's greatest admirers admit that his sense of persecution and emotional volatility helped bring about his own worst nightmare: being abandoned by his friends, particularly Diderot. Throughout his writings, Rousseau had professed a love of humanity that knew no bounds; his real problem was getting along with actual humans, with their foibles, their inconsistencies, and their self-absorption, especially when it got in the way of his own. But Diderot, too, had contributed to their break by mismanaging his friend's distrust and paranoia. In addition to giving Rousseau heavy-handed advice, as would a big brother, Diderot did not hold back from telling his friend that he was being judged and perhaps even maligned back in Paris. One of the more famous episodes occurred in March 1757, when Diderot slipped an aphorism into his recently published play, _Le fils naturel_ (_The Natural Son_), that Rousseau interpreted as a personal attack. The proverb in question — "The good man is a member of society, and only the evil man is alone" — sent the antisocial Rousseau into a rage.[49] Upon seeing this sentence, Rousseau dashed off a letter to Diderot to object to this "injurious" maxim. On March 10, Diderot wrote back, ostensibly to ask Rousseau's forgiveness. But by the time that he actually got to the apology, in the postscript, Diderot also slipped in a little joke: "P.S. I ask your forgiveness for what I say to you about the solitude in which you live... Forget what I say to you about it, and rest assured that I will speak no more about it. Adieu, Citizen! Although a Hermit makes for a very peculiar Citizen."[50]

Rousseau, who often had a hard time digesting Diderot's insouciance and his sense of humor, was not amused. Three days later Rousseau wrote to Madame d'Épinay to let her know that his friend had written him a letter that was "piercing [his] soul."[51]

Diderot's somewhat insensitive apology was not the only perceived affront. Rousseau frequently complained that Diderot neglected their friendship, often canceling their appointments at the last second. This had certainly been the case in 1756 and 1757, an era during which Diderot studiously avoided traveling to the Hermitage. Diderot's letters during these increasingly difficult years as editor of the *Encyclopédie* also reveal a new and palpable exasperation with his friend's unbecoming anxiety and relentless mistrust. Even the slightest interaction with the hermit now seemed to generate sanctimonious high drama.[52] By November 1757, Diderot brutally informed Rousseau that his constant suspicion had cost him all his friends in Paris with one exception: Diderot himself. In a revealing analogy, he went on to explain that he had decided to maintain his tortured relationship with his reclusive friend despite his better judgment: you are like a "mistress," he wrote to Rousseau, "whose faults I know well, but from whom my heart cannot free itself."[53]

The final split between the two men began taking shape that same month. It was about this time that Rousseau confided in Diderot that he had fallen desperately in love with Sophie Élisabeth Françoise Lalive de Bellegarde, Comtesse d'Houdetot, a vibrant, jovial, and quick-witted twenty-seven-year-old noblewoman who briefly introduced a bit of light into Rousseau's generally morose existence. Entering into a relationship with Madame d'Houdetot had its problems. Not only was she Madame d'Epinay's sister-in-law, but the mistress of the Marquis de

Saint-Lambert, an army officer, Encyclopedist, writer, and, ostensibly, friend of both Rousseau and Diderot.

Diderot was dismayed. An adulterous husband himself, he did not object to this love affair because Rousseau was theoretically committed to his longtime companion, Thérèse Levasseur. On the contrary, Rousseau had violated a far more sacred rule within polite society: one does not appropriate a friend's mistress while her lover is at war. During their discussion of this ethical problem, Diderot implored Rousseau to write Saint-Lambert to confess all and tell him that he was breaking off his relationship with Madame d'Houdetot. Rousseau did indeed write, but the ambiguous letter revealed very little about what was happening at the Hermitage.

Shortly thereafter, Saint-Lambert returned from war and passed through Paris, where he stopped by the rue Taranne to see Diderot. While they chatted, Diderot soon brought up Rousseau's love for Madame d'Houdetot while (supposedly) under the impression that his friend at the Hermitage had already broken the news to Saint-Lambert. This turned out not to be the case, and Saint-Lambert returned to Montmorency and demanded that Madame d'Houdetot end her relationship with Rousseau. Rousseau was incensed, and rightly so. In addition to having to end his friendship with d'Houdetot, he was now convinced that the manipulative Diderot had carefully and artfully created this situation, not only playing with him like a puppet, but engineering a public scandal designed to destroy him.

By February 1758, Rousseau decided to settle the score with the philosophes, Encyclopedists, and Diderot. The forum he chose was an open letter to d'Alembert on the subject of the prohibition of theater in Geneva, one of the themes the mathematician had touched on in his famous *Encyclopédie* article. Before getting to the heart of his subject, however, Rousseau stated that, in an earlier era in his life, he would have submitted this essay to an esteemed friend for preliminary comments before publishing it. This person, everyone knew, was Diderot. Rousseau then stated melodramatically, "I no longer have him; I no longer want him; but I will miss him forever, and my heart misses him more than my writing." He later appended this observation with a Latin citation from Ecclesiasticus that left little doubt about what he now thought of his oldest and dearest comrade: "If you have drawn your sword on a friend, do not despair; there is a way back. If you have opened your mouth against your friend, do not worry; there is hope for reconciliation; but insult, arrogance, betrayal of secrets, and the stab in the back — in these cases any friend is lost."[54]

Over the years, Diderot had been accused of a host of transgressions by the anti-Encyclopedist cabal. Yet Rousseau's accusation of treachery in the *Lettre à d'Alembert sur les spectacles* (*Letter to d'Alembert on the Theater*) wounded Diderot far worse than any other public attack he had suffered. The fact that this had come from his oldest confidant, a man who had loved him and whom he had loved, made it unbearable. Unwilling to enter into a public fracas that would have been too pleasurable for his enemies, Diderot nonetheless jotted down an uncharacteristically fierce reaction to what he deemed to be his ex-friend's betrayal in a notebook of reflections called *Tablettes*. Rousseau, Diderot wrote, had become a charlatan and a liar in order to better vex his friend; he was simultaneously "false, vain like Satan, unappreciative, cruel, hypocritical and mean." "In truth," Diderot concluded, "this man is a monster."[55]

1759, ANNUS HORRIBILUS

Diderot's painful break with Rousseau overlapped with the most difficult months of the *Encyclopédie* project. In February 1758, Voltaire predicted that Diderot, d'Alembert, the *Encyclopédie*, and the fledgling republic of letters were entering a new and dangerous era, one where religious "fanatics and rascals" had formed "huge battalions" that were now slitting the philosophes' throats "one by one."[56] Writing from the safety of Geneva, he urged both d'Alembert and Diderot either to quit or to leave Paris quickly, and move the entire *Encyclopédie* project to the court at Potsdam or Saint Petersburg. From there, he assured Diderot, the full potential of the *Encyclopédie* could finally be realized, as volume after volume of uncensored ideas would flow back into France, dropping like bombs on the Church.

Diderot was well aware that remaining in Paris had its risks and liabilities. But, as he made clear in a letter to Voltaire, there were also numerous reasons to stay. To begin with, he was hamstrung by the simple fact that the book manuscript was not his to drag around the world. It was the property of Le Breton and his partners: "the project of finishing the *Encyclopédie* in a foreign country," he wrote, "is a fantasy. It is the editors who signed agreements with the contributors; the manuscripts that they have acquired belong to them, and would not belong to us." Even more importantly, however, Diderot let Voltaire know in no uncertain terms that leaving would amount to a cowardly retreat: "To abandon the enterprise, would be to turn our backs on the battle and to do exactly what these rogues desire...What shall we do? What it suits people of courage to do: scorn our enemies, pursue them, and take advantage, as we have done, of the stupidity of our censors."[57]

This courageous stance was put to the test at the end of July, when one of the most radical texts of the eighteenth century, Claude-Adrien Helvétius's *De l'esprit* (*On the Mind*) began flying out of booksellers' shops. Helvétius, an extremely wealthy tax farmer and Versailles courtier who had purchased the position of maître d'hôtel to the queen, had actually gone through the proper channels before publishing this two-volume treatise. The first edition of the book, which was printed by the *Encyclopédie*'s Laurent Durand, bears the censor M. Tercier's declaration that he saw nothing problematic in the book.

Helvétius's *On the Mind* was anything but inoffensive, however. In this systematic rendering of the human mind and its motivations, the irreligious writer went further than Diderot had ever gone in reducing the human condition to a series of mechanical reactions to either pleasure or pain. Humans, he theorized, conduct their lives solely based on their ability to derive sensual gratification or to sidestep discomfort and agony, be it physical or psychological. This understanding of the human psyche, in addition to challenging the notion of the soul, the utility of religion, and the long-standing Christian concept of innate ideas, also called for a radical reorganization of society.

Helvétius's ideas were so far-reaching and inflexible that most philosophes — even those who shared the same materialist beliefs as he did — found the publication of the book to be terribly ill-advised.[58] The reaction at Versailles proved the philosophes right. The extremely religious dauphin, who had received a copy of *On the Mind* from Helvétius himself, reportedly stormed out of his apartment after reading it, screaming that he was going to show the queen some of the "beautiful things" that her maître d'hôtel had printed.[59] In short order, the book was banned and burned, the privilege revoked, and the censor sacked. Helvétius lost his position at court, despite publicly stating, on three separate occasions, that he regretted having ever published the book.

The aftermath of *On the Mind* ushered in the darkest days of the *Encyclopédie* project. Reminiscent of how critics had effectively coupled the abbé de Prades's thesis with the *Encyclopédie*, an even larger league of religious, literary, and royal authorities now ascribed Helvétius's indiscretions to the permissive intellectual climate fomented by the Encyclopedists. Among the more significant critics, Abraham-Joseph de Chaumeix, the protégé of the conservative dauphin, published a vociferous, six-volume refutation of the project entitled *Préjugés légitimes contre l'*Encyclopédie (*Legitimate Prejudices against the* Encyclopédie). His warning against the project was unequivocal: reading the *Encyclopédie* was akin to ingesting "venom" disguised as nourishment.[60]

Such literary indictments were seconded at the Paris Parlement by the attorney general of France, Omer de Fleury, who delivered a fierce denunciation against both Helvétius and the *Encyclopédie* in January 1759, stating that "impiety [was now] walking with its head held high" and that thinkers including Diderot and Helvétius were attempting to "disseminate materialism, destroy religion, inspire a spirit of independence, and corrupt morals."[61] Parlement issued a new proclamation against the *Encyclopédie* later that same month, voting overwhelmingly to prohibit printers and any other persons from selling or distributing it.[62] Two other royal interdictions were also issued, the latter being a final "stop order" coming from the king's council on March 8. The *Encyclopédie* had once again become illegal.

Diderot had never lacked for labor or drama in his tenure as the editor of the *Encyclopédie*, but this was a breaking point. Shortly after Diderot received word that the pope had also put the *Encyclopédie* on the Index — the list of publications that Catholics were forbidden from reading — he was horrified to discover that an anonymous defender of the dictionary project had produced an anticlerical (and very successful) satire targeting Abraham Chaumeix, the man who had dedicated his career to destroying the *Encyclopédie*. Conservative elements at Versailles understandably believed that this was Diderot's work and clamored for his imprisonment.[63]

The king did not sign a lettre de cachet, but did command Malesherbes to confiscate the *Encyclopédie* manuscripts. The curious way in which this order played out was perhaps the only thing to work in the Encyclopedists' favor in the early spring of 1759. Much as Malesherbes had presumably done several years before, the chief censor and director of the book trade not only alerted Diderot the day before this seizure was scheduled, but volunteered to take possession of the thousands of collated articles that Diderot had filed in wooden boxes at his rue Taranne office. That very night, according to Diderot's own account, he was able to sneak these cartons down the five flights of stairs to a waiting coach. The next day, at the same time that the police were canvasing Paris for any sign of the manuscripts, Malesherbes was safeguarding them at his own house.

The best summary of the tense atmosphere at this time comes from Diderot himself, who documented the heady events of the early spring in a very long letter to Grimm. Faced with the unfortunate prospects of prison or exile, as well as the possible relocation of the project to Holland or Russia, Diderot relates how he called a meeting to discuss strategy at Le Breton's house on the rue de la Harpe. Present that night were the four printers, the Baron d'Holbach, Louis de Jaucourt, and d'Alembert:

> We sat down at four o'clock in the afternoon. We were cheer-
> ful. We drank, we laughed, we ate; and when night fell, our atten-
> tion turned to the matter at hand [i.e., continuing the *Encyclopédie*
> despite its interdiction]. I explained the project of completing the
> manuscript. I cannot tell you how surprised and impatient my
> dear colleague [d'Alembert] was as he listened to me. He launched
> into one of his characteristically puerile and reckless tirades,
> treating the editors like servants, the continuation of the project
> as a folly and, while he was at it, saying disagreeable things about
> me that I felt obliged to swallow.
>
> The more d'Alembert grew in opposition and foolishness, the
> more I responded with moderation and calm. It is clear that the
> *Encyclopédie* has no enemy more determined than that man...
>
> And our friend the baron, in your opinion, what face was he
> making during [d'Alembert's rant]? He was squirming in his chair.
> I was afraid that at any moment d'Alembert's senseless remarks
> would unhinge the baron and make him enter the fray. However,
> he contained himself, and I was quite happy with his discretion.
> As for the Chevalier de Jaucourt, he didn't say a word. He had his
> head lowered and appeared dumbfounded. D'Alembert finally
> stammered, cursed, turned on his heel, and left, and I haven't
> heard from him since.
>
> When we were free of that little fool, we returned to the proj-
> ect that had brought us together. We examined it from all angles;
> we made arrangements; we encouraged each other; we swore to
> see the task to completion; we agreed to work on the next vol-
> umes with the same freedom as the first ones, and, if needed, to
> print them in Holland.[64]

In the ensuing weeks, d'Alembert withdrew his support from what remained of the *Encyclopédie* project. Diderot and his now much smaller team of collaborators nonetheless continued to produce articles for the project, albeit separately and behind closed doors. D'Holbach spent many days consulting his three-thousand-book library on the rue Royale in order to write many of the remaining articles on natural history, metallurgy, chemistry, philosophy, and history. Diderot, too, characterized his existence in 1759 as monastic and monotonous: getting out of bed at the crack of dawn and climbing the stairs to his sixth-floor office, where he alternated between writing plays, composing unsigned *Encyclopédie* entries, and editing tens of thousands of articles for the remaining volumes.

Diderot certainly worked prodigiously during this time, but the majority of the remaining articles were written by Louis de Jaucourt. A well-off aristocrat who, despite his rank, had chosen to become a medical physician, the Chevalier de Jaucourt had begun his career as an Encyclopedist modestly, in 1751, when he was forty-seven. At the time, Jaucourt was still recovering from the heartrending loss of an enormous manuscript that he had spent decades preparing for publication. This book, a multivolume dictionary of anatomy, had ended up on the bottom of the North Sea the previous year when the ship carrying it to his prospective publisher foundered off the coast of Holland. Nine years later, when the chevalier confronted the possibility of the end of the *Encyclopédie*, he could not stomach a similar loss. Dedicating himself entirely to the project for the next six years, Jaucourt soon earned the nickname "the slave of the *Encyclopédie*." Working ceaselessly and coordinating his labor with several copyists and secretaries that he hired from his own funds, the self-effacing chevalier ultimately handed over 17,000 articles to Diderot.[65] He was, in effect, the third and unrewarded editor of the *Encyclopédie.*

LOUIS DE JAUCOURT, ENGRAVING

In the preface to the eighth volume, Diderot ultimately showed deep gratitude to the chevalier for his herculean efforts, admitting that if he and the remaining Encyclopedists were now able to shout out "land ho" like sailors, this was thanks to the prodigious effort expended by the chevalier.[66] In private, however, Diderot often maligned the book's savior as dull and uninspiring, a copyist and vulgarizer more than an original thinker. Some of this lack of appreciation surely came from the disappointment that Diderot felt about the quality of the final volumes of the project. In his opinion, many of these lacked the verve, intelligence, and waggishness of what the former team of contributors had produced for the *Encyclopédie*'s early tomes.

Yet if the chevalier admittedly lacked the wit of a Voltaire, the vision of a Diderot, or the intellectual profile of a d'Alembert, this journeyman dictionary maker arguably provided one of the most progressive and, for its time, radical arguments to appear in the *Encyclopédie*. In an era when the abolitionist movement was only just budding, Jaucourt made use of his platform to denounce slavery in a way that no one had ever done in France. Forcefully contradicting a number of proslavery articles that also appeared in the *Encyclopédie* — these were generally penned by experts on the colonial world — the chevalier unambiguously proclaimed that slavery "violates religion, morality, natural law, and all the rights of human nature."[67] He also declared that those Africans who had been taken as slaves, regardless of the conditions of their enslavement, had the right to declare themselves free.[68] From his view, all justifications for human bondage, be they scientific, religious, or economic, are disallowed by humankind's defining principle: liberty. To drive home this last point, Jaucourt proclaims memorably that he would prefer that the European colonies in the Caribbean "be destroyed" rather than allow such a horrific practice to continue.[69] These ideas, which Jaucourt synthesized from a variety of sources, became the foundation of even more incisive and violent condemnations of the slave trade, some of them put forward by Diderot himself years later.

Jaucourt's tireless and self-sacrificing work on the *Encyclopédie* cost him his fortune. Diderot's cost him his health. Beginning in 1759, his recurrent stomach discomfort, cramping, and terrible diarrhea had returned with a vengeance. Often citing an inextinguishable burning sensation above his breastbone, Diderot gave up the delight of wine and food for the deceiving comfort of a milk diet. Digestive problems were nothing, however, in comparison with the pain that Diderot felt after his father died of acute pulmonary edema in early June 1759. Having hesitated and finally decided against visiting the old cutler for fear of giving the impression that he was fleeing the capital, Diderot had missed the opportunity to comfort and say goodbye to his father. For the rest of the summer, he entered into a period of guilt-fed inactivity. When he finally returned to work several months later, his plan was simple: slog through his gloom. "Work," as he wrote, "is the only thing I have to distract myself from my pain. Thus, I work a lot... If my sorrow persists and my colleagues [continue to] support me, I will be done with this much sooner than I had promised."[70] Six years would pass, however, before the last of the letterpress volumes of the *Encyclopédie* would finally be printed.

THE NEW *DICTIONNAIRE DE TRÉVOUX*

During the fall of 1759, those who opposed both the philosophes and the *Encyclopédie* had good reason to feel satisfied with their crusade. In addition to obtaining the Parlement's condemnation and a second ban issued by the king's council, their efforts had prompted Pope Clement XIII to issue a "damnation" of the project that not only declared the *Encyclopédie* blasphemous, but directed those people who still owned any of its seven published volumes to turn them over immediately to their local priest—to be burned.[71] The most clever attempt to deal the project a death-blow, however, had come in July when the Parlement voted to order the printers to reimburse each of their 4,200 subscribers at seventy-two livres apiece. Ostensibly carried out in order to compensate those people who had already paid for volumes that were no longer forthcoming, this crippling transfer of three hundred thousand livres was also intended to disrupt—once and for all — the relationship between the public's hunger for scandalous ideas and the printers' ability to meet it.

As seemingly effective and wide-ranging as these tactics were, one oversight cost the project's detractors the war. In crafting their overall strategy, Diderot's enemies focused their attacks on the letterpress volumes alone, and did not attempt to block the as-yet unpublished tomes dedicated to the era's technologies and trades. This allowed the printers to ask for a separate privilege, which was granted in September 1759. Once the printers had obtained this authorization, they let their subscribers know that the seventy-two-livre "reimbursement" could be applied to their upcoming payment for the forthcoming volumes of plates. The small victory saved the *Encyclopédie*: no one, as the printers were proud to point out, asked for repayment for the unpublished letterpress volumes.

Permission to publish the *Encyclopédie*'s illustrated volumes breathed new life into the project. Diderot and his few remaining colleagues now had cover to work on the remaining letterpress volumes. The printers could also now deploy their capital more freely. This allowed Le Breton and his associates to solve the thorny problem of where to print the remaining volumes of the *Encyclopédie*. Although it surely pained the printers not to make use of their own workshops in Paris — even with Malesherbes's tacit approval, this would have been too perilous   the men began shopping for a printing facility that could not only print 42,000 volumes (ten volumes times 4,200 subscribers), but house them until they were ready for distribution. In 1760, after considering moving the project to either Holland or Switzerland, Le Breton and his associates furtively purchased a large printworks in Trévoux, 446 kilometers to the southeast of Paris.[72]

Trévoux was a tactical choice. In addition to being far from Versailles, the Parlement, and the strictures of the Parisian printing guild, Trévoux (currently a suburb of Lyon) had a long-standing tradition of producing dictionaries. Most famously, the city's press had lent its name to the Jesuits' famous *Dictionnaire de Trévoux*; it has also printed a clandestine sixth edition of Pierre Bayle's *Historical and Critical Dictionary*.[73] Yet Le Breton and his associates were also drawn to Trévoux and its facility for another very important reason: situated within the principality of Dombes, this small city was technically outside of French jurisdiction.[74] Rather than delegate the printing of the final volumes to a foreign press, Le Breton and the Associated Printers had simply bought one themselves.

Though the specifics about what occurred here remain entirely unclear — were all of the letterpress volumes printed here? Or just some? — it is quite probable given the printers' secretive investment that a circumspect group of workers produced two or so volumes a year in Trévoux starting in 1760. That the *Encyclopédie* would ultimately be finished in the city that had lent its name to the most famous Jesuit publications of the century — the *Dictionnaire* and the *Mémoires de Trévoux* — was a symbolic victory to say the least: in the clash between Jesuits and Encyclopedists, the *Encyclopédie* had not only supplanted the Jesuits' *Dictionnaire de Trévoux*, it had become it.

By the time the printing of the final volumes had been completed in 1765, 18,000 cubic feet of books, worth 800,000 livres (about twelve million dollars), must have been stacked in the Associated Printers' facility in Trévoux. Each and every one of these books began with the *Encyclopédie* project's final ruse: a title page featuring the name and insignia of Samuel Fauche

and Company, booksellers and printers of Neuchâtel, Switzerland. This bogus imprint, which the editors arranged by paying
off the uninvolved Swiss editor, now allowed Le Breton and his
colleagues to distribute the *Encyclopédie*, as if they had no role in
printing it.

THE LAST VOLUMES

By the fall of 1765, the final ten volumes (8–17) of the *Encyclopédie*
were ready to be handed over to their subscribers.[75] Two events
ultimately helped to make this politically possible. The first was
the downfall of the powerful Jesuit order, which had not only
lost its influence at court by 1762, but had been disbanded in 1764
after the Society refused to bend its knee to the Gallic Church.[76]
The second significant shift in the political climate came a year
later, when Louis XV's son, the thirty-six-year-old dauphin, died
in December 1765. More than any other single event, the death of
the influential and conservative voice at Versailles seems to have
prompted Le Breton and the Encyclopedists to work with the
new chief of police, Antoine de Sartine, to secure permission to
deliver the remaining books.

Distributing the ostensibly illegal *Encyclopédie* nonetheless
remained a touchy matter. As was often the case in the history of
this controversial book, yet another bit of caution was required.
Working in conjunction with Sartine, who happened to be an
old school friend of Diderot, Le Breton and his associates received
permission to take out advertisements announcing, first, that
the Swiss publisher Samuel Fauche had bought the manuscripts
and printed the last volumes in Neuchâtel, and second, that the
remaining books would soon be available for distribution to their

subscribers. As a concession to conservative elements, however, Parisian subscribers were also told that the book could not be freely distributed in the capital. For several months, subscribers' coaches and lackeys made their way outside of Paris to retrieve the remaining volumes of the *Encyclopédie*. Although the final volume of the plates did not appear for another seven years, the battle of the *Encyclopédie* had been won, at least from Le Breton's point of view.

TITLE PAGE OF VOLUME 8 OF THE *ENCYCLOPÉDIE*, 1765

Sometime in January 1765, Diderot received his own copy of the final letterpress volumes. Although relieved to see this portion of the project to completion, he was far from content with the final result. Much of this disillusionment and resentment had actually set in during 1764, a year before the delivery of the final volumes. While consulting the proofs of the fourteenth volume, Diderot was horrified to find that his 16,000-word article on *"Sarrasins"* (an ethnic and religious term for Muslims) had been carefully redacted by Le Breton without his approval.[77] The printer, clearly fearing backlash for a book that had lost its privilege, had excised the heart of the article, some eight hundred words, including Diderot's ethnological explanation of the relationship between religion and philosophy: "It is a general observation that religion increasingly sinks into discredit as [the prevalence of] philosophy grows. People will conclude — either pro or con — regarding the usefulness of philosophy or the truth of religion; but I can tell you that the more philosophers one finds in Constantinople, the less often people will be undertaking pilgrimages to Mecca."[78]

Censorship of *"Sarrasins"* turned out to be the tip of the iceberg. In methodically examining the volumes, Diderot discovered that Le Breton had truncated dozens of potentially touchy articles in a number of volumes, including entries on morality, political oppression, philosophy, royal power, and religion. In the article *"Luxure"* ("Lust"), the editor had cut the quip (italicized) at the end of the following phrase: "In the Christian religion, lust is one of the seven deadly sins; *one can imagine how many people must be damned since the slightest sin in this category is damning."*[79] Le Breton made far deeper cuts to the article *"Paradis"* ("Paradise"), which, before being edited, had mocked theologians for trying to find the physical location of heaven, and for having a tendency to build things "out of air."[80] Likewise, the editor blue-penciled a biting sentence in "*Pythagorisme*" that reduced all miracles either to the product of superstition or the result of "entirely natural events."[81] At other points Le Breton had simply dropped articles or sub-articles altogether, including entries for "Protestant Religion," "Scholastic Theology," "Tolerance," and the disingenuous article on "Christian Denominations," which began by announcing insincerely that it would be quite useful to determine which of the many conflicting versions of Christianity actually led to salvation.

Diderot's anger was without bounds. In November, he wrote a blistering note to Le Breton: "So this is the result of twenty-five years of labor, exertion, expenses, dangers, and mortifications of all kinds! An incompetent, an Ostrogoth, destroys everything in a moment!"[82] Faced with what he called the mutilation of the *Encyclopédie*, Diderot began a period of soul-searching. For more than two decades, he had sacrificed his larger literary aspirations to the *Encyclopédie* project, enduring repeated episodes of royal and religious harassment along the way. The whole enterprise now seemed to be of little worth to him.

What Diderot did not fully realize, in 1765, was that he had carried the ideas of the Enlightenment forward in a way that no person, not Voltaire, and certainly not Rousseau, had done before. Despite his own dissatisfaction with the result, he had unquestionably reached the goals he had set forth: as well as "serving humanity," he had produced "a revolution" in the minds of his readers by giving them the tools not only to think for themselves, but to stand up to the world's "tyrants, oppressors, [religious] fanatics, and bigots."[83] Under his direction, knowledge had been transformed into a form of political warfare. Perhaps more importantly, this spirit of *Encylopédisme* lived on well after the last volume appeared in 1765. By 1782, printers in Switzerland and Italy had produced another twenty thousand copies of the Enlightenment's bible.

But there was another positive aspect to his years as Encyclopedist that Diderot never fully seemed to understand.[84] Poring over tens of thousands of articles for twenty-five years had been far from a sterile exercise. Although he rarely said a positive word about the *Encyclopédie* after the final volumes appeared, his labor had given him a panoramic understanding of knowledge that few people have ever achieved. Indeed, decades of self-inflicted intellectual labor, coupled with his prodigious memory and an ability to see well beyond his own era, had prepared Diderot for the second and undoubtedly greatest phase in his career, the one he carried out in the shadows.

PART TWO

LATE HARVEST

One only communicates with force
from the bottom of the grave;
that is where one must imagine oneself;
and it is from there
that one should speak to mankind.
— DIDEROT, *Essay on the Reigns
of Claudius and Nero*, 1782

VI

ON VIRTUE AND VICE

In assuming the editorship of the *Encyclopédie*, Diderot knew that he would receive his fair share of abuse. Character assassination during the ancien régime was simply too exhilarating, too effective, and, for some of his critics, simply too lucrative. His earliest detractors labeled him a militant atheist and a shameless bootlegger of other people's ideas. Several years later, a fresh group of critics accused him of being the leader of a group of malicious scoundrels whose true intention was to bring about the ruin of the country. By 1755, yet another cabal began spreading rumors that Diderot had published several new irreligious tracts, which was simply not true.

Working under such conditions was difficult; maintaining a presence as an independent author of philosophical works was even more problematic. Diderot nonetheless attempted to continue his career as a stand-alone writer in the early 1750s. In 1751, he received tacit permission from Malesherbes to publish his *Lettre sur les sourds et les muets* (*Letter on the Deaf and Dumb*), a nonheretical—but philosophically dense—exploration of the gestural origins of language.¹ Two years later, in 1753, he also brought out a series of pithy essays on scientific methodology that he entitled *Pensées sur l'interprétation de la nature* (*On the Interpretation of Nature*). This short book avoided the type of polemical materialism that he had preached in the *Letter on the Blind*, but it also implored a new generation of savants to embrace the power and unpredictability of a true and radical investigation of nature, one where the scientist does not seek preordained answers, but simply truth.²

On the Interpretation of Nature was the last work of pure philosophy that Diderot published while working on the *Encyclopédie*.³ Yet he had not given up entirely on his desire to speak to his own generation. Sometime the following year, he came up with the idea for a far more visible project after reading Carlo Goldoni's Italian-language play *Il vero amico* (*The True Friend*). Goldoni, who was far and away Italy's best-known playwright and dramatic theorist, had successfully transformed his country's theater by rejecting many of the conventions associated with the centuries-old commedia dell'arte.⁴ Inspired by the Venetian's campaign for more realistic acting and plots, Diderot decided that he, too, would attempt to usher in a similar renewal of French theater.

In 1757, he published his first play, a moralistic drama titled *Le fils naturel, ou Les épreuves de la vertu* (*The Natural Son, or The Trials of Virtue*). As a supplement to this drama, he added an imagined dialogue that had purportedly taken place between himself and "Dorval," the main character and supposed author of the play. These so-called *Entretiens sur le fils naturel* (*Conversations on the Natural Son*) provided Diderot with the opportunity to enter into a theoretical discussion where he, like Goldoni, called for an end to the hackneyed stock roles that were the backbone of French theater. These fixed character types — *tipi fissi* in Italian — included servants, valets, masters, doctors, domineering fathers, monarchs, governesses, widowed mothers, cowardly soldiers, and lovers, the so-called *innamorati*. In their place, Diderot envisioned putting a range of real and believable characters onstage, be they merchants, philosophes, politicians, or magistrates. Likewise, he advocated for a more faithful and complex rendering of the familial roles that regular people played in life, as fathers, mothers, daughters, sons, or friends.[5] By far the most revolutionary innovation that Diderot theorized for French theater was a *bourgeois tragedy* whose realistic and heartrending ending would elicit an unprecedented emotional impact from the audience. These potent moral dramas, he mused, might be so affecting that they would strike fear into the public's hearts. Audiences might "tremble while going to the theater," he said, "but they would not be able to stop themselves from doing so."[6]

Diderot never realized his dream of completing a working-class tragedy. Yet in 1757 and 1758, he took time out from overseeing the seventh and eighth volumes of the *Encyclopédie* to compose two bourgeois dramas. These plays, both of which were departures from traditional French theater, straddled the divide between light and meaningless comedy and the deadly seriousness of aristocratic tragedy. The basic idea was to tell a moral story that has a happy ending, but, at the same time, recalls the unpretentious nobility of France's lower and middle classes. This was precisely what one of Diderot's favorite painters, Jean-Baptiste Greuze, had achieved in the visual arts.

Diderot hoped that theatergoers who attended these realistic and stylistically unaffected plays would "believe that they were among their family, and [would] forget that they were at the theater."[7] In describing just how such plays should be staged, Diderot is generally credited with inventing what is now commonly referred to as the theory of the fourth wall. Beseeching future actors to forget the audience and their highly codified and stylized forms of acting, he writes: "Imagine a great wall on the edge of the stage that separates you from the parterre. Act as if the curtain did not rise."[8]

The theoretical underpinnings of these plays are, alas, far more interesting than the plays themselves. The first of Diderot's plays, the aforementioned *Le fils naturel*, tells the tale of a virtuous yet parentless man named Dorval who falls in love with his friend's fiancée, Rosalie. Caught between friendship and love, our hero Dorval suffers until Rosalie's father shows up and acknowledges Dorval as his own son. Discovering that the woman he loves is actually his sister, Dorval is not only able to escape a terrible ethical dilemma, but is now able to marry his friend's sister, while Rosalie can get married to her original fiancé. Filled with dripping sentimentality and heavy-handed moralism, Diderot obviously designed this artificial ending with tears in mind.[9]

The second bourgeois drama that Diderot wrote during this period was *Le père de famille* (*The Father of the Family*, 1758). Based loosely on his own courtship of Toinette, the plot follows the adventures of a young and somewhat impetuous man who hopes to marry a beautiful young woman of inferior social standing. Diderot assigned the name Saint-Albin to the young lover playing his quasi-autobiographical self in the play; more remarkably, he named Toinette's character Sophie, in honor of his mistress Sophie Volland.

The intrigue in *Le père de famille* recalls his own family's efforts to dissuade him from marrying beneath his station. The benevolent father in the play first tries to reason with his son; his uncle is far more violently opposed to the wedding and threatens to lock

Sophie up in a convent, much as Diderot's own father had done to him.[10] Sophie is only saved from this cruel fate when it is discovered that she is actually the niece of the so-called *commandeur*, the father's brother-in-law. Thanks to this coup de théâtre, the play is able to conclude happily with the engagement of the young couple and the blessing of Saint-Albin's father. We in the audience are once again supposed to weep as love triumphs over distress and class tensions.

The syrupy and tedious plots of Diderot's theater now make his dramas all but unplayable. Yet in 1759 the naturalistic style and nonaristocratic characters of *The Father of the Family* resonated deeply with European audiences. By 1761, dramaturges had staged the play in Bordeaux, Toulouse, Lyon, Marseille, Hamburg, Frankfurt, and Vienna. As Diderot received an increasing number of positive reviews about these productions from the provinces—hoping all the while that the play would ultimately be staged in the capital—he was convinced that he had entered an entirely new phase in his writing career, one where he might preach simple family values while repairing his reputation as a militant atheist in the process.[11]

PALISSOT'S LAMPOON

Diderot's critics, who had generally targeted him in his capacity as editor of the now-banned *Encyclopédie*, reacted violently to this whiff of theatrical success. In the pages of the *Année littéraire*, Élie Fréron accused Diderot of shamelessly pilfering *Il vero amico*.[12] Far more effective than this particular allegation, however, was a satirical comedy called *Les philosophes* that Charles Palissot had written. This malevolent and, from Diderot's point of view, untalented playwright had also achieved something that Diderot had not: he had secured a place for his play on the stage of the Comédie-Française, the country's premier theater.[13] The irony was almost too much to bear. At the precise moment that Diderot had hoped to create a new kind of theatrical work where the audience would share in a common and uplifting moral experience, the snakelike Palissot was using the same genre to spit venom on him.

Palissot's three-act play opened on Friday, May 2, 1760. Much to Diderot's dismay, this turned out to be the theatrical event of the season. On opening night, unruly crowds waited for hours on the Fossés-Saint-Germain-des-Prés for tickets. The subsequent publication of the play, by one of Le Breton's colleagues, Nicolas-Bonaventure Duchesne, was also a windfall for its publisher. While most people realized that Les philosophes lacked the style and grace of the best French comedy — Palissot, to put it mildly, was no Molière — the fact that the playwright was satirizing Diderot and the country's "vile flock of Encyclopedists" had created a sensation: some twelve thousand people would buy tickets to Les philosophes over the next three months, making it one of the more popular comedies of the century.[14]

Truth be told, Palissot's play is clever enough to merit a quick synopsis. The basic story line follows a traditional "forced marriage" plot. A rich widow named Cydalise falls under the influence of an unethical band of "philosophes." Swooning under their pretentious and ridiculous ideas, she orders her daughter to abandon her current fiancé for Valère, one of the group's pseudo-savants.[15] By the end of the play, the forsaken lover, Damis, wins his way back into his future mother-in-law's heart after unmasking the play's villainous philosophes, thinly disguised versions of Helvétius, Duclos, Rousseau, and Diderot.

SCENE FROM THE SATIRICAL PLAY
LES PHILOSOPHES, 1777

All four of these philosophes take a good beating. During one
particularly comical scene, Damis's valet, Crispin (played by the
famous actor Préville), poses as a traveling philosophe living by
the precepts of Rousseau. Crawling out onstage like an animal, he
proclaims (in a satire of Rousseau's praise of the state of nature)
that he has decided to return to humankind's primal origins. The

biggest gag comes when the disguised Crispin takes a mouthful from a head of lettuce that he pulls out of his pocket. (The French did not eat raw vegetables in the eighteenth century.) Palissot's treatment of Diderot's character, Dortidius, is even more brutal.[16] In addition to identifying him as the "leader of the sect" who allows his disciples to transcend "their status of insect," the playwright maligns the philosophe as an untalented writer, an unprincipled liar, a self-centered scoundrel, and a shameless plagiarist.[17] At one point in the play, Palissot even has Diderot's character admit to being antipatriotic, at a time when the French were deeply engaged in the Seven Years' War against England and Prussia: "I care little about my own nation / The true sage is a cosmopolitan."[18]

Much of the uproar generated by the play finally died down toward the end of the summer. In fact, the public's initial fascination with Palissot's satire had given way to an unpleasant taste in the mouth. While audiences had initially relished this mocking satire, every person who had attended or read the play knew that the three-act comedy violated one of the fundamental rules of the French theater: playwrights had the right to ridicule specific professions or even what we now call social classes, but it was bad form to target individuals. By fall, the backlash against Palissot was such that Diderot breathed a sigh of relief. "Six months ago," he wrote, "people were dying of laughter at Les philosophes. Where is it now? It is at the bottom of an abyss that readily accepts such uninspired, amoral productions, and ignominy belongs to its author."[19]

In December Diderot received even better news: the Comédie-Française had accepted The Father of the Family into their repertoire. On February 21, the play finally opened to a large and enthusiastic crowd. Diderot, so nervous and excited that he could not bring himself to attend, asked his friends to let him know how the performance went. After the third night, which was even more successful than the first two, he finally let himself believe that had a huge hit on his hands. Puffed up by this success, he dashed off a note to Voltaire, whom he had still not met, but who certainly was considered the greatest playwright of his generation. Diderot's letter was fairly modest — perhaps falsely humble — but gratification and delight nonetheless dripped from his pen when he related that, during the many curtain calls, someone from within the parterre screamed out, "What a response to [Palissot's] *Les philosophes!*"[20]

Diderot's victory celebration turned out to be premature. While his letter was still en route from Paris to Voltaire's château in Ferney, attendance at the play began to wane. By the sixth performance, the hall had dwindled to less than half capacity. After the seventh, *The Father of the Family* disappeared from the Comédie-Française's playbill. While this was still a decent run, Diderot had hoped for an undisputed triumph. This disappointment was even harder to swallow knowing that his friend-turned-nemesis Jean-Jacques Rousseau had just published what would become the best-selling novel of the eighteenth century, *Julie, ou La nouvelle Héloïse* (*Julie, or The New Heloise*).[21] The success of this epistolary novel — the tragic story of the love between a sensitive young teacher, Saint-Preux, and his beautiful student Julie — was so great that printers could not keep up with the demand.[22]

Diderot did not seem to dwell on this letdown. And yet, if there was one thing that continued to preoccupy him, it was actually the stinging blow that *Les philosophes* had dealt to his dignity. Sometime in the spring of 1761, he sat down at his desk at the rue Taranne and began writing a satire with the intention of targeting the sordid members of Parisian society behind *Les philosophes*, a group that not only included politically motivated writers such as Palissot himself, but the conservative aristocrats, politicians, ecclesiastics, and bankers who were promoting the antiphiloso-phe agenda as well. Diderot called this work his *Second Satire*; we now know this playlike dialogue by the other title that was even-tually scrawled at the top of the manuscript: *Rameau's Nephew*.

As this "conversation" opens, Diderot (his character is called Moi, or Me) introduces himself to us as he appeared in 1761. The forty-eight-year-old writer sits contentedly on a bench in the Pal-ais Royal gardens, dressed in his shabby jacket, flimsy waistcoat, woolen (not silk) stockings, clumpy shoes, and an old-fashioned wig.[23] He is engaged, so he reports, in his daily habit of watch-ing a hoard of would-be seducers pursuing the courtesans and harlots flitting about the garden's alleys and passages. Long out of the business of chasing skirts himself, the middle-aged philo-sophe muses that the garden's zigzagging *amants* remind him of the impulsive drifting of his own mind:

> It is a habit of mine to go for a walk in the Palais Royal pleasure gardens every afternoon at five, whatever the weather. That's me you see there, always by myself, daydreaming on d'Argenson's bench. I have conversations with myself about politics, love, taste, or philosophy. I give in to my mind's every fancy. I let it be master and allow it to pursue the first idea that comes to it, good or mad, and to behave just like those young libertines of ours we see chas-ing some flighty, pretty courtesan with bright eyes and a snub nose along Foy Walk, leaving her for another one, stalking them all and sticking to none. In my case, my thoughts are my sluts.[24]

It is this mental libertinage—which does not distinguish between high and low, good and bad, or crazy and prudent—that opens the door to a conversation with a man as peculiar as Jean-François Rameau.

According to numerous contemporary accounts, the real Jean-François Rameau was a washout, something of a madman, and a terrible disappointment to his family. Born three years after Diderot, in 1716, he was the son of a well-respected organist from Dijon. After a stint in the army and a time as an abbot, he decided to follow his family's tradition and become a musician. At age thirty, he moved from Dijon to Paris, hoping to benefit from the celebrity and influence of his uncle, the great Jean-Philippe Rameau (1683–1764). Living in the shadow of one of the most celebrated theorists and composers of French Baroque music turned out to be far more difficult than he had anticipated. Comparatively untalented and, as a result, unable to live up to the family name, Rameau ultimately made a meager living for himself by giving lessons and recitals, as well as by lending his musical abilities to Palissot and the burgeoning anti-*Encyclopédie* movement.[25]

Rameau's greatest claim to fame, however, had more to do with his behavior than his musicianship. A few years after arriving in the capital, the nephew of the famous composer created a scandal when he forced his way onto the stage of the Paris Opéra and entered into a shouting match with one of the directors.[26] Refusing to leave, Rameau was arrested "for disorder and insults" and sentenced to several weeks in the For-l'Évêque prison, which was generally reserved for felonious actors.[27] His uncle was not pleased. Shortly after this incident, the great composer wrote to the secretary of state to request that his nephew be forcibly put on a merchant ship and sent to the colonies. (His request was not granted.)

Over the years, the often penniless and underemployed Rameau built up his dubious reputation by making a spectacle of himself in numerous cafés. One chronicler reported that Rameau loved to proclaim that everything that we do, be it a selfless act of bravery or a great scientific discovery, is nothing more than a means of filling one's belly: the world operates, as he put it, according to the "law of mastication."[28] Even his closest friends found his views and behavior to be outlandish. A fellow Dijonnais, the writer Jacques Cazotte, described him as "never saying what he wanted to say, nor what others would have wanted him to say, but always saying what neither he nor you would have expected him to say: and both of you, after exploding in laughter, not knowing what he said!"[29] By the mid-1760s, a guidebook published by the city's booksellers identified him as one of the capital's biggest fools.[30]

SUPPOSED COPY OF A LINE DRAWING
OF JEAN-FRANÇOIS RAMEAU

Casting Rameau as the main character in his satire must have seemed like an inspired choice to Diderot in the spring of 1761.

How better to highlight the moral bankruptcy of Palissot and his malicious band of mudslingers than by featuring a conversation with the most repugnant and unusual member of their group? Yet as Diderot reworked this manuscript over the course of the next twenty years, the character of Jean-François Rameau outgrew the role he had been assigned. Initially brought to life as Diderot's whipping boy, the character of Rameau (referred to as *Lui* or Him in the dialogue) ultimately became a strident voice for the philosophe's most nagging doubts. By the time Diderot finished this curious book, he knew he had achieved something monumental. In addition to creating a new type of literature that allowed him to interrogate his deepest beliefs, he had also shown that philosophy could be much more than a positive set of ideas. It could come alive, twist itself, contain the roots of its own contradiction, and be a vehicle for rendering the tremendous complexity of the human mind.

RAMEAU'S NEPHEW

In this imagined encounter, Diderot (*Moi*) bumps into Rameau (*Lui*) in the famous Café de la Régence near the Palais Royal. Rameau has a wretched air about him, having recently been banished from a sumptuous town house where he had provided sordid entertainment in exchange for a monthly stipend and food. As *Moi* describes *Lui* to us, he lets us know — perhaps in a snottier voice than Diderot himself might employ — that he does not generally truck with such oddballs. And yet *Moi* also admits that he respects the way in which this noncomformist speaks honestly about his sloth, greed, and cowardice.[31] Men like *Lui*, he continues, have one real asset: they have a liberating effect on those who take the time to speak with them. Highlighting and disrupting the "annoying uniformity that our education, social conventions, and codes of conduct have inculcated in us,"[32] the Rameaus of the world function like a "pinch of yeast" that ferments among us, bringing out the truth.[33]

For the rest of the afternoon, *Moi* and *Lui* enter into a no-holds-barred discussion where they face off on a number of subjects. They converse about genius, the differences between Italian and French music, the education of children, and whether philosophy should have a role in society and what it should be. During each of their debates, and especially when they take up the all-important question of ethics, *Lui* acts as a sparring partner armed with a metastasized version of Diderot's own philosophy, especially his materialism.

Lui was far from the first materialist or atheist character to take the floor in Diderot's writing. His earliest works of philosophy, including the *Philosophical Thoughts* and the *Letter on the Blind*, conjured up irreligious characters in heated debate with Christian or deist believers (or beliefs). In *Rameau's Nephew*, however, Diderot engineered something altogether different by presenting an intellectual dispute between two confirmed materialists, both of whom implicitly concede that matter is the only substance in the universe, that the immortal soul is a myth, and that God and the afterlife are both fairy tales. *Lui* and *Moi*, in short, do not waste their time debating or even discussing their atheism. What they ponder are the biggest questions that the specter of materialism raises. If God does not exist, is there really a basis for morality? Is it really possible to be virtuous? And what, if anything, separates humankind from the amorality and potential ruthlessness of the animal world?

Like the real Diderot, *Moi* fights tooth and nail to save morality from the dangers of this materialist worldview. To do so, he
maintains that all humans—even *Lui*—are inescapably drawn to
the beauty of doing good. This notion was one of the most idealistic and long-lived aspects of Diderot's thought. From his first
days as translator of Shaftesbury until his dying breath, the philosophe never gave up on his belief in the fundamental goodness of
humankind and the possibility of a natural and universal ethics.
People became virtuous, he believed, not because someone had
scribbled down some guidelines on a scroll some two thousand
years before, but because moral actions themselves were beautiful, a natural extension of the secular trinity of truth, beauty, and
the good.[34]

Lui counters such optimism with a far more hedonistic understanding of the human condition. Why go to the trouble of getting satisfaction by doing good deeds, he asks, when the world
offers a veritable buffet of pleasure without any self-denial or
martyrdom? Indeed, if there is a lifestyle one should emulate, *Lui*
asserts, it is surely not that of the city's starry-eyed philosophes:
it is, rather, that enjoyed by the well-heeled bankers of the Faubourg Saint-Germain who worship money and lounge around all
day in elegantly appointed town houses drinking "good wine,"
gorging themselves silly on "delicate morsels," rolling around
"with pretty women," and sleeping in "lovely soft beds."[35] Rejecting *Moi*'s altruistic view that individuals should aspire toward
creating an honorable and principled future for those generations
who come after them, *Lui* makes clear that our objective should
be to seek out immediate gratification—starting with food—on a
daily basis. In his view, one can best measure the quality of one's
existence by tallying the number of times that one goes "easily,

freely, pleasurably, and copiously on the chamber pot every evening. *Ô stercus pretiosum!*"[36]

Lui's foulmouthed bit of Latin—which we can translate as
"Oh, joyous turd"—sums up Rameau's philosophy (or antiphi-
losophy) admirably. But *Lui*'s ethics are far more than a simple
tribute to high living and debauchery. Often arguing like a philosophe himself—though he denies being one—*Lui* attacks *Moi*'s
prescriptive and impracticable moral codes, all of which are not
only illusions from his point of view, but patently unfair. How
dare this philosophe impose such a dry and boring philosophical system on him when he is perfectly content to remain "a lay-
about, a greedy pig, a coward, and a real old scumbag."[37] Even
more compelling, *Lui* claims that he had little choice in who he
became; both his upbringing and what we would now call his
genetic makeup have determined his fate. To make his point, *Lui*
diagnoses two anatomical anomalies that have led him down the
path of depravity. The first, from his view, is a misfiring or absent
"moral fiber," which makes him blind to the supposed charms
of virtue. The second is the Rameau family's notorious "obtuse
paternal molecule," an inborn liability that makes the males cold-
hearted and amoral.[38] This genetic glitch, according to Rameau,
is also clearly present in his own son: "He is already greedy,
duplicitous, thieving, lazy, and a liar. I fear [the molecule] runs in
the family."[39]

The body of the Rameau family itself seems to bristle at the
possibility of universal human values. As a connoisseur of his
own natural depravity, *Lui* has not only accepted these liabilities;
he also makes use of them to his benefit in society. His strategy,
which he discusses at length, is a version of trickle-down economics, albeit explained from the perspective of the downtrodden.

Embracing his role as freeloader and fawning bootlicker, *Lui* brags about how he sponges off the opulent — catering to their egos, tutoring their children (often poorly), taking their money, and eating at their tables. Many of *Lui*'s most striking observations on the subject of this dog-eat-dog world simultaneously harken back to Thomas Hobbes and foreshadow Karl Marx and the theory of Social Darwinism. From his perspective, life in Paris is little more than a massive conflict among different ranks, a war of sorts that is reminiscent of the war that pits the world's animals against each other. In nature, as *Lui* puts it, "all species prey on each other; in society, people of all stations prey on each other too."[40]

By the end of *Rameau's Nephew*, *Lui* has left much of *Moi*'s benevolent humanism — and what will later be called the philosophy of the Enlightenment project — in tatters. *Lui* reduces virtue, friendship, country, the education of one's children, and achieving a meaningful place in society to nothing more than our vanity, to our tainted, narcissistic desire to make ourselves more attractive to our entourage. No matter who we are, he suggests, we are all corrupted, acting out various pantomimes to get what we want and to take advantage of those around us. The only difference between *Lui* and us is that Rameau is honest about his role and we are not.

As far as anyone knows, Diderot never showed the unpublishable *Rameau's Nephew* to anyone other than his friend Grimm. In addition to the fact that the dialogue is filled with some of the most disquieting cynicism ever to appear in the French language, Diderot had directed a litany of insults at the county's musicians, politicians, and financiers that would presumably have sent their author directly to the Bastille. He describes Palissot, by way of example, as a man who has "taken depravity to new depths, who'd make his friend renounce his religion for the hell of it, who'd steal his associates' possessions, who lacks all faith, principles, and feeling, who's only after the money and will do whatever it takes *per fas et nefas* [by hook and by crook], who measures his life in wicked deeds."[41]

But this is only the most obvious reason why the writer never let *Rameau's Nephew* circulate. Even more disturbing is the fact that this text repudiates his own role as *le philosophe*, not to mention the power and the authority of reason and philosophy itself.

THE TIME BOMB

Despite his reluctance to share *Rameau's Nephew* with his contemporaries, Diderot nonetheless passed on a manuscript version of the dialogue to his copyist for duplication in the 1780s. One of the resulting copies went to his daughter, another was passed on to Grimm, and the third one was dispatched to Catherine the Great in Saint Petersburg along with Diderot's other manuscripts. It was this last copy that first came to light when a German bibliophile and manuscript hunter named Maximilian Klinger was sniffing around in the Hermitage Library at some point in 1800 or 1801; knowing that he had found something important, Klinger quickly arranged to have a clandestine copy made of Diderot's lost satire. Several months later, this manuscript ultimately made its way to Germany, where it came into the possession of the poet, philosopher, and playwright Friedrich Schiller.

Schiller, who had read and even translated some of Diderot's unpublished works into German a few years earlier, took great pleasure in this witty series of dialogues. Shortly after reading it, he passed the manuscript on to his longtime colleague and friend,

Johann Wolfgang von Goethe, who was stunned by the unknown text, claiming he had never encountered anything "more insolent and more restrained, more talented and more audacious, more immorally moral."[42] That same year, in late 1804, he set about translating the manuscript into German.[43] The experience, as he explained it to Schiller, swept him away: "At first, one steps into the water and fancies that one can very well wade through it, but as it becomes deeper and deeper, one finds oneself at last obliged to swim."[44] Once he had finished his translation, Goethe described Diderot's absorbing tribute to even the most grotesque expressions of liberty and thinking as a "bomb" poised to explode "right in the middle of French literature."[45]

As explosives went, *Rameau's Nephew* turned out to have a long fuse. To begin with, the only French manuscript version that anybody had heard of—the one from which Goethe based his 1805 translation—disappeared shortly after the German author made his translation. Some fifteen years later, however, enterprising scoundrels in the Parisian publishing industry came up with an idea worthy of Jean-François Rameau himself. Working from a copy of Goethe's *Rameaus Neffe*, they undertook a back-translation from the German and subsequently published what they claimed was the long-lost French manuscript. This 1821 publication was quickly denounced as a fraud, most notably by Madame de Van-deul, who had been sitting on her own unpublished version of the manuscript for nearly forty years. Family pride soon overcame her reluctance to publish such an infamous work, however, and in 1823 she allowed a doctored and more genteel version of *Rameau's Nephew* to appear in print. Although this text was more accurate than the German "translation," a great deal of incertitude hovered over this version of *Rameau's Nephew* for almost seven more decades. This remained the case until a librarian named Georges Monval stumbled across a copy of *Rameau's Nephew* (entitled *Satire seconde*) in Diderot's telltale script while perusing the *bouquinistes* along the Seine in 1890. This precious manuscript now lies in a vault in the Pierpont Morgan Library in New York City.

Rameau's Nephew came into being because its author was willing to subject his own beliefs to the same brutal method of interrogation that he had used when cross-examining religion. Reconciling such an amoral experiment within Diderot's varied corpus (and life) is not an easy task. What kind of an author, after all, creates tear-jerking bourgeois dramas — morally edifying plays designed to enlighten and uplift his fellow citizens — while simultaneously giving birth, like Dr. Frankenstein, to a monster who utterly overwhelms the most cherished ideas of his creator?

The genius of this book lies precisely in this contradiction. Perhaps in large part thanks to the book's almost postmodern view of morality and truth, *Rameau's Nephew* now seems like a modern hymn to the individual's right to reject any unbending worldview — religious or secular — that impinges on the right to live freely. Fully conscious of the kind of text he had produced, Diderot consigned this manuscript to a locker filled with his other unpublishable texts. And yet this lively rendering of *Moi*'s conversation with *Lui* is the lynchpin to understanding the second half of Diderot's writing career. Before our very eyes, Diderot is evolving past his role as philosopher, Encyclopedist, and playwright of sentimental dramas. While he continued to embrace the role of philosophe — the leader of the group of public intellectuals responsible for rationalizing human existence and knowledge — he had also learned to render the complexity of his own conflicted mind, giving a stage, in the process, to the most intemperate opinions and ideas.

Diderot soon applied this method in other areas of his thought as well, particularly as he matured into the century's most forward-thinking art critic during the 1760s. For here, as was the case in *Rameau's Nephew*, he ultimately came to realize that the best way to write about art was not simply to describe or assess the painting in front of him, but to take the time to have a conversation with himself.

VII

ON ART:

DIDEROT AT THE LOUVRE

s sole proprietor of the *Literary Correspondence*, Melchior Grimm earned a sizable income by dispatching his secret, handwritten newsletter to several princes and princesses, two kings, a queen, one Russian empress, and the ruler of the Holy Roman Empire. The annual fee for this bimonthly journal ranged from one thousand to two thousand livres, depending on the distance Grimm needed to send the bulletin. All of the faraway nobles paid gladly. Receiving the *Correspondence* gave subscribers access to the capital's tittle-tattle and scandals, as well as to in-depth reviews of the theater and opera scene. But there was also something far more intriguing in Grimm's tabloid: an unending stream of otherwise unpublishable essays, literary experiments, and philosophical musings produced by Denis Diderot.[1] Over the course of the twenty-five years that the Paris philosophe provided material to Grimm (and Grimm's successor, Meister), the *Correspondence*'s readers received early versions of *The*

Nun, D'Alembert's Dream, The Supplement to Bougainville's Voyage, On Women, Jacques the Fatalist, as well as a number of other essays, short stories, and reviews.

Diderot plainly enjoyed communicating with Europe's most enlightened rulers. For once, his writing had an appreciative audi-ence. Yet being the chief contributor (and sometimes editor) of Grimm's so-called *boutique* often felt like a thankless chore. This was particularly true every two years during the "Salon season" at the Louvre, when the members of the Royal Academy's Salon of Painting and Sculpture exhibited what they believed to be the best examples of their painting, drawing, and sculpture. It was Grimm who had initially begun providing cursory reviews of these exhi-bitions in the mid-1750s. By the end of the same decade, however, he had profitably delegated this task to Diderot, his workhorse of a friend. From 1759 until 1781, the Encyclopedist, philosophe, and polymath took on the role of art critic for the *Correspondence*, pro-viding reviews of nine Salons, two of them as extensive and origi-nal as anything else he wrote in his entire career.[2]

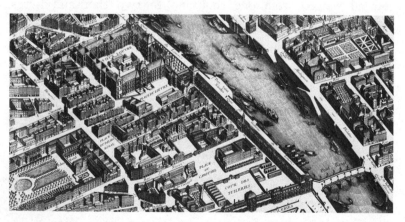

THE LOUVRE AND SURROUNDINGS
ON TURGOT'S MAP OF PARIS, 1734–39

THE SALON

The opening day of the Royal Academy's Salon of Painting and Sculpture was invariably August 25, the king's feast day. Though Diderot generally preferred spending the dog days of summer at d'Holbach's estate in Grandval, during "Salon years" he made an effort to return to the capital by early or mid-September, at which point he fell into the routine of art critic. This involved making a twenty-minute trip from the rue Taranne to the Louvre on almost a daily basis.

THE WESTERN SIDE OF THE LOUVRE,
PAINTING BY PHILIBERT-LOUIS DEBUCOURT

The Louvre that Diderot knew had long ceased to be the primary seat of the French monarchy. Shortly after Louis XIV had moved himself and his family to Versailles in 1682, much of the

palace had been transformed into the cultural and intellectual
nerve center of the kingdom.[3] In addition to housing the Académie
française, the Royal Academy of Sciences, the Academy of Inscrip-
tions and Belles-Lettres, the Academy of Architecture, and the
Royal Printing Press, many of the former royal chambers were converted to "grace and favor" apartments and studio spaces destined
for the members of the Royal Academy of Painting and Sculpture.

THE SALON DU LOUVRE OF 1787, ENGRAVING

Even outside of the Salon season, Diderot spent more time in
or around the Louvre than most philosophes. Sometimes he simply came to watch some of his painter friends bring a canvas to
life; on other occasions, he made the trip to dine with his friend
Louis-Michel van Loo and his wife. But when the Salon was open,
Diderot did not head for the large eastern section of the château
where the artists had their apartments and studios; he went
directly to the Salon Carré (Square Room), the exhibition space
from which all other art Salons ultimately derived their name.

Like most people, Diderot found the biennial Salons as draining as they were exhilarating. On an average day, more than a thousand people shoehorned themselves into the relatively small four-thousand-square-foot space. To make matters worse, the only access to the Salon was by way of a narrow and congested stairway. One of Diderot's contemporaries, the art critic Pidansat de Mairobert, claimed that navigating this passage was like running a gauntlet into an "abyss of heat" where the air was so "pestilential and impregnated with the exhalations of so many unhealthy persons" that one expected either "lightning" to strike or "plague" to break out.[4]

Diderot tended to arrive as early as possible in order to avoid both the heat and the crowds. By midmorning, swarms of people hovered around the sculpted heads, frescoes, and small-format artwork exhibited on the long tables in the center of the room. An even bigger throng crowded in front the paintings hanging on the Salon's four walls. The outer ring of spectators peered at the portraits, genre paintings, and still lifes exhibited at eye level. Others positioned themselves behind this first group, analyzing the medium-sized narrative paintings, landscapes, and large-format portraits. The final band of people lingered at the center of the room, craning their necks and squinting at the outsized history canvases suspended from the Salon's moldings, thirty feet in the air.

Despite the exhibition's challenges, it would be difficult to overestimate the thrill of seeing this vibrant mosaic of oil paintings, some of which were still wet. On the most obvious level, painting was the sole medium that provided a truly suggestive, color-rich rendering of Greek mythology, Roman history, or even the king himself. Large landscape canvases also allowed the public, most of whom had never seen a mountain range or the ocean, to imagine the natural wonders of the world. But the exhilaration of the biennial Salon not only came from the visual or mimetic qualities of the works being exposed; it also stemmed from painting's status as the highest expression of artistic modernity, as well as from the fact that these masterpieces were destined to disappear forever after the exhibition, carted off to richly appointed *hôtels particuliers*, provincial châteaux, or palaces.[5]

The obvious purpose of organizing such Salons, at least from the Academy's point of view, was presenting (and ultimately selling) its members' paintings and sculptures to the country's elite. Yet the legacy of these exhibitions is actually quite different. In stark contrast to what happened in other spaces of eighteenth-century high culture — the Paris Opéra and Comédie-Française for example — the Louvre's Salons did not limit or control their audiences through ticket pricing or hierarchical seating. Indeed, the Academy (at the king's invitation) opened the Louvre's doors to anyone who was interested in seeing the art. Free and open to the public, the Salon drew both the expected audience of foreign diplomats, aristocrats, financiers, tax farmers, rich merchants, and budding artists, and a range of so-called commoners, including laborers and servants. These working-class communities joined the fray, commenting on, interpreting, and evaluating the art that they would probably never see again. While the paintings and sculptures exhibited at the Louvre could only be owned by the very, very rich — some paintings cost a hundred times a typical worker's annual salary — the Salon nonetheless planted seeds for the democratization of art culture.[6]

Not everybody thought this was a great thing. Many members of the Royal Academy of Painting and Sculpture resented any encroachment on their royally sanctioned monopoly on taste. In

the Academy's view, to be a connoisseur of painting and sculpture, one necessarily had to be a practitioner; simple amateurs or
self-proclaimed lovers of the fine arts could never rival what the
artists themselves understood about their creations.[7] For many
sculptors and painters, the only thing worse than uninformed
crowds voicing their loathsome and ignorant opinions while staring dully at the art on display, had been the anonymous art critics
of the 1740s who had dared to publish illegal pamphlets criticizing the Academy's artists.[8] This situation had so vexed the members of the guild that the Academy went on strike in 1749, refusing
to hold another Salon until such time that the police had put an
end to these illicit publications.[9]

Diderot certainly sympathized with the artists; he, too, had
often been on the receiving end of cynical and disparaging criticism. And yet, unlike many members of the Academy, he appreciated the company of the nonartists who came to the Salon.
Indeed, during the hours that he spent slipping in and out of the
crowds at the Louvre, he took great pleasure in listening in to the
"verdicts of old men," "the thoughts of children," "the judgments
of men of letters," "the opinions of sophisticates," and "the views
of the people."[10] These varied perspectives, he wrote, infused his
own thinking on art. If he undoubtedly believed that a discrim-
inating palate was a real and measurable thing—a capacity to
sense the "true and the good, along with the circumstances rendering it beautiful"—he was also convinced that anyone could
acquire an appreciation of beauty and art through "reiterated
experience," by investing the time to understand "nature or the
art that copies it."[11] He, of course, was the living proof: the son of
a provincial cutler who became the century's most noteworthy
art critic.

HOW TO THINK AND WRITE ABOUT ART

To write about the Louvre's Salons, Diderot embraced a free-form journalistic voice that was filled with his own personality. Addressing Grimm directly in the introductory remarks to his second Salon review, in 1761, he informed his associate and editor (along with the subscribers to the *Correspondance*) that this "letter" would be filled with his own sometimes haphazard and muddled comments: "Here, my friend, are the ideas that passed through my head when I saw the paintings exhibited this year at the Salon. I am throwing them down on paper without worrying about sorting them or expressing them [fully]."[12]

Despite this deceptively slapdash method, Diderot was anything but a lighthearted dilettante. In the same way that he had studied medicine, natural history, music, and mathematics, he had also pored over Leonardo da Vinci's *Traité de la peinture* (*Treatise on Painting*), Jean Cousin's *La vraie science de la portraiture* (*The True Science of Portraiture*), Roger de Piles's *Abrégé de la vie des peintres* (English translation: *The Principles of Painting*), Roland Fréart de Chambray's *Parallèle de l'architecture antique et de la moderne* (*The Parallels between Modern and Classical Architecture*), and Charles Le Brun's *Méthode pour apprendre à dessiner les passions* (*Method for Learning to Draw the Passions* [emotional states]).[13] He had also been deeply interested in aesthetics as early as 1750, reading Plato, Augustine, and Wolff in order to write the article "*Beau*" ("Beauty") for the first volume of the *Encyclopédie*.[14]

But most important, Diderot made an effort to see as much art as possible. He visited the collections at Versailles, at the Luxembourg Palace, and at the Palais-Royal, and made arrangements to view collections belonging to private enthusiasts. He also consciously absorbed and developed his technical vocabulary and artistic sensibility by visiting the Louvre's Salons with the Academy's painters and sculptors themselves. This produced something of a paradox in his criticism since, as he put it, "if it sometimes happens that I wound artists, very often it's with weapons that they themselves have sharpened for me."[15]

Diderot had also begun to think quite seriously about what art criticism should be by the time that he attended his third Salon, in 1763. As he looked at the range and variety of the 127 paintings displayed that year, he mused that the best way to write about art would be to attune himself to the style of the artist, and to deploy a corresponding number of prose styles.

> To describe a Salon to my liking and yours, do you know, my friend, what one would need? All sorts of tastes, a heart sensitive to all charms, a soul susceptible to an infinity of different passions, a variety of styles that responds to the variety of brushes; to be grand or voluptuous with Deshays [the painter of huge and powerful religious and mythological subjects], simple and true with Chardin [the master of the still life], delicate with Vien [the forerunner of simplistic Neoclassical scenes], poignant with Greuze [the genius of doleful genre scenes], and to conjure up all sorts of illusions with Vernet [the unparalleled master of landscapes].[16]

Four years later, in 1767, Diderot shared an even more all-encompassing desire. In order to write about art in a more encyclopedic and comprehensive way, he said that he would need to travel and study the vast collections of Italian, Flemish, and French masterpieces that were either hundreds of miles away or sequestered in private residences. Gaining access to this far-away or hidden art was only his first objective, however. In order to best describe art that would never be seen by the subscribers to the *Correspondence*, he dreamt of commissioning sketches of the paintings and sculptures he was reviewing. This combination of text and image, he promised, would allow him to produce "a totally new Salon" that would highlight "the treatment and handling of a modern artist" compared to his predecessors.[17]

Time, logistics, and feasibility prevented Diderot from bringing this illustrated, pan-European history of art into being. And yet, the very fact that Diderot recognized the incongruity of writing about decontextualized paintings (for people who would never see the art itself) led him to compensate by creating an entirely different kind of art criticism. By the time that he wrote his longest and most famous Salon reviews, those of 1765 and 1767, he was not only entering into an imagined dialogue with the painters and sculptors who had produced the art; he often plunged directly into the compositions himself, sometimes as a character in the painting and sometimes as a fellow artist. In his hands, art criticism became far more than simple evaluation; it became a space of crisscrossing exchanges between the artist, the artwork, and the spectator, an opportunity to comment on and sometimes re-create the aesthetic experience of viewership.

TALKING TO ARTISTS

In his most euphoric moments, Diderot gushes with fervent and passionate praise about the art he saw at the Salon. This was certainly the case when he reviewed Étienne Falconet's sculptural depiction of the myth of Pygmalion and Galatea at the Salon of 1763. Falconet, who took his cue from Ovid's legendary tale of how a sculptor falls in love with his own statue, posed Pygmalion on

his knees in front of *Galatea* at the precise moment the goddess
Venus breathes life into the statue. The sculptor's ability to capture the complexity of this emotional moment prompts Diderot
to suggest that his friend had achieved something miraculous:
"Falconet! How is it that you were able to place surprise, joy, and
love all together in a piece of white stone? Imitator of the Gods, if
they did indeed animate statues, you have replicated this miracle
by animating this one. Come, let me embrace you."[18]

FALCONET'S *PYGMALION AND GALATEA*

Measuring his own pleasure was just the beginning of how
Diderot envisioned his role as a critic. Steeped in the vocabulary of the artists whom he came to know over the years, he also

evaluated art against a series of formal criteria. For a piece of art to be successful, from his perspective, it needed a unified composition whose formal elements—these included rendering, staging, conceptual clarity, contrast, and execution—achieved or even surpassed the potential of its medium. This was especially true for his favorite genre, oil painting.

What Diderot prized above all in a painting was the illusion of artlessness. This was a tall order, in his opinion, since the medium was perhaps the most "deceitful" of the fine arts. Whereas dancers move their own bodies in order to produce art, singers produce sound from their own vocal cords, and sculptors "release" their sculptures from a block of marble, the painter has a much more convoluted task.[19] What the artist "blends on his palette," as Diderot wrote poetically of the Salon of 1763, "is not flesh, blood, wool, sunlight, and air from the atmosphere, but soil, plant sap, calcined bones, shredded stones, and metallic lime."[20] The "best and most harmonious painting," as he put it, is "a web of lies that cover each other."[21]

Of all the members of the Academy, it was the master of color, Jean-Baptiste-Siméon Chardin, who was the best liar in Diderot's estimation. Chardin, who was one of the philosophe's closest friends at the Academy, specialized in what were ostensibly the lower genres of painting: domestic scenes, portraits, and, especially, still lifes. Yet the painter's understated compositions coupled with his virtuosity as a colorist seduced Diderot completely: "Back away, move in close, the illusion is the same [in a Chardin painting], there's no confusion, no artificiality, no distracting flickering effects; the eye is always diverted, because calm and serenity are everywhere. One stops in front of a Chardin as if by instinct, just as a traveler exhausted by his trip tends to sit down, almost without noticing it, in a place that's green, quiet, well watered, shady, and cool."[22]

In his first Salon review, in 1759, Diderot was so inspired by two Chardin still lifes that he proclaims that he could "grab the bottles" that the artist has painted "by the neck."[23] Four years later, while looking at the painter's remarkably lifelike rendition of some olives floating in water alongside some "biscuits," the philosophe calls out to his artist friend and exclaims: "Oh Chardin, it is not white, red, and black that you blend on your palate; it is the very substance of the objects; it is the air and light that you dip with your brush, and that you stick to your canvas."[24]

THE RAY, PAINTING BY JEAN-BAPTISTE SIMÉON CHARDIN

Diderot was even more in awe of Chardin's paintbrush when he stood in front of *The Ray*, a haunting still-life masterpiece featuring the ghostly, humanlike face of an eviscerated stingray hanging on a hook amidst a handful of scattered oysters. After praising the artist for the powerful and lifelike rendering of the skin and blood of the dead animal, Diderot concludes that only Chardin could redeem such a gruesome image with his supreme "talent."[25] While Diderot never came up with a theory to explain the precise source of his appreciation, his glowing review nonetheless reflects an ability to oscillate freely between attraction and repulsion.[26]

By the mid-1760s, Diderot was impatient to experience more of this kind of art, art that might make him recoil, yet delight him aesthetically. In his review of the Salon of 1765, he proclaims that "I hate all the mean, petty [actions] that indicate merely a base soul, but I do not hate great crimes, first, because they make for beautiful paintings and fine tragedies; and also because grand, sublime actions and great crimes have the same characteristic energy."[27]

Some of Diderot's fascination with the aesthetic power of suffering, terror, or evil flows directly from Edmund Burke's 1757 A Philosophical Enquiry into the Origin of Our Ideas of the Sublime, which the philosophe had reviewed for the Literary Correspondence. Like the Irish philosopher and statesman, Diderot believed that there is a fundamental difference between the classical notion of beauty and the feeling brought on by something that is so morally or physically immense that it defies our ability to rationally process what we are experiencing. Such overwhelming moments of aesthetic shock, in his opinion, were a perfect antidote to the boredom of eighteenth-century rococo pastorals. A great painting, as he put it in his Notes on Painting, sometimes required a subject that was "savage, crude, striking, enormous."[28]

There are times, when Diderot writes like this, that he seems to be whispering into the ears of nineteenth-century Romantic painters, daring them to produce the type of color-rich scenes of orgiastic excess, chaos, and ferocity that are best embodied by Eugène Delacroix's 1844 *Death of Sardanapalus*.[29] Such calls for a new form of painting relying on the rawness, shock, or primal energy of life remained little more than passing notions in his criticism, however. Far more prominent in his Salon reviews was the (seemingly contradictory) belief that art should have a salutary moral influence on its spectator. The visual arts, he often maintained, had a duty to become more relevant to the middle class and, like the Enlightenment project as a whole, to communicate values leading to a more just and honest society. "To make virtue attractive, vice odious, ridiculousness salient," he proclaims solemnly in his *Notes on Painting*, "such is the project of any honest man who takes up the pen, the paintbrush, or the chisel."[30]

Diderot's tendency to prescribe a moral foundation for the fine arts remains one of the more curious aspects of his entire career. Its source, quite frankly, is up for debate. Is this simply the logical extension of the philosophe's role as earnest reformer of society's morals? Is this an undigested part of his bourgeois upbringing? Or could this moralism stem from Diderot's tangible desire to distance himself from his own somewhat salacious reputation as an author of smut? Whatever the case, the occasional eruption of heavy-handed moralism in his Salon reviews not only leads him astray from his otherwise freethinking inclinations; it prevents him from appreciating the genius of some of his era's best painters.[31] This is certainly the case for François Boucher. By the mid-1760s, the sixty-year-old Boucher had produced a sizable and impressive body of work that included beautifully lit landscapes, subtle genre paintings, large historical and mythological

canvases, and exquisite portraits (including several of his great
admirer and patron, Madame de Pompadour).[32] Named the official "Painter of the King" in 1765, Boucher was among the richest
and most successful artists of the era.

BOUCHER'S *THE BLONDE ODALISQUE*

Diderot never denied Boucher's greatness; he stood in awe,
in fact, of the painter's virtuosity, especially his ability to master
the play of light and shadows in his compositions. Yet from the
philosophe's point of view, the artist was wasting his talent by
producing an unending stream of imagined pastorals and landscapes featuring overdressed shepherdesses, fawning lovers, dec-
orative animals, and vine-covered architectural elements: "What
colors! What a variety! What richness of objects and ideas! This
man has everything, except truth."[33] Boucher's biggest liability

was that his frivolous canvases never let the viewer forget that he was standing in front of a meaningless painting designed — above all — to please a generation of unthinking courtiers.[34]

The Boucher paintings that drew Diderot's most censorious response were his licentious domestic tableaux, the most famous of which were his *Brown Odalisque* and his *Blonde Odalisque*. In both paintings, the painter had combined the erotic atmosphere of the Turkish seraglio with the velvet-adorned world of a Versailles or Parisian boudoir. The telltale traits of the rococo — of which Boucher was a directing figure — abound in both of these compositions. Sensual light illuminates rich textiles, jewelry, and ceramics as well as the flushed flesh of the two languid women, both of whom press their bodies heavily into the sheets. The model for *Blonde Odalisque* was supposedly one of Louis XV's mistresses; the model for *Brown Odalisque* was apparently none other than the painter's wife. Nearly two decades after Boucher had painted the *Brown Odalisque* (1745), Diderot was still bellyaching about the painting in his Salon of 1763 review, asserting that the artist had incited a generation of artists to "paint chubby and ruddy asses."[35] Four years later, he once again went back to the same subject, libelously maintaining that Boucher "didn't blush at prostituting his own wife" when he cast her as the painting's subject.[36]

Such sermonizing and censure seem somewhat jarring, coming as they do from one of the era's most unrepentant apologists of pleasure.[37] Yet, both philosophically and ideologically speaking, Diderot was convinced that rococo artists like Boucher would have been better served by turning away from decadence and frivolity, and treating more serious and heroic subjects and sentiments. What Diderot longed for, as he once put it, was an artist who could "paint in the same way people spoke in Sparta," which was to say fearlessly, candidly, and without ornamentation.[38] This was not, as it might seem, a recommendation that painters imitate the best works of antiquity, as had been suggested by the great German art historian Johann Joachim Winckelmann. It was, rather, the desire that a new generation of painters combine the power of a serious and evocative subject with the purity and perhaps even geometrical simplicity of classical models.[39]

DAVID'S *BELISARIUS BEGGING FOR ALMS*

Late in life, Diderot ultimately witnessed the triumph of this precise Neoclassical aesthetic at the Salon of 1781. Exhausted and unwell as he dragged himself around the exhibition, he was nonetheless struck by the young Jacques-Louis David's critically acclaimed reception piece, *Belisarius Begging for Alms*.[40] A large-format history painting that David presented for his admission to the Academy, *Belisarius* depicts the fate of a once-heroic Byzantine general who (according to legend) ran afoul of the Roman emperor Justinian and was blinded as part of his punishment. David's painting depicts the old soldier propping himself up against a large column while both sheltering a child and begging for alms from a beautiful young woman. This moving scene is witnessed by one of the general's former soldiers, who throws up his arms with astonishment when he sees his commanding officer. Here, finally, was what Diderot had been craving: a brilliantly executed moralizing drama whose theme echoed the unaffected and natural nobility of its characters as well as its artist.

GREUZE

Well before Diderot saw some of the first examples of what would become French Neoclassicism, his hope for an alternative to putti and pastorals had focused on the master of the domestic drama, Jean-Baptiste Greuze. This self-taught artist had first triumphed at the 1755 Salon with his earnest genre painting, *A Father Reading the Bible to His Family*. In stark contrast to the other paintings at the Salon, Greuze's small-format canvas depicted a simple and touching domestic scene that glorified the upright moral life of France's lower classes.[41]

Diderot's appreciation of Greuze was a perfect example of a philosophy finding the right artist. The first time he wrote about the painter was for his review of the Salon of 1761, after he had finally braved the crowds long enough to stand in front of the artist's greatest achievement, his 1761 *L'accordée du village*, or *The Marriage Contract*.[42] Sadness and emotion brim over in this depiction of a sober father who has just signed the marriage papers that will give his daughter to another man. The patriarch, who is one of the two primary foci in the painting, ignores both the notary, who sits to his left, and his future son-in-law, who now clutches the dowry. Instead, he reaches out to his daughter, either to embrace her, say goodbye, or offer a final word of advice. (The Salon attendees hotly debated this point.) The daughter, who looks subdued, casts her eyes downward, while a younger sister and mother both hang on her, sagging with emotion. Diderot praised this portrayal of the future bride, including the way in which Greuze brought out her honest, subtle, and natural eroticism.

JEAN-BAPTISTE GREUZE'S *THE MARRIAGE CONTRACT*

The philosophe was similarly swept away two years later, in 1763, when Greuze produced what appeared to many observers to be a sequel entitled *Filial Piety*. This canvas depicts the same or a similar family at a later stage in life; this time, however, the father now lies paralyzed and on his deathbed, surrounded by a downcast and troubled household. Diderot applauded Greuze for producing yet another example of his "moralistic art," and implored him to continue to "preach" in his paintings.[43]

GIRL WITH A DEAD CANARY, PAINTING BY GREUZE

It is often said that Greuze's paintings (much like Boucher's) brought out one of the few conservative and unadventurous streaks in Diderot's otherwise freethinking mind. Yet some of Greuze's canvases also elicited a far more morally ambiguous reaction from the *philosophe*. At the Salon of 1765, for example, Diderot was particularly drawn to a small oval study of a young flush-cheeked girl weeping over the death of her bird. Diderot began his review by announcing that this "pretty elegy" was "delicious" and "the most attractive and perhaps most interesting" painting in the Salon."[44]

Allegorically minded spectators who stood before Greuze's painting readily understood that this scene was rife with symbolic content. If cages signaled some form of imprisonment or confinement, then the open birdcage in the painting surely signified some kind of liberation or release. Diderot sensed this as well. Yet rather than reveal exactly what this might be, he speaks directly to the distraught sixteen-year-old in the painting in order to tease out the truth.

> Come, little one, open up your heart to me, tell me truly, is it really the death of this bird that's caused you to withdraw so sadly, so completely into yourself?... You lower your eyes, you don't answer. Your tears are about to flow. I'm not your father, I'm neither indiscreet nor severe. Well, well, I've figured it out, he loved you, and for such a long time, he swore to it! He suffered so much! How difficult to see an object of our love suffer![45]

Once he has identified the source of her suffering—her lover—Diderot quickly outlines what transpired that same morning:

> [U]nfortunately, your mother was absent; he came, you were alone; he was so handsome, his expressions so truthful! He said things that went right to your soul! And while saying them he was at your knees; that too can easily be surmised; he took one of your hands, from time to time you felt the warmth of the tears falling from his eyes and running the length of your arm. Still

your mother didn't return; it's not your fault; it's your mother's fault…My goodness, how you're crying! But what I say to you isn't intended to make you cry. And why cry? He promised you, he'll keep all his promises to you. When one has been fortunate enough to meet a charming child like yourself, become attached to her, give her pleasure, it's for life…Your mother, she returned almost immediately after his departure, she found you in the dreamy state you were in a moment ago; one is always like that. Your mother spoke to you and you didn't hear what she said; she told you to do one thing and you did another.[46]

Just before he is about to tell his readers why the girl is so despondent, Diderot is "interrupted" by his editor Grimm, who mocks him for talking to the painting: "Why, my friend, you're laughing at me; you're making fun of a serious person who amuses himself by consoling a painted child for having lost her bird, for having lost what you will…"

Changing tone completely, Diderot goes on to explain to Grimm why he has been so taken with the portrait of this young girl. The composition of this painting is so sly and "cunning" that many of the people who stood before it did not understand what the artist was trying to communicate, namely, that this young woman is not only lamenting the loss of her bird, but her virginity as well.[47]

Like much of his art criticism, Diderot's appraisal of the *Girl with a Dead Canary* reveals the writer's amusing tendency to interrupt himself, and to leap from one point of view to the next. When Diderot first addresses the young girl — this allegory of dis- traught femininity — he shows his empathy for her anguish and tries to dry her tears. As he turns back to Grimm, he dispenses with this mawkishness and admits that, while contemplating her alluring image, he had also imagined himself playing the role of the seducer: "I don't like to trouble anyone," he confesses, "yet I wouldn't be too displeased to have been the cause of her pain."[48] This is arguably one of the more significant moments in his Salon reviews. Shifting from sentimentality to unvarnished eroticism, Diderot demonstrates the depth and complexity of his own splin-tered relationship to the art. Ironically enough, it was Greuze, the well-known master of the sentimental family drama, who helped the critic move beyond the heavy-handed moralism that the phi-losophe preached elsewhere. If Diderot remained impervious to the frivolous displays of flesh that filled Boucher's canvases, Greuze's charming vignette of a young girl mourning the death of her bird lured the author of the *Indiscreet Jewels* out from hiding.

THE ART OF SUGGESTION

In the most playful passages within Diderot's Salon reviews, the art is no longer an object of study; it is a living thing. In Diderot's account of the two portraits that Roland de la Porte (an excellent painter of still lifes) submitted to the Salon of 1765, the canvases actually speak up, rebuking their creator for attempting a new genre: "Monsieur Roland, lend an ear to your two portraits, and you'll hear them tell you in a loud voice, despite their apparent weakness and dullness: 'Go back to inanimate objects.'"[49]

Much more memorably, at the Salon of 1767, Diderot takes a leisurely "promenade" through a series of charming landscapes painted by his friend Claude-Joseph Vernet. This imaginary voy-age begins when Diderot interrupts his review and suddenly announces to Grimm: "I was about to review [Vernet's works] with you, when I left for a country close to the sea that is cele-brated for the beauty of its sites."⁵⁰ Stepping "into" these paint-ings along with an unnamed abbot who engages the art critic in conversation, Diderot then begins strolling through each of the seven "sites." In addition to luxuriating in Vernet's representa-tions of mountain summits, seascapes, waterfalls, castles, and the final port scene that ends the promenade, he occasionally infuses this travelogue with theoretical digressions on art itself.

COAST SCENE:

GENOA LIGHTHOUSE AND THE TEMPLE OF MINERVA MEDICA,

PAINTING BY CLAUDE-JOSEPH VERNET

One of the more important topics to surface during his walk and discussion with the abott is the artist's role vis-à-vis nature itself. Reacting to his companion's suggestion that a landscape painter should attempt to mechanically replicate the nature

around him as well as possible, Diderot argues that the best artists produce a carefully crafted dialogue between the real and the
imaginary. This is, of course, precisely what Vernet achieves in his
paintings:

> If you'd spent more time with [Vernet], perhaps he'd have taught
> you to see in nature what you don't see now. How many things
> you'd find there that needed altering! How many of them his art
> would omit as they spoiled the overall effect and muddled the
> impression, and how many he'd draw together to double the
> enchantment! [If] Vernet had taught you to see nature better,
> nature, for her part, would have taught you to see Vernet better.[51]

A great artist, Diderot makes clear, not only perceives the
essence of nature, but captures and reconstitutes its spirit, stimulating our imagination to enter into the painting in the process.
This was also what Diderot was demonstrating in his criticism:
by leading his readers into imagined versions of Vernet's landscapes, he was creating a world that initially seems entirely natural, but ultimately reveals itself to be inspired art.

Such moments—when Diderot attempts to translate the
full experience of art spectatorship via the medium of his writing—are the high points of his Salon reports. The most stunning
example of this type of art criticism came in 1765, when Diderot
reviewed the most popular painting of that year's Salon, Jean-
Honoré Fragonard's ten-foot-by-seventeen-foot acceptance piece,
The High Priest Coresus Sacrificing Himself to Save Callirhoe.

In stark contrast to the paintings for which Fragonard
would later be known—erotic domestic scenes and figures of
fantasy—the source for this massive history painting (which
Louis XV purchased) was a second-century CE anecdote from

Pausanias's *Description of Greece*. Recently adapted for the French stage, the story itself was well known to the French public. During a time of plague, the inhabitants of the ancient Greek city of Calydon ask the oracle at Dodona how they might end the plague that has fallen upon the population. The oracle replies that they must sacrifice a beautiful girl named Callirhoe or find someone to die for her. At the climax of the story, the victim is brought to the temple where the head priest, a man named Coresus, who has always loved Callirhoe, has the task of slaying her to save the city.[52]

FRAGONARD'S *THE HIGH PRIEST CORESUS
SACRIFICING HIMSELF TO SAVE CALLIRHOE*

In his manipulative review of the painting, Diderot does not provide a straightforward reaction, explanation, or description of Fragonard's rendering of this scene. Claiming that he could not

get close enough to view the canvas itself—the crowds once again
determining what one could or could not see at the Salon—the
critic informs Grimm that he has decided, instead, to relate a
hazy, hallucinatory dream. This strange and elaborate reverie
ultimately culminates in Diderot's own rendering of the events
portrayed in *Coresus and Callirhoe.*

After a lengthy evocation of plague and pandemonium, as well
as the divine decree that sentences the beautiful young Callirhoe
(or her surrogate) to die, Diderot cuts to a scene in the temple
where the sacrifice is about to take place. Recounting this cli-
mactic moment as if he is witnessing it himself, Diderot gives a
gripping account of Coresus's decision to kill himself in place of
the woman he loves. This is, of course, the precise moment that
Fragonard depicts in his painting:

> At that very instant the high priest grips the sacrificial knife, he
> raises his arm; I think he's about to strike the victim, to plunge it
> into the breast of she who had scorned him and whom the heavens
> had now delivered to him; not at all, he strikes himself. A general-
> ized shriek pierces and rends the air. I see death's symptoms make
> their way over the cheeks, the forehead of the loving, generous
> unfortunate; his knees give way, his head falls back, one of his arms
> hangs limp, the hand wielding the knife still fixes it in his heart.[53]

Seemingly breathless as he describes the priest's suicide,
Diderot then moves through the rest of the painting, scanning the
gallery of faces, all of which are frozen in horror. After fixing on
the acolyte at the foot of the candelabrum, several female atten-
dants, and the "cruel" priests who were attending to the ritual,
Diderot's gaze lands on a haunting old man in the bottom left portion of the painting.[54] It is here where he ends his dream: "I see his

eyes, I see his mouth, I see him lurch forward, I hear his screams, they awaken me, the canvas withdraws…"[55] Writing alongside the painter as a partner and an equal, Diderot also allows us to feel how he himself felt when he first saw this canvas, wide-eyed and mouth agape.[56]

Diderot's digressive and trancelike account of *Coresus and Callirhoe* numbers among the most compelling examples of his dynamic art criticism.[57] In addition to replicating the illusionist atmosphere of Fragonard's canvas, Diderot compels his reader to live through the most intense moments of the painting's drama.[58] Yet the most noteworthy moment within this same review is not Diderot's "translation" of Fragonard or the saga of Coresus: it is, rather, the retelling of Plato's allegory of the cave that actually opened this long dream sequence.[59]

Diderot's dreamlike version of Plato's cave initially seems very much like what we find in *The Republic*. The dream begins in a dark cavern in which there are a "multitude of men, women, and children," all of whom are prisoners and forced to watch a series of projected images, echoes, and silhouettes of reality on one of the cavern's walls.[60] The most obvious message behind both Plato's and Diderot's parables is not dissimilar: most people are prisoners of their own perception, going through life with only a hazy or illusion-filled idea of reality.[61] The difference, however, is that Diderot has inflected his version of the allegory with a biting message about contemporary politics. The characters in Diderot's dream, unlike those in Plato's cave, do not confuse the shadows of reality with a higher, Platonic realm of forms; they are, rather, compelled to watch a coercive spectacle (which seems very much like modern cinema) designed to seduce and bully them into believing a series of manufactured lies.

All our hands and feet were chained and our heads so well secured
by wooden restraints that it was impossible for us to turn them.
[Our] backs were turned to the entrance of this place and we
could see nothing but its inner reaches, across which an immense
canvas had been hung.

Behind us were kings, ministers, priests, doctors, apostles,
prophets, theologians, politicians, cheats, charlatans, masters of
illusion, and the whole band of dealers in hopes and fears. Each of
them had a small set of transparent, colored figures corresponding to his station, all so well made, so well painted, so numerous
and diverse that they were able to represent all the comic, tragic,
and burlesque scenes in life.

These charlatans...had a large hanging lamp behind them, in
front of whose light they placed their little figures such that their
shadows were projected over our heads, all the while increasing in
size, and came to rest on the canvas at the back of the cave, composing scenes so natural, so true, that we took them to be real,
now splitting our sides from laughing at them, now crying over
them with ardent tears, which will seem a bit less strange when
you know that behind the canvas there were subordinate knaves,
hired by the first set, who furnished these shadows with the
accents, the discourse, the true voices of their roles.[62]

To understand the audacity of his review one needs to once
again recall that Grimm was dispatching this periodical to a group
of royals including the Count Dalberg, the Duke and Duchesse
of Saxe-Gotha, the Margrave of Ansbach, the princes of Hesse-
Darmstadt and of Nassau-Sarrebruck, the queen of Sweden, the
king of Poland, and Diderot's and Grimm's imperial benefactress,
Catherine of Russia.[63] The message embedded in this review

would have been hard for the *Correspondence*'s subscribers to miss: as monarchs, they, along with their ministers, priests, and profiteers, were complicit in running a massive illusion factory whose function was to control the minds of the people.

Nowadays, 250 years after Diderot's so-called *Salons* first left Paris for various courts throughout Europe, scholars continue to revel in this eccentric art criticism. In addition to providing firsthand details about the politics and personalities of the Academy of Painting and Sculpture, Diderot's reviews take us back to a time when critics were lawbreakers, taste was a controlled substance, and the production, evaluation, and ownership of art was consciously limited to a tiny percentage of the French population. But perhaps more importantly, "listening" to Diderot as he unabashedly composes alongside the Salon's artists serves another purpose. As the philosophe flouts the preconceptions of his era, he also invites us to question the conventions and expectations put in place by our own academies, and to make the viewing of art as personal and inspired as possible.

VIII

ON THE ORIGIN OF SPECIES

In the final paragraphs that Diderot wrote for his review of the Salon of 1769, the philosophe explained why he thought that the best days of the biennial were over. Tastes, he believed, were changing, and not for the better. Younger Parisians now had less appreciation for the fine arts, philosophy, poetry, and traditional sciences; they were far more preoccupied with "administration, commerce, agriculture, imports, exports, and finance." While the philosophe did not dispute what he called "the beauty of the science of economics," he also lamented that this trend would eventually transform his countrymen into "morons." Money, in his opinion, was the enemy of human imagination. Great artists (and true aficionados like himself) understood this: not only did they scorn art's financial value, they became so obsessed with the quest for the perfect canvas or statue that they tended to become "unspeakably neglectful" of their own private lives.[1]

Not surprisingly, Diderot's assessment of the Salon of 1769 was shorter than that of either 1765 or 1767. This was not only the art's fault. In addition to the fact that Diderot now found far fewer paintings and sculptures that inspired him, he was thoroughly occupied with writing a beguiling and unpublishable piece of science fiction recounting the godless origin of the human species. Diderot had first gotten the idea for this text during a dinner party in August 1769 at the so-called Synagogue, a sumptuously appointed four-story townhouse on the rue Royale belonging to his friend Paul Henri d'Holbach. If there was one place in Paris where Diderot would have been able to speak with impunity about such heretical ideas, it was at this temple of impiety, just north of the Louvre.[2]

BARON D'HOLBACH, ENGRAVING

D'Holbach, who had inherited two immense fortunes from his father and uncle, purchased this imposing building in 1759, and transformed it into the greatest freethinking salon of the eighteenth century. On virtually every Thursday and Sunday afternoon when he was not at his country estate at Grandval, the baron (and his coquettish wife) invited between fifteen and twenty-five people to his house for conversation and a multicourse feast.[3] In addition to Diderot, who was one of the regulars, guests included

Grimm, Buffon, Condillac, Condorcet, d'Alembert, Marmontel, Turgot, La Condamine, Raynal, Helvétius, Galiani, Morellet, Naigeon, Madame d'Épinay, Madame d'Houdetot, and Madame de Maux. Quite frequently, the baron also welcomed illustrious foreigners on Sundays, including Adam Smith, David Hume, Laurence Sterne, and Benjamin Franklin. Invitees knew the ritual well. Meals began at two p.m. sharp and ran until seven or eight p.m.; exquisite fare and superb wines were always on the menu; and anyone who came to the rue Royale was encouraged to engage in unbridled freethinking and debate. What was discussed at the so-called *hôtel des philosophes* stayed at the *hôtel des philosophes*.

All was not simply cuisine and chitchat behind the walls of d'Holbach's townhouse, however. As well as organizing his celebrated gastronomic salon, the baron financed and presided over an enormous and clandestine atheism factory. Drawing inspiration and material from the extensive three-thousand-volume library that he maintained on the premises, d'Holbach wrote, translated, and collaborated on more than fifty books, about ten of them with provocative and anticlerical titles like *Christianity Unveiled* (1761), *The Sacred Contagion* (1768), *Critical History of Jesus Christ* (1770), and *System of Nature* (1770).[4] Though Diderot wisely left no traces of his own participation in these projects, it is evident that he contributed at least marginally to some of the attacks that d'Holbach levied against the Church. This was particularly true for *System of Nature*, one of the best-selling works of atheism ever published.

Despite his support for the baron's scorched-earth campaign against all forms of spirituality, Diderot was far less interested than d'Holbach or his disciple, Jacques-André Naigeon, in disseminating straightforward atheism by the 1760s and 1770s. Rather than contradicting Scripture or trumpeting godlessness—especially

in print—Diderot generally preferred thinking through the problems that remained unanswered *after* atheism was established as
a given. These far headier questions began with What is life? and
extended to natural history puzzles such as Who are we? Where
did we come from? How are we changing as a species, both morally and physically? And can matter actually think?

Diderot had been asking questions such as these one afternoon at d'Holbach's house when, according to his own description of events, he and a number of irreverent dinner guests began
making jokes about the first humans. One can imagine the guf-
faws as someone directed the conversation to the contents of
Eve's ovaries and Adam's testicles. Were the organs of these first-
generation humans normal? Or were they swollen with the seeds
of all future generations, compressed into smaller and smaller
spores, like matryoshka dolls? After the dinner wound down and
the guests had all left, Diderot lingered. It was at this point that
he and d'Holbach perhaps shared a glass of Malaga—d'Holbach
often served his friend this prized dessert wine—while discussing a series of related and far more serious subjects including the
birth of new types of animals, the natural history of the human
species, and the likely destruction and revival of the world.[5] The
speculative biology discussed that night did not dissipate with
the wine. Over the course of the next month, Diderot wrote three
short dialogues, the sum of which constitute the most engaging
proto-evolutionary book of the eighteenth century.

D'ALEMBERT'S DREAM

The August 1769 heat wave numbered among the most oppressive
that Diderot could remember. Toinette and Angélique had already

fled the summer heat in July, preferring the riverbanks of Sèvres to the sweltering Faubourg Saint-Germain. Most of the philosophe's friends were also avoiding the capital: d'Holbach had retreated to Grandval; Grimm was traveling to various courts in Germany; and the Volland sisters had settled into life at their family château, near Vitry-le-François. Diderot, however, remained in Paris, submerged in work. Every morning, after breakfast, he climbed the stairs from his apartment to the sixth-floor office, where he wrote under the building's rafters and slate roof. Spending time in this stifling atticlike atmosphere had only one advantage: unlike the tenants on the first and second floors, he was not privy to the foul stench of the street.

Much of what Diderot needed to accomplish that summer involved a tremendous amount of editing. In addition to being surrounded by illustrations "from head to foot" as he proofed the copy for the sixth volume of plates, he had also temporarily inherited the unpleasant chore of reviewing a number of books for the *Literary Correspondence* while Grimm was in Germany. (He described this as writing some "pretty good things about some really bad ones.")[6] His final task was to polish one of the most modern economic treatises of the era, Abbé Galiani's *Dialogues sur le commerce des blés* (*Dialogues on the Commerce of Wheat*). In the midst of all this editing, however, Diderot somehow managed to compose *D'Alembert's Dream*.

By August 31, he announced to his lover Sophie Volland that he had begun doing what he had really wanted to do: transforming his thoughts from his silly evening at d'Holbach's into a series of outrageous philosophical dialogues.[7] When he had first thought about casting characters for this discussion, he considered assigning the two major roles to the pre-Socratic philosophers

Democritus and his mentor Leucippus. At first glance, these ancient Greek thinkers had seemed like excellent intellectual surrogates; like Diderot, they believed the world could only be explained as the result of physical forces, matter, and chance.

As Diderot began composing the *Dream*, however, he came to the conclusion that this classical framework would hinder the discussion. Having spent thirty-five years following advances and debates in the contemporary life sciences, he ultimately decided to delegate his ideas to present-day thinkers instead. Democritus, Leucippus, Hippocrates (and ancient Greece in general) soon gave way to a series of imagined Left Bank conversations between people Diderot knew in real life: d'Alembert, Mademoiselle de l'Espinasse (d'Alembert's would-be lover), the eminent doctor, physician, and philosophe Théophile de Bordeu, and, in the first dialogue, Diderot himself.

As the curtain opens on this three-act materialist drama, we join the fifty-five-year-old Diderot and the similarly middle-aged d'Alembert in the midst of an intense debate. The rendition of Diderot that we see here differs markedly from the tepid version of the philosophe who took the stage in *Rameau's Nephew*. Closer to the real Diderot, this is a far more commanding thinker, a projection of the man known throughout Paris as one of the most forceful conversationalists of his generation. And, true to form, this particular version of Diderot is bullying his friend, d'Alembert, in an imagined clash of Enlightenment geniuses.

Diderot's goal in this conversation is quite straightforward: to convince his friend — the mathematical prodigy, illustrious member of the Académie des sciences, winner of the Berlin Academy of Science prize, member of the Académie française, and former coeditor of the *Encyclopédie* project — to accept an entirely materialist understanding of the universe. This is a world, Diderot points out, where everything that exists, from the movement of the stars to an idea that flits across our consciousness, is composed of or the result of the activity of matter.

The first step toward accepting this philosophical doctrine, from Diderot's point of view, involves admitting that there simply is no valid reason to continue to believe in God. As the dialogue opens between the two men, d'Alembert seems inclined to concede this point:

> I grant you that a Being who exists somewhere but corresponds to no one point in space, a Being with no dimensions yet occupying space, who is complete in himself at every point in this space, who differs in essence from matter but is one with matter, who is moved by matter and moves matter but never moves himself, who acts upon matter yet undergoes all its changes, a Being of whom I have no conception whatever, so contradictory is he by nature, is difficult to accept.[8]

Deity or no deity, however, d'Alembert quickly points out what he believes to be a major flaw in Diderot's system: his friend has not explained the seemingly unbridgeable gap between the immaterial and physical worlds. Echoing elements of Descartes's theory of human existence, which distinguishes between the body (as an unthinking extension in space) and the mind or soul (which exists on an immaterial plane of being), d'Alembert challenges Diderot to demonstrate conclusively that there really is only one substance — matter.[9] Prove to me, he says, that the entire world is cut from the same cloth.

To convince his skeptical friend, Diderot does not engage with Descartes's dualism. Instead, he decides to demonstrate that all matter has a latent ability to become sensitive and, under the right circumstances, to sense and cogitate. Ever the skeptic, d'Alembert retorts that, if this is true, then "stone must feel."[10] Diderot's reply — "Why not?" — leads to one of the most playful thought experiments in the *Dream*: the conversion of a stone statue into conscious human flesh.

The statue that d'Alembert proposes for this thought experiment is Étienne Falconet's *Pygmalion and Galatea*, the same masterpiece that Diderot had reviewed at the Salon of 1763.[11] That the two men settle on Falconet's statue is an inside joke. In the year before he wrote the *Dream*, the real Diderot had engaged in a heated correspondence with his friend Falconet about the role of posterity in the creation of art.[12] Diderot argued that artists produce their best works in order to speak to future generations, perhaps even from the grave. (This was what he himself was counting on.) Falconet rejected this idealistic view of the artist. Speaking from his own experience, he maintained that once his sculptures were wheeled out of his studio, he forgot about them: they were, as he put it, "pears that fall from trees, right into pastries."[13] For this reason, Falconet's statue was an excellent choice for pulverization: after all, "the statue has been paid for, and Falconet cares very little about his present reputation and not at all about it in the future."[14]

But there was an even more salient reason why d'Alembert and Diderot settled upon Falconet's *Pygmalion and Galatea*: this work of art depicts the story of a statue coming to life. Such a scene not only provides an obvious thematic link to the materialist animation proposed by Diderot, but also draws attention to the boundaries that separate matter and thought, and the living and the nonliving. Just how Falconet's statue comes alive in the

Dream differs markedly from the myth of Pygmalion, however. In lieu of gentle kisses and divine intervention, Diderot engineers a multistep mechanical process that involves breaking the statue into pieces, grinding it up in a mortar, and transforming it into something that he can then eat and animalize into himself. This speculative science reads something like a recipe:

> DIDEROT: When the marble block is reduced to the finest powder, I mix this powder with humus or compost, work them well together, water the mixture, let it rot for a year, two years, a century, for I am not concerned with time. When the whole has turned into a more or less homogeneous substance—into humus—do you know what I do?
>
> D'ALEMBERT: I am sure you don't eat it.
>
> DIDEROT: No, but there is a way of uniting that humus with myself, of appropriating it, a *latus*, as the chemists would call it.
>
> D'ALEMBERT: And this *latus* is plant life?
>
> DIDEROT: Precisely. I sow peas, beans, cabbages, and other leguminous plants. The plants feed on the earth and I feed on the plants.[15]

By the time that Diderot has proposed assimilating the statue into his own being—demonstrating conclusively the atomic mobility of the statue's elements—the philosophe has made his point. All molecules have the latent potential to achieve sensitivity, to move from the realm of the inanimate to what humans call "the living" and the "thinking realm." D'Alembert is amused by this good-humored thought experiment: "It may be true or it may not," he states, "but I like this transition from marble to humus, from humus to vegetable matter, and from vegetable matter to animal, to flesh."[16]

Diderot's next step in his argument, which is to provide an entirely materialist account of d'Alembert's own existence, is far more disconcerting. This story begins with the very brief introduction of the mathematician's famous unmarried birth mother, the beguiling novelist and *salonnière* Claudine-Alexandrine-Sophie Guérine de Tencin (1682–1749), a woman who had started out life as a nun in Geneva before renouncing her vows and moving to Paris in 1712.[17] Diderot then introduces us to d'Alembert's biological father, a libertine and artillery officer named Louis-Camus Destouches (whom Diderot refers to as "La Touche"). The final biographical element alludes to the defining aspect of d'Alembert's early life, the fact that his mother left him as a swaddled newborn on the steps of a small church on the Île de la Cité. The rest of Diderot's chronicle, however, is little more than a series of seminal fluids, gestational processes, and nutritive assimilation:

DIDEROT: Before taking another step forward, let me tell you the story of one of the greatest mathematicians in Europe. What was this wondrous being in the beginning? Nothing.

D'ALEMBERT: Nothing! How do you mean? Nothing can come from nothing.

DIDEROT: You are taking words too literally. What I mean is that before his mother, the beautiful and scandalous Madame de Tencin, had reached the age of puberty, and before the soldier La Touche had reached adolescence, the molecules which were to form the first rudiments of our mathematician were scattered about in the young and undeveloped organs of each, were being filtered with the lymph and circulated in the blood until they finally settled in the vessels ordained for their union, namely the sex glands of his mother and father. Lo and behold, this rare seed takes form; it is carried, as is generally believed, along the Fallopian tubes and into the womb. It is attached thereto by a long pedicle, it grows in stages and advances to the state of fetus. The moment for its emergence from its dark prison has come: the newborn boy is abandoned on the steps of Saint-Jean-le-Rond, which gave him his name, taken away from the Foundling Institution and put to the breast of the good glazier's wife, Madame Rousseau; suckled by her, he develops in body and mind and becomes a writer, a physicist, and a mathematician.[18]

What is compelling about Diderot's retelling of his friend's life is not the fact that this abandoned child grew up to become famous, but that the animal called d'Alembert—like Falconet's statue—is no more than a temporary assemblage of atoms arising from, and soon to return to, a bubbling, material universe.[19] The process, as Diderot explains it, is as simple as it is inevitable: "[T]he formation of a man or animal need refer only to material factors, the successive stages of which would be an inert body, a sentient being, a thinking being, and then a being who can resolve the problem of the precession of the equinoxes, a sublime being, a miraculous being, one who ages, grows infirm, dies, decomposes, and returns to humus."[20]

Much more powerfully than the neutral and amusing pulverization of Falconet's statue, the literary staging of d'Alembert's life rewrites the mathematician's (and our) understanding of humankind's relationship with the material world. By the end of this somewhat unnerving conversation, the doubtful mathematician informs Diderot that he has had quite enough of this exhaust-ing repartee and will be returning to his house to go to sleep. Diderot warns d'Alembert (correctly, of course) that he will soon be dreaming about their exchange. The reverie that ensues intro-duces us not only to the confused biology of the sleeping mind, but also to a much more complete history of the human and the world, a history that is inaccessible to d'Alembert's waking and skeptical mind. Once Diderot had completed this second and much longer dialogue in the last days of August, he set aside all false modesty and boasted to Sophie that "it was actually quite clever to put my ideas in the mouth of a man who is dreaming. One often has to lend an air of folly to wisdom."[21]

AS D'ALEMBERT SLEEPS

Act 2 of the *Dream* opens with Mademoiselle de l'Espinasse at the bedside of the dreaming and apparently delirious d'Alem-bert. For hours, de l'Espinasse has been carefully jotting down all his garbled and seemingly irrational mutterings. While de l'Es-pinasse does not yet understand the torrent of ideas that she is transcribing, d'Alembert's dreaming body is communicating the feeling of awe as he contemplates the significance of his life (or lack thereof) within a materialist universe.

D'Alembert's dream begins precisely where he and Diderot had left off in their earlier conversation, with a reprise of his own progressive development from inert matter to responsive and con-scious being: "A living point...No, that's wrong. Nothing at all to begin with, and then a living point. This living point is joined by another, and then another, and from these successive joinings there results a unified being, for I am a unity, of that I am certain."[22]

MADEMOISELLE DE L'ESPINASSE,
WATERCOLOR AND GOUACHE

Metaphors and analogies flow freely as d'Alembert attempts to explain just how these diverse particles, elements, and compounds ultimately became *him*. Initially, he proposes that living molecules fuse together "just as a globule of mercury joins up with another globule of mercury."[23] He then shouts to Mademoiselle de l'Espinasse that progressive creation of identity is like a swarm of bees, a mass of tiny individuals that come together and communicate through various forms of tiny pinching: "the whole cluster will stir, move, change position and shape,... a person who had never seen such a cluster form would be tempted to take it for a single creature with five or six hundred heads and a thousand or twelve hundred wings."[24]

When initially speaking with Diderot, d'Alembert had not taken such views of identity seriously. The dreaming geometrician, however, is far more adventurous asleep than awake, not only proposing that organs might contribute to his psychological identity, but also theorizing that a given animal might be split or divided into smaller groups of individuals according to organic subdivisions. To explain how this might happen, he once again conjures up the image of a swarm of bees that is functioning as an individual. This time, however, he proposes surgically altering the mass by cutting them apart where they were fused together, which would result in the production of new identities: "Now carefully, very carefully, bring your scissors to bear on these bees and cut them apart, but mind you don't cut through the middle of their bodies, cut exactly where their feet have grown together. Don't be afraid, you will hurt them a little, but you won't kill them. Good—your touch is as delicate as a fairy's. Do you observe how they fly off in different directions, one by one, two by two, three by three?"[25]

THÉOPHILE DE BORDEU, ENGRAVING

FRESHWATER POLYPS, ENGRAVING AND WATERCOLOR, 1755

Dr. Bordeu interjects that d'Alembert's bee swarm is a very useful image; this bee animal, he points out, is akin to a massive freshwater hydra or polyp that can be cut up into smaller individuals and "that can be destroyed only by crushing."[26] That Bordeu would choose to conjure up a freshwater hydra or polyp at this point in the *Dream* comes as no surprise. Diderot's generation had been fascinated with these small creatures since 1744, when the Swiss naturalist Abraham Trembley first published his "observations" on these multicellular, half-inch-long aquatic invertebrates. Adorned with a varying number of leaflike appendages, the hydra looked like a plant, yet was also quite predatory, extending its tentacles far beyond its body to coil around small crustaceans and insect larvae. Even more shocking, and of particular interest to materialists, were the polyp's regenerative powers. Cut a hydra in half — exactly like Diderot's swarm of bees — and two entirely new hydras would swim off. In a world where the sanctioned belief was that God had formed animals on the fifth and sixth days of Creation, here was seeming proof that life could be generated (and even self-generate) in the present.

The polyp's asexual reproduction is hardly scandalous to modern-day scientists or theologians. Yet the hydra's stunning ability to self-perpetuate posed a seemingly unsolvable problem to theologically oriented savants who subscribed to preformationism, which was the prevailing (and scripturally compatible) understanding of "generation" or reproduction at the time. Handed down to eighteenth-century naturalists from ancient science, the belief that all beings developed from miniature versions of themselves ("seed germs") gained scientific currency during the seventeenth century thanks to the work of the "microscopists" Marcello Malpighi and Jan Swammerdam. Studying spermatozoa, both men published tremendously influential studies asserting that these small swimming "individuals" were complex enough to have souls. Egg-oriented anatomists working on human ova reached similar conclusions, positing that the location of the soul could be found in the human egg. Whether spermist or ovist, however, all preformationists believed that reproduction was the extension of a single act of Creation that had produced — all at once — generations and generations of homunculi (Latin for "tiny men") or eggs. This theory was pushed to its logical, albeit absurd, conclusion, when the celebrated philosopher, priest, and theologian Nicolas Malebranche asserted, in *De la recherche de la vérité* (*Search after Truth*, 1674–75), that each egg must contain all future generations within it.

D'Alembert, who channels Diderot's own view of "gener-ation," implicitly refutes this religion-tainted embryology.[27] Indeed, his polyp-based understanding of procreation allows him to fantasize that humans on faraway planets might "reproduce" by "budding," exactly like a hydra. D'Alembert lets out "bellows of laughter" as he relates this flight of the imagination: "Human polyps in Jupiter or Saturn! Males splitting up into males and females into females — that's a funny idea…"[28] As is often the case throughout the dream, d'Alembert's mutterings underscore the remarkable fertility of nature. But they also give rise to what was an unthinkable idea at the time: the use of technology to inter-vene in the production of human specimens. Anticipating a form of embryo storage, d'Alembert first proposes that scientists might collect these dividing human hydras for future use. The result would be "myriads of men the size of atoms which could be kept between sheets of paper like insect-eggs, which…stay for some time in the chrysalis stage, then cut through their cocoons and emerge like butterflies." This spawn, d'Alembert claims, might even produce "a ready-made human society, a whole province populated by the fragments of one individual…"[29]

This clonelike propagation fantasy bleeds into yet another of Diderot's remarkably prescient ideas. Still visualizing the possi-bility of divisible humans, d'Alembert proposes distilling specific genetic types from "tendencies" located within a particular part of the body. Cackling uncontrollably at this point, the mathemati-cian immediately seizes upon the humorous image of a new breed of humans whose character and traits would be derived exclusively from either the male or female sex organ: "doesn't the splitting up of different parts of a man produce men of as many different kinds? The brain, the heart, chest, feet, hands, testicules...Oh, how this simplifies morality! A man born [from a penis]...A woman who had come from [a vagina]..."[30]

At this point in the discussion, the still-decorous Mademoiselle de l'Espinasse censors the specific details of what kind of people might come forth from the powerful organic drive of these *indiscreet jewels*. Instead, she moves on to the technology that might make this possible: a genetic storage chamber that she describes as a "warm room, lined with little phials," each of which would contain a seed germ bearing a vocational label: "warriors, magistrates, philosophers, poets—bottle for courtiers, bottle for prostitutes, bottle for kings."[31] Such is the delightful eccentricity of Diderot's understanding of the universe: the staggering unpredictability of nature is only matched by humankind's ability to control it.

LUCRETIAN MUSINGS

Many of the stimulating ideas in *D'Alembert's Dream* have their roots in Lucretius's *De rerum natura*.[32] This was not the first time that the philosophe had drawn from the Roman poet's unpredictable, vibrant, and destabilizing understanding of nature. Lucretius's ideas infused much of Diderot's early writing on God, most famously in the deathbed scene that he inserted into his 1749 *Letter on the Blind*. In *D'Alembert's Dream*, however, Diderot went further, combining the Roman's Epicurean worldview with contemporary scientific knowledge and discoveries. Such is the case when the dreaming d'Alembert conjures up the "reality" of spontaneous generation, long considered an Epicurean touchstone. Peering into an imaginary container of macerating meat and crushed seed broth, exactly as the Irish naturalist John Needham had done in a famous experiment undertaken in 1745, d'Alembert proclaims that he can see rotting, inorganic matter sprouting to life and perishing before his very eyes. As he describes the "microscopic eels" that he sees swimming about (these were simply bacteria), he bellows excitedly that this microscopic universe contains a lesson about all life forms:

> In Needham's drop of water everything begins and ends in the twinkling of an eye. In the real world the same phenomenon lasts somewhat longer, but what is the duration of our time compared with eternity?...Just as there is an infinite succession of animalculae in one fermenting speck of matter, so there is the same infinite succession of animalculae in the speck called Earth. Who knows what animal species preceded us? Who knows what will follow our present ones? Everything changes and passes away, only the whole remains unchanged.[33]

Needham and Diderot, of course, were entirely mistaken about spontaneous generation. But the "reality" of this churning universe nonetheless gives rise to one of the most powerful moments in the *Dream*. This is when d'Alembert realizes that the human race, too, is but a fleeting occurrence within this endless invention and reinvention of nature: "Oh, vanity of human thought! oh, poverty of all our glory and labors! oh, how pitiful, how limited is our vision! There is nothing real except eating, drinking, living, making love and sleeping..."[34]

Diderot had no compunction about facing down the potential bleakness of his materialist worldview. He had underscored the ethical problems raised by his "own devil of a philosophy" in *Rameau's Nephew*, and he certainly conjures up the emptiness of the material world in the *Dream*. Yet d'Alembert's character, and the

Dream as a whole, do not get bogged down in existential pathos. Indeed, immediately after the mathematician laments the lack of anything real and durable in his life, his gaze shifts from this men- acing world of self-replicating eels and focuses on what is import- ant to him in his own life: the alluring Mademoiselle de l'Espinasse. Dreaming of his companion, d'Alembert then becomes sexually excited and masturbates in front of the object of his fantasy. This comical moment is, we should recall, recounted by de l'Espinasse herself, who is entirely unaware of what is transpiring in front of her, as she diligently continues to take notes:

> [D'Alembert said:] "Mademoiselle de L'Espinasse, where are you?" "Here." Then his face became flushed. I wanted to feel his pulse, but he had hidden his hand somewhere. He seemed to be going through some kind of convulsion. His mouth was gaping, his breath gasping, he fetched a deep sigh, then a gentler one and still gentler, turned his head over on the pillow and fell asleep. I was watching him very attentively, and felt deeply moved without knowing why; my heart was beating fast, but not with fear.[35]

After d'Alembert's "convulsion," as Mademoiselle de l'Espinasse describes it, the restless mathematician finally enjoys a temporary respite for several hours. When he again begins dreaming, at two o'clock in the morning, he returns to the book's biggest questions: Just what does it mean to be human? Where did our species come from? And who are we within the infinite contexts of space and time?

THE HUMAN STORY

Diderot was painfully aware that science had done little to illu- minate the history of the human race. Such a subject simply did not lend itself to the kind of disinterested and probing empirical examination that Diderot promoted. Well into the eighteenth century, nature remained laden with inflexible, religious-inspired concepts. To begin with, there was the orthodox understanding of time, which, at least officially, maintained that animals and humans had come into existence at the time of the Creation, 5,769 years before.[36] The second related notion was that animals and humans had appeared in their present forms during this biblical drama. The final, and perhaps less obvious, sacrosanct idea had to do with humankind's supposedly exceptional place within God's kingdom. According to Christianity's sacred writings, man was unique on earth: he was a "rational" animal infused with a higher spiritual nature — a divinely bestowed soul — that separated him from the other beasts. Fashioned from the slime of the earth, this fallen creature nonetheless stood apart.

Diderot was one of the first to discredit all three of these Christian tenets in one work. But he was not the only person to disrupt the supposedly immutable barriers between animals and humans. By the late seventeenth century, an increasing number of anatomists began underscoring the undeniable physiological correlations between humans and the animal kingdom, particularly the great apes.[37] This blurring reached a turning point in 1735 when the Swedish naturalist Carl Linnaeus assigned humankind a spot in the world's bestiary, right next to sloths and apes.[38] The most important elements of Diderot's proto-anthropology, however, did not stem from Linnaeus's trenchant classification scheme; instead, they came from Diderot's friend, the renowned naturalist Georges Louis Leclerc, Comte de Buffon.

Buffon's tremendous influence on Diderot had begun during the latter's imprisonment in 1749. Once he had been allowed books at Vincennes, Diderot pored over and annotated the first three volumes of Buffon's recently published *Natural History*. Among the key portions of this groundbreaking text was a 150-page inventory of the human species that, at first glance, appears to be a simple geographical catalogue of racial phenotypes. But behind this mapping of the world's different "varieties," as Buffon called them, was the theory that these dissimilar groups all came from a prototype race that mutated as it moved across the globe into different climates, ate dissimilar foods, and created new and diverse customs for itself.

COMTE DE BUFFON, ENGRAVING

Buffon, who was the keeper of the king's garden and wrote the *Natural History* at the monarch's pleasure, was extremely careful not to question or even bring up the biblical Genesis in this account. Yet his theory of human degeneration, as it was called, represented the single biggest reconceptualization of the history of the human species during the eighteenth century. People who read this best-selling account of a once unified, but now bifurcating, human race now had something far superior to the biblical tale of how Noah's sons wandered off into the wilderness to start the different branches of the human family. They had a physical, scientific explanation of where we came from that was, from a European point of view, tremendously reassuring. After all, the prototype species that Buffon hypothesized was white. The other groups — the maligned and marginalized peoples of Africa and other antipodal regions — were thus, by definition, accidents of history.[39]

The version of the human degeneration story that Diderot conjured up in the *Dream* is even more forceful. Instead of retelling Buffon's reassuring story of difference emerging from an archetype, Diderot (via d'Alembert's dreaming) concentrates on what eighteenth-century naturalists believed to be the most degenerated variety of humans on the planet: the Laplanders. From d'Alembert's dreaming perspective, this supposedly wretched and snow-dwelling branch of diminutive humans was not only misshapen, but on the verge of extinction, perhaps like the human race itself: "Who knows whether that shapeless biped a mere four feet in height, which is still called a man in polar regions, but which would very soon lose that name if it went just a little more misshapen, is not an example of a disappearing species? Who knows whether this is not the case with all animal species?"[40]

Anything but preordained, planned, or eternal, from d'Alembert's point of view, the birth and the demise of the human species is no more significant than the delivery of a freakish two-headed pig.

D'Alembert's character is the most despondent of the four voices that Diderot created for his *Dream*. As the math wizard progressively accepts the implications of materialism, he lets go of the reassuring (but spurious) concepts that give meaning to the human identity: individuality, species, and even the separation between what is normal and monstrous. By the end of his dream, d'Alembert has come to realize that humans come into this world as contingent flukes, lead their lives without knowing who they really are, and return to a bewildering world of matter without ever knowing why.

Bordeu and de l'Espinasse react far more creatively and cheerfully to these destabilizing ideas. During the *Dream*'s substantial discussion of monstrosity, for example, Bordeu does not deconstruct his own identity, but rather proposes an amusing Frankenstein-like thought experiment in teratogeny, the fabrication of monsters.[41] Casting himself as something of a mad scientist, the doctor imagines intervening in the gestation process by manipulating the speculative genetic material of embryos, what Diderot calls "threads." This prescient scene not only debunks the supposed "miracle" of conception, but foreshadows our own world, one in which scientists have claimed the right to refashion human biology at the embryonic level.

> BORDEU:...Now do mentally what nature sometimes does in reality. Take another thread away from the bundle — the one destined to form the nose — and the creature will be noseless. Take away the one that should form the ear and it will have no ears or only one ear, and the anatomist in his dissection won't find either the olfactory or auditory threads, or will only find one of the latter instead of two. Go on taking away threads and the creature will be headless, footless, handless. It won't live long, but nevertheless it will have lived.[42]

As the willing assistant in this thought experiment, Mademoiselle de l'Espinasse immediately seizes upon the most important

philosophical implications of what is transpiring. Considering
the misshapen humans she and the good doctor are producing
together, she realizes that no human endeavor — not science and
certainly not religion — can even begin to understand the limits
and possibilities of nature.

By the end of the *Dream*, Bordeu and de l'Espinasse have become
our accomplices in a new and heady venture to better understand
the universe through the frontiers of procreation. This openness
to experiment reaches a boiling point during the last section of
the *Dream*. In this tête-à-tête between the good doctor and de l'Espinasse (d'Alembert has finally left his bedroom on the rue de Bel-
lechasse to have supper elsewhere), the two new friends sip sweet
Malaga wine and let their imaginations run wild. Mademoiselle
de l'Espinasse, in fact, has taken over as the more aggressive freethinker and is pushing the conversation to its limits. Liberated
from d'Alembert's presence, and out of earshot of the servants,
she finally has the opportunity to ask a question that has been
vexing her for hours: "What do you think about crossbreeding
between species?"[43] This query leads to an even more shocking
idea: bestiality, the possibility of crossing humans with animals
to produce a new race of beings.[44]

Bordeu is only too happy to take up this and all other racy
subjects. Ridiculing the moral qualms of those people who
have prevented more intensive "experimentation," the doctor proposes the (hypothetical) creation of a new life form, a
goat-human hybrid born from a human-animal coupling. After
Bordeu discusses the technical aspects of engendering such offspring, de l'Espinasse directs her friend to start the process without any delay: "Quick, quick, Doctor, get to work and make us
some goat-men!"[45] While the couple eventually pulls back from

this hypothetical trial — Mademoiselle de l'Espinasse suddenly objects that these goat-human hybrids might turn out to be unrepentant sex fiends — the two would-be empiricists have made their point: by playing with nature, one can readily prove that the human race is anything but immutable. Not only do human varieties change over time — shifting and twisting as a function of their climate and food — but the species itself can be altered, combined, and perhaps even improved. This last provocative section of *D'Alembert's Dream* is far more than libertine chitchat; it mocks humanity's supposedly special place in the universe, and invites us in the process to reconsider the eternal categories that supposedly define us, be they man and woman, animal and human, and even monstrous and normal.

In the weeks after he finished the *Dream* in the fall of 1769, Diderot read the manuscript aloud to a small group of his friends at d'Holbach's estate at Grandval.[46] One can only imagine how those in attendance must have whooped, in particular, at the last section. In this entertaining mixture of the lofty and the scabrous, Diderot had put forward a purely materialist understanding of human sexuality that explored questions related to masturbation, homosexuality, and even bestiality. Outraged, amused, or cowed into silence, what Diderot's audience could not understand in 1769 was that, in addition to everything else, the philosopher was something of a prophetic sexologist as well.

IX

THE SEXOLOGIST

As philosopher, woeful husband, and persistent adulterer, Diderot spent a great deal of time thinking about both sex and love. Just how the two fit together (or not) preoccupied him throughout his entire adult life. In his more flippant moments, the philosophe reduced the sex act to a simple biomechanical occurrence, nothing more than a quick "rubbing of intestines."[1] But he also saw far beyond this entirely carnal and utilitarian view of lovemaking. Toward the end of his life, in the notes he jotted down for his unfinished *Elements of Physiology* (1781), he explains that the sex act is both akin to and fundamentally different from the state of being hungry. The big distinction, as he puts it, is that when it comes to hunger, "the fruit doesn't have the desire to be eaten," whereas we do. This dashed-off metaphor is not immediately obvious, but it appears that Diderot is saying that we, as sexual beings, are both *the person who eats* as well as *the meal*.

Sex, in short, was surely far more complicated than most people thought.[2] This comes out in Diderot's varied writings on the subject. Over the course of his forty-year career as a writer, he alternatively described the sex act as a time of intoxication, a time of complete focus, a time of intimacy, a time of playful eroticism, a time of ferocity, a time of devotion, a time of submissiveness, a time of corporeal confusion, and a time when one experiences (or not) the sovereign pleasure of orgasm with someone you love. Lovemaking, while perhaps not synonymous with love, certainly benefited from it.

Diderot also assumed that the complicated world of sex was rarely only about procreation. Once again beating Freud to the punch, he was convinced that human sexuality did not confine itself to what happened in the bedroom. Regardless of how people spend their lives, he stressed, they are invariably embracing, sublimating, or reacting against nature's most potent impulse. This was the case for abstinent monks, libertines, and even the most honorable and principled members of society. No matter who you are, as he admits about himself as well, there is always a bit of "testicle" lurking even in "our most sublime feelings and purest affection."[3]

HUMAN JEWELS

Diderot's understanding of sex was a marked departure from what he had learned as a child in Langres. Catechism had taught the boy that erotic desires, far from being a natural part of our being, only came about after Eve grasped the forbidden apple from the tree of knowledge, saddling humankind with a regrettable craving for "delicious agitation" in the process.[4] Langres's clergy, including Diderot's teachers at the collège Jésuite, built on this foundation, not only condemning the dirty and unmentionable sex act itself, but lashing out at social entertainments that might lead toward "criminal commerce" and wantonness of all sorts.[5] Theater, in Langres, was portrayed as a school for scandal where mixed audiences banded together in a dark room to initiate themselves in the most criminal of human passions.[6] Dancing was worse; its spiraling minuets were supposedly a sinful vestige of Roman bacchanalia.[7]

Some of these warnings, especially those related to the potential lustiness of the body, apparently weighed heavily upon Diderot during his adolescence. According to Madame de Vandeul, her father briefly adopted something of an ascetic lifestyle when he was thirteen, not only fasting and sleeping on straw, but wearing a prickly *cilice* or haircloth shirt under his abbot's cassock.[8] Why Diderot eventually gave up this regime is anyone's guess, but one can imagine that he soon discovered that tormenting himself was not all that gratifying. Ten or so years later, as he reached his early twenties, he presumably reached a similar conclusion about the priesthood and a lifetime ostensibly without sexual pleasure. In his first work, the *Philosophical Thoughts* (1746), he condemned both asceticism and abstinence (as well as his austere and priestly brother, Didier-Pierre), claiming that fleshly enjoyments and passions make us who we are.[9]

Diderot was far from the only person to be writing favorably about humankind's quest for pleasure in the 1740s. Julien Offray de La Mettrie, a physician-philosopher and self-avowed libertine who was obliged to take refuge at the court of Frederick II of Prussia in 1747, produced two daring works of philosophy celebrating and prescribing the joys of the body: *La volupté* (*Ecstasy*, 1745) and *L'art de jouir* (*The Art of Pleasure*, 1751). Enterprising pornographers and writers of libertine fiction also fabricated dramatic versions of this same philosophy of pleasure. Diderot himself jumped on this bandwagon in late 1747, when he wrote the *Indiscreet Jewels*. Supposedly the result of a bet or a challenge, *Indiscreet Jewels* was a conscious imitation of the type of licentious best seller made popular by Claude-Prosper Jolyot de Crébillon in the 1740s. Crébillon's most famous novel in this vein, *The Sofa* (1742), tells the tale of an Indian aristocrat who is not only magically transformed into a divan by Brahma, but sentenced to spend his life banished between couch cushions until such time that two virgins consecrate their love "on" him. His episodic adventures as a sofa, during which he is bumped about in a variety of ways, provide the salacious content of the novel.

Diderot's *Jewels* borrows simultaneously from Crébillon and the kind of enchanted orientalism present in Antoine Galland's famous *Mille et une nuits* (*One Thousand and One Nights*, 1704–17). The events of Diderot's tale take place at the court of Congo, a thinly veiled, Africanized version of Versailles. The main character is a Congolese sultan named Mongogul (Louis XV), who obtains a magic ring from a genie named Cucufa (derived from *cocu* or "cuckold"), which gives him the power to make women's vaginas speak. For twenty-one chapters, Mongogul uses his newfound power to coerce a wide variety of "jewels" to reveal their iniquitous, clandestine adventures. After thirty such interviews, he finally decides to turn the ring's power on his mistress, his beloved Mirzoza (an obvious version of Louis XV's paramour, Madame de Pompadour). In an evident gesture of respect to this supporter of the philosophes and to the king himself, this particular jewel soon reveals that Mirzoza/Pompadour is the only woman who has remained faithful. All the other women we hear about, regardless of class or nationality, have made cuckolds of their unsuspecting partners. Such is the unfortunate fate of the pitiful Sélim, a courtier who, upon his return from a mission abroad, asks Mongogul to use his magic ring to determine if his mistress, Fulvia, has remained true to him in his absence. As happens inevitably in each of the book's short chapters, Fulvia's effusive and exhausted vagina has a lot to say when given the floor, not only proclaiming that Fulvia is anything but faithful, but that the poor organ is leading the life of a "galley slave. [T]oday it's one, tomorrow it's another..."[10]

Unsurprisingly, the talkative and unfaithful jewels that Diderot first brought to life in late 1747 have drawn the attention of scholars working on gender in the academic world. Some have attributed the overall framing of this novel to the era's (or even Diderot's) misogyny; others have countered this idea by pointing out that the men in the novel are themselves no more virtuous than the women, and that Diderot's *Jewels* gave a voice to the authority and legitimacy of female sexuality, which was rare at the time.

Whatever his real intentions, Diderot ultimately regretted publishing the scandalous *Jewels*. The book may have seemed funny in 1748, but it was far less amusing in subsequent years, when his enemies mocked the earnest editor of the *Encyclopédie* for being the author of this "piece of trash."[11] Diderot's friend and literary heir, Jacques-André Naigeon, reported that Diderot frequently claimed that if he could somehow undo this dreadful mistake by cutting off a finger, he would not hesitate to do so.[12] This, however, may have been something of a public stance. Sometime in the early 1770s, he composed several new manuscript-only chapters—including some of the most pornographic of the whole book—presumably for his own amusement, and that of his closest friends.

_____

WOMEN, NUNS, AND SEX

Diderot's unpublished musings on human sexuality include, among other things, speculations on the genealogy of sexual ethics, writings on human anatomy, and conjecture regarding the source of homosexuality. This mass of written material does not reduce tidily into a clinical book on humanity's erotic appetites and responses. On the contrary, Diderot's wide-ranging observations, scattered as they are among philosophical dialogues, personal correspondence, novels, and in more serious-minded notes on human physiology, are less an attempt at science than an interpretation of nature that broadcasts the belief that sexual contact is the most natural and desirable expression of our humanity.

Diderot did hold certain fixed beliefs, however. If man generally initiated the sex act, it was undoubtedly the woman who had the far more complicated role. Having studied numerous books of natural history and medicine—particularly Albrecht von Haller's eight-volume *Elementa physiologiae corporis humani* (*Elements of Human Physiology*, 1757–66)—Diderot was under the impression that women had been poorly served by nature: in addition to the fact that it was far more difficult for them to achieve orgasm, they were saddled with a monthly malaise and the peril of childbirth.

Worse yet, the era's foremost naturalists had concluded that women's problematic anatomy held them back from being the equal of men. What really separated the two sexes was not physical size, strength, or overall intelligence, but the fact that women had a "fierce" and "unruly" reproductive organ—the womb—that had no counterpart in men. This despotic body part, Diderot himself came to assert, often acted unilaterally and selfishly, sometimes "strangling" other organs as would "an angry animal."[13] Here, for many men of Diderot's generation, was the source of the overall corporeal anarchy that not only filled the female imagination with strange visions, but produced the tremendous swings in emotional states that made the sex "beautiful like Klopstock's Seraphs" or "terrible like Milton's devils."[14]

Diderot's views on female anatomy and psychology have been perceived as among the few truly rearguard aspects of his thought. Yet these prejudices coexist with a more compassionate understanding of the plight of women during his era. During those moments where Diderot abandoned anatomy for what we might call proto-sociology, he proclaimed that the world's women were trapped within an unforgiving system that was engineered by men for men, and that produced misery for one-half of the planet's population. Once a woman was no longer beautiful, he wrote pessimistically in a short 1772 essay entitled "On Women," she becomes a person who is "neglected by her husband, forgotten by her children, nothing in society, and for whom her only and last resort is religion."[15] This sad state of affairs dovetailed with the overall miserable situation of women, for whom "the cruelty of civil law has conspired with the cruelty of nature... They have been treated as stupid children."[16]

Diderot never came close to proposing a coherent theory of sex roles and human sexuality, particularly in a condensed and contradictory piece like "On Women." His most successful attempts at grappling with the intricacies, contradictions, and morality of sexuality, as it turned out, came in his fiction. That Diderot looked to an *imagined* world as the best place to think through such questions makes sense. Fiction not only freed him from the constraints of scientific truth, but allowed him to force his characters to confront and negotiate their own desires in light of a variety of moral, religious, and societal codes.

Diderot's fictional treatments of love and sex extended into several genres. In 1770, he dashed off two short stories—"This Is Not a Story" and "Madame de la Carlière"—that take up the problems that tend to beset couples, be they of the couple's own making or due to society's ludicrous laws and expectations. More famously, in his novel (or antinovel) *Jacques le fataliste*, which he composed over the course of twenty years beginning in the 1760s, Diderot let slip a pessimistic assessment of love and sexual desire, namely, that both are destined to evaporate before our eyes, revealing the emptiness of any pledges we may have made in our youth: "The first time that [man and woman] swore undying love to each other was at the foot of a crumpling crag. They bore witness to their constancy beneath the canopy of heaven that is constant only in changing. They themselves were changing even as they spoke and all changed around them, and they believed that their feelings were immune to change! Children! Eternal children!"[17]

Diderot's most comprehensive presentation of sexuality came in his one and only realist novel, *The Nun*. Recounted from the point of view of a nun who wishes to renounce her vows, this moving first-person memoir leads us deeply into the psychosexual sadism and sexual abuse that he associated with cloistered life. Not surprisingly, *The Nun* remains Diderot's most controversial work. Only fifty years ago, when Jacques Rivette adapted the book for the cinema in 1966, the state information secretary under Charles de Gaulle censored the film for its conflation of religious ceremony, cruelty, and lesbian love.[18] Even today, *The Nun* strikes a nerve.

Despite the somber and despairing tone of *The Nun*, the novel began as a mirthful practical joke. Diderot himself recounted the circumstances behind the prank — as well as the subsequent birth of the novel — to his readers in the *Literary Correspondence*.[19] As he tells the story, he, Grimm, and Madame d'Épinay were sad that their friend, the affable Marquis de Croismare, had deserted them for his faraway estate in Normandy. A year after his departure, in 1759, the small group of friends decided that they would come up with a scheme to lure the aristocrat back to the capital. Knowing full well that the marquis had intervened on behalf of a nun who had sought to leave the sisterhood, they decided to write to Croismare in the voice of this same holy sister, beseeching the provincial aristocrat to come help her out in Paris. Reading of the letters that Diderot sent to Croismare, as well as the marquis's responses, supposedly became the highlight of dinner parties held by d'Épinay at her château at La Chevrette.[20]

If we are to believe Diderot's account, Croismare was entirely taken in by the invented nun's pleas for help. The problem, from the conspirator's point of view, was that the kindhearted marquis had no inclination to return to the capital. Instead, he informed the nun that she should take a coach to his estate in Normandy, where he had arranged for her to serve as a governess for his daughter. Faced with Croismare's reluctance to return to Paris, and perhaps feeling a bit uncomfortable that their friend had gone to the trouble of making special preparations, Diderot and his friends wrote a note from the nun's landlord announcing her death in May 1760.[21]

The demise of Suzanne was not the end the story, however. During the same months that the pranksters were writing false letters to the marquis, Diderot began to flesh out a far more detailed first-person account of the nun's life. Chronicling the horrors of this poor woman—Diderot ultimately called her Suzanne Simonin—was apparently quite an affecting experience. Diderot recounts in the book's preface that the actor Henri-Louis d'Alainville came to pay him a visit at his rue Taranne office while he was composing the nun's memoir; he found the author "immersed in pain and bathed in tears."[22]

Suzanne's memoir, very much like the letters that Diderot and his friends had sent to Croismare, is ostensibly destined for the kind marquis as well. The chronicle begins with a synopsis of the ill treatment that Suzanne received at the hands of her parents and her two siblings. Suzanne's first exposure to convent life, she explains, came at sixteen, after she informed her mother that one of her sister's suitors was actually interested in courting her. Four days after this episode, Suzanne finds herself behind the walls of the Convent of the Visitation on the rue du Bac, as a *pensionnaire*. Suzanne initially believes that this is a temporary measure, since it was common practice at the time for young girls to spend a few years in a convent before returning to society to get married. To her chagrin, however, she soon receives a visit from her mother's spiritual adviser, who informs her that her parents supposedly have no more money for an eventual marriage and she has no other choice but to take the veil.

At the end of a two-year probationary period, Suzanne remains firmly opposed to this forced vocation, and refuses to take her vows. Having embarrassed and infuriated her parents, she is whisked home and locked in a room for six months. Toward the end of this house arrest, Suzanne's mother reveals why she has treated her daughter so abominably over the years: Suzanne is the illegitimate child of an illicit affair, a living and hateful reminder of her mother's sexual infidelity and guilt. Despite the abuse she has suffered from both her parents, Suzanne ultimately sympathizes with her mother's difficult situation and agrees to return to convent life and take her vows. Several months later, the once-reluctant Suzanne goes through the profession ceremony at a different convent, Longchamp, where she joins a community of nuns who have dedicated their lives to God, but who remain women with sexual energy that must be expressed, repressed, or, at times, sublimated into violence and perversion.

As an interpreter of monastic life, Suzanne is often Diderot's proxy, churning out philosophe-like maxims that sound as if they were penned by Voltaire: "a life of poverty is degrading," she writes, but "a life cut off from society is depraving."[23] Yet as perceptive as Suzanne is in some ways, she is also quite blind to the homosexual desire that breeds organically at Longchamp, where she quickly becomes the "favorite" of the house's Mother Superior, Madame de Moni.

A benevolent and deeply spiritual leader who is exceedingly kind to Suzanne, Moni is known for her uncanny ability to conjure up the Holy Spirit during her prayers. Throwing herself and those around her into a trance of sorts, Moni seems to commune sexually with God. Suzanne, who describes herself as generally impassive, is anything but immune to Moni's stimulating prayer sessions: "You would leave her room with your heart on fire, joy and ecstasy radiating from your face, and weeping such sweet tears…I think that I too might have reached such a state if I had become more used to the experience."[24] This relatively pleasant stage in Suzanne's life ends, however, when Moni realizes that she has fallen deeply in love with Suzanne, thereby losing her ability to connect with God.[25] Racked with guilt, she becomes melancholic and increasingly insane, castigating herself for an undisclosed sin before expiring. Suzanne is distraught, but never suspects the real cause of Moni's shame.

Moni's replacement, Sainte Christine, proves to be an entirely different type of Mother Superior. Intent on imposing fasts, vigils, and self-mortification, the new ruler of the convent instills a regime of the worst kinds of superstition. Her reign in Longchamp is without a doubt the most somber part of the book: a study not only in how the community turns against Suzanne, but how repressed female desire, from Diderot's point of view, can take the form of persecution and violence.

Suzanne falls immediately afoul of this pitiless and austere new Mother Superior. In addition to reading the New Testament (and thinking for herself), Suzanne courageously burns her hair shirt and throws away her discipline (a paddle used to hit oneself). Perceived as a threat to Sainte Christine's authority, she is soon spied upon, condemned to spend weeks praying on her knees by herself in the middle of the chapel, given only bread and water to eat, and locked up in her cell. Over the next few months, a collective psychosis develops; tormenting Suzanne becomes "a game, a source of fun for fifty people in league against [her]."[26] Eventually, the convent's nuns rip her clothes off, dress her in a sack, parade her through the convent, starve her, take away her furniture, mattress, shoes and stockings, and throw her into a cell in the basement of the house. The most emblematic moment of persecution comes after the Mother Superior discovers that Suzanne has filed suit to leave Longchamp. Calling the rest of the community to worship (while Suzanne is confined to her cell), Sainte Christine declares that this insubordinate nun is now dead to the community. Suzanne, who is able to escape from her room, recounts what follows once she is outside the chapel:

[I] managed to break open the lock, and I went down to the door to the choir which I found closed…I lay on the ground, with my head and back against one of the walls and my arms crossed across my chest, and with the rest of my body I stretched out and blocked the passageway when the office finished and the nuns came to leave. The first one stopped short and the others did as well. The Mother Superior guessed what had happened and said: "Walk over her, she's just a corpse."[27]

Suzanne is unexpectedly saved from what looks like certain death by Monsieur Manouri, the lawyer whom she had hired to help her with her suit. Through his intervention and financial support, she soon receives word that she will be moving to her third and final convent, Sainte-Eutrope, twenty-six miles due south of Paris, in Arpajon. As her carriage pulls up to the massive square residence, she is startled to see a highly irregular sight: two or three nuns staring down out at her from each of the convent's bedroom windows. This is, of course, a sign of things to come. In stark contrast to the regime of self-denial and absti nence that she left at Longchamp, Sainte-Eutrope has given in to the lure of desire.

Shortly after she arrives, Suzanne meets the Mother Superior at Sainte-Eutrope, who is languorously sitting up in bed and casting her half-open eyes over her charges like an oriental despot. Suzanne watches as Madame de **** (we are spared the Mother Superior's real name) rises from her somnolent state and begins inspecting her nun-filled harem:

She did not sit with us but instead walked around the table, placing her hand on one nun's head, gently tilting it backwards and kissing her on the forehead; lifting up another nun's gimp, placing her hand underneath it and leaning against the back of her chair; walking past another nun and as she did so letting one of her hands stray over her or touch her mouth; and nibbling some of the food that had been served and then offering it to this nun or that.[28]

Suzanne describes a number of such scenes candidly, completely oblivious to the sexual implications of what she is witnessing or experiencing. Despite the fact that this narration sometimes seems far-fetched, Suzanne's supposed naïveté is the most brilliant conceit of the novel. In addition to the fact that this allows Diderot to delegate the book's indictment of convent life to a blameless Christian—and not to an atheist like himself—Suzanne's ignorance allows for a curiously detached account of her own sexual awakening. Unaware of what is transpiring as she gets to know the Mother Superior, the young nun can only describe the curious physiological changes taking place in her new friend and in her own body. The narrative effect, as in the Mother Superior's "harpsichord lesson," produces a curious form of pornography where the reader, through Suzanne, witnesses what transpires from the point of view of an oblivious sexual object:

I followed her in [to her cell]. In an instant she had opened the harpsichord, produced a book, and pulled up a chair, for she moved briskly. I sat down. She thought I might be cold, so she took a cushion from one of the chairs and placed it in front of me, then bent down, took my feet and placed them on the cushion; then she went and stood behind my chair and leant against it. At first I played some chords, then I played some pieces by Couperin, Rameau, and Scarlatti. While I was playing, she had lifted up a corner of my gimp, her hand was now resting on my bare shoulder and the ends of her fingers were touching my breast. She sighed, it was as if she felt oppressed, she had difficulty breathing. The hand she had placed on my shoulder at first held me tightly, then not at all, as if all strength and life had drained from her, and her head fell against mine. In truth, though mad, she was extremely sensitive and had the keenest interest in music. I have never known anybody on whom music has had such an extraordinary effect.[29]

"SHE PLAYS AND SINGS LIKE AN ANGEL,"
ENGRAVING FROM DIDEROT'S *LA RELIGIEUSE*, 1804

Over the next few months, Suzanne increasingly becomes the source of the Mother Superior's masturbatory pleasure. Over time, however, the Mother Superior seeks to move beyond this charade by letting the innocent girl in on the secret of Sainte-Eutrope. Convent life, she hints to Suzanne, can be a place of intense sensuality, despite the constraints of the monastic setting. One has but to listen to the "language of the senses," as the Mother Superior puts it, making very clear to Suzanne that bodies have an innate way of expressing and communicating between themselves.

Suzanne not only spurns this indirect invitation to a far more explicit sexual relationship, but ultimately speaks with her confessor about the altered states that Madame de **** seems to enter when the two women exchange "innocent" caresses. The fear that Suzanne, too, might soon give in to this lesbian lifestyle is very much present in her unconscious mind; she describes the Mother Superior's intense pleasure during their encounters as an "illness," a malady that she thinks might be contagious. Her confessor, Father Lemoine, is equally alarmed and instructs Suzanne to avoid this "devil" at all costs.

As soon as Suzanne begins to shun the Mother Superior, the titular head of the convent begins to realize that she has been guilty of a tremendous transgression. Like Madame de Moni, she begins a slow descent into insanity: from "melancholy to piety and from piety to delirium."[30] The final pages of Suzanne's memoir relate the Mother Superior's agonizing hysteria in detail. Swinging wildly between her love for Suzanne and a crushing culpability, Madame de **** calls out for her former lovers, roams the halls naked, foams at the mouth, rambles, screams obscenities, whips herself, and finally succumbs, convinced that the spirits of hell are dragging her down as she does so.

After the Mother Superior dies, the convent once again turns on Suzanne; she is immediately accused of "bewitching" Madame de ****, of leading her into mortal sin, and causing her death. Faced with the prospect of the same sort of persecution that she suffered at Longchamp, she makes the fateful decision to escape with Don Morel, a sympathetic confessor who has suffered similar persecution under his superiors. Her escape is yet another station of the cross; in the final (and quite cursory) pages of the memoir, Suzanne describes an attempted rape at the hands of her would-be savior, her arrival in Paris at a bordello of sorts, a stay at an institution for wayward women on the rue Saint-Denis, and her last days as a laundress.

In the months after *La religieuse* first appeared in print in 1796, both the champions and detractors of the book agreed with the assessment that this was "the cruelest satire of cloisters ever written."[31] And yet, as powerful and shocking as this story must have appeared to eighteenth-century readers, Diderot was not targeting the Catholic faith itself in this book; rather, he was condemning the long-standing tradition of creating a "sect of virgins" that deprived the French state of tens of thousands of citizens and their potential offspring. One of these individuals had been, of course, his younger sister Angélique, who, at age twenty-eight, had lost her mind and died behind the thick, limestone walls of the Ursuline convent in Langres.

But beyond this distressing link to Diderot's life, his novel also allowed the writer to explore what he believed to be the specific psychological and physiological effects of cloistering on the mind and body. That Diderot chose to limit his investigation to the convent as opposed to the monastery is hardly a surprise. If, in his opinion, same-sex seclusion inevitably led to perversion and degeneracy, women risked far greater harm in such situations because of their uterus. The Nun is perhaps the first "realist" novel to portray the presumed influence of this impulsive sex organ, beginning with the otherwise quite reasonable Suzanne herself, a woman who becomes subject to fainting, temporary fits of madness, and, finally, sexual arousal at the hands of Madame de ****. Diderot's depiction of the other cloistered nuns is even more dramatic; whether they express their repressed sexual energy in sadistic or forbidden sex acts, these sequestered females seem to march in lockstep toward collective hysteria. The liabilities of female physiology, Diderot seemed to lament, were ideally matched to the folly of the convent.

SEX IN TAHITI

Diderot began to write The Nun in his midforties. Twenty-three years later, in 1782, he put the finishing touches on the novel. Much of the tone and some of the structure of this heartrending story must be credited to the English novelist Samuel Richardson, whom Diderot not only admired greatly, but for whom he composed an epitaphic tribute in the Journal étranger in late 1761. Richardson, in Diderot's opinion, had opened the door to the moral and psychological potential of long-form fiction, ushering in the era of the novel as we know it. The Englishman's novels, in stark contrast to most books belonging to this once-disreputable genre, did not transport his readers to faraway places inhabited by cardboard characters leading improbable lives; instead, books like his Pamela, or, Virtue Rewarded (1740) and Clarissa, or, the History of a Young Lady (1747–48) conjured up the tiny, recognizable details of human existence and realistic people whose stories conveyed the complexity and cruelty of their existence. In writing *The Nun*, Diderot not only seized upon the muckraking potential of such realistic fiction; he had added his own innovation: staging human sexuality from the perspective of a first-person narrator who was, incredibly enough, often oblivious to the desires, perversions, and arousal that she herself was experiencing.

Suzanne's suffering — which Diderot forces us to feel from her first-person perspective — is designed to inspire a hatred of forced religious vocations by bringing us to tears. Diderot's second-most famous treatment of sex, his *Supplement to Bougainville's Voyage*, could not be more different. In stark contrast to the sexual perversion and buried desires of the convent, the *Supplement* leads us to an island of sexual and sensual openness — Tahiti — while often attempting to make us smile and laugh in the process.

Like many of Diderot's most important works, the light-hearted series of philosophical dialogues that form the *Supplement* had humble origins. Many of its themes — including its long mediations on infidelity and the inanity of marriage — stem from personal experience. But the actual genesis of the *Supplement* grew from the notes that Diderot took while reading Louis-Antoine de Bougainville's best-selling *Voyage autour du monde* (*A Voyage around the World*, 1771), presumably to review it for the *Literary Correspondence*.[32]

Admiral Bougainville, in the early 1770s, was a household name. Much like Captain James Cook, this sailor, navigator, and mathematician not only traversed the globe, but wrote a compelling account of his adventures while doing so. Setting sail on *La boudeuse* (*The Sulker*) and *L'étoile* (*The Star*), the admiral and his crew of three hundred men sailed around Africa and proceeded to Île de France (Mauritius), the islands of the South Pacific, the Straits of Magellan at the tip of South America, and along the coast of Brazil before arriving back in France. The three-year log (1766–69) is full of absorbing stories of storms, scurvy, new lands, fallen masts, and the occasional group of belligerent natives.[33] His readers, including Diderot, were most enchanted, however, with the description of Bougainville's landfall in Tahiti.

LOUIS-ANTOINE DE BOUGAINVILLE,
ENGRAVING

Bougainville's crews first spied the lush forests and mountainous terrain of the island in April 1768. The land seemed utopian. When the men finally set up camp, they slept peacefully and comfortably near a warm, insect-free beach where abundant food supplies, rich in vitamin C, quickly cured the scorbutic sailors.[34] What was more, the warmhearted islanders were among the friendliest and best-looking they had encountered in their travels. The men were tall, strong, and perfectly proportioned. Indeed, they seemed far healthier than the Europeans, living to a "happy old age," never losing their teeth, and rarely falling sick.[35] But

Bougainville was most fascinated by the island's striking women, with their tattooed breasts and buttocks, flower-filled garlands, and seemingly unabashed sexuality.[36] He labeled the island the New Cythera in honor of the fabled isle where Venus — the goddess of sex, desire, fertility, and love — was born.[37]

Bougainville's account abounds with anecdotes that made eighteenth-century European minds (particularly male minds) swirl. When his sailors were invited into various Tahitian households, they were supposedly offered both light meals and, quite often, a young girl, who was told to fulfill other "duties" for the men.[38] Indeed, by the end of his report, Bougainville himself seemed to suggest that he had given in to the climate of love while on the island. How could he resist? "The air that we breathe [here], the singing, the dances which are almost always accompanied by lascivious postures, everything at every instant recalls the sweetness of love, everything cries to give in to it."[39]

Diderot, too, fell under the spell of life on Tahiti. As he began writing his "supplement" to Bougainville's book, he imagined the possibilities of a world where spurious religious conventions did not interfere with nature's highest calling. To give form and zest to his ideas, he staged a discussion between two witty and inquisitive men ("A" and "B") who have both read Bougainville's book. Their initial conversation moves quickly: the men discuss how people came to inhabit the isolated islands that Bougainville and his crew encountered in the South Pacific, how morality arose in these remote lands, and how the physical configuration of the continents indicates that they must have "drifted" apart. They then turn their attention to a supposedly unpublished manuscript that they have discovered sandwiched within Bougainville's travelogue that is filled with recorded "conversations" on the subjects of nature, colonialism, and morality's relationship to human sexuality. As they pore over this document together, the two men often interrupt the tale to discuss the implications of what they are reading.

The first part of the lost manuscript features a speech by an old Tahitian man who lashes out at what he predicts will be the inevitably nefarious consequences of colonialism and exploration — a prescient speech if there ever was one. Calling out to his fellow islanders to rebel, he predicts an era of new diseases, enslavement, and perhaps the eventual annihilation of the Tahitians: "Weep, wretched Tahitians, weep — but rather for the arrival than for the departure of these wicked and grasping men! The day will come when you will know them for what they are. Someday they will return, bearing in one hand that piece of wood [a cross] you see suspended from this one's belt and in the other the piece of steel [a sword] that hangs at the side of his companion."[40]

After this anti-European diatribe — one of the first true post-colonial moments in French literature — we arrive at the absorbing question of Tahitian sexuality. The focus of the discussion at this point is not the Tahitians themselves, but a thirty-five-year-old French chaplain who has sailed to the island with the ship's crew. As is the case with the other sailors, we learn that the man of religion is assigned to live with an island family, in his case at the house of the respected patriarch Orou. Not surprisingly, the chaplain's vows of sexual abstinence will be put to the test in this overly welcoming household:

> Orou's family consisted of his wife and three daughters, who were called Asto, Palli and Thia. The women undressed their guest, washed his face, hands and feet, and put before him a wholesome though frugal meal. When he was about to go to bed, Orou, who

had stepped outside with his family, reappeared and presented to him his wife and three girls — all naked as Eve — and said to him: "You are young and healthy and you have just had a good supper. He who sleeps alone, sleeps badly; at night a man needs a woman at his side. Here is my wife and here are my daughters. Choose whichever one pleases you most, but if you would like to do me a favor, you will give your preference to my youngest girl, who has not yet had any children"...The chaplain replied that his religion, his holy orders, his moral standards and his sense of decency all prevented him from accepting Orou's invitation.[41]

To this, Orou "naively" replies,

I do not know what this thing is that you call "religion," but I can only have a low opinion of it because it forbids you to partake of an innocent pleasure to which Nature, the sovereign mistress of all, invites everybody. [This religion] seems to prevent you from bringing one of your fellow creatures into the world...Look at the distress you have caused to appear on the faces of those four women — they are afraid you have noticed some defect in them that arouses your distaste.

Hoping not to offend his gracious hosts, the chaplain stammers an answer that the Tahitians do not understand — he has made a vow of celibacy to his God and his religion: "It is not that: they are all four equally beautiful: but my religion! My holy orders!"

Shortly thereafter, of course, temptation nonetheless gets the best of the poor priest and he surrenders to the inevitable:

Providence had never exposed [the chaplain] to such strong temptation. He was young, he was excited, he was in torment. He turned his eyes away from the four lovely suppliants, then let his gaze wander back to them again. He lifted his hands and his countenance to Heaven. Thia, the youngest of the three girls, threw her arms around his knees and said to him: "Stranger, do not disappoint my father and mother. Do not disappoint me!"...The poor chaplain records that she pressed his hands, that she fastened her eyes on his with the most expressive and touching gaze, that she wept, that her father, mother and sisters went out, leaving him alone with her, and that despite his repetition of "But there is my religion and my holy orders," he awoke the next morning to find the young girl lying at his side. She overwhelmed him with more caresses.[42]

The next day, Orou and his wife are delighted with the chaplain's "generosity." Orou nonetheless asks his guest to explain why his God would have objected to something so wonderful and natural. While his questions initially seem quite naive, by the end of his discussion with the chaplain, the Tahitian is educating the chaplain as would an Enlightenment philosophe. What kind of deity, Orou asks pointedly, would create moral edicts (such as chastity and lifelong marriage) that are simultaneously nonsensical, counterproductive, and impossible to follow? "I find these precepts contrary to nature, and contrary to reason. I think they are admirably calculated to increase the number of crimes and to give endless annoyance to [God]...Take my word for it, you have reduced human beings to a worse condition than that of the animals. I don't know what your great workman is, but I am very happy that he never spoke to our forefathers, and I hope that he never speaks to our children..."[43]

After belittling the absurd and sad state of European society and its illogically "great workman," Orou describes the superior, nature-based sexual customs of Tahiti. According to Orou, there is no shame, crime, or guilt attached to the sex act. Women, in particular, cannot lose their "honor" for having sex, because there is no honor in chastity. As for marriage, it, too, is based on the natural inclinations of the species. Far from the lifelong burden that marriage is in Europe, wives and husbands are free to switch partners after a month.

All of these unfamiliar conventions are linked to Tahiti's primary preoccupation: producing children. The Venus of Tahiti is "a fertile Venus," as Orou puts it, not the coquettish Venus of Europe. The effects of this child-oriented ethics shape every aspect of life on the island. Infanticide, a widespread fact of life in eighteenth-century Europe, is unthinkable on the island because every child is seen as a national treasure. The importance of fertility has even determined Tahiti's aesthetic standards. To emphasize this point, Orou tells the tale of an ugly Tahitian woman who encounters a good-looking acquaintance: "You are beautiful enough," the first woman says to the better-looking friend, "but the children you bear are ugly; I am ugly, but my children are beautiful, so the men prefer me."[44]

This obsession with fertility extends well beyond the aesthetic realm. Since Tahitians universally believe that all sexual contact should be productive, their rules exclude the nonfertile from the sexual economy: prepubescent girls wear white veils to signal their unavailability; women who are menstruating must wear a gray veil; and infertile women or those past the age of fertility must adorn themselves with a black veil to ward off potential suitors. Similar restrictions extend to boys as well: until the adult community has determined that a boy's seminal fluid has achieved a certain quality, he must wear a tunic and a chain, and not cut the fingernail on the middle finger of his right hand.[45]

That fertility is the foundational consideration in matters of ethics also explains Tahitian views on incest and adultery. This discussion is by far the most audacious moment of the book:

THE CHAPLAIN: May a father sleep with his daughter, a mother with her son, a brother with his sister, a husband with someone else's wife?

OROU: Why not?

THE CHAPLAIN: Well! To say nothing of the fornication, what of the incest, the adultery?

OROU: What do you mean by those words, *fornication, incest,* and *adultery*?

THE CHAPLAIN: They are crimes, horrible crimes for which people are burned at the stake in my country.

OROU: Well, whether they burn or don't burn in your country is nothing to me. But you cannot condemn the morals of Europe for not being those of Tahiti, nor our morals for not being those of Europe. You need a more dependable rule of judgment than that. And what shall it be? Do you know a better one than general welfare and individual utility? Well, now tell me in what way your crime of *incest* is contrary to the two aims of our conduct; if you think that everything is settled once and for all because a law has been promulgated, a derogatory word invented, and a punishment established. Why don't you tell me what you mean by incest?[46]

Not surprisingly, Diderot's insouciant remarks on incest scandalized a certain segment of the population when they appeared in print in 1796. His most severe critics maliciously accused him of legitimizing the practice in order to justify his love for his own daughter, Angélique.[47] More subtle readers understood that Diderot had simply created an island laboratory, a tropical thought experiment designed to make us laugh and think.

WE ARE ALL HERMAPHRODITES

Diderot's imagined trip to Tahiti allowed him to probe some of his era's long-standing sexual taboos. One notable exception, however, was the subject of homosexuality. Tackling the question of same-sex desire simply did not make sense in the context of this procreation-based island. Had Diderot's fictive Tahitians confronted the practice on their island, they would have surely dismissed it as an unproductive form of libertinage — a waste of time, energy, and precious seminal fluid.

Homosexual sex raised far more serious questions back in France. Categorized alongside bestiality, same-sex encounters were considered a crime "against nature," an abhorrent vice, and a sin against the law of God. The French penal code actually specified that sodomites (this included women) be burned to death, whether their crime be committed *cum bestia, inter masculos,* or *inter fœminas.*[48] The last execution of homosexuals in France took place in July 1750, when a shoemaker named Bruno le Noir and a servant named Jean Diot were strangled to death before being reduced to ashes on the place de Grève.[49]

Philosophes waged war against various forms of intolerance during the era, but the persecution of homosexuals was not one of them. Indeed, in his capacity as editor of the *Encyclopédie*, Diderot followed long-standing tradition in labeling homosexual acts as both immoral and warped. Such is the case in the anonymous article "*Tribade*" ("Lesbian"), which Diderot likely wrote himself. In addition to defining a lesbian as a "woman who has passion for another woman," this entry carefully specifies that such acts constitute "a type of odd depravity that is as inexplicable as that which inflames one man for another."[50]

An article such as "*Tribade*" stands in stark contrast to Diderot's more substantive writings on the question of homosexuality, all of which languished in manuscript during his lifetime. Diderot staged his most radical philosophizing on same-sex desires and acts during the last scene of *D'Alembert's Dream*. Here, over an after-dinner digestif, Mademoiselle de l'Espinasse and Dr. Bordeu flirt with a theory of sexual pleasure that is entirely free of religious, moral, and reproductive constraints.

Bordeu—as a medical practitioner—begins this conversation by underscoring the utility of masturbation for both men and women. As he explains it, both sexes can suffer from pent-up and potentially deleterious surpluses of sexual energy. After cheerfully volunteering that sometimes one simply needs to give "nature a hand on occasion," he then moves on to the question of other nonprocreative sexual acts, including those between members of the same sex.[51] Mademoiselle de l'Espinasse's objection that such coupling is "against nature" incites an authoritative reply from Bordeu that numbers among the boldest statements in Diderot's entire corpus: "Nothing that exists can be against nature or outside nature…"[52] Same-sex attraction and love is entirely natural, according to this principle, by dint of the simple fact that it exists.

Bordeu and de l'Espinasse's freethinking discussion foreshadows shifts in the understanding of human sexuality that did not come to pass until the twentieth century. While Bordeu carefully dissociates himself from the actual practice of homosexuality, and even attributes same-sex attraction to a series of pathological conditions (e.g., "abnormality of the nervous system in young people, softening of the brain in the old," "a shortage of women," or "a fear of the pox"), he effectively concedes its place in the natural world. This is particularly true when one considers one of the doctor's other explanations for homosexual acts: sometimes they simply happen because of the "seductive power of beauty."[53]

Diderot himself seemingly pondered this last possibility during his own life. In the late 1750s and early 1760s, he spent months both savoring and fearing the relationship that he assumed existed between Sophie Volland and her alluring younger sister, Marie-Charlotte (a story to which we will return). But Diderot had also guardedly admitted in 1762 that he, too, had been drawn to another man. This somewhat camouflaged confession came about during a larger discussion about the effect that total honesty would have on the letters he was sending to Sophie, his then-lover and confidante:

> My letters are a fairly accurate history of my life...[I]t would require a lot of courage to hide nothing. One might more readily admit to plotting a great crime than to a small, vile, and murky unintelligible feeling. It might cost less to write in one's diary: "I desired the throne at the expense of the one who now sits on it," than to write: "One day when I was in the public bath among a large number of young men, I noticed a man of surprising beauty, and could not prevent myself from approaching him."[54]

It would be a stretch to assert that Diderot was a homosexual himself, or that this scene is a "veiled confession" of bisexuality "muted by shame and fear."[55] And yet it is certainly true that Diderot recognized the possible allure of male bodies, particularly in his Salon reviews. His most famous (and blasphemous) exploration of same-sex desire is found in the *Notes on Painting*, where he reimagines the wedding scene at Cana in Galilee in which Jesus famously turned water into wine. Conjuring up a drunken Christ, the philosophe goes on to describe the Godhead's bisexual quandary where he is simultaneously caressing the breasts of one of the bridesmaids and Saint John's buttocks, "uncertain if he would remain faithful to the apostle with the down-dusted chin."[56]

Whatever Diderot's actual proclivities, his overall philosophical orientation led him to reconsider both sexual norms and the immutability of gender categories. Some of this broad-minded stance may flow directly from his understanding of sexual anatomy. By the late 1760s, Diderot was not only convinced that the two sexes shared common anatomical structures in utero, but that the categories of gender themselves had also emerged from a biologically fluid past where, as he put it in *D'Alembert's Dream*, "perhaps man is only a freakish form of woman, or woman a freakish form of man."[57]

Diderot's belief that the categories of man and woman were not as trenchant as most people believed carried over into his own relationships. He often called Sophie a hermaphrodite in recognition of her supposedly malelike ability to reason. But he also used the same word in a seemingly more literal sense to describe his treasured companion, Melchior Grimm. Diderot explained how Grimm earned this nickname in two letters that he sent to Falconet. In the first, Diderot said that Grimm "combined the grace

and elegance of one sex with the force of the other."[58] In the second, he specified that "the one that I love, the one who has the
softness of the contours of a woman and, when he desires, the
muscles of a man; this rare blend of the Medici Venus and the
Gladiator; my hermaphrodite,... it is Grimm."[59]

GRIMM AND DIDEROT, DRAWING

How exactly this effusive and seemingly erotic relationship
played out on a daily basis comes through in a letter that Diderot

sent to Sophie almost eight years before. At the time, Grimm had
been absent from Paris for eight months.

> What a pleasure to see Grimm and to have him back again. With
> what warmth we hugged each other. I was unable to speak, nei-
> ther was he. We kissed each other without saying a word, and I
> was crying. We had given up waiting for him for dinner. We were
> all eating dessert when he was announced: "It's Monsieur Grimm,
> it's Monsieur Grimm!" I repeated with a shriek as I got up. I ran to
> him, I wrapped my arms around his neck. He sat, and did not eat
> a lot, I believe. As for me, I could not unclench my teeth, neither
> to eat, nor to drink, nor to talk. He was next to me. I was holding
> his hand and I was looking at him ... [The others] treated us like a
> lover and his mistress for whom one would have respect."[60]

The playwright and draftsman Louis de Carmontelle seized
on this or a similar moment in a c. 1760 sketch that he did of the
two friends. The erotic undercurrent of their connection is hard
to miss.

Among the many joys of reading Diderot as he navigates the
murky waters of eighteenth-century sexuality (including his
own) is the fact that he had the courage to distance himself from
his era's accepted norms and beliefs. Not surprisingly, when the
Supplement, the *Dream*, and *The Nun* finally became known over the
course of the nineteenth century, conservative critics attacked
the writer for what they deemed to be his valueless philosophical orientation on sex, one where bestiality, homosexuality, and
fornication had no conceptual difference from the sexual relations sanctioned by the Church. And yet, despite the fact that
Diderot's provocative thoughts on sex sought to question the
stranglehold that Christian morality had on humankind, his

goal was rarely to titillate or overthrow established customs; it was, rather, to incite us to consider a fuller understanding of our nature as sexual beings. This was, as it turned out, often far easier and more entertaining for Diderot than managing his own love life.

X

ON LOVE

Like many people who reach middle age, Diderot sometimes looked back with nostalgia at his more memorable
sexual escapades. Perhaps the most cherished and titil-
lating was a bit of neighborly philandering that he had engaged
in before getting married to Toinette. When recounting this episode to a lady friend years later, after it was but a distant memory,
Diderot emphasized the physical freedom and splendor of youth:

> [W]here did the days go when I had long hair floating in the breeze?
> In the morning, the collar of my shirt would be open and I would
> take off my nightcap, and my hair would fall down in great unruly
> locks onto my pale and silky shoulders. My neighbor, who got up
> early and left her husband's side, would open her curtains and feast
> her eyes on the sight, something of which I was well aware. This is
> how I seduced her from one side of the street to the other.[1]

Decorum dictated that Diderot withhold the subsequent
details of the liaison: he makes no mention of the suggestive
chitchat, the first kiss, the inevitable lovemaking, or the poor
cuckolded husband. Instead, he wakes himself from this reverie

in order to lament how much his life has changed since these carefree days: "It is all gone now," he sighs palpably, "my blond hair, the candor, and the innocence."[2] The lesson is one of carpe diem, or perhaps of youth being wasted on the young, but there is another morality tale here: as sad as it may be to watch one's youthful body bend and wither, the more devastating disappointment is no longer feeling the thrill of being coveted by another. This sad situation had become the case for Diderot, at least at his apartment on the rue Taranne.

Time and again, Diderot expressed two major regrets in his life. The first was wasting his best years toiling on the 74,000-article *Encyclopédie*. The second was marrying a perpetually tetchy woman; of the two blunders, he perhaps regretted the second one more. Though he thought and wrote a great deal about love and sex—not to mention the fact that our primary responsibility in life is to be happy—the flesh-and-blood Diderot often felt that his marriage was a brutal chore.

Voltaire and Rousseau had both avoided the burdens of marriage, each in his own way. Voltaire chose to content himself with a series of long-term lovers, most notably the brilliant savant Émilie du Châtelet and, later, his own niece, Marie Louise Mignot. Rousseau had been even more adamant about avoiding the yoke of marriage. Though he spent most of his life with Thérèse Levasscur, and ultimately entered into an informal and invalid marriage with the ex-laundress at age fifty-six, he not only rejected any formalized relationship between man and woman, but forced his companion to abandon their five children. A century or so later, Friedrich Nietzsche put into words how Rousseau and Voltaire had lived their lives. In his view, an efficient and successful philosopher should avoid all conventional and entangling alliances at all costs.³ A "married philosopher," as he put it, "belongs in comedy."⁴ This, of course, was Diderot's fate; by marrying Toi-nette Champion in 1743, he had cast himself in a gloomy version of his own *Father of the Family*.⁵

EARLY LOVE

When Diderot had first fallen in love with Toinette at age twenty-eight, he adored her with his entire being. Yet it was patently obvious, even then, that they had little in common. Where she was unschooled, closed-minded, and devout, he was erudite, unreserved, unrepentant, and hedonistic. Early in their courtship, Toinette seemingly understood these differences far better than her future husband. While her letters to Diderot on this subject are lost, the responses he sent to Toinette reflect her acute anxiety about their relationship. In February 1742, a full year before they married, he pleads with her to believe in his love: "You would be the most unjust of all women, if you continue to suspect the sincerity of my promises."⁶ In another letter that he presumably wrote shortly thereafter, he not only declares their love to be eternal, but explains that he is no longer the sexually unrestrained man who went around seducing his neighbors: "I may have deserved the name of young libertine, but the fire that burns in such people is made of straw, and burns out quickly for the wife of one's neighbor, and then blows out forever. But the fire [that burns in the heart] of an honest man — a name I now deserve because you have made me good — will never go out."⁷

Diderot's devotion to Toinette did burn out. Some three years later, he fell in love with Madame de Puisieux, the feminist author and fellow freethinker. We know little about this relationship,

presumably because Diderot destroyed his correspondence with
Madeleine for fear of it falling into Toinette's hands. Yet we can
easily surmise just how he felt about this *femme de lettres* from a
thinly veiled description of her that he slipped into his 1747 *The
Skeptic's Walk*:[8] "She was blonde...and had a fine and light waist
that came along with plenty of plumpness. I have never seen more
vibrant colors, a more animated skin, nor more beautiful flesh.
Coiffed simply, and wearing a lined, pink-colored straw hat, her
shimmering eyes breathed only desire. Her speech revealed an
opulent mind; she loved to reason."[9]

The time that Diderot spent with Madeleine during these
early years understandably took a toll on his marriage. Frequent
absences, excuses, and his obvious unfaithfulness fueled Toinette's
insecurities and, increasingly, her fury. According to numerous
accounts, Toinette had (or soon acquired) an unfortunate tendency to fly into a rage, and not only with her husband. On one
documented occasion, in April 1750, she had a violent run-in with
a servant who worked in their apartment on the rue de la Vieille
Estrapade. According to a contemporary police report, "Madame
Diderot" accused the domestic, a certain Maguerite Barré, of being
"insolent." (One is tempted to imagine, with no proof of course,
that jealousy may have had something to do with the episode.)
After a ferocious exchange, Toinette allegedly chased the servant
down the street, punching her, kicking her, and pulling her by
the hair before ultimately smashing her head against a stone wall,
which opened up a gaping wound.[10] The formal complaint, which
Barré filed with the commissioner of the Châtelet prison, noted
that the victim lost a great deal of blood. It added that she required
the attention of a surgeon who, following standard procedure,
made an incision in her arm and bled her some more.

This was not the only example of violence attributed to Toinette. Sometime in 1751, Diderot's wife supposedly had an altercation with Madame de Puisieux. While this particular tale was perhaps embellished (or entirely fabricated), Diderot's ex-mistress allegedly pulled up in a carriage in front of the Diderots' apartment on the rue de la Vieille Estrapade with the intent of berating Toinette for forcing her husband to put an end to their affair. Calling up to Madame Diderot, who was then looking out from the second-story window, Madeleine supposedly pointed at her own two children (they were not Diderot's) and screamed out: "Over here, Madame She Monkey, take a look at these two youngsters; they belong to your husband, who never did you the honor of doing as much for you."[11]

According to the account of this episode in a Dutch newspaper called *La Bigarrure*, Toinette immediately ran down the stairs and threw herself at Diderot's former mistress, initiating the most "energetic and ludicrous fight to ever take place between two women." After several minutes, the brawl apparently became so brutal that members of the crowd decided they needed to break it up, which they did by dousing the women with several pails of water. The journalist reporting this torturous episode in Diderot's life clearly enjoyed informing his readers that the famous philosophe remained holed up in his office during the entire skirmish, preferring "to write up some philosophical and moral thoughts about the pleasures of marriage and the character of women" rather than enter the fray.[12]

Whether this particular episode is true or not, Toinette's violent temper and irritability weighed heavily on Diderot. Unable to remedy the situation himself, he seems to have tried to delegate this task to others. In 1752, when Toinette traveled by herself to

Langres to visit her in-laws, Diderot secretly wrote to his child-hood friend from the city, Madame Caroillon La Salette, and asked her to reach out to Toinette with some friendly advice: be more considerate and polite with her husband.[13] Another time, in 1759, after suffering through a brutal "domestic fight that was still shooting off sparks," Diderot took the highly unusual step of reaching out to Toinette's longtime spiritual adviser, insist-ing that he inform his wife that if the atmosphere in his house did not improve, she would find herself out on the street.[14] It is worth pointing out that Diderot did not dare communicate this message himself.

Despite the misery of his home life, Diderot never gave up entirely on his marriage. This became particularly evident in times of desperation. In 1762, when Toinette fell deathly ill with a bloody cough, he attended to her every need for six weeks. On another occasion, when she was suffering from a terrible case of sciatica that confined her to bed, he spent hours giving her mas-sages. Perhaps most revealing, Diderot rose to her defense when people mocked her. On one occasion, when Diderot's friend the abbé Morellet imitated Toinette's uneducated manner of speech during a dinner at d'Holbach's house, Diderot informed the jokester that if he did not cease immediately, he might find him-self thrown through the window.[15]

Much of the emotional energy that Diderot devoted to his family nonetheless went to his daughter, Angélique. From her ear-liest years, he hoped that he might prevent Toinette from stuffing her head with the same religious foolishness and inanities that he was attacking in the *Encyclopédie*.[16] In the interest of (relative) domestic peace, however, Diderot contented himself with small victories: keeping Angélique out of the convent where Toinette and his own brother Didier-Pierre had conspired to send her, taking her on long walks where they talked of ethics and philosophy, and making sure that she had a relatively progressive education. In addition to arranging music lessons for her — according to one English musicologist who was passing through Paris, she had become one of the city's best harpsichordists by the time she was eighteen — Diderot also organized a remarkable and highly unusual sexual education for her. Shortly before Angélique was to marry Abel François Nicolas Caroillon de Vandeul at the Church of Saint-Sulpice, he decided to prepare her, psychologically, for "the nuptial bed" and a healthy and happy life as a married woman. To do so, Diderot asked his friend the famous anatomist Mademoiselle Marie-Catherine Biheron to instruct Angélique in the subtleties of female sexuality by showing her some of the wax models that Biheron had created for her small anatomical museum. Exposing a young woman to the functioning of her own sexual organs was, at the time, an unconventional idea to say the least.

Diderot considered such paternal duties to be quite distinct from and, indeed, far more vital than those he had taken on as a husband. For at least thirty of the forty years that he was married to Toinette, he not only disregarded the commitment he had made to her, but wished for a different type of wife, one who might cheerfully tolerate a string of infidelities while never committing such a sin herself. True to his era, Diderot never acknowledged this sexual double standard in his life. Nor did he concede the fact that his own behavior must have contributed to Toinette's petulance. What he did condemn himself roundly for, however, was not being able to share his life with the one woman that he seems to have truly loved, Sophie Volland.

―――――

LOVE STORIES

How the undeniable, flesh-and-blood urge for both sex and love could be reconciled with the strictures of marriage preoccupied Diderot throughout his entire career. When he took up the question as a philosophe, he often suggested that humankind's sexual impulses could not be squared with the order and well-being of civil society as it existed in Europe.[17] Anticipating much of what Freud would say in *Civilization and Its Discontents*, he bemoans the fact that we are constantly confronted by sexual and moral choices that tear us apart and separate us from our true nature.

In his own life, Diderot tried to sidestep this conflict. While he certainly regretted some of the choices he made in his love life, he never evinced guilt about his desire for women outside his marriage. Even the sanctimonious and prudish version of himself that we find in *Rameau's Nephew* feels the pull and gratification of giving in to sexual desire. While *Moi* earnestly declares that the sex act pales in comparison to the real gratifications in life — helping the unfortunate, writing a page of "good prose," or whispering a few tender truths to the woman he loves — this same Diderot character also proclaims that "I too have a heart and eyes, and I love to see a pretty woman, I like to feel the firm round flesh of her bosom in my hands, to press my lips to hers, to feel aroused when I look deep into her eyes, and expire with pleasure in her arms."[18]

Diderot's only true love story began three or four years after he and his first mistress, Madame de Puisieux, had parted ways. It was actually Jean-Jacques Rousseau who was partly responsible for this adventure. Sometime in the spring of 1755, Rousseau introduced the forty-two-year-old Diderot to a pair of well-off brothers, Nicolas Vallet de La Touche and Pierre Vallet de Salignac, the latter of whom held the important post of *receveur de finances* (minister of finances) for the Duc d'Orléans. Soon thereafter, Vallet de Salignac invited Diderot to pay a visit to his mother-in-law's flat on the stylish rue des Vieux-Augustins, near the Palais Royal. It was here that Diderot came to know the twice-widowed Élisabeth Françoise Brunel de La Carlière and her three daughters.

Madame de La Carlière's girls had all been born over the course of her first marriage to Jean-Robert Volland, the wealthy director of the unpopular salt tax.[19] By the time Diderot met the family, the eldest daughter, Marie-Jeanne Volland, was already married to the aforementioned Pierre Vallet. Marie-Charlotte, the youngest in the family, had wed a prominent architect named Jean-Gabriel Le Gendre. But the middle daughter was a frail, bespectacled, whip-smart, and often-melancholy thirty-eight-year-old spinster. This was Louise-Henriette Volland, the woman who would arguably become the most important person in Diderot's life.

We now know Louise-Henriette by the distinctive Greek-inspired nickname that Diderot gave to her: Sophie, which evoked her *wisdom*. Over the course of thirty years, Diderot sent Sophie Volland 553 letters, of which 187 survive. These intimate and often very candid dispatches are incontestably the greatest window into Diderot's private life. In addition to containing a tremendous amount of Enlightenment-era gossip related to his friends and associates—his ups and downs with Rousseau, Grimm, d'Holbach, and the *Encyclopédie* project—his letters to her also reveal his aspirations, unrealized projects, and complicated emotional longings.

Much has been destroyed from what must have been an exchange of a thousand letters. Sometime late in life, Sophie burned the first four years of correspondence that Diderot had sent her, surely because they chronicled the most intimate portion of their relationship. She then added to this mutilation by selectively purging dozens of other letters. Ultimately, toward the end of her life, she also requested that Diderot return all the letters that she had sent him, which she presumably consigned to a fireplace shortly thereafter. The loss of these letters (and her voice) is immeasurable. Her prose and personality must have been captivating, especially when one considers that Diderot would only have spent so much time composing some of his most memorable writing for a woman who could return the favor. Unfortunately, Louise-Henriette Volland is a ghost to us now.

Diderot and Sophie would not have written as much as they did had they both lived in Paris throughout the year. As it happened, and as is always the case in any worthwhile epistolary exchange, the lovers were often living apart for large stretches of time. In the early years of their relationship, it was actually Madame de La Carlière, Sophie's mother, who made sure that they were separated. Not terribly keen on having her daughter frequent a married man, she often obliged Sophie to accompany her for six months out of the year to their family château at Isle, in Champagne, about two hundred kilometers to the east of Paris. Things were not much easier when the two lovers were lucky enough to be in the capital at the same time. To gain access to Sophie's room during the early years of his relationship, Diderot initially had to act like a teenage scoundrel, sneaking up to his lover's bedroom via the servant's staircase to avoid the watchful eye of Madame de La Carlière.

Even exchanging and receiving letters was a challenge. This was especially true since Diderot could not receive any correspondence at the rue Taranne for fear of invoking Toinette's wrath. Accordingly, Sophie sometimes sent her letters to Diderot at Grimm's house on the rue Neuve-Luxembourg, just north of the Tuileries. More often than not, however, both she and Diderot sent their letters either to or from Étienne Noël Damilaville's office on the quai des Miramiones.[20] Damilaville, an ardent materialist and good friend of both Diderot and Voltaire who was often present at d'Holbach's dinners, was an ideal confederate for the lovers. As collector of the *vingtième* — the French poll tax — he could dispatch letters throughout the kingdom at no charge. Diderot took ample advantage of his personal mailman, particularly when Sophie was in Champagne.

The first surviving letters from Diderot to Sophie were written in the spring and summer of 1759, five years after the couple first met each other. The most delightful note from this otherwise nerve-racking time in Diderot's life — the *Encyclopédie* had been shut down and he was in grave danger of being imprisoned — was penned on a summer night while he was waiting in the dark outside the Volland apartment:

> I am writing without being able to see. I came. I wanted to kiss your hand and return home quickly thereafter. I will return without that gift... It is nine o'clock. I am writing you that I love you; I at least want to write it to you, but I don't know if the pen is bending to my will. Won't you come down so that I can tell you this, and then flee?
>
> Adieu, my Sophie, good night. Your heart must not be telling you that I am here. This is the first time that I am writing in the dark. This situation should arouse loving thoughts in me. I am

feeling only one; it is that I am unable to leave. The hope of seeing you for a moment is holding me back, and I continue to speak to you, without knowing if I am actually forming letters. Wherever you see nothing [on this paper], read that I love you.[21]

Diderot's letters to Sophie are filled with numerous such declarations of love. Yet Mademoiselle Volland was far more than a simple object of affection for the philosophe. He cherished the fact that he could treat her as he might another (male) philosophe: she was honest and brainy, and blessed with, as one of Diderot's *Encyclopédie* colleagues put it, the "quick wit of a demon."[22] In stark contrast to those women who found his conversation overwhelming, outrageous, or off-putting, Sophie had transcended the supposed prudery and weaknesses of her sex. It was this that had earned her the title of "hermaphrodite."[23]

Diderot's claims that Sophie embodied both male and female attributes may also be related to his views about her sexuality. Sometime in 1759 or 1760, her mother, Madame de La Carlière, seems to have informed Diderot that Sophie's younger sister, Marie-Charlotte, not only had lesbian tendencies, but that she loved Sophie a great deal, perhaps romantically.[24] Diderot himself noticed the erotic tension supposedly existing between Sophie and her sister, at one point mentioning to Sophie how Marie-Charlotte "leans on you, with her fingers singularly pressed between your own."[25] Sophie's mother had also further incited Diderot's suspicions about Marie-Charlotte when she let him know that her youngest daughter had had a "predilection" for a certain nun when she was an adolescent.[26] That these thoughts were floating around in Diderot's head at the same time he was composing *The Nun* was surely not a coincidence.

We certainly cannot conclude very much about the Volland sisters' long-vanished erotic inclinations for each other, if they did, in fact, exist.[27] Suffice it to say that the prospect of some sort of lesbian relationship between Sophie (the woman "he loved the most in the world") and Marie-Charlotte Legendre was often on Diderot's mind. In the late 1750s and early 1760s, each time that Diderot's separation from Sophie left her in proximity to Marie-Charlotte, he could not prevent himself from imagining their lips pressed against each other: "We will come closer together, my beloved, we will come closer together; and these lips will press against those that I love. While waiting, only your sister is allowed access to your lips. This does not vex me; I might even admit that I like coming after her. As such it seems to me that I am pressing her soul between yours and mine like a snowflake that will melt between two burning coals."[28]

The idea that Diderot had entered into a curious triangular relationship with Marie-Charlotte and Sophie surfaced on numerous occasions. At times, he seemed genuinely excited by the prospect of this sisterly passion. Under other circumstances, he became so jealous that he could not bear to hear Sophie speaking about the indisputable charms of Marie-Charlotte. In a letter dated September 7, 1760, that Diderot sent from Madame d'Épinay's house at La Chevrette, Diderot comes off as a nervous wreck, pleading with Sophie to stop "singing the praises" of her sister in her letters.[29] The following week, still writing from the same estate in Montmorency, he seems even more anxious and asks pointedly, "Are you forgetting me in the tumult of parties and in the arms of your sister?" This fretful question is followed by a bit of disingenuous advice: "Madame, be aware of your health, and remember that pleasure may cause fatigue."[30]

In addition to expressing concern about a possible lesbian relationship, Diderot sometimes complained to Sophie about the kind of sexual gratification that they found together. Though Diderot's letters reveal an intimacy that was anything but sexless, there is also ample evidence that Sophie carefully limited the physical part of their relationship. In a telltale letter written in May 1765 — ten years after he had first met her — the philosophe reproaches Sophie for denying herself the ecstasy that she has presumably seen and appreciated on his own face many times:

> Since the face of a man who is transported by love and pleasure is so beautiful to see, and since you can control when you want to have this tender and gratifying picture in front of you, why do you deny yourself this same pleasure? What folly! You are delighted when a man in love with you [he is referring to himself] looks at you with eyes full of kindheartedness and passion. Their expression passes into your soul, and your soul trembles. If his burning lips touch your cheeks, the heat they produce arouses you; if his lips press into yours, you feel your soul rise to unite with his; if, in that moment, his hands clutch onto yours, a delicious quivering takes hold of your entire body; all of this heralds an infinitely greater moment of bliss; everything is leading you there. And yet you do not want to die of ecstasy, and make another person die of pleasure alongside you! You refuse yourself a moment in time that has its own folly... If you leave this world without having known this pleasure, can you consider yourself ever to have been happy or to have made someone else happy?[31]

Well before he wrote this somewhat pestering note, Diderot had accepted the fact that the physical part of his relationship with Sophie would never hold a candle to their tender devotion to one another. While he certainly remained an ardent apologist of sexual pleasure — including in his letters to Sophie — he also frequently referenced this intensively spiritual version of love. In 1759, Diderot even admitted that base lust paled in comparison to this most transcendent variety of affection. As he then put it, "What are the caresses of two lovers, when they can't do justice to the infinite love that two people feel for each other?"[32]

For the better part of fifteen years, Diderot considered his love for Sophie to be the most vital component of his life. In 1767, when his friend Falconet was trying to lure him to Catherine the Great's court in Saint Petersburg, he demurred, explaining that his devotion to Sophie prevented him from leaving Paris:

> What shall I tell you? That I have a friend; that I am linked by the strongest and sweetest emotion with a woman to whom I would sacrifice a hundred lives, if I had them. Listen Falconet. I could see my house burn to cinders without caring. I could see my freedom imperiled, my life compromised, and all sorts of misfortunes visited upon me without complaining, provided that she remained with me. If she told me, give me your blood, I want to drink some, I would drain myself to satisfy her.[33]

Despite such hyperbolic declarations, things began to change between Diderot and Sophie after 1765. To begin with, he no longer addressed her by her famous pet name; she had once again become *ma bonne amie* or "Mademoiselle Volland." Even more significantly, Diderot replaced his burning, personal, and secret dispatches to her with letters that he wrote to her entire family. This was perhaps inevitable. Over the years, after courting, corresponding with, and longing for Sophie (and perhaps even for Marie-Charlotte at times), he had proven himself to be far more than a transitory figure for the three Volland sisters and their mother. Indeed, on many occasions, he took on the role of extended member of the family. Among other things, in October 1762, he intervened on behalf of the once-suspicious and skeptical Madame de La Carlière with the tax authorities in order to help her escape a penalty for not paying the *vingtième*. Another time, when Marie-Charlotte fell gravely ill with a terrible fever and perhaps pneumonia, he stayed by her bedside, nursing her, coordinating with the doctor, and sending updates to the rest of the family, who were then at Isle.[34] Diderot also took an active interest in the affairs of Sophie's older sister, Marie-Jeanne de Salignac, who had suffered tremendously after her husband, a fraud, went bankrupt and fled Paris in 1760. Having once tiptoed stealthily around the Volland apartment, the charming and generous Diderot had become an integral part of the family's social fabric and identity. Sometime during the 1760s, Madame de La Carlière went so far as to purchase and proudly display a bust of the famous *philosophe* in their salon.

As Diderot's relationship with Sophie became more companionable and less physical, he opened himself up to other possibilities, including a brief affair with Jeanne-Catherine de Maux, the eye-catching wife of a Paris lawyer. Diderot had probably first heard of Jeanne-Catherine years before from her father, Quinault-Dufresne, a famous actor whom Diderot knew quite well. But the *philosophe* only began to see Jeanne-Catherine on a regular basis in the mid-1760s, first in the company of their mutual friend Madame d'Épinay and then, on at least one other occasion, at d'Holbach's town house on the rue Royale.[35] In all likelihood, however, Diderot became infatuated with her over the course of several months in 1768 when both he and Jeanne-Catherine tended to Étienne Noël Damilaville as he lay on his deathbed.

When Damilaville finally succumbed to painful throat cancer in December, Diderot had lost a dear friend and Madame de Maux had lost her lover. Her solace, however, was double: not only had Damilaville left her a clay bust of Diderot sculpted by Marie-Anne Collet, but he had left her Diderot as well.

MADAME DE MAUX, HER DAUGHTER MADEMOISELLE DE MAUX, AND MONSIEUR DE SAINT-QUENTIN, WATERCOLOR (DETAIL)

Jeanne-Catherine was enchanting, sophisticated, and brainy. As the (illegitimate) daughter of two actors, she was also a very talented performer, often singing arias from contemporary opéra comique to the delight of her friends.[36] Charles Collé, a contemporary of Diderot's, summed up her many talents as "divine,"[37] and Diderot certainly concurred. In the short time that he entered into correspondence with her sparkling and inquisitive mind, he excitedly wrote to her about painting, embryology, materialist philosophy, colonialism, seventeenth-century libertine thinkers, astronomy, and love.

Jeanne-Catherine surely had much of the same appeal as Sophie. But his new lover also had something that Sophie did not: she was far more enticed by the physical side of love.[38] This, in fact, led to problems with Diderot when, during the summer of 1770, she took another lover. This painful story (for Diderot) began in early August of the same year, when he and Grimm set off to Langres with the intention of meeting up with Jeanne-Catherine and her daughter, Madame de Prunevaux, in the neighboring city of Bourbonne. Diderot, whose father had traveled to the city to partake of its thermal springs, presumably recommended the spa to his new love interest when she told him that her daughter was suffering from an "obstruction in one of her ovaries after a difficult childbirth."[39] Meeting up with Jeanne-Catherine in Bourbonne had advantages that went beyond the strictly therapeutic, of course. Far removed from Paris and Toinette, Diderot could spend days on end here with Madame de Maux without a care in the world. And this he did, during two separate eight-day trips.

As wonderfully as the summer of 1770 had started, it soon became one of the more emotionally complicated times in Diderot's life. On the way back to Paris from Langres (and Bourbonne), he was invited to stop by the Vollands' château in Isle in mid-September, an offer he accepted. After spending a week with Sophie and her family, he then journeyed to Châlons-sur-Marne (also in Champagne) to spend yet another few days at his friend Duclos's house, knowing full well that Jeanne-Catherine would also be arriving at the same time. As planned, his lover and her daughter appeared, but, much to Diderot's astonishment, they had come with an uninvited guest: the Chevalier de Foissy, a handsome, thirty-year-old aristocrat, who was the Duc of Chartres's squire.

Diderot initially wrote about Foissy with a great deal of admiration; for a young man, he implied, this squire had the sensibility and intelligence of someone twice his age. Upon his return to Paris, however, Diderot came to understand that Madame de Maux and Foissy were lovers. In mid-October, Diderot reported to Grimm that he had had words with the young Foissy. The poor man was apparently terribly upset, at least initially. Dressed down by this famous philosophe and bulldog of a talker, Foissy confessed his sins, apologized, cried, and initially suggested that he would slink off and leave Madame de Maux to her own devices. Madame de Maux had other ideas. Far less compliant than her young lover, she explained to Diderot that the poor boy "had desires" that needed to be met.[40] Later in the month, she proposed the simplest solution to Diderot: why should you not both be my lovers? Diderot, who had no problem sharing himself with Toinette, Sophie, and now Madame de Maux, recoiled at the idea and issued an ultimatum that would prove the end of the amorous portion of their relationship.

Weeks after the dust settled, Diderot still smarted from the slight. In a letter to Grimm, who had actually attempted to patch things up between Diderot and his independent-minded lover, the philosophe complained bitterly that Jeanne-Catherine's treachery had made his heart as "hard as a rock."[41] It was perhaps time, he suggested, to finish with these youthful pursuits. The "season of *needs*," as he put it bluntly, was over.[42]

In the ensuing months and years, Diderot settled into a less tumultuous relationship with the women in his life. This actually began at home. After decades of acrimony, Diderot finally admitted, in his sixties, that he had married "an honest woman whom I love and to whom I am dear because," as he joked, "whom will she scold when I am longer here?"[43] Part of this improved relationship actually came about as a result of Toinette's newfound interest in reading. Having noticed that her mood improved markedly after she began reading Le Sage's *Gil Blas*—a picaresque story of a witty valet who makes good despite a series of thieving masters—he quickly volunteered to be her reader. Three times a day, he reported, he administered a "dose" of the novel. In a joking letter that he sent to his daughter about this new habit, he wrote out a fake prescription for a much happier Toinette: "eight to ten pages of *Don Quichotte*, a well-chosen paragraph of the *Roman comique*, four chapters of Rabelais. [Then] infuse all these with a reasonable quantity of *Jacques le fataliste* or *Manon Lescaut*."[44]

During the same years that his home life quieted down, Diderot had also settled into a more platonic relationship with Sophie. This seems to have been perfectly acceptable to both parties. After a turbulent couple of months in the late 1760s when Sophie had surely suspected that something was afoot with Madame de Maux, she and Diderot both recognized that they had entered into a new stage in their lives, one where they were moving deeply into the decline of old age.

Sophie nonetheless revealed how important Diderot remained to her in her last will and testament, the sole surviving piece of paper that we have in her own hand. After commending her soul to God, and leaving her money, property, beds, cushions, clothes, books, slippers, and furniture to her servants and members of her family, Sophie singles out her former lover as her most important heir, bequeathing to him two precious and symbolic objects. The first of these was an eight-volume edition of Montaigne's *Essays* bound in red leather, which Sophie had consulted, according to Diderot, on a daily basis for years. This was more than an old book. Montaigne's essays embodied what Diderot loved most about Sophie: her unflagging honesty, openness to new ideas, and inquisitiveness. The second gift that she willed to the philosophe was even more personal: an iconic ring that she called "her Pauline."[45]

Thirteen years before the aged Mademoiselle Volland sat down to write her last will and testament, Diderot too took the time to think about their inevitable deaths and separation. At the time, his passion was so strong that he could not help but fantasize about how he and Sophie might somehow continue to love each other long after they had both died. His solution, to be entombed beside his "Sophie," gives way to an enchanting materialist fantasy:

> Those people who are buried next to each other are perhaps not as crazy as one might think. Their ashes might press and mix together, and unite. What do I know? Maybe they haven't lost all feeling or all the memories of their first state. Perhaps there is a flicker of heat that they both enjoy in their own way at the bottom of the cold urn that holds them. Oh my Sophie, [if our ashes were put together in such a vessel] I could touch you, feel you, love you, look for you, unite myself with you, and combine myself with you when we are no longer... Allow me this fantasy. It is sweet and it would assure me an eternity in you and with you.[46]

Diderot's materialist pipe dream obviously echoes his belief that death is not really an ending, but a simple shifting of forms. But this fantasy also contains a powerfully erotic message. As

Diderot's and Sophie's bodies break down over the centuries, he imagines that his dusty remains might start to quiver and, through molecular attraction, seek out the vestiges of his mistress. True love, in this letter, functions on an atomic level. Like iron dust being attracted to a magnet, Diderot's molecules scurry about in a quest for the carnal and intellectual joy that he had felt in an earlier life. This search culminates in the highest tribute one could make to a lover: fusing together to create "a whole" or "common being."[47] Such was the love that the materialist philosopher felt for the enchanting Mademoiselle Volland.

XI

A VOYAGE TO RUSSIA:

POLITICS, PHILOSOPHY,

AND CATHERINE THE GREAT

After Mademoiselle Volland, the second-most important Sophie in Diderot's life was a Prussian princess by the name of Sophia Augusta Fredericka. We know her, as did Diderot, by a different name, Екатерина Алексеевна or Catherine the Great, empress of all the Russias.

Sophia was born in 1729, some sixteen years after Diderot. Growing up in the Baltic seaport of Stettin (now part of Poland), she was raised in the great tradition of Prussian nobility, with a range of tutors who schooled her in music, dancing, and various forms of etiquette.[1] In addition to being exposed to the protocols and pastimes associated with life at court, the princess also received an education dispensed by a dogmatic army chaplain who forced her to memorize what he believed to be the main points of history, geography, and the Lutheran religion.[2] Sophia's most fruitful instruction, however, came from her Huguenot governess, Elisabeth (Babet) Cardel. In addition to introducing the princess to the fables of Lafontaine and the plays of Molière, Corneille, and Racine, the tutor taught her student the joys of thinking and writing in the continent's lingua franca.[3]

Sophia brought her love of French culture and literature with her when she moved to Saint Petersburg in 1744, at age sixteen, to wed the heir to the Russian Empire. (It was at this point in her life that she took the name Catherine.) Effectively alone in a foreign country, and now married to the abusive and alcoholic Grand Duke Peter, the grand duchess found sanctuary in the era's literature and philosophy. In the mid-1750s, she willed herself through her horrible marriage and postpartum depression by reading Voltaire on world history, Montesquieu on the varied political systems found around the globe, and abbé Prévost's compilation of travel writing from Asia to the New World.[4] During these unhappy years, Catherine also had occasion to pore over the first seven volumes of the astonishing *Encyclopédie*, though she, along with the book's other subscribers, was disappointed when the dictionary was banned after the letter *G*.

Her relationship with the faraway world of French ideas, culture, and literature changed abruptly after she led the successful coup d'état against her husband, Emperor Peter III, in June 1762. Among the first things that the new empress did after coming to power was to reach out to the French luminaries whom she had so admired. This "cultural offensive" began with Diderot.[5] Contacting the French writer through one of her chamberlains in Paris, she made the Encyclopedist a remarkable offer: leave France and its repressive intellectual climate behind, come to Riga, and publish the remaining volumes of the *Encyclopédie* without constraint.[6] She also contacted Diderot's former partner, d'Alembert, and asked him to serve as tutor to her son, Grand Duke Paul, for the colossal annual salary of one hundred thousand rubles.

Both men politely declined. Diderot explained that he was honored but, for better or for worse, he was unable to leave Paris. D'Alembert sent back a gracious letter that claimed that he was not qualified to teach a prince about matters of government. The two philosophes also had other reasons for not relocating to what they believed to be a violent and politically unstable country. D'Alembert quipped that he would have made the trip to Saint Petersburg, but he was too "prone to hemorrhoids, and they are far too dangerous in that country."[7] This was, of course, a joke made at Catherine's expense: the Russian government had announced to the world that her late husband had died from complications related to piles, although virtually everybody knew that he had actually been murdered shortly after the coup by Catherine's lover's brother.

Bons mots about the empress's ruthlessness notwithstanding, the news that this cultured and enlightened despot was willing to sponsor the contentious *Encyclopédie* project solidified her reputation among the philosophes; it also opened up what would be a line of communication between Diderot and the sovereign.[8] While the intimacy and frequency of their correspondence pale in comparison to the exchange between Voltaire and Catherine, the empress ultimately had a far greater effect on the Encyclopedist's life than she did on Voltaire's. Her most dramatic gesture toward Diderot came in 1765, only months before the final ten volumes of the *Encyclopédie* were to appear. At the time, the philosophe was both delighted to be bringing this thankless task to completion and apprehensive about losing the relatively stable income that he had been receiving for years.

Diderot was hardly an extravagant spender; his basic expenses—food, rent, and the salary that he paid to the family's servant and various tutors—were actually quite restrained. But one sizable financial burden loomed large: the dowry that he was preparing for the future husband of the then eleven-year-old Angélique Diderot, who would soon be old enough to marry. Faced with the prospect of this substantial disbursement at the same time that his income was about to drop, Diderot fell upon the idea of selling his one possession of real value: his personal three-thousand-book library, most of which had been funded by the publishers of the *Encyclopédie* as part of his salary.

In early 1765, Diderot began hinting in various circles that he would be willing to sell his books to a French bibliophile. Grimm had a better idea: why not inform one of the philosophe's foreign admirers that he had fallen on hard times and that he was now willing to part with this legendary collection? On February 10, 1765, Grimm sent off a note to Catherine's chamberlain and unofficial cultural minister, General Ivan Ivanovich Betskoy, not only proposing the sale of Diderot's books, but suggesting an asking price of 15,000 livres. When the empress received news of this proposition, she immediately agreed to the terms and sent back orders that the deal be concluded on two conditions, both of which were to Diderot's benefit. First, she insisted that Diderot remain in possession of the books during his lifetime. The second condition was equally warmhearted: she appointed Diderot as curator of his own library with an annual stipend of one thousand livres.

Catherine surpassed this act of goodwill the following year after her plenipotentiary minister in France, Prince Dmitry Alekseevich Golitsyn, discovered that Diderot had not received his annual fee as curator. According to Naigeon's account of what happened next, Diderot supposedly told Golitsyn that he had not even thought about this money because he was perfectly satisfied with the sum that had come from the purchase of the library.[9] The ambassador brushed off Diderot's modesty and pointed out that these were not the terms of the arrangement. Shortly thereafter, he sent off a note to Betskoy informing him of the Russian treasury's administrative oversight.

The exchange between Paris and Saint Petersburg obviously took time. But several months later, Betskoy informed "Monsieur Diderot" that the empress had no interest in letting some underling delay or overlook her librarian's stipend in the future; accordingly, she had decided to pay him for his services fifty years in advance. In due course, he was told, he would receive the staggering sum of fifty thousand livres. The empress had also added an amusing addendum stipulating that, at the end of this half-century (Diderot's 102d birthday), the two parties would once again renegotiate the terms of the contract. Diderot was "stupefied." Writing to the empress via Betskoy, his gratitude poured out from his pen: "I prostrate myself at your feet. I reach my arms out toward you, I would like to speak, but paralysis grips my soul, my mind is hazy, my ideas confused, and I melt like a child, while the true expressions of what I feel inside me expire on the edge of my lips."[10] Diderot's fascination with Russia's enlightened despot — and international politics in general — had entered a new era.

ART COLLECTING, DITHERING, AND A PAINFUL WEDDING

The large sum that came into Diderot's possession — the rough equivalent of perhaps $700,000 — had no real expected quid pro

quo. Diderot nonetheless made clear to Catherine's Russian emissaries that he intended to live up to this act of generosity by serving as her cultural attaché in several capacities. To begin with,
he helped Prince Golitsyn convince a number of artists, teachers, and even the occasional physiocrat philosopher to resettle in
Saint Petersburg.[11] Diderot's most successful recruit was the great
sculptor Étienne-Maurice Falconet, whom Catherine commissioned to produce the twenty-foot-tall bronze statue of Peter the
Great that now stands in Saint Petersburg's Senate Square. Alluding to this and other such examples of successful conscription,
Diderot boasted that he and Golitsyn made an excellent team: the
prince, he explained, weakened the will of their targets with his
"generosity, kindness, affability, [and] honesty," while Diderot's
job was to "finish them off."[12]

Over the next few years, Diderot also became one of Catherine's most important art brokers, jubilantly spending her money
(in consultation with Golitsyn) on what he believed to be the best
available canvases and sculptures. His most significant impact as
cultural agent began in 1768, after Golitsyn left Paris to become
ambassador to Holland. Collaborating far more closely at this point
with Grimm and François Tronchin—the latter a Genevan art
enthusiast who would later sell his own collection to Catherine—
Diderot utterly transformed the empress's burgeoning holdings.

The foundational contribution that the philosophe made to
Catherine's art collection, which the empress had begun only
two years after her coup d'état, was negotiating the purchase of
five hundred superlative paintings that had belonged to Louis-
Antoine Crozat, the baron of Thiers, who had died in December
1770.[13] Crozat's collection was generally considered the second-
most important in France at the time, not only containing

Raphael's transcendent small-cabinet painting *Saint George and the Dragon* (c. 1504), but numerous Rembrandts and Van Dycks, as well as selected works by Rubens, Veronese, Correggio, Dürer, Titian, Poussin, Watteau, and Chardin.[14] When this assortment of canvases finally arrived in Saint Petersburg in 1772, it became the core of the Hermitage Museum.

That a French collection of this magnitude and value — Catherine bought it for 460,000 livres — could leave the country for Saint Petersburg caused quite a stir in both Versailles and the capital. The Marquis de Marigny, who was then serving as the director of the "households" of the king of France (including the Louvre and Versailles), lamented that the pitiful financial state of the kingdom prevented the crown from competing for these paintings.[15] Diderot was unmoved by this hand-wringing. Indeed, he seemed to take a certain amount of satisfaction in the impotence of the once-great French state. If the collectors, artists, and the wealthy were all up in arms, he suggested, it was because they were both ashamed and envious, ashamed that "we [France] are obliged to sell our paintings during a time of peace," and envious that "Catherine can purchase them while waging war [against the Turks.]"[16]

Some of this cosmopolitan nonchalance regarding the exodus of France's best paintings stemmed from Diderot's gratitude to Catherine. But the philosophe had also become bitterly disappointed with the state of affairs in France. Life in the capital, he lamented, had changed a great deal in the decade after the expensive and humiliating Seven Years' War, which had ended in 1763. Besides the fact that this world conflict had deprived France of much of North America — unimaginably huge swaths of land stretching from Louisiana to the shores of Nova Scotia — the expenses and compounding debt incurred during the conflict had pushed the crown toward near bankruptcy.[17] Bad weather on a seemingly annual basis during the late 1760s made things worse. Terrible grain shortages not only drove the price of bread to unaffordable levels, but gave rise to rumors that the crown had cunningly organized a "pact of famine" in order to produce yet more profits.[18] By 1770, riots had broken out across much of the country, and thousands of businesses began to fail, leading to further, crippling falloffs in tax revenue.[19] Diderot summed up these dire days with trepidation: "half of the nation is going to sleep financially ruined, and the other half is afraid of hearing their own ruin broadcast in the street when they wake up."[20]

Contributing to the country's difficulties, from Diderot's point of view, was what he believed to be France's descent into despotism. In 1771, he and many of his fellow philosophes were outraged when France's chancellor, René Nicolas Charles Augustin de Maupeou, used the king's musketeers to disband the Paris Parlement and the country's sovereign courts.[21] While the Parlement was anything but a friend of the philosophes, Diderot was nonetheless a firm believer in maintaining this important check on monarchical power. Lamenting the fact that the pope would now be able to disseminate bulls in France without the mediation or approval of the Parlement, he sighed that the country was regressing to the medieval era.[22]

The depressing political situation in France led Diderot to think far more seriously about accepting an open invitation to travel to Saint Petersburg to meet his benefactress. Although the philosophe was well aware that Catherine was an autocrat of the first order, he also considered her a *souverain civilisateur*, a monarch who had declared herself interested in promoting a tolerant, enlightened empire. Indeed, in the same years that the aging Louis XV had begun veering toward despotism and religious conservatism, Catherine had actually convened a commission of elected representatives from a broad cross section of Russian society, charging them with the task of helping her reform the *Ulozhenie*—the archaic and feudal code of laws enacted in 1649. Even more significantly, Catherine wrote a series of directives for this commission, which she published in both French and English in 1767 under the title of *Nakaz* or *Instruction.* Drawing heavily from Montesquieu's *Spirit of the Laws* and the Italian jurist Cesare Beccaria's *On Crimes and Punishments,* Catherine showed herself to be open to some of the most liberal reforms ever advanced by a sitting monarch, including progressive penal and judicial reforms that outlawed torture.[23]

Catherine never implemented the most important changes that she discussed in the *Nakaz.* Yet her best-selling book, much like her magnanimous gestures toward Diderot, functioned as effective propaganda outside her empire. By publicly advocating for a significant restructuring of her empire based on the ideas of some of France's greatest thinkers, she consciously differentiated her own philosophical values from those of the more conservative monarchies to the west. This message was not lost on Diderot. Unlike Louis XV, who had blocked the *Encyclopédie* on two occasions, signed the lettre de cachet that sent him to jail, and even personally interceded to deny the philosophe's admission to the Académie française, Catherine seemed to be actively sponsoring the liberal ideas proposed by the French philosophes. While Diderot was under no illusions regarding the feudal society upon which the Russian nobility depended—millions of serfs who were little more than slaves—the political climate in

Russia seemed utopian compared to that in France. Not only had the Russian monarch proposed to finance the *Encyclopédie*; she had also made sure that Diderot was named a member of the Imperial Academy of Arts of Saint Petersburg in 1767. By 1772, Diderot had concluded that there was a fundamental cultural and intellectual realignment taking place in Europe, one where "science, art, taste, and wisdom are traveling northward," while "barbarism and all it brings in its wake, is coming south."[24]

In addition to the political regression in France, there were also a number of personal reasons that pushed Diderot toward Saint Petersburg. By 1772, the last volume of *Encyclopédie* plates finally appeared, which freed him from any responsibility vis-à-vis his employers of twenty-five years. Of even greater consequence, however, was that his once intense love life in the capital had seemingly come to an end. Not only had his passionate relationship with Sophie Volland faded by the late 1760s, but his breakup with Madame de Maux continued to bedevil him in 1772; it was, as he put it, a "pain in the flank."[25] In May of that same year, he confessed to Grimm that he felt timeworn and unappealing, like one of those "old pieces of furniture that you shouldn't move too much" because "their planks are wobbly and separated and you can't put them back together very well."[26]

The most painful change in Diderot's life, however, occurred later that fall, when his daughter Angélique married Abel-François-Nicolas Caroillon de Vandeul, the son of a distinguished family of Langrois industrialists whom Diderot had known for forty years.[27] Despite (or perhaps because of) his own love story with Toinette, Diderot had claimed the right to decide whom his daughter should marry. But he had also insisted on bringing Angélique and Abel together to see if they approved of this decision. In March 1770, Diderot invited the twenty-four-year-old Abel to the rue Taranne. While all concerned were favorably inclined to this union — Angélique, Diderot, Toinette, and Abel — the philosophe and patriarch successfully put off the day that his daughter would leave the household for three years by declaring that both these children were far "too young" to be married immediately.[28] Abel readily agreed to this prolonged engagement, but he soon proved to be far more hardheaded when it came to matters of money. In the final year and a half before the wedding, Abel and his future father-in-law entered into often-painful and protracted negotiations concerning the all-important marriage contract. When they finally had this document notarized on the night before the wedding, the young man had negotiated a prodigious dowry of thirty thousand livres. The whole process had not endeared Abel to Diderot; he found him to be grasping and money-oriented.

The actual ceremony took place on September 9, 1772, in the Saint-Sulpice parish. This turned out to be smaller and far less joyous than Diderot had hoped. Toinette had refused to let Diderot invite any of his impious friends to the wedding: certainly not d'Holbach, not Grimm, and not Madame d'Épinay. Those present included a few members of the Caroillon family and Diderot's own sister, Denise. Diderot's brother, Didier-Pierre, had not only refused to come to Paris, he had actually done his best to ruin the wedding.

A month before the ceremony, Angélique had attempted to repair the enormous rift in the Diderot family by writing her "dear uncle" in Langres. She not only pleaded with the priest to reconcile with her father, but to officiate at the wedding itself. Didier-Pierre's answer surely numbers among the most caustic letters that he ever penned. Informing Angélique that he regarded Caroillon as an unworthy unbeliever like her own father—this was far from the truth—he then went on to threaten that he would no longer consider her as his niece if she went through with the marriage. The only people he recognized as family, he put it curtly to her, were the truly "devout."[29]

Angélique never saw this letter until much later in her life. A few weeks after the wedding, Diderot, who apparently intercepted the letter, replied ferociously on his daughter's behalf. Accusing Didier-Pierre of dishonoring his vows, he asks the priest to imagine himself on his deathbed and think back on his past actions before predicting: "you will see that you are a bad priest, a bad citizen, a bad son, a bad brother, a bad uncle, and an evil man."[30]

In the weeks after marrying off Angélique, Diderot entered into a somewhat depressive state. Alienated from his only brother, married to the ill-tempered Toinette, forsaken by Madame de Maux, and now abandoned by his daughter, Diderot complained of feeling terribly alone. In a revealing note that he sent to Abel's mother, who had been one of Diderot's childhood friends in Langres, he lamented that life without his daughter would have been easier had he had been married to a woman who would have helped him "forget [his] loss."[31] This, alas, was not the case.[32] Several days after the wedding, Diderot summed up his psychological state to his married daughter, whom he now addressed as Madame Caroillon:

> I am letting you go with a pain that you will never be able to understand. I will gladly let you off for not suffering the same agony. I am now alone, and you have followed a man whom you must adore...Adieu, my daughter, adieu, my dear child. Come press yourself one final time against my chest. If you sometimes found

me more stern than I should have been, please forgive me. Rest assured, however, that fathers are cruelly punished for the tears that they caused in their children, be they justified or not. You will know that one day, and you will excuse me...I don't understand other fathers. I see all their worries evaporate the moment that they separate themselves from their children; it seems to me that mine are beginning. I was so happy to have you under my wing! God willing, I hope the new friend that you have chosen will be as good, as tender, as loyal as me.

> Your father,
> Diderot.[33]

The philosophe's mood improved in the following months, and sometime in November or December 1772, he announced to Falconet, who had been living in the Russian capital since 1766, that he was coming to Saint Petersburg to pay his respects to Catherine. Diderot also had two other thinly concealed objectives. The first was to act as a sort of political counselor to the empress, to encourage her to initiate programs of reform that, while compatible with monarchical power, would nonetheless inch Russia toward a more representative government. The second was to convince the Russian empress to champion a new and uncensored version of the *Encyclopédie* that would serve as a "literary monument to her."[34]

PETERSBURG

Diderot initially hoped to head off to Russia on or around June 1, 1773. As was often the case, he ultimately dithered for more than a week. This indecisiveness came to a head on June 9, the day before he was finally scheduled to depart. At midday, he, Toinette, and the then-pregnant Angélique all sat down to what everyone in the room thought might be their last meal together. None of them ate; no one spoke; all three sobbed with grief. It was, as Diderot described the moment, the "cruelest scene" that he as a "father and husband" had endured during his life.

Later that same night he announced to his friend Jean Devaines, who had stopped by to say goodbye, that he was going to cancel this dangerous trip: "I am staying, I have decided; I am not going to abandon my wife and my daughter."[35] According to Devaines, who recorded these events, this conversation was interrupted by Madame Diderot, who had suddenly barged into the office, as if on cue. Standing in the doorway with her fists ground into her hips, a dainty bonnet incongruously tied under her chin, she supposedly screeched at Diderot: "Well, well, Monsieur Diderot, what are you doing?... You are wasting your time talking nonsense, and you are forgetting your packing. You need to leave tomorrow morning early...Oh, what a man! What a man!"[36] This scolding perhaps helped Diderot change his mind yet again. The next morning he began the months-long voyage to Saint Petersburg.

Five days and five hundred kilometers later, Diderot arrived in The Hague, the first real stop in the journey. He had come to this Dutch town for several reasons. The first was to meet up with the empress's chamberlain, Aleksei Vasilyevich Naryshkin, with whom he had arranged to continue on to Saint Petersburg.[37] He had also wanted to spend time with his good friend Prince Golitsyn, whom he had not seen for four years.

Diderot enjoyed a two-month stay in this small foreign city of 38,000. Having never really traveled outside the somewhat humdrum corridor between Langres and the Paris region, he now had the luxury of becoming a sightseer for the first time in his life. The first thing he did upon arriving was to make the short trip from Golitsyn's house on 22 Kneuterdijk to see the sea for the first time.[38] In addition to contemplating "Neptune and her vast empire," as he put it, Diderot soon relived his days as art aficionado by traveling with Golitsyn to Leyden to see the city's Dutch paintings and engravings.[39] During his stay he also visited Amsterdam, Haarlem, Zaandam, and Utrecht.

Living away from Paris had many advantages. Freshly caught ocean fish impressed Diderot no end. "The more I get to know this country," he wrote to Sophie and her sister in July, "the more I get used to it. The sole, the herring, the turbot, the perch, and everything they call *waterfish*, are the finest folk in the world."[40] In addition to enjoying the food and escaping from his less-than-perfect life on rue Taranne, he was also able to concentrate on his own writing. Among other things, he completed a draft of his *Paradoxe sur le comédien* (*Paradox of the Actor*), a philosophical dialogue in which one of the speakers maintains, against prevailing opinion, that the greatest actors are those who master themselves completely, who replicate emotional states without feeling any passion or sentiment themselves. Stanislavsky would later say that the *Paradox*, published posthumously in 1830, was among the most important theoretical works on acting ever written.[41]

Two months after arriving at The Hague, on August 20, 1773, Diderot finally set off to Saint Petersburg with his traveling companion. After only 230 kilometers, the sixty-year-old philosophe had to interrupt the journey in Duisberg (Germany) to seek medical help for a serious gastroenterological infection. The next major stop along the way was Leipzig, where Diderot apparently made quite a spectacle of himself by preaching atheism in front of a crowd of savants and merchants, including the younger brother of the German writer Gotthold Ephraim Lessing.[42]

While traveling, Diderot spent much of his time preparing for his upcoming meetings with the empress. The first document he composed en route was a sweeping assessment of the state of French politics entitled a *Historical Essay on the Police in France* that moved from Clovis to the overthrow of the Parlement by Maupeou. The message contained in this relatively large essay was unambiguous: with the exception of several bright spots — including the efficient police force managed by his friend Sartine — France was not a country to imitate.[43]

Weeks upon weeks of monotonous travel also gave Diderot time to compose a number of short poems, some of them quite obscene indeed. A month after leaving The Hague, Diderot and Naryshkin stopped for the night at a tavern in the port city of Riga where they apparently laid eyes on a beautiful servant in whose honor the philosophe composed a poem entitled "The Auberge of the Cloven Hoof":

> She is cute, very cute,
> For all of Riga she is a hoot,
> Oh the servant of the *Cloven Hoof.*
> For an *obol*, one day, I lifted her pleat.
> For a double *teston* — for a double *teston*,
> Oh yes! What did I get? I grabbed her teet.

The rest of the poem — it becomes far ruder — culminates in the servant providing each and every one of her favors, as well as a case of syphilis.[44] Diderot, who often expressed his aversion to such houses of ill repute, presumably played the role of the poet here only for dramatic effect.

Several weeks after Diderot produced this smutty rhyme, Naryshkin and Diderot finally rolled into Saint Petersburg. After 2,400 juddering kilometers through what is now Poland, Lithuania, and Latvia, both men were no longer laughing. Naryshkin had come down with a terrible respiratory infection and a throbbing toothache. Diderot's chronically weak digestive system had also rebelled against foreign microbes and contaminated water. Suffering worse than ever from fever, cramps, and terribly inflamed intestines — presumably dysentery — he forced himself to soldier on for the last 150 kilometers, arriving "more dead than alive" as he pulled up to what he thought was his final destination, Falconet's flat on Millionnaia Street.[45]

Falconet had always been a dear friend, and yet an enigma for Diderot. Sometime before he left for Saint Petersburg, he had described the sculptor as "hard and tender, sophisticated and argumentative, eager for praise and scornful of posterity; envious of the kind of talent he lacked, and caring little for the one he possessed; loving passionately, and cruelly tyrannizing over those he loved; rich in talent, and a hundred, a thousand more times so in self-esteem...; made up of all sorts of contradictions."[46]

Falconet added to his list of inconsistencies on the day that Diderot landed on his doorstep. In the months leading up to his voyage, the sculptor had promised his writer friend a warm welcome and lodging in the apartment that he shared with his mistress and fellow sculptor, Marie-Anne Collot. Diderot had accepted and had actually imagined a moving scene where the three friends would fall into each other's arms after years of separation. "What a moment this will be for [the three of] us," he wrote to Falconet, "when I knock on your door."[47]

As it turned out, the reception was hardly what Diderot had

imagined. Greeting Diderot rather coldly, the sculptor rescinded his invitation, explaining that he had given the guest room to his son, who had arrived unexpectedly two months before. While Diderot graciously accepted his friend's explanation, Madame de Vandeul later wrote that her father was "wounded forever" by this humiliating brushoff.[48] Unwell and adrift, the weary traveler quickly got back in touch with Aleksei Naryshkin, with whom he had just spent two months. The young chamberlain immediately arranged for Diderot to stay with him and his brother, Semën Vasilyevich Naryshkin, in their majestic three-story town house in the heart of the city. The so-called Naryshkin Palace, built twelve years before, was ultimately far more convenient for Diderot. In addition to its comparative luxury, the building was but a short walk or coach ride to Catherine's quarters in the Winter Palace.

CATHERINE

Obliged to remain close to a chamber pot for the first few days in Russia, Diderot finally had the opportunity to meet the empress at a masked ball (at the Hermitage) about a week later. True to his sartorial preferences, Diderot wore the understated and distinctive uniform of the philosophe, which is to say black breeches, waistcoat, and dress coat. In a courtly world where one was measured as much by one's finery as by anything else, it was hardly a surprise that Petersburg's ambassadors, dignitaries, and nobles mocked this Frenchman who took himself for a modern-day Diogenes. Their scorn soon turned to envy, however, when it became clear that Catherine intended on welcoming the famous philosophe in a way that few if any of them would ever experience.[49]

CATHERINE II, PAINTING

Diderot had actually appeared in the capital at an opportune
time. During his five months' stay in the capital, the forty-four-
year-old Catherine was effectively "between lovers," something
that was exceptional for her.[50] The turmoil in her love life had
begun sixteen months before, when she replaced Count Grigory
Orlov — the father of at least one of her children — with a young
member of the Horse Guards named Alexander Vasil'chikov. By
the time that Diderot arrived in the capital in October 1773, the
empress had become so bored with this fetching yet character-
less man that Diderot had far less competition for her time than
he might have had otherwise. Among other things, the philosophe traveled with the empress to visit the Smol'ny Monastery,
a school for aristocratic girls for which Diderot had recruited

several professors, and of which he had been named the official counselor. In early December, Catherine also invited him to be her guest in Tsarskoe Selo, at the so-called Catherine Palace—named after Catherine I—which is about twenty kilometers outside of Saint Petersburg.

But the vast majority of the meetings that Diderot had with Catherine took place at the Little Hermitage, the three-story Neoclassical town house and art gallery that the empress had built as an addition to the 700,000-square-foot Winter Palace.[51] By Diderot's own account, he was introduced into Catherine's study three or sometimes four afternoons a week. Outside of these meetings, Diderot spent much of his time feverishly preparing a series of essays for her—these are now known collectively as the *Memoirs for Catherine II*—that served as the point of departure for their discussions.

On the afternoons that the philosophe arrived on time—he was frequently late—Diderot entered Catherine's study at three p.m. The empress tended to sit on a sofa, at times occupying herself with needlework while Diderot generally took a seat in front of her in an armchair.[52] The intensity (and the lack of ceremony) that Diderot brought to their conversations in the Little Hermitage is now a thing of legend. During sometimes heated exchanges, the philosophe cajoled, contradicted, and even reached out and pounded on Catherine's leg as he would while speaking to d'Holbach or Grimm. In a letter that the empress sent to Voltaire in January 1774, she admitted to being impressed by the limitless imagination of the most "extraordinary man" she had ever met.[53] Diderot, too, felt a similar exhilaration, as he explained to Toinette: "Do you know that I have my interviews every day at three p.m., at her Imperial Majesty's house? You should know that this is a notable honor, and that I cannot not appreciate its worth. I swear to you that the Empress, this astonishing woman, does everything in her power to lower herself to my level, but it is in this very movement that I find her a hundred cubits tall."[54]

In the first weeks that he met with Catherine, Diderot believed that the empress might be the rarest of all beasts, a monarch who was not only a member of the republic of letters (she ultimately produced two dozen plays, a history of Russia, fairy tales for her grandsons, and her memoirs), but also willing to let Diderot help her liberate Russia from its irrational traditions and medieval institutions. How wonderful, he clearly thought, to put the values of the Enlightenment into practice in Russia, particularly since they certainly did not seem to be taking root in France.

POLITICS AT THE LITTLE HERMITAGE

Well before Diderot had arrived in Saint Petersburg, Catherine had a pretty good understanding of the philosophe's political and intellectual inclinations. As the driving force behind the *Encyclopédie* project, Diderot had become famous for waging a protracted battle against superstition and religious bigotry. But he had taken up more explicitly political questions in his dictionary as well, among them the biggest one of all, namely, what gave a handful of European kings and queens (and one Russian empress) the right to rule over 160 million human beings?

In the few instances where Diderot himself wrote on this sensitive topic — his entries are generally more courageous than innovative — he categorically rejects the long-standing belief that God himself granted monarchs the authority to rule over their subjects.[55] The right to command, as he makes clear in the article "Political Authority," flows directly from the consent of the people and the natural and civil codes that define their relationship.[56] While Diderot believed that princes had the validated right to rule over their nation, they still had an obligation to reflect or embody what he called the "general will" of the nation. In exchange, he explained, the people were bound to respect and preserve the sovereign's power and right to govern.

Diderot's overall political philosophy during his *Encyclopédie* years was the reflection of what might be characterized as moderate humanism. Anything but a demagogue or a revolutionary, he was primarily a reformer in the 1760s: one of the philosophes interested in persuading the era's monarchs to restructure their institutions so that individuals would be protected under the rule of law from the abuses of the state and the Church.

Catherine had had no qualms about inviting someone who held such opinions to her court. In addition to the fact that Diderot had served as her cultural attaché for years, he was also a generous and creative thinker, not to mention a legendary communicator. What was more, both she and Diderot had drawn their political theory from the same well, from the basic contract theory of Grotius, Pufendorf, and Montesquieu. On paper, they seemed like a good match: an openminded reformer and an enlightened Russian autocrat who was, as she wrote for the inscription of her own tombstone, "goodnatured, easygoing, tolerant, broadminded... with a republican spirit and a kind heart."

As liberal thinkers went, Diderot was certainly more palatable and far less threatening to Catherine than someone like Rousseau. Rousseau's early political career, very much like Diderot's, had begun in the pages of the *Encyclopédie*. After the mid1750s, however, the socalled citizen from Geneva had also begun publishing a series of increasingly influential political works that combined a powerful interpretation of humanity's moral potential with quotable, maxim-driven criticism of Europe's "social system." (The most famous of these is undoubtedly "Man is born free, but everywhere he is in chains.") Advocating for much more than superficial changes to the era's political institutions, Rousseau sought to revolutionize not only the way people thought about themselves, but their political birthright as well. More than any other thinker before him, he positioned the subjugated peoples of Europe on the right side of history.

Rousseau's most influential book of political theory, *Du contrat social* (*The Social Contract*), appeared the same year that Catherine came to power, in 1762. Building on many of the same criticisms that he had levied against the "social system" in general, Rousseau claimed provocatively that monarchies were necessarily inferior to more democratic forms of government since they could only function thanks to self-interest, political corruption, privilege, and venality. His remedy for what he believed to be rampant inequality was nothing short of a wholesale transformation of society: the creation of a new binding political pact that would replace the individualism and self-love of current society with a form of absolute democracy and collectivism guaranteed by the general will of the population. The dialectical message proposed by Rousseau was that the people were supposed to sacrifice their freedom in order to be truly free. Those who violated this trust, he argues in *The Social Contract*, must be put to death.

Diderot did not supply Catherine with the type of long, abstract political treatise at which his former friend excelled. Though he had written entries on political questions for the *Encyclopédie* — including the articles "City," "Citizen," and "Political

Authority"—he limited himself during his stay to the more isolated nuts-and-bolts questions associated with her political
regime, such as how can the Russian relationship between government and the individual be improved? and how can the state
use its power in such a way that it succeeds in getting people to
accept its policies?

To her credit, Catherine seemed to have been more than willing to discuss these ideas with Diderot. The wide-ranging memoranda that he left behind examine a number of subjects, including
the relationship of religion to the throne, the importance of a mer-
itocracy in Russia, the situation of the country's Jews, the source
of revolutions, the definition of tyranny, the importance of public schools, the administration of justice, and the role of luxury,
divorce, universities, and scientific academies. Diderot invariably
embedded suggestions in all these disquisitions. He encouraged
Catherine to mandate that her schools teach young girls about
their sexuality with lifelike wax models, as he had done with
Angélique. More brazenly, he cited a litany of political and military reasons why the empress should move her court back to
Moscow. Having a "capital at the end of an empire," he writes
somewhat mockingly, simply did not make sense; it was like having "an animal whose heart would be at the end of its finger, or its
stomach at the end of its big toe."[57]

Perhaps Diderot's most telling and radical essay was his meditation on "Luxury." Lashing out against a world where, as he
had already suggested in Rameau's Nephew, gold was the only real
"God," Diderot provocatively crowns himself as "King Diderot"
in order to right the wrongs of a country that seems a lot like
France. To begin with, this philosophe monarch decrees that he
must secularize the religious orders and nationalize the clergy's

property, essentially predicting what the French Revolutionary government would enact fifteen years later. In another attempt to raise capital and pay off the state's debts, he then proposes to sell off much of the realm's land and properties, significantly reducing the number of stables, hunting grounds, pensions, useless voy-ages, ambassadors, and foreign offices.[58] (It is worth remembering that Diderot would have read this indictment of luxury and royal pomp out loud to the most powerful woman in the world, while they both sat comfortably in the Little Hermitage, surrounded by some of the greatest treasures in existence.)

By December, Diderot had shared dozens of such forward-thinking memoranda with the empress. And yet he also began to realize that she was not taking his ideas to heart. According to an account that circulated in the 1780s, Diderot interrupted their discussion one day to ask the empress, who always was very attentive during their conversations, why none of his suggestions had been implemented. Her answer spelled out very clearly just where Diderot's jurisdiction began, and where it ended.

> Monsieur Diderot, I have listened with the greatest pleasure to all the inspirations flowing from your brilliant mind. But all your grand philosophies, which I understand very well, would do mar-velously in books and very badly in practice. In your plans for reform, you forget the difference between our two roles: you work only on paper which consents to anything: it is smooth and flex-ible and offers no obstacles either to your imagination or to your pen, whereas I, poor empress, work on human skin, which is far more prickly and sensitive.[59]

Before this decisive moment, Diderot had probably had at least one other indication that Catherine was unlikely to change course so easily. In November, the French ambassador to Saint Petersburg had dragooned him into using his supposed influence with the czarina to float the idea of signing a peace treaty with Turkey, a country with which Russia had been at war for five years. Catherine was immediately vexed that Diderot had the audacity to go beyond his normal "sphere"—that of the philosophe—and had made a point of throwing the proposed terms prepared by the embassy into the fire.[60]

Though Diderot continued to prepare essays for Catherine during the first two months of 1774, he also began to fall into a somewhat lethargic and deflated state. By February, the volume of his correspondence, often an indicator of his mood, dropped to almost nothing. Some of this disenchantment surely came from a realization that his hope of transforming Russia into a beacon of enlightenment was destined for failure. But he also had an additional concern. As if to chase him from the capital, the other supposedly enlightened monarch on the continent, Frederick of Prussia, had taken it upon himself to make Diderot's life miserable during his last weeks in Petersburg.

FREDERICK AND THE RETURN HOME

Long before Catherine had become the darling of the philosophe coterie, Frederick had established himself as the greatest enlightened monarch of the era. An ardent lover of the era's philosophy, a talented musician, as well as a strong believer in the freedom of the press and religious tolerance, this top-down authoritarian and warlord also saw himself as a public intellectual, writing and publishing, among other things, an influential historical account of the modern era in 1746. But the most alluring part of his reputation among the French philosophes did not come from his books; it stemmed from the fact that he often offered sanctuary to persecuted members of their cohort. When Voltaire, the abbé de Prades, La Mettrie, and Helvétius, among others, were exiled from France, the German monarch immediately welcomed them to Berlin.[61]

Despite Frederick's generosity, Diderot had always remained far more wary and skeptical of the Prussian ruler than most of his friends. Indeed, in 1770, Diderot forever soured on the ostensibly enlightened despot when Frederick published a scathing attack on d'Holbach's *Essai sur les préjugés* (*Essay on Prejudices*).[62] D'Holbach's book, to which Diderot had presumably contributed some of the ideas during a stay at Grandval in 1769, called for more social equality, more religious tolerance, and more freedom of thought.[63] As importantly, the *Essay* did not advocate for political reform by speaking to the continent's enlightened monarchs; it addressed the people themselves. It was this, as much as anything else, that had incited Frederick's caustic and disdainful seventy-page retort. Shortly after the Prussian monarch's so-called *Examination on the Essay on Prejudices* appeared, Diderot wrote a response (unpublished) in which he sounds more like Danton than Diderot: "I will no longer patiently put up with a highborn wretch who insults me because he is the last of his race — me, who am perhaps the first of mine."[64]

Three years later, Diderot took great pleasure in turning down Frederick's invitation to spend a few days in Berlin on his way to Russia. The Prussian monarch, who had fully expected the philosophe to pay his respects, was annoyed and quickly evened the score by writing a blistering review of Diderot's literary career for the December 1773 issue of the *Nouvelles littéraires* (*Literary News*).[65]

As soon as this mean-spirited piece of journalism was published, Frederick dispatched multiple copies to Saint Petersburg, where Diderot had been meeting with Catherine for several months. The article, not surprisingly, found an enthusiastic audience among the Russian courtiers, virtually all of whom resented the philosophe's atheism, his unaffected simplicity, and, above all, his privileged relationship with the empress.[66]

As the Russian capital became frostier, Diderot planned his trip home. Despite his increasing disillusionment and homesickness, he nonetheless felt a certain amount of sorrow to be leaving Catherine, a ruler whom he described on numerous occasions as having the soul of "Caesar with all the charms of Cleopatra."[67] Catherine, too, had grown attached to the aging philosophe, and had actually "forbidden les adieux," presumably to avoid a tearful goodbye.

In one of his last meetings with Catherine, Diderot had nonetheless asked three favors of the empress: safe passage back to France, a traveling companion to accompany him as far as The Hague, and a keepsake or "trifle" that his friend the empress had actually "used." Catherine granted these wishes and more. In addition to providing for his travel, she gave the philosophe the considerable sum of three thousand rubles for his travel expenses.[68] She also had a new English coach (a dormeuse) especially equipped for him with a bedstead and mattress so that the philosophe could lie down and sleep during the trip. Her final and most symbolic gesture took place at court, on Friday, March 4, the day before Diderot set off for home. Rising to speak in front of a group of court aristocrats, Catherine conspicuously took a ring off her finger and asked her chamberlain to approach her. She then carefully handed the ring over to the court official while making an announcement in front of all those present: Monsieur Diderot "wanted a trifle, and this is one. He wanted me to have used it, and you will tell him that I wore it."[69] Later that day, the chamberlain delivered the cameo ring to the departing philosophe. As Diderot held the ring between his two fingers, he realized that he was looking at a portrait of the empress herself. According to Madame de Vandeul, her father cherished this present for the rest of his life. More than a simple gift, the ring symbolized the powerful yet undoubtedly complex relationship between autocrat and philosophe.

XII

LAST WORDS:

SPEAKING TO DESPOTS

AND AMERICAN INSURGENTS

On Saturday, March 5, 1774, Diderot's well-appointed English carriage headed out of the Russian capital back toward The Hague. The return trip, in general, proved far easier than the trip east had been. His fragile intestines, now accustomed to foreign bacteria, had ceased to rebel. The weather cooperated as well. By Riga, he and his traveling companion, an amiable Greek aristocrat named Athanasius Balla, were marveling at temperatures that were more reminiscent of summer than spring. The journey was not entirely without incident, however. Only 570 kilometers from Saint Petersburg, Diderot's coachman attempted to take the four-horse team and carriage across the frozen Dvina River. This turned out to be a poor decision. As the carriage began rolling across the frozen waterway, the river's ice started to give way beneath the heavy load. According to Diderot's very cursory account of this potential disaster, the driver quickly tried to navigate his way over a "crystal bridge" that was sinking and resurfacing while the passengers looked on in horror.[1] Though Diderot never explained precisely just how the three men managed to escape the rising waters — it seems that he climbed painfully into a boat while thirty men attempted to carry the coach to shore — drowning had seemed a real possibility.[2]

The remainder of the journey back from Russia was relatively straightforward. The only real detour took place in Germany, where Diderot once again ordered his driver to bypass the capital and its spiteful monarch, Frederick the Great. Despite the fact that Grimm had pleaded with Diderot to pay a visit to this flute-playing patron of the arts, the philosophe clearly had no intention of fawning in front of a repugnant despot whom he now described as "malicious as a monkey."[3]

A week after rebuffing Frederick, on April 5, 1774, Diderot arrived in The Hague. As had been the case the previous year, the philosophe prevailed upon his friend Prince Dmitry Golitsyn and his wife for accommodations. In the first letters he sent to friends and family after he arrived, he crowed about the good weather and his equally good health. Yet the philosophe was, in reality, dog-tired from traveling almost nonstop over 2,400 kilometers of jarring, rut-plagued dirt roads that had ultimately spelled the death of three carriages.[4] Quickly returning to the comfortable bed that he had left behind almost nine months before, he apparently spent most of the week sleeping.

Soon after recuperating under the Golitsyns' care, Diderot entered into yet another period of feverish work. His primary task in The Hague was an imperial commission: overseeing a French-language edition of edicts and plans related to Catherine's educational reforms and charitable work.[5] In addition to this assignment, which Diderot assiduously completed during the first five months of his stay in Holland, he also began reworking some of his unpublished manuscripts with the intention of finally producing a proper collection of his complete works. Yet the project that most enthused him during his second stay in The Hague was one that would never come to pass: editing a new, Russian-sponsored version of the *Encyclopédie*. Writing to Toinette shortly after arriving, Diderot claimed that he had all but signed a contract for this new book project. After revealing that this deal would be worth an unimaginable 200,000 livres — more than twice the amount he made on his first dictionary project — he instructed his wife to start looking for a far nicer apartment: "this time around," he proclaimed to her, "the *Encyclopédie* will be worth something to me and will not cause me any problems."[6]

Two months later, despite further assurances that he would soon receive a down payment, Diderot had still heard nothing concrete from Saint Petersburg. In reality, the empress had decided that she had actually very little to gain by associating her name with the new *Encyclopédie*, a book that Diderot had repeatedly claimed would be far bolder than the first one. Rather than inform him of this decision herself, however, Catherine asked the man who had first gotten in contact with Diderot, General Ivan Ivanovich Betskoy, to string the philosophe along until the project died of its own accord. By fall, Diderot would finally understand that the silence coming from Saint Petersburg meant there would be no *Encyclopédie russe*. This decision had an unexpectedly emancipatory effect on the last decade of his life; unburdened by the massive task of yet another dictionary, Diderot now had far more time to think and write critically about the European monarchs he had come to know late in life.

DIDEROT'S POLITICS

Before he left Russia, Diderot had promised Catherine that he would never betray her trust by badmouthing her or her regime, at least publicly. A man of his word, he studiously kept this vow. Before leaving the capital, he burned the notes that he had compiled about his experience in the Russian capital. Upon his return to The Hague and, eventually, Paris, he also tended to emphasize the positive aspects of his trip, especially Catherine's intelligence, good intentions, fair-mindedness, and ability to relate to a philosophe "man to man."[7]

And yet, by the time he arrived back in Holland, Diderot had realized that his view of the world's monarchies had shifted dramatically. Interestingly enough, the first person to whom he hinted about this change was Catherine herself. In September 1774, he divulged that he had been amusing himself by rereading Tacitus — not only the most venerated historian of the Roman Empire, but a proponent of free speech and freedom and a fierce critic of the corruption of the empire's power politics. More significantly, he told the empress that he had dashed off a political pamphlet entitled *Principes de politique des souverains* (*Political Principles of Sovereigns*). Catherine did not ask to see this document and Diderot did not send it to her for good reason. These so-called *Principles* were, in fact, a series of Machiavellian political maxims written from the perspective of a malevolent despot for the benefit of his (or her) fellow rulers. Chock-full of fiendish pieces of advice — among them, one should "only form alliances in order to sow hatred"[8] and never, ever "raise one's hand without striking"[9] — this guidebook of autocratic duplicity, self-interest, and brutal militarism was designed to satirize the increasingly autocratic rule of Diderot's bête noire, Frederick II. Yet the ruthless outlook of this manual for tyrants obviously applied to Catherine's reign as well.

The *Political Principles of Sovereigns* was not the only piece of political writing that Diderot alluded to in his letters to Catherine. Surely far more worrying to the empress, her onetime resident philosophe also admitted that he had had the audacity to pore over her *Nakaz*—her best-selling book of legal and political philosophy—with his "pen in hand."[10] Diderot's host in The Hague, Prince Golitsyn, was well aware of this new and impertinent document as well. Toward the end of Diderot's stay in The Hague, in fact, the Russian diplomat felt compelled to break into the locked chest where the writer kept his manuscripts—perhaps on Catherine's orders—and stole (and presumably burned) the so-called *Observations on the Nakaz*. Diderot, who often said that trust and honesty among friends were among humanity's most important virtues, was both despondent and livid. The rest of his stay with the Golitsyns, as one might suppose, was frosty.

As luck would have it, however, Diderot had another copy of note-based version of this document that he ultimately reworked upon his return to Paris. At first glance, the final version of the *Observations* appears to be little more than mini-essays on the various articles that Catherine developed in her *Nakaz*. In actuality, this small book is the first time that Diderot took it upon himself to speak entirely openly (and as an equal) to the empress. If, in the past, he had begrudgingly conceded that the sovereignty of the Russian Empire resided with its monarch, he now stipulates quite clearly that the right to govern can only be delegated by and never taken away from the people: "There is no sovereign except the nation; there can be no true legislator except the people."[11]

More radically, he then goes on to explain that the contract between the sovereign and the nation gives the people the right to defy, depose, and, in extreme cases, condemn a tyrannical ruler to death, should this same monarch flout the law.[12] As demonstrations of popular sovereignty went, Diderot could hardly have been much clearer.

Catherine did not receive or read the *Observations* until 1785, the year after the philosophe died. Despite the fact that the reference to justified regicide had been scratched out, perhaps by Madame de Vandeul or her husband, there were plenty of other things in the *Observations* that made her seethe. In the pointed "debate" that Diderot had staged with her, he not only accuses the empress of failing to bring about the far more representative type of government that she had promised in the *Nakaz*, but predicts that, without a new legal code, it is likely that the next rulers of Russia will not be as benevolent or as freethinking as she is. Diderot did not mince words in the *Observations*: although he praised her for being a magnificent person, he also stated quite brutally that she was a despot masquerading as an enlightened monarch.[13]

Notwithstanding the misgivings that Diderot had progressively developed about Catherine's reign, he nonetheless remained more than willing to spend long hours working on her behalf, particularly if he thought he might actually have a positive effect on her politics. His best chance to effect change came in March 1775, when the empress requested that he submit a plan for a new educational system designed to lead Russian students from their ABC's through to university.[14] By the fall, he finished the assignment and dispatched a substantial 170-page manuscript to the empress that he entitled *Plan d'une université pour le gouvernement de Russie* (*Plan of a University for the Government of Russia*).

The time for toadying and subtlety had come to an end. Diderot began the *Plan* with several powerful maxims that reflected his view that the function of education was not to produce a better-educated aristocracy; it was a weapon to be deployed against superstition, religious intolerance, prejudice, and social injustice. "To instruct a nation," Diderot writes in the first line of the *Plan*, "is to civilize it."[15] Education, as he went on, not only "gives man dignity"; it has a necessarily emancipatory or transformative effect on both the enslaved and the ignorant: "the slave [who is instructed] soon learns that he was not born for servitude" while the "savage loses the ferocity of the forest."[16]

Diderot's conviction that education could be the motor of social and moral progress required a radical rethinking of what a university should be. In stark contrast to the reality of the institutions of higher learning that he himself had experienced in France—closed-door faculties dominated by religiously trained scholars whose highest goal was to replicate themselves and their beliefs—he called on the new Russian *universitet* to replace the teaching of theology with that of tolerance. He also believed that the various faculties should be staffed by well-paid functionaries who would welcome "all the children of a nation" into their classrooms. Perhaps the most radical aspect of his plan took place on a general curricular level: anticipating the birth of the great research universities of the future, he knocked Greek and Latin from their privileged pedestal, and called for a far more practical and concrete course of study that gave pride of place to the teaching of math and experimental science, the latter in a laboratory setting. This new type of pedagogy, he insisted, would finally allow experimentation to take precedence over received ideas.

A free, secular, and empirically driven education for the nation's children was not only a question of benevolence and fairness from Diderot's point of view; it was in the nation's best interest.[17] In addition to "civilizing" the country in general, Diderot argued that educating the largest swath of the population made the most sense, mathematically speaking. If, as he reasoned, there was only a one-in-ten-thousand chance that the next Newton would be born in a palace rather than within the general population, it was a fool's bet to invest all educational resources in only the highest-born men. The more people the state instructed, in short, the more chances it had to cultivate virtuous and talented men, not to mention the occasional prodigy.[18]

Catherine seems to have first consulted the philosophe's *Plan* in the spring of 1777. As was the case for many of his proposals, she felt that his views on education were either too radical or ill-suited for implementation in imperial Russia. Soon after they were read, they joined the philosophe's other political musings in the archives, never to be acted upon. Yet if Diderot's political ideas fell upon deaf ears in Saint Petersburg, his voice was far from silenced during the 1770s. Indeed, during the second half of the decade, he arguably became the most influential, progressive (and often radical) voice in the years leading up to the French Revolution.

OLD AGE

The France to which Diderot returned on October 21, 1774, had changed significantly. This shift began the previous spring, when Louis XV, who had reigned for fifty-one years, died of an agonizing case of smallpox. Given the fact that his two sons had predeceased him, the throne passed to his nineteen-year-old grandson, Louis-Auguste, who made it a point to distinguish himself from his grandfather's conservative outlook on life. Among the new king's first acts was making the very public and political decision to have himself and the rest of his family inoculated with a small amount of the (live) smallpox virus, something that his grandfather had obviously chosen not to do.

LOUIS XVI, ENGRAVING

Far more importantly, from Diderot's point of view, Louis XVI began his reign by endorsing a series of progressive policies. Several months after coming to power, the new king took the unprecedented step of putting a check on his own authority by reinstating the parlements that his grandfather had disbanded. Equally as significant, he surrounded himself with an entourage of reformist counselors and cabinet ministers, many of them friends or colleagues of Diderot. Anne-Robert-Jacques Turgot, the prominent Encyclopedist and physiocrat, became secretary of state of the navy, before ultimately occupying the prominent role of controller-general or minister of finances. Antoine de Sartine, the lieutenant-général de police who had done his best to protect Diderot from the ecclesiastical party during the final years of the *Encyclopédie*, succeeded Turgot as secretary of state of the navy. Diderot's friend Malesherbes also became part of the government. Four years after Louis XV had banished the former director of the book trade from Versailles for protesting the coup against the parlements, Malesherbes took on the role of secretary of state of the king's houses. Among the many tasks he performed during the early months of Louis XVI's reign, the liberal aristocrat was tasked with providing recommendations regarding the political status of the country's Protestants and Jews. The proposal he finally submitted — recommending that both groups be admitted to full citizenship — was rejected by the king. Some things simply remained too radical for the new monarch.[19]

Regardless of the vestigial conservatism of the ancien régime, Diderot believed that some of France's smartest men were attempting to usher in a new era. The most challenging problem that the new government addressed in its first year was reforming the inefficient grain market. This task fell to Turgot, a staunch believer in the advantages of economic liberalism. By September 1774, the country's controller-general had convinced Louis XVI to sign legislation allowing for the free flow of grains throughout the kingdom for the first time in French history. The hope was that, by relaxing the country's byzantine set of laws, taxes, and trade protocols, France would unleash the full potential of the most fertile land in Western Europe, simultaneously benefiting property owners, tenant farmers, and the millions of peasants for whom bread was a staple.

Unfortunately for Turgot and the rest of the country, these reforms were enacted during a spell of repeatedly poor harvests. This not only led to a dramatic spike in grain and bread prices, but insurrections that foreshadowed the next decade's Revolution. By 1775, riots, looting, and violent uprisings had reached the point that the crown was forced to station soldiers outside of the country's *boulangeries* and grain facilities. Though Louis XVI continued to support Turgot during this time of upheaval, this was the beginning of the end of his reform agenda. By the spring of 1776, a reinvigorated chorus of critics—this included the newly reinstated parlements, the financial interests involved in the grain trade, and Marie-Antoinette herself—had effectively turned the king against Turgot's proposals and policies.[20] The controller and finance minister sealed his own fate, however, when he declared himself unwilling to support the American fight for independence against the British for fear of further indebting the state. By May, the king asked Turgot to step down; Malesherbes left shortly thereafter. Almost two years to the day after Diderot had first written that France had entered a new and promising era, the philosophe looked on glumly as his friends either left or were dismissed from the government.

Diderot wrote very little about Turgot's and Malesherbes's short-lived political appointments. Part of this presumably had to do with the fact that the philosophe actually disagreed with the liberalization of the grain market, but did not want to come out publicly against Turgot. Some of it was also surely related to his declining health. In addition to suffering from various digestive flare-ups, he lamented that his teeth were now "tottering," his eyes would not cooperate after dark, and his legs had "grown very lazy, endlessly multiplying the need for canes."[21] It was his heart, however, that had become his most serious problem. The previous year, during July and August 1775, he had been laid low by painful angina, which he described as an "affection" of the chest.[22] In a letter that he sent to Grimm in August 1776, he even hinted that his friend should cut short his trip to Saint Petersburg if he wanted to see him alive when he got back. He had arrived at a point in his life, as he put it, where one "counts the years, which is very close to the age where one counts the months, which is very close to the age where one lives from day to day."[23]

Much of his hermitlike existence during his last years was spent hiding either "under the gutters" at the rue Taranne or in Sèvres, in his friend Étienne-Benjamin Belle's guesthouse, which looked out on the Seine and the old stone Pont de Sèvres. Among the many projects he worked on during his last years, he wrote a play that he would eventually entitle *Est-il bon? Est-il méchant? (Is He Good? Is He Wicked?)*.[24] In stark contrast to his far more earnest and moralizing bourgeois dramas, this short comedy recounts a day in the life of Hardouin, a Parisian man of letters who, very much like Diderot himself, experiments with the idea that working in the interest of the greater good often means moral compromise, if not downright dishonesty.[25] Acting as a sort of puppet master, Hardouin seeks to resolve three problematic situations through various forms of deception: he helps bring about a resolution to a seemingly endless lawsuit by hoodwinking a lawyer; he helps a widow obtain a pension for her boy by claiming that he (Hardouin) is the child's father, ruining the reputation of the widow in the process; and finally, he convinces his former mistress to allow her daughter to get married by informing her, untruthfully, that her daughter is pregnant. This little play, which is designed more as after-dinner entertainment than for the grand stage, is far closer to *Rameau's Nephew* in sensibility than it is to *The Father of the Family*. As one critic correctly points out, it is the only truly funny play ever written by Diderot.[26]

In 1776, Diderot had also agreed to provide a short biographical postface to a new, six-volume translation of the works of Lucius Annaeus Seneca (1 BCE–65 CE) that d'Holbach and especially Naigeon had helped translate.[27] Summarizing the life and works of one of the most important philosophers of the Roman imperial period, he knew, would not be a simple task. On the positive side of his legacy, Seneca had exposed the philosophes of Diderot's generation (not to mention Erasmus's and Montaigne's) to the foundational ideas of Stoic philosophy. In a series of celebrated essays and philosophical dialogues with titles such as *On Providence*, *On the Firmness of the Wise Person*, and *On the Tranquillity of Mind*, Seneca had asserted that true happiness does not come from either our health or our wealth, but from doing good and leading a virtuous life.[28] The challenge of writing about Seneca was not his philosophy; it came from the fact that the man had supposedly not lived up to his own values. To begin with, Seneca had famously condemned the allure of money, but nonetheless amassed one of the largest fortunes in Rome. His far greater sin, however, was supposedly serving as Nero's tutor, allegedly conspiring alongside the bloodthirsty emperor to murder Agrippina, the ruler's own mother. For the vast majority of eighteenth-century thinkers this hugely important Stoic was guilty of hypocrisy.

As a young man, Diderot had been among those who castigated Seneca for his supposed inconsistencies, at one point accusing the famous Stoic of enabling Nero's various desires while "valiant citizens were put to death."[29] Three decades later, in what ultimately became a five-hundred-page account of Seneca's life, philosophy, and ethics, he now sought to rehabilitate the Roman philosopher from "eighteen centuries of calumny."[30]

Appearing in print in late 1778, Diderot's *Essai sur la vie de Sénèque* (*Essay on the Life of Seneca*) is an argumentative and often digressive intellectual biography that, for the most part, lacks the verve and wit of Diderot's famously spirited dialogues. Yet the *Essay* is nevertheless an intriguing work. To begin with, Diderot's unwavering defense of Seneca's relationship with Nero certainly serves to justify his own role vis-à-vis Catherine, empress of all the Russias.[31] What was more, as well as allowing him to grapple with the fact that he, like Seneca, had sidled up to a despot, the *Essay* also became a forum for Diderot's first public assessment of his fraught relationship with Jean-Jacques Rousseau.

In an ideal world, Diderot would surely have preferred to forget his painful breakup with Rousseau, particularly his former friend's allegation that Diderot had not only betrayed him but engineered a malicious conspiracy against him. By the late 1770s, however, putting Rousseau out of his mind had become impossible. Diderot, like many others in d'Holbach's set, was dreading the impending publication of Rousseau's *Confessions*, a tell-all autobiography that he believed would be full of paranoid half-truths targeting him and the other philosophes. Diderot had, of course, already suffered a fair share of defamation in the past, but this was different. Unlike the other writers who had taken up the pen to lambaste him, Rousseau was not a third-rate playwright or an unimaginative journalist; he was arguably the most influential writer of his day. What was more, Rousseau knew far more about Diderot's life than his other enemies. What was at stake, for Diderot, was nothing less than his beloved posterity and his reputation as an upright, generous, and honest soul who served his friends faithfully.

Diderot's solution to this threat was to lash out at Rousseau. Using the *Essay* to strike before the *Confessions* appeared in print, he compared Rousseau to Seneca's detractors, and inserted a series of footnotes into his text that accused his former friend of being derivative, an obfuscator, a hypocrite, and an intellectual thief whose best ideas were borrowed from Seneca, Plutarch, Montaigne, and Locke.[32] There was, of course, no mention of Diderot's own role in exacerbating Rousseau's paranoia by being aloof, by neglecting him, and by often mocking his fears as unwarranted.

As fate would have it, Diderot's invectives against Rousseau appeared in print in late 1778, only months after Rousseau had died. This was unfortunate timing. To almost anyone who picked up the book, Diderot's name-calling seemed petty and overly vindictive and soon prompted a hailstorm of negative criticism. Diderot's response to the reviews was to spend yet another two years rewriting and expanding the *Essay*, reframing and retitling the book the *Essay on the Reigns of Claudius and Nero*. In addition to further strengthening his defense of Seneca's career and responding to his critics, he added an entirely new and far more brutal section dedicated to Rousseau's sins. After claiming that it had been the Genevan's perverse and irrational outlook on life that had cost him "twenty respectable friends," Diderot went on to ask an important question: how was it that this onetime philosophe ultimately became the most ardent antiphilosophe of his era? The answers are piercing:

> In the same way that he became Catholic among the Protestants, Protestant among the Catholics, and professed to be a deist and a Socinianist among Catholics and Protestants...

In the same way that he wrote against theater, after writing comedies...

In the same way that he lashed out against literature, after cultivating it his entire life...

In the same way that, while preaching against loose morals, he composed a licentious novel.

The most painful inconsistency in this list of falsehoods and hypocrisy concerned Diderot himself: "In the same way that he vilified that man who admired him the most..."[33]

Diderot's violent tirade against Rousseau's duplicity appeared in 1782, the same year the first volumes of Rousseau's *Confessions* appeared as well. While both men had hoped to claim the moral high ground in their final public clash, the written accounts of this twenty-five-year-old dispute did little to settle who was at fault. Indeed, more than anything else, the combination of spite and regret that drips from both men's pens is a poignant testament to what they continued to have in common: the fear of mutual slander and the searing pain of lost companionship.[34]

HOLDING FORTH ON THE WORLD

Diderot's last published book was arguably his least successful. Before the second (1782) version of the *Essay* had even appeared, a number of Diderot's friends, including Naigeon, had pleaded with the aging philosopher to make serious revisions or cuts to the manuscript before publishing it. The author demurred. When the book finally appeared in print, even his staunchest supporters were scandalized. In an emblematic review that appeared in the *Nouvelles de la république des lettres*, Pahin de la Blancherie not only derided Diderot for his fawning praise of Seneca, but for "sinking the knife even deeper" into Rousseau's back.[35]

There is, however, a great irony related to this time in Diderot's career. During the same years that the literati were shaking their heads at the writer's one-sided apology of Seneca, the philosophe had also invested far more efficiently in his legacy by penning hundreds of critical pages for the best-selling book of the last quarter of the eighteenth century, abbé Guillaume Thomas Raynal's *Philosophical and Political History of the Two Indies.* It is no exaggeration that these anonymous contributions to Raynal's project not only changed the book, but history as well.[36]

FRONTISPIECE FOR
GUILLAUME THOMAS RAYNAL'S
HISTOIRE DES DEUX INDES, 1780

Diderot had known Raynal for thirty years before getting involved in the *History of the Two Indies.* Like Diderot himself, Raynal had initially come to Paris with the intention of pursuing an ecclesiastical career. A short, solemn-faced man with a deep, penetrating gaze — he was known to wear a black suit and a bluish cloth cap that looked very much like a turban — Raynal first established his reputation by writing books on Holland and the English parliament, as well as by editing two journals: the *Nouvelles littéraires*, the precursor of the *Literary Correspondence*; and the *Mercure de France*, one of the premier journals of the day. The direction of Raynal's career changed significantly in the early 1760s, however, when Étienne François de Choiseul, the foreign minister in charge of both the navy and France's overseas colonies, asked the writer to produce a manual of modern warfare, which was ultimately published in 1762.[37] Shortly thereafter, Choiseul commissioned a far larger project, the multivolume examination of European colonization from India to North America. This book would ultimately become Raynal's testament.

Very much like the *Encyclopédie*, the *History* was not supposed to be a *machine de guerre* at the outset. To the extent that Choiseul encouraged Raynal to adopt a "philosophical" or critical point of view, he presumably asked the author to prod the government into implementing a more forward-thinking foreign policy that would help stimulate the French economy, which had been battered by the Seven Years' War.[38]

The scope of such a project was daunting. In order to produce such a comprehensive survey of European ventures abroad, Raynal consulted thousands of documents from the foreign ministry, while also entering into correspondence with a wide variety of colonial administrators, diplomats, and settlers scattered across the globe.[39] The former editor was also shrewd enough to understand that processing this material was beyond his abilities, and engaged a number of ghostwriters who, while eager to contribute to a critical examination of European colonization, preferred to do so anonymously. The most important of these nameless "political philosophes" was Diderot, who secretly began collaborating with Raynal sometime in the late 1760s.[40]

The first edition of the *History* (dated 1770) was ultimately printed in The Hague in 1772. The French reading public had never encountered anything quite like this before. In addition to a far-reaching survey and history of European commercial activities, the book had replaced the *Encyclopédie* as the venue for some of the era's most liberal positions on both global *and* domestic politics. Despite the fact that the *History*'s disparate points of view often come into direct contradiction—the inevitable pitfall of multiple authors—the most powerful portions of the book unequivocally put forth a vision of history according to which tyrants, magistrates, and priests had not only instituted various forms of despotism in Europe, but had exported it to the world's colonies. French censors had no illusions about the implications of the *History*. Shortly after the book became widely available in France, it was banned by an *arrêt du Conseil* in December 1772.

Diderot's contributions to the first iteration of the *History* pale in comparison to what he would ultimately provide for the subsequent two editions. Yet Raynal immediately understood the power of the philosophe's pen. Well before the first edition of the *History* had even appeared in print, he was already asking Diderot if he would once again provide new material for a revised edition. While the philosophe grumbled about this new task, he ultimately agreed and doubled his anonymous contributions for the next version of the book, which appeared in 1774. Shortly after Diderot returned from Russia that same fall, Raynal again prevailed upon him, soliciting even more text for the third and final volume. While Diderot was increasingly unhealthy—and occupied with his essays on Seneca and other projects—he nonetheless soon found himself working far more intensely than he had on either of the first two editions. By the time that he handed over his final manuscript to Raynal at the end of the decade, he had become responsible for fully 20 percent of the entire ten-volume book.

Diderot's contributions to the *History*, which vary from a few sentences to chapter-length interventions, functioned as the capstone to his diverse political writings. Though Raynal had theoretically limited the scope of the *History* to the East and West Indies, Diderot was among those contributors who forcefully turned the critical focus of the book back on Europe itself. One of the more interesting contributions that he furnished for the third edition of the *History* is a cheeky note that he directed to Louis XVI himself. Having picked up the habit of addressing monarchs in a familiar tone, Diderot speaks to the young king in the informal and forward *tu* form. He warns the doomed Louis XVI that the country as a whole is a powder keg: "Cast your eyes over the capital of your empire and you will find two classes of citizens. Some, wallowing in wealth, flaunt a luxury which provokes indignation among those not corrupted by it."[41] A paragraph later, the aging philosophe predicts that empires such as his own "cannot endure, without morals and virtue," then asks the king why he continues to condone the "insatiable greed" of his courtiers, allowing all the "protected men" of his kingdom to shelter themselves from the burden of taxation while the people "groan" under the weight of their levies.[42] Toward the end of this diatribe, Diderot gives his king a choice: accept the infamy of the do-nothing tyrant or transform the country and achieve true glory. Diderot embedded many other such messages in the *History* as well, even when he was not speaking to the king directly. On the subject of freedom of the press, for example, the philosophe was categorical: "Wherever the sovereign does not allow people to express themselves freely on economic and political subjects, he provides the most convincing evidence of his inclination to tyranny."[43]

As influential as Diderot's views on the French monarchy would ultimately become in the years leading up to and during the Revolution, his writing on the colonies was at least as significant. In addition to underscoring the fundamental injustice of much of the colonial enterprise as a whole—repeatedly condemning his era's conquerors for appropriating lands that did not belong to them—Diderot forcefully attacked what he believed to be his era's most glaring evil: the ongoing business of African chattel slavery.

By the time that Diderot became involved in the *History of the Two Indies*, French slave traders were delivering thirty thousand enslaved Africans to the Caribbean on an annual basis, adding to the half million slaves who were already toiling on the three major French Islands of Guadeloupe, Martinique, and especially Saint-Domingue (Haiti). In all, French ships had carried well over a million souls to the islands since the trade had begun in earnest, 120 years before.[44]

The varied and generally anonymous writers who provided material for the *History* reacted to the plight of the African in different ways. One of the contributors uncritically summarized the era's spurious race science, providing a long disquisition on how the so-called *nègre* or Negro had serious anatomical and cognitive deficiencies that seemingly destined the "species" for slavery. Other writers with more liberal tendencies advocated for an "enlightened form of slavery" that encouraged plantation masters to treat their slaves with more respect and kindness. Raynal also included more "progressive" voices. One of the sections in the *History* advocates for the eventual emancipation of African populations, once they had understood Western laws and customs. Most famously, however, Raynal also included violent antislavery outbursts interjected by thinkers including Jean de Pechméja, who penned one of the book's most memorable sentences: "whoever justifies [slavery] merits a contemptuous silence from the *philosophe* and a stab of the dagger from the Negro."[45]

Diderot added to and rewrote much of what Raynal and his other ghostwriters had put forward on the subject of slavery. In addition to rejecting the era's illegitimate race science, he attributed the existence of the trade, which had always been blamed on Africans themselves, to European greed. He also solemnly informed readers of the *History* that the responsibility for the forced enslavement and murder of millions of Africans not only lay with slave merchants and planters, but regular Europeans as well: "The insatiable thirst for gold has given birth to the most infamous and atrocious of all trades, that of slaves. People speak of crimes against nature and they do not cite slavery as the most horrific. The majority of Europeans are soiled by it, and a vile self-interest has stifled in human hearts all the feelings we owe to our fellow men."[46]

Diderot's most prescient and rhetorically awe-inspiring passages on slavery come, however, when he predicts the rise of a Black Spartacus who will wave the "banner of liberty" and lead an army of former slaves against their masters, leaving the ground stained with their former oppressors' blood. This is, of course, precisely what happened in Saint-Domingue a decade later, when a brilliant tactician and Revolutionary soldier named Toussaint

Louverture — some historians maintain that he probably read the *History of the Two Indies* — began the struggle that would ultimately lead to the freedom of Haiti.[47]

AMERICA

Like many of the contributors to the *History*, Diderot was convinced that the brutal reality of chattel slavery was the defining feature of the New World. Yet in the same years that he was castigating the horrors of the plantation system, he was also applauding the birth of a new kind of country in "Septentrional" or North America: a federation of independent states that combined the freedom of democracy with the political strength of a monarchy.[48] If this new republic were only able to rid itself of human bondage, he believed, it might actually become the promised land.[49]

Diderot had been a so-called *américainiste* — a supporter of the colonists' struggle against the British — well before the Declaration of Independence was signed in 1776. As early as 1769, he had been on the receiving end of a letter of recommendation from Benjamin Franklin, asking him to meet with a young, upstanding physician named Benjamin Rush. Diderot gladly received the future signatory of the Declaration of Independence in his rue Taranne office, where the two men reportedly discussed the best way to resist British tyranny.[50] Diderot may also have met with Franklin himself in 1767, when the American spent six weeks in Paris, or sometime in 1776 or 1777, when he returned to France to secure both financial and military support for the ongoing rebellion in the American colonies.[51] While there is little concrete proof of this meeting, one can certainly be forgiven for imagining an encounter between the two effervescent and wigless polymaths, both of whom would presumably have battled to get a word in, Diderot in his stilted English and Franklin in his broken French.

Franklin and Diderot's relationship, whatever it may have been, was undoubtedly quite limited. Yet Diderot was nonetheless very much connected to Franklin and the American cause through Raynal. The abbé had met Franklin in 1767 and had remained in touch ever since. Throughout the 1770s, in fact, Raynal repeatedly solicited Franklin for information (for his collaborators) on subjects such as the "population, state of trade, shipping, agriculture, [and] produce related to North America."[52] Similar requests continued until the last edition of the *History*. Indeed, shortly before the third volume appeared, Raynal sent a final appeal to the American statesman and scientist for more detailed data about the colonies, including the precise demographic breakdown of blacks and whites in each of the states.[53] This last question might very well have come from Diderot, who was then rewriting the entire section on American slavery.

Franklin was well aware that Raynal's overall positive assessment of the American colonies was having more of an impact on French public opinion than any other published work at the time.[54] In 1775, the eminent scientist decided to recognize the French writer's contributions by inducting him into the American Philosophical Society, of which Franklin was both founder and president. What both Franklin and his Philadelphia colleagues did not realize, however, was that the most important French philosophe advocating for the mutinous Americans was not Raynal at all; it was actually Diderot.

In the 1774 edition of the *History*, Raynal had treated the possibility of complete independence from England somewhat warily, suggesting that, justified or not, separation from the mother-land might cause religious and cultural problems in the future.[55] When Diderot rewrote this section for the 1780 edition, he gave it an entirely different thrust. In addition to asserting that the American colonies had the absolute moral and political right to unshackle themselves from their oppressive mother country, he provided an enthusiastic summary of the political foundations and ideology of the new nation, not only translating portions of Thomas Paine's 1776 *Common Sense* and summarizing the main points of the Declaration of Independence, but analyzing the new country's Articles of Confederation as well.[56] It is no exaggeration that Diderot was the single most important French interpreter of the remarkable political experiment taking place on the other side of the Atlantic.

Diderot confessed that he regretted being too old to travel to this "land of tolerance, morals, laws, virtue, and liberty."[57] Yet he did not let this obstacle deter him from giving advice to the "American insurgents," as he called them. In addition to repeat-edly urging the New World revolutionaries to lay down their lives before sacrificing the smallest part of their liberty, he also cau-tioned these same men to avoid the mistakes that had plagued the European continent for centuries.

> People of North America: may the example of all those nations that have preceded you, and especially that of your motherland, be your guide. Beware the abundance of gold that brings about the corruption of morals and the scorn of law; beware of an unbal-anced distribution of wealth that will produce a small number of opulent citizens and a horde of citizens in poverty...[58]

The real threat to American democracy, as Diderot had also

suggested in his *Essay on Seneca*, came less from foreign powers than from the unintended consequences of future success: luxury goods, the rise of class tensions, political corruption, venality, and, in the worst scenario, perhaps even a dictator.

Diderot's musings in the *History of the Two Indies* often hint at what the philosophe believed might be a series of coming revolutions. In addition to predicting the violent end of slavery on Saint-Domingue, he also made very clear that it was likely that all forms of repression — be it the brutal trade monopolies forced on the various colonies or the despotic monarchies in Europe — would ultimately be defied and, in many cases, overthrown. Addressing the downtrodden and oppressed directly at one point in the *History*, Diderot asks: "[you] whose roar has made your masters tremble so often, what are you waiting for? For what moment are you reserving your torches and the stones that pave your roads? Pull them up."[59] Publishing such passages, Diderot knew only too well, was as audacious as it was dangerous. In one telling anecdote, he recounts how he asked Raynal who would dare print the incendiary passages that he was producing. The editor of the book supposedly replied, "Me, me, I tell you, keep going."[60]

When Raynal published the 1770 and 1774 editions of the *History*, he had wisely done so anonymously. Associating his name with the third and increasingly militant version of the book was far more dangerous. Yet as he prepared the final 1780 version of the *History* for publication, he not only put his name on the title page, but added a portrait of himself for the new frontispiece. Decked out in his writer's dressing gown and signature turbanlike cap, Raynal stares out intensely at us while the caption under his image reads: "Guillaume Thomas Raynal, Defender of Humanity, Truth, and Liberty."[61]

The far more audacious content of the 1780 edition of the *History* quickly incited the wrath of the king, Parlement, and Church, and was burned on the place de Grève in May 1781. Raynal, who was under orders to be arrested, quickly fled to Prussia, where he spent the next seven years. Persecution and interdictions notwithstanding, bookstores could not keep the new version of the *History* in stock; by the end of the century, the *History of the Two Indies* would run to twenty French editions and forty or so pirated foreign editions. Along with several other key books and documents — Montesquieu's *Spirit of the Laws*, Rousseau's *Social Contract*, and the American Declaration of Independence — Raynal's *History of the Two Indies* would also play a major role in inspiring a number of French Revolutionary figures, including Danton, Desmoulins, Robespierre, and even Charlotte Corday, the young Girondin sympathizer from Normandy who plunged a dagger into Marat's heart while he sat in his bathtub.

Diderot did not live long enough to witness the influence that his anonymous contributions to Raynal would have on the next generation. Yet he was well aware how divisive the book was, even among his own friends. Shortly after the third edition of the *History* appeared in the spring of 1781, Raynal and the man who had been Diderot's most cherished friend for nearly thirty years, Grimm, got into a heated scrap about the book. Grimm not only maligned the *History* as ill-conceived and irresponsible, but attacked Raynal personally by presenting him with a seemingly insolvable puzzle: "either you believe that the [monarchs] you attack cannot retaliate against you, in which case you are a coward; or you believe that they can retaliate, and are likely to do so, in which case it is folly to expose yourself to their anger."[62]

Two days later, Diderot met up with Grimm at the Vandeuls'

apartment. Unaware that Diderot had been the most important contributor to Raynal's *History of the Two Indies*, Grimm gleefully recounted to Diderot how he had treated Raynal as a fool for publishing such a misguided work. Diderot was incensed, and felt personally attacked by this powdered flatterer who had given up a literary career to fawn over Europe's monarchs. While he chose not to enter into direct conflict with Grimm in front of his daughter, upon his return to the rue Taranne he jotted down his thoughts about the incident in an (unsent) note.[63] Making clear that he would sooner die than stop "loving" Grimm, Diderot nonetheless chastises his friend as "gangrenous" and for letting his soul grow "thin" in the "antechambers of the great."[64] But it was in the postscript that Diderot was the most cutting, declaring emphatically that "one is not capable of heroic actions if one condemns them; and one condemns them only because one is not capable of them."[65]

Diderot's unsent letter allowed the philosophe to express his fury without breaking off his friendship with Grimm entirely. Perhaps as important, it also gave him the opportunity to clarify what he believed was the moral responsibility of the philosophe: being honest, resolute, and audacious in the pursuit of truth, whether one trumpets one's name, as Raynal had done, or whether one writes in the shadows, as he himself often chose to do.

A year before this run-in with Grimm, Diderot had summed up his curious career far more fully in the final paragraph of the 1780 edition of Raynal's *History*. Acknowledging that he had not published a masterpiece during his lifetime, he then expressed the hope that the ideas that he interjected into Raynal's book — and elsewhere — would change society for the better. This pleasing thought, he admitted, would comfort him as he got closer and closer to the grave:

I do not flatter myself into thinking that, when the great revolution comes, my name will still survive.... This feeble work [the *History of the Two Indies*], whose sole merit will be to have inspired better books, will undoubtedly be forgotten. But at least I will be able to tell myself that I contributed as much as possible to the happiness of my fellow men, and prepared, perhaps from afar, the improvement of their lot. This sweet thought will for me take the place of glory. It will be the charm of my old age and the consolation of my final moment.[66]

Epilogue

WALKING BETWEEN

TWO ETERNITIES

In mid-December 1776, the eighty-three-year-old Voltaire pulled out a piece of paper and dashed off a note to Diderot. Having been exiled from Paris for more than twenty-five years, the now wizened and virtually toothless philosophe lamented the fact that the two men had never laid eyes on each other: "I am heartbroken to die without having met you…I would gladly come and spend my last fifteen minutes in Paris in order to have the solace of hearing your voice."[1]

Fifteen months later, Voltaire rolled into the capital in his blue, star-spangled coach. Quite ill with prostate cancer, the famous humanitarian, essayist, and playwright nonetheless organized a feverish schedule for himself. In addition to finishing work on a five-act tragedy—he lived long enough to attend the premiere—Voltaire spent most of his days holding court in a friend's *hôtel particulier* on the corner of the rue de Beaune and the quai des Théatins. Here, for hours at a time, Voltaire received visits from a long list of adoring friends and dignitaries, among them Benjamin Franklin and his son. Sometime during Voltaire's three-month stay, Diderot also came to pay his respects. Journal-ists who wrote about the meeting hinted that some relationships are best conducted solely by correspondence.

HOUDON'S BUST OF VOLTAIRE

Diderot and Voltaire had first exchanged letters in 1749 when the "prince of the philosophes" had invited the then up-and-coming Diderot to dinner. In addition to hoping to get to know the clever author of the *Letter on the Blind*, Voltaire had presum-ably hoped to help the newly appointed editor of the *Encyclopédie* rethink his atheism. Diderot decided to dodge both the invitation and the sermon. One might wonder what kind of young writer turns down lunch with the most famous public intellectual ever to live. The answer, in 1749, was pretty clear: a proud and unre-morseful unbeliever who had no interest in having his philosophy questioned by an unbending deist.

The two philosophes nonetheless remained in contact (from

afar) over the course of the next twenty-eight years. Voltaire sent fifteen more letters. Diderot replied nine times. The relationship, which actually deepened as time went by, was cemented by mutual friends, mutual interests, and a deep reciprocal respect for each other's intelligence. And yet, well into the 1760s, a continued sense of wariness existed on both sides. In addition to their divergent views on religion—Voltaire remained a Newtonian deist whereas Diderot had long declared himself an unbeliever—the two men evidently had ambivalent feelings about each other's respective literary careers. Both had invested heavily in the theater, and each also believed that the other was on the wrong path. Voltaire, from Diderot's point of view, continued to churn out an endless string of rearguard classical dramas and comedies; as for Voltaire, he secretly found Diderot's bourgeois dramas to be a sad testament to the direction of the theater.

What did these two old men talk about when they finally sat in front of each other in 1778? The battles they had waged, won, and lost? The dark days of the *Encyclopédie*, when Voltaire repeatedly tried to convince both Diderot and d'Alembert to drop the project? The friends who had died over the years, especially the beloved Damilaville? Voltaire's failed attempt to get Diderot elected to the Académie française? Their mutual friend Catherine the Great? Diderot's curious book on Seneca? His secret contributions to Raynal? Or how much Diderot was in deep admiration for Voltaire's defense of the family of the Protestant Jean Calas, who had been falsely accused of killing his son after he converted to Catholicism?

The only real accounts we have, alas, focus on an argument that the two men had regarding the merits of Shakespeare. Convinced of the superiority not only of French theater but of his own art,

Voltaire supposedly asked Diderot how it was possible to "prefer this tasteless monster to Racine or Virgil."[2] In the discussion that ensued, Diderot conceded that the playwright lacked the polish of some of the greatest poets, but that the Englishman nonetheless possessed a sublime energy that transcended the "gothic" aspects of his writing. He then went on to compare Shakespeare to the massive fifteenth-century statue of Saint Christopher that stood just outside the doors leading into Notre Dame Cathedral. While perhaps crude and rustic, this colossus was very much like Shakespeare, according to Diderot, because "the greatest men still walk through his legs without the top of their head touching his testicles."[3] The implication was clear. Voltaire, who rightly considered himself the greatest French poet and playwright of his generation, did not measure up either. According to one journalist's account of this exchange, Voltaire was not "excessively happy with Monsieur Diderot" after this comment.[4]

Diderot's unrestrained tongue had reportedly irked Voltaire as much as it had captivated him. After years of exchanging letters — with Diderot, the epistolary mode had the distinct advantage of allowing the other person to respond without being interrupted — Voltaire had finally witnessed the Encyclopedist's legendary ability to leap from one idea to the next without stopping to take a breath. After Diderot left the quai des Théatins, Voltaire reportedly remarked to some friends that his visitor had lived up to his reputation as a tremendous wit, but that nature had refused him "an essential talent, that of true conversation."[5] Diderot, too, summed up his meeting with the brilliant yet failing Voltaire. He reported that the man was like an ancient "enchanted castle whose various parts are falling apart," but whose corridors were "still inhabited by an old sorcerer."[6]

Diderot's visit with Voltaire was the first and last time that these two figureheads of the Enlightenment era would see each other in person. Not long after his visit, on May 30, the old sorcerer succumbed to his cancer. This turned out to be the first of two significant deaths in 1778. A little more than a month later, on July 2, Jean-Jacques Rousseau would die as well. The story told throughout Paris was that Rousseau had felt ill after taking a morning stroll through the gardens at the château d'Ermenonville, twenty-five miles north of Paris. Upon returning to the cottage where was he staying, he nervously informed his longtime companion, Thérèse Levasseur, that he had a stabbing pain in his chest, a strange tingling sensation on the soles of his feet, and a ferociously throbbing headache. Soon thereafter, the Citizen of Geneva collapsed and died.[7]

Rousseau and Voltaire's deaths signaled the beginning of an era where many more of Diderot's close friends, associates, and enemies would also die. By 1783, all the main players with whom he had worked on the *Encyclopédie* — this included d'Alembert, Jaucourt, and the project's four printers including André François Le Breton — were gone. This ever-expanding necrology also came to include Madame d'Épinay and several of his painter friends as well, among them Jean-Baptiste Chardin and Louis-Michel van Loo. Diderot's generation was disappearing.

WELCOMING THE NOOSE

Repeated bereavements surely contributed to Diderot's decision to live a far simpler life during his last years. While he continued to work on a variety of projects, the philosophe consciously withdrew from the hubbub of Paris society. In addition to retreating

with Toinette to the calm of his friend Étienne Belle's house in
Sèvres, Diderot also spent far more time at his daughter's apart-
ment, not only to see his two grandchildren, but to eat dinner and
supper with the family. Madame de Vandeul's brother-in-law,
who was often at the house, provides us with a few clues about
Diderot's increasingly domestic existence in late 1778: "Monsieur
Diderot comes every day to the house and sups with us. Madame
Diderot remains [at the rue Taranne] and is generally quite ornery.
These days she is quite distressed by the death of her little dog,
who had been blind for three months. Madame Billard [Toinette's
older sister] sat on him by mistake, and broke his back. Since that
moment, Madame Diderot has been berating her constantly."[8]

Diderot, who surely recounted the story of Toinette's little tragedy to his daughter and son-in-law, was indeed paying
more attention to his family. His sole pleasure outside of the rue
Taranne and Angélique's apartment, as he confessed somewhat
misanthropically some months later, was taking a coach to the
Palais Royal every afternoon where he treated himself to a glass
of ice cream at the Petit Caveau. Flavors of the day included fresh
fruit, butter, almond milk, or kirsch.[9]

Diderot's very limited correspondence at this time is dotted
with allusions to both boredom and impending death. The end
of life did not seem to worry him in the least, however. To begin
with, as a disciple of both Montaigne and Seneca, he knew that
the only thing one accomplished by dreading the inevitable was
ruining the present. Yet more than simply accepting Montaigne's
tenet that "to philosophize is to learn how to die," Diderot had
also cultivated a thoughtful atheist understanding of life and
death. In the materialist primer that he worked on well into the
1780s — the *Elements of Physiology* — he summed up what he believed

to be the important things in life: "There is only one virtue, justice; one duty, to make oneself happy; and one corollary, not to exaggerate the importance of one's life and not to fear death."[10]

Diderot often drew comfort from his materialism. In the late 1750s, he once told Sophie that he had fantasized about being buried with her so that that their atoms might seek each other out after death and form a new being. His fiction, too, reflects the intellectual joy he took in thinking about a godless world. In *D'Alembert's Dream*, his own character — "Diderot" — jubilantly force-feeds the core ideas of materialism to a fictional representation of d'Alembert, who later confronts the fact (while dreaming) that he, and the human race in general, are nothing more than cosmic accidents. Even more courageously, in *Rameau's Nephew*, Diderot gave life to a character who cheerily embraces the idea that humans seem, at times, to be little more than pleasure-seeking meat machines.[11]

In contrast to other materialist writers, however, Diderot never forgot the compensatory and often comic aspects of the human condition. While perfectly aware of the threat that materialism presented to *la morale*, he preferred to let the bleakest elements of his philosophy dance joyfully in front of us, much as they did in his own mind. This is also the case in the last of his dialogue-driven experiments in fiction, *Jacques le fataliste*, which he was finishing in the same months that Voltaire and Rousseau both died.[12] It is in this book that Diderot consciously took up the problem of existence in a materialist world.

Unlike *D'Alembert's Dream* and *Rameau's Nephew*, Diderot does not appear as a named character in this nested and digressive tale. Instead, the writer's personality infuses the entire book, especially the "character" of the narrator as he attempts, and perhaps fails, to pull together a hodgepodge of anecdotes related to a man-servant named Jacques and his master. To read the first words of *Jacques the Fatalist* for the first time is to be struck by the stagger-ing modernity of this cheeky storyteller:

> How had they met? By chance, like everybody else. What were
> their names? What's it to you? Where were they coming from?
> From the nearest place. Where were they going? Does anyone
> really know where they're going? What were they saying? The
> Master wasn't saying anything, and Jacques was saying that
> his Captain used to say that everything that happens to us here
> below, for good and for ill, was written up there, on high.[13]

Jacques is the most joyful, lighthearted, and yet perhaps pro-found of Diderot's books. In the hands of Diderot's rascally narra-tor, the contingencies of life and our destiny all seem like fodder for a good laugh. And yet, despite the amusing tenor that defines this novel, the book raises some of the thorniest questions that the writer confronted within his philosophy: in a world that lacks a divine creator, where all beings necessarily obey the same mechanical rules that explain the material world, just what is human reality? And can we really consider ourselves free if what we do and what we think are necessarily preordained by our physiology and our environment?

It is the manservant Jacques who provides the doctrinaire answer to these questions, an answer that he learned from "his Captain" during his career as a soldier. Humans, according to this Spinoza-derived worldview, live out their lives with no free will. Each and every thing we do is ultimately determined by the effect of other preceding causes: we cannot be or think anything other than what is taking place in front of us in the present. To break free from this inescapable chain of events would be impossible; to do so would mean that we were actually *someone else*.[14]

Diderot never wavered from the core tenets of this determinist view of human existence.[15] Yet the haphazard adventures and capricious narration that characterize *Jacques* seemingly work against the so-called fatalism that is at the heart of the book and, perhaps, our lives. As the master and his valet travel throughout France with no real destination in mind, they are never dragged down by Jacques's potentially gloomy, closed shop of a philosophy. Instead, they luxuriate in their curious friendship, revel in the long and frequently interrupted story of Jacques's loves, and are enthralled or exasperated by the bewildering people they meet along the way. What is more, Jacques never bows down before the inevitability of his destiny; his modus operandi is to act and react. In his travels, he confronts dangerous bandits in a tavern, sets off to find his master's watch, scraps with a talkative innkeeper, and arranges for his master to fall off his horse. This is, to say the least, a tongue-in-cheek understanding of fatalism.

There are many messages that one can derive from this jolly and zigzagging story. Perhaps the most critical is that we as a species are far more than automata; we are self-conscious beings who can both manipulate the causes that determine who we are and delight in the complexity of human experience while doing so. Determinism, it would seem, has the space for action, if not total psychological freedom. One of the wonders of this book is that Diderot does not tell us this directly: we absorb this message through the act of reading and laughing, which is part of the philosophical experience.[16]

From the *Encyclopédie* on through to *Jacques the Fatalist*, Diderot entreats us to make the most of what Jacques calls the great scroll of life. This view of our existence certainly includes how we should greet death as well. Like many philosophers, Diderot believed that our final moments on earth define or establish, once and for all, the essence of our character. The most beautiful death, from a philosophical point of view, was of course Socrates' suicide: the moment when the Greek philosopher triumphed over his captors and death by pleasantly greeting his accusers, drinking the hemlock, and dying simply, truthfully, and serenely.[17]

Diderot was so fascinated with this powerful moment in Plato's *Phaedo* that he actually considered adapting it for the stage. While he never got around to writing this play, he nonetheless returned to Socrates' *belle mort* one final time in *Jacques the Fatalist*. In a long speech that seems to arise out of thin air, the master suddenly announces that Jacques is, like Socrates, surely destined to die a philosopher's death. "If it is permitted to read the events of the future from those of the present and if what is written up above is ever revealed to men long before it happens, I predict that...you will stick your head in the noose with as much good grace as Socrates."[18] This was also Diderot's hope in the late 1770s and early 1780s: to die with the same equanimity as the great Greek philosopher.

1784

Sometime in mid-February 1784, Diderot presumably composed the last letter he would write. Scrawled in an unsteady, chicken-scratch hand, this one-paragraph note was destined for Roland Girbal, the copyist who had helped him compile his unpublished manuscripts for years. The tone is prickly: Diderot is clearly a bit annoyed that Girbal had not yet returned one of his plays: "And my comedy, Monsieur Girbal? You promised me that you would give it back to me soon. Keep your word because it is the only one of my manuscripts that I'm missing."[19]

A week or so later, Diderot finally abandoned the task of collating his manuscripts for posterity; it was now time to focus on the unpleasant chore of dying. Being very ill was nothing new of course. As had been the case for years, his intestines continued to send him shuffling off to *la garde-robe*. Far more problematically, his fading, oxygen-starved heart not only triggered frequent and uncomfortable chest pain, but filled his lungs and legs with fluid. This painful dropsy, as edema was called at the time, made it hard to breathe, let alone climb five flights of stairs at the rue Taranne.

Diderot's first real brush with death came on February 19, when a small blood vessel ruptured in one of his lungs. A stroke followed several days later. According to Madame de Vandeul, who happened to be present during this second vascular episode, Diderot quickly diagnosed the malady himself. After tripping over a sentence and realizing that he could not move his hand, he went over to a mirror and calmly put a finger to a part of his mouth that had gone slack. "Apoplexy," he murmured. He then called Toinette and Angélique over to him. After reminding them to return some books that he had borrowed, he kissed them both goodbye, tottered over to his bed, and soon fell into a trancelike state.

Fittingly enough, the impact of this stroke did not affect what was arguably Diderot's defining attribute: his astonishing ability to *talk*. In the three days and nights after the attack, Madame de Vandeul reported that her father entered into a "very sober and rational delirium."[20] Much like the scene that Diderot himself had conjured up in *D'Alembert's Dream*, where a fictional representation of Mademoiselle de l'Espinasse sits at d'Alembert's bedside as he hallucinates, Diderot's own daughter now stood watch over her rambling father as a lifetime of erudition bubbled up from his brain: "He discoursed on Greek and Latin epitaphs and translated them for me, held forth on tragedy, and summoned up beautiful lines from Horace and Virgil and recited them. He talked throughout the entire night; he would ask the time, decide it was time for bed, lie down in his clothes and rise five minutes later. On the fourth day his delirium ceased, and with it all memory of what had taken place."[21]

On February 22, while he was still recovering from his stroke, the greatest love and closest friend that Diderot had had in his life, Sophie Volland, breathed her last. Diderot had not seen her nearly as much as he had in the past, but he nonetheless shed some tears, consoling "himself by the fact that he would not survive her for long."[22]

Word of Diderot's declining health traveled quickly. As letters describing his worsening state began arriving throughout Europe, a deathwatch began. In the Netherlands, the philosopher François Hemsterhuis alerted Diderot's Dutch friends and colleagues that the French philosophe had fallen back into his "second infancy."[23] Meister, in his capacity as the new editor of the Literary Correspondence, announced to a dozen European courts that Diderot was at death's door. Grimm, who had become Catherine the Great's agent in Paris, not only informed the empress of Diderot's ill health, but requested permission to secure better quarters for the ailing philosophe, who was still living at his fifth-floor apartment on the rue Taranne.

Catherine received Grimm's note six weeks after Diderot's stroke. Dismayed to discover that Diderot was living in such unsuitable quarters, she chided Grimm for not acting on his own and instructed him to find a better flat for the philosophe. Five weeks later and 2,500 miles away, Grimm received the empress's note and began seeking out a well-appointed garden-level flat for his friend.[24]

While Catherine and Grimm were corresponding about new lodgings for Diderot, the philosophe himself was undergoing agonizing and intrusive medical treatments. In happier years, Diderot had remarked that "the best doctor is the one you run to, but that you cannot find."[25] Now that he had lived past the time in his life where avoiding the doctor was the best course of action, the medical profession began a series of treatments that Diderot described as the "very nasty things" keeping him alive. Concerned about his water retention, physicians gave him emetics to make him throw up and bled him repeatedly (three times in one day on one occasion).[26] A certain Dr. Malouet gave him herbs and cauterized his arm with a hot poker, a treatment designed to dry the liquid within the body. When his legs also began to swell, Diderot asked the famous Alsatian physician, Georges-Fréderic Bacher, to come to the house. Bacher coordinated a series of different treatments, including his own special pills and the application of "vessicatories" on the back of Diderot's thighs and back. These painful, burn-producing plasters, which were composed of ground blister beetles or Spanish fly, actually provided Diderot with a certain amount of relief. On one occasion, Madame de Vandeul reported, the open wounds produced by this treatment actually rendered a "bucket" of fluid from his legs.[27]

Over the course of the next several months, Diderot's daughter and wife fretted as they watched him decline, knowing full well that his vibrant presence would soon be only a memory. One of their worries was what would happen to the body of this declared atheist once he died. In an era where the Church had an effective monopoly on a proper burial, the Vandeul and Diderot families were only too aware that a majority of Paris ecclesiastics would be delighted to see the philosophe's remains consigned to the *voirie* or garbage dump along with the city's prostitutes and disreputable actors. How the clergy had reacted after Voltaire's death six years earlier was clearly on everybody's mind.

Voltaire had had the misfortune to die in the same reactionary parish where Diderot was now ailing — Saint-Sulpice. Though the famous playwright had actually signed something of a "recanta-tion" of his irreligious behavior shortly after arriving in Paris, the archbishop of Paris ultimately wanted a more concrete proof that Voltaire had accepted the divinity of Jesus Christ. In late May, when word arrived in the parish that the writer was on his death-bed, the archbishop dispatched a doctrinaire curate from Saint-Sulpice, Jean-Joseph Faydit de Terssac, to attempt to extract a fuller revocation from the impenitent philosophe. Despite multi-ple solicitations, Voltaire seems to have held firm; his last words to the priest were reportedly "let me die in peace."[28] This rebuff led the Church to refuse the writer a suitable burial in one of the parish graveyards; some clergy even called for tossing his remains into a mass grave.

As it turned out, Voltaire's larger-than-life reputation prob-ably saved him from this humiliation. Louis XVI, who had care-fully followed the aged writer's apotheosis during his return to Paris, was surely as wary of his corpse as he had been of the liv-ing philosopher. To avoid the martyrdom that would come from any disrespectful handling of the cadaver, a coward's compro-mise was ultimately arranged: namely, allowing the body to leave Paris as if it were still alive. De Terssac provided a letter certifying that the Church had relinquished any "parochial rights" over the affair. The men responsible for Voltaire's remains also received documentation guaranteeing safe passage out of the capital. On May 31, 1778, under cover of night, Voltaire's body was propped up in his carriage as if he were still alive and taken out of Paris. He ultimately received a full Christian burial, two days later, in Romilly-sur-Seine.[29]

Diderot's soon-to-be lifeless body was likely to be in a far more precarious situation. This was already a matter of some speculation eight months before he died. In November 1783, a journalist writing for the *Mémoires secrets* related that the clergy was already sharpening its knives in anticipation of the infamous atheist's death. Since, as the newspaper explained, "this atheist...does not belong to any academy, is not related to any great family, has no imposing public status in his own person, and does not have powerful associates and friends, the clergy plan on avenging themselves upon him and making his cadaver suffer every religious snub unless he satisfies the externals [by recognizing the divinity of Jesus Christ and the Christian God]."[30]

The pious Toinette was torn about what to do about this. While she "would have given her life for [Diderot] to be a believer," she also wanted to prevent her husband from being coerced into accepting Christ in order to ensure himself a decent burial. At some point, she nonetheless decided that giving him the opportunity to return to the Church was worth a try. To this end, either she or perhaps the Vandeuls arranged for the same Saint-Sulpice vicar who had visited Voltaire, Jean-Joseph Faydit de Terssac, to come by the rue Taranne.

Having failed in Voltaire's case, de Terssac was eager to convert the best-known atheist of his generation. According to

Diderot's son-in-law, who was present during some of the meetings, the abbé got on exceedingly well with the affable philosophe. (Diderot was far more tolerant of the clergy than Voltaire.) Madame de Vandeul even reported in her memoirs that Diderot and de Terssac came to an agreement regarding a shared set of moral principles.[31]

Accounts of these promising meetings soon reached Langres, where they generated a certain amount of hope that the godless philosophe might finally recant. By late April, however, de Terssac had gone too far, proposing that Diderot publish a short set of moral *pensées* that would contain a repudiation of his earlier works. According to Madame de Vandeul, Diderot categorically rejected this idea since, as he informed the curate, writing such a retraction "would be an impudent lie."[32]

Shortly after this discussion, and perhaps to escape any more metaphysical pestering from de Terssac (or perhaps even his own brother, who was apparently threatening to come to Paris), Diderot suggested that they leave Paris for Belle's house in Sèvres. Diderot and Toinette ultimately spent two months in the country, during which time the writer's health improved a bit. By mid-July, however, they decided it was time to return to the spacious new quarters that Grimm (and the czarina) had rented for them on the rue de Richelieu.

Diderot's final apartment occupied the entire second floor of a majestic limestone town house that was formerly known as the Hôtel de Bezons. Madame de Vandeul reported that her father was enchanted by the neighborhood and flat. In addition to the fact that he only had to climb one flight of stairs, the apartment had four massive floor-to-ceiling windows that let light cascade into a large reception room. Diderot was charmed. As Madame de Vandeul described it, he had always been lodged in hovels, but now "found himself in a palace."[33]

The greatest advantage of this Right Bank flat was not its light or décor, however; it was the fact that it was situated within a few blocks of the Church of Saint-Roch, a parish with a long tradition of providing a suitable burial for writers and even philosophes: Fontenelle, Maupertuis, and even Helvétius had managed to be buried there. Soon after he arrived on the rue de Richelieu in mid-July, Diderot sensed that he, too, would soon be making the journey to Saint-Roch.

On July 30, he was sitting in the apartment when two workers arrived with a more comfortable bed that had been ordered for the philosophe. Once the workmen had assembled the frame, they politely asked its future occupant where he would like it placed. Diderot, whose morbid sense of humor was apparently still very much intact, reportedly replied, "My friends, you are giving yourself a lot of trouble for a piece of furniture that will only be used for four days."[34] That same night, Madame de Vandeul came by the apartment as she usually did to spend some time with her father, and watched contentedly as he held court with a few friends. Shortly before she left, she heard him paraphrase a famous quote from the *Philosophical Thoughts* that summed up his entire career: "The first step toward philosophy," he apparently said, "is incredulity." These were the last words she heard him say.

The next morning Diderot felt better than he had for months. After spending the morning receiving visits from his doctor, his son-in-law, and d'Holbach, the philosophe sat down with Toinette to his first proper meal in weeks: soup, boiled mutton, and some chicory. Having eaten well, Diderot then looked at Toinette and asked her to pass him an apricot.[35] Fearing that he had already eaten too much, she tried to dissuade him from continuing the meal. Diderot reportedly replied wistfully: "What the devil type of harm can it do to me now?"[36] Popping some of the forbidden fruit in his mouth, he then rested his head on his hand, reached out for some more stewed cherries, and died. While having anything but a heroic death à la Socrates, Diderot had nonetheless expired in a way that was perfectly compatible with his philosophy: without a priest, with humor, and while attempting to eke out one last bit of pleasure from life.

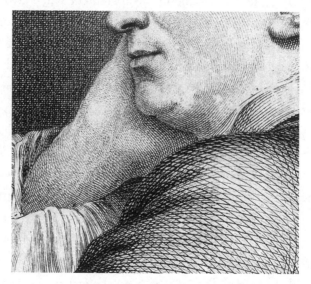

ENGRAVING OF DIDEROT AFTER GARAND (DETAIL)

The thirty-six hours after Diderot died were filled with preparations, prayers, and official visits. Upon receiving word that the ailing writer was no longer among the living, Saint-Roch's parish priest dispatched a vicar to sit and pray with the body at the apartment. Diderot's cantankerous old artist friend,

Jean-Baptiste Greuze, also came by to sketch a memento mori of the departed philosopher, who was now lying in state. Greuze's portrait of Diderot in death is crowlike and drawn, his nose even more prominent in death than it was in life.

DEATH PORTRAIT OF DENIS DIDEROT,
DRAWING BY JEAN-BAPTISTE GREUZE

At some point after the painter had left, an autopsy was also performed on Diderot's cadaver, something that the patient had insisted upon before he died. This dissection, according to Madame de Vandeul, generated a ghastly report summing up the various corporeal failings that had plagued her father: though his brain supposedly remained as "perfect and well conserved as that of a man of twenty…one of his lungs was filled with fluid, his heart was terribly enlarged, and his gallbladder was entirely dry, without any bile despite containing twenty-one stones, the smallest as big as a hazelnut.[37]

Diderot's burial took place on Sunday, August 1. Shortly before seven in the evening, Toinette, Madame de Vandeul, Abel-

François-Nicolas Caroillon de Vandeul and several other Caroillon family members descended the stairs of the apartment alongside the body of Denis Diderot. From there, the funeral cortege, which included fifty priests that the now very prosperous Vandeuls had hired, moved south on the rue de Richelieu toward rue Saint-Honoré and the Church of Saint-Roch. After the funeral mass, Denis Diderot's lead coffin was lowered into the large central crypt under the church's Chapelle de la Vierge. It was at this point that the long story of Diderot's afterlife really began.

THE AFTERLIFE

In the months before he died, Diderot had prepared for what he hoped would be a postmortem afterglow. Writing for future generations, as he had revealed in the *Encyclopédie* article "Immortality," had been the single biggest motivating factor in his highly policed and self-censored career: "We hear in ourselves the tribute that [posterity] will one day offer in our honor, and we sacrifice ourselves. We sacrifice our life, we really cease to exist in order to live on in their memory."[38]

Diderot was far from the only writer to chase the fame that comes after death. He is, however, perhaps the only one who speaks from the grave, pleading with us to pay attention to his work: "O holy and sacred Posterity! Ally of the unhappy and oppressed; you who are fair, you who are righteous, you who avenge the honest man, who unmask the hypocrite, and who punish the tyrant; may your comfort and your steadfastness never forsake me!"[39]

As it turned out, posterity did not discard Diderot in the years right after his death. His naturalistic and sentimental play,

The Father of the Family, continued to enjoy a strong resurgence on stages throughout France well into the 1790s. New and pirated editions of the *Encyclopédie* also continued to circulate throughout Europe at the same time that the editors of the new *Encyclopédie méthodique* were warmly crediting him for inspiring them to undertake their own massive inventory of human knowledge. And yet something dramatic would also happen to Diderot's legacy after the French Revolution broke out in 1789; five years after this champion of human rights and freedom had died, he was increasingly being lambasted as an enemy of the people.

PORTRAIT OF A MAN WITH A BUST OF DENIS DIDEROT,
PAINTING BY JEAN-SIMON BERTHÉLEMY

Why Revolutionaries would consider the most progressive thinker of the Enlightenment at odds with their liberal values may not seem immediately obvious to us.[40] And yet the politically astute leaders of the Revolution realized that there was no better way of dooming the movement than by letting it be contaminated by the atheism that Diderot represented. To do so would deprive the French citizenry not only of a God, but the comforting prospect of some form of afterlife. Bearing this in mind, most Revolutionary era leaders, regardless of their own beliefs, turned away from godlessness while simultaneously barring Diderot from their pantheon of intellectual heroes. Maximilien Robespierre, who was both a deist and a disciple of Rousseau, articulated Diderot's sins far more succinctly. Since, from his point of view, the Revolution required a Supreme Being both to guarantee transcendence for its citizens and to justify the terror needed to purify the body politic, Diderot and the Encyclopedists were necessarily de facto counterrevolutionaries: they were corrupt, immoral, and contaminated as much by their ideas as by their proximity to the aristocracy.[41]

Diderot's reputation did not fare much better after the Revolution turned on Robespierre in 1794. A year after the Jacobin politician was guillotined on the place de la Révolution, a former philosophe and acquaintance of Diderot's named Jean-François La Harpe published a well-received book that held the departed writer responsible for the worst crimes of the Terror. This was, of course, terribly ironic. Having been castigated for his supposed royalist and aristocratic tendencies by Robespierre only months before, Diderot was now being associated with the execution of 17,000 French citizens, including hundreds of priests and nuns. That Diderot had somehow helped precipitate these heinous acts was seemingly confirmed two years later when his poem "Les éleuthéromanes" ("The Maniacs for Liberty") appeared in print for the first time. Within this ceremonious Pindaric ode was a verse that soon became synonymous with the writer's supposedly murderous politics: "And with the guts of the last priest let us wring the neck of the last king."

Diderot had composed "Les éleuthéromanes" as flippant entertainment for a small audience, and had never circulated the poem before the Revolution.[42] Yet its appearance in two major journals in 1796—the same year *The Nun* and *Jacques the Fatalist* were published—cemented his reputation as the most godless and extreme of the philosophes.[43] This turned out to be quite a dubious accomplishment: Diderot had not only been crowned the "Prince of the Atheists," but was now being seen as a bloodthirsty ideologue hell-bent on the destruction of "all virtues and their principles."[44]

Over the course of the next 130 years, the avant-garde and France's traditionalists tussled over Diderot's reputation. For the first eighty or so years after his death, conservative writers, monarchists, and the clergy had the upper hand in this quarrel. During the decades that France lurched from the Directory to Napoleon's empire, back to monarchy, to constitutional monarchy, to republic, and then from yet another empire to yet another republic, traditionalists effectively portrayed Diderot as a godless radical, a sex fiend, a peddler of smut, and one of the causes of the nineteenth century's unbridled secularism, individualism, and moral decline.

Diderot's rehabilitation with the general population began in earnest in the final quarter of the nineteenth century when the Third Republic's radicals, Freemasons, positivists, and scientists began publicly correcting so-called misconceptions regarding the writer's career. This was an audacious effort. In lieu of shying away from the writer's atheism and materialism, liberally minded thinkers now praised Diderot as something of a persecuted Galileo who had had the courage to storm the "intellectual Bastille" that had propped up the Church and the ancien régime. In stark contrast to the unsavory image of the writer that the right had been describing, his apologists now cast him as positivism's predecessor: a torchbearer who had had the courage to lead his country away from the haven of piety and "to reorganize the world without God or a king."[45]

DIDEROT AND HIS THIRTEEN MISTRESSES,
FRONTISPIECE FROM A PUBLISHED SCREED
AGAINST DIDEROT, 1884

By July 1884, exactly a century after Diderot had reached for his final piece of stewed fruit on the rue de Richelieu, posterity had seemingly understood the writer. Celebrations in his honor took place in various cities across France, including Langres, Moulins, and Nîmes. His adopted city of Paris, which had already named one of Haussmann's new avenues the "boulevard Diderot" in 1879, organized several events as well.[46]

THE SALLE DES FÊTES AT THE TROCADÉRO PALACE, PARIS,
WHERE CEREMONIES HONORED DIDEROT IN 1884

On Sunday, July 27, 1884, over three thousand people squeezed into the Trocadéro Palace's Salle des Fêtes to listen to the philosopher and positivist Pierre Laffitte describe Diderot as one of the most wide-ranging "geniuses to have ever lived."[47] Later that same day, a thousand Freemasons and their families also gathered in the eastern portion of the capital for a banquet and ball to honor the

godless philosophe. These ceremonies were a prelude to a more concrete tribute to Diderot on the following Wednesday: the inaugu-
ration of a statue at the intersection of the relatively new boulevard
Saint-Germain and the rue de Rennes, only steps away from where
the philosophe had spent thirty years of his life on the rue Taranne.[48]

GAUTHERIN'S STATUE OF DIDEROT
ON THE BOULEVARD SAINT-GERMAIN IN PARIS

The artwork's creator, Jean Gautherin, portrayed the writer
as a brawny, combative, and long-boned man whose muscles
bulge from his waistcoat and stockings. Diderot leans forward,
plume in hand, head cocked probingly to the left, a vision of the

freethinker and writer who dared defy censors, Versailles, and the Church.[49] In the days after the dedication of this statue, one liberal journalist mused,

> Of all the eighteenth-century philosophes, the most in vogue is now Diderot, without a doubt. Rousseau is falling, because he is sentimental and a deist. Even Voltaire has fallen because, despite his war against *l'infâme*, he was sometimes wrong to believe in God...Voltaire was a man who dared rip out the guts of the last priest, but he would not have used them to strangle the last king. Only Diderot, after a bit of hesitation, and a few distractions without consequence, showed himself to be as much a democrat as he was an atheist.[50]

Catholic newspapermen did not miss out on the significance of this politically motivated public artwork either. It was hard to miss that this latest example of republican *statuemania* had been positioned in such a way that Diderot appeared to be looking out distrustfully at the spire of the neighboring Church of Saint-Germain-des-Prés, like a "secular sentinel."[51]

Neither Diderot's detractors nor his disciples were wrong to emphasize the author's career-long campaign against God. And yet, today, incredulity is far from the most compelling aspect of his writing. What really distinguishes him from his peers is what he accomplished *after* doing away with the deity. Although Diderot is undoubtedly the steward of the age of the *Encyclopédie*, he is also, paradoxically, the only major thinker of his generation who questioned the rational perspective that is at the heart of the Enlightenment project.

Writing in an era of powerful systems and systemization, Diderot's private thinking opened philosophy up to the irrational, the marginal, the monstrous, the sexually deviant, and other non-conformist points of view.[52] His most important legacy is arguably this cacophony of individual voices and ideas.[53] Readers today continue to be amazed by his willingness to give a platform to the unthinkable and the uncomfortable, and to question all received authorities and standard practices — be they religious, political, or societal. As philosophers go, Diderot is neither a Socrates nor a Descartes, nor did he ever claim to be.[54] Yet his joyful and dogged quest for truth makes him the most compelling eighteenth-century advocate of the art of thinking freely.

Acknowledgments

Writing a book about a genius—when you are not one—is a daunting process. In order to attempt to do justice to a mind like Diderot's, I have shamelessly called upon the expertise of numerous friends and colleagues. Among those who engaged most deeply with the project, I would first like to thank Patrick Graille, with whom I have collaborated fruitfully for twenty years on virtually everything I have ever written. Other generous friends who spent a lot of time helping me think through the book include Sophie Audidière, Catherine Chiabaut, John Eigenauer, Marie Leca-Tsiomis, Alex Lee, David Mayo, Anne and Walter Mayo, Kelsey Rubin-Detlev, and Caroline Warman. I would also like to thank the attentive team at Other Press who engaged with the manuscript, particularly Yvonne Cárdenas, Julie Fry, Alexandra Poreda, and Walter Havighurst. Finally, I would like to thank my editor, friend, and mentor at the press, Judith Gurewich, who proposed that I write this book in the first place. This book would not be the same without her.

I am also indebted to a whole group of other friends and colleagues. Some read portions of the manuscript or talked to me about what they expected from the genre of biography; still others suggested how I might structure such a curious and full life. Bearing these many and varied contributions in mind, I would like to recognize Nadja Aksamija, Steve Angle, Marco Aresu, Amy Bloom, Emmanuel Boussuge, Jeffrey Burson, Andrew Clark, Lisa Cohen, Nicholas Cronk, Carolyn Curran, Claire Curran, Clayton Curran, Michel Delon, Jane Dieckmann, Colas Duflo, Anne Duthoit, Dan Edelstein, Deren Ertas, Pierre Franz, Alden Gordon, Violette Graille, Arthur Halliday, Paul Halliday, Thierry Hoquet, Joyce Jacobsen, Katherine Kuenzli, Stéphane Lojkine, Christine Lalande, Michael Maglaras, John C. O'Neal, Murielle Perrier, Michael Roth, J. B. Shank, Courtney Weiss Smith, Victoria Smolkin, Joanna Stalnaker, Gerhardt Stenger, Suzy Taraba, Terry Templeton, Sawyer Tennant, Helen Thomson, Cassie and Jean-Baptiste Toulouse, Kari Weil, and Stephanie Weiner. Many more of my colleagues in the Department of Romance Languages and Literatures have also been wonderful interlocutors during this process.

Over the four years that I wrote this book, I have also met (and talked on the phone) with dozens of kind and patient archivists, librarians, and curators. Although there are too many people to thank individually here, I would notheless like to express my gratitude to colleagues at the Musées d'art et d'histoire, Geneva; the Bibliothèque de l'Assemblée nationale; the Bibliothèque nationale de France; Brown University Libraries; the Musée Carnavalet; the Musée Condé; the Musée Girodet; the Metropolitan Museum of Art; the McCain Library and Archives at the University of Southern Mississippi; Princeton University Libraries; the Musée Jean-Jacques Rousseau, Montmorency; Wesleyan University Special Collections and Archives; the Walters Art Museum in Baltimore; the Wellcome Library; Williams College Libraries;

and Yale University Libraries (particularly the Beinecke Rare Book and Manuscript Library).

I must also thank the people of Langres. One of the most rewarding aspects of writing this book was getting to know the city of Diderot's birth, along with the people who, among their many other tasks, are charged with preserving the writer's legacy. I would like, first, to express my gratitude to David Covelli (Langres's *Responsable du Service Patrimoine*) for his intellectual generosity, logistical support, private tours, and especially helping me locate key images for the book. I also want to thank the great historian of Langres, Georges Viard, for making time to meet with me. And finally, I am indebted to Olivier Caumont, director of Langres's Museum of the Enlightenment, for providing numerous illustrations (and great conversation related to Diderot). Other kind Langrois include Jean-François Feurtriez of the Tourist Bureau and Yves Chevalier, the bighearted owner of the Hôtel du Cheval Blanc and the excellent Restaurant Diderot.

Projects like these, which require substantial travel, are really not possible without institutional or foundation support. I have been lucky to have had both. Initial research was made possible by a semester-long National Endowment for the Humanities Public Scholars grant. Later stages of the book were made possible by Wesleyan University, which not only granted me a year-long sabbatical, but summer travel funds.

Lastly, I want to thank my wife Jennifer for her patience, terrific sense of humor, and the brilliant insight she brought to this project.

Chronology

1677
Angélique Vigneron (d. 1748), the mother of Denis Diderot, is born.

1685
Didier Diderot (d. 1759), master cutler and the father of Denis Diderot, is born.

1694
Voltaire (d. 1778) is born in Paris.

1710
Anne-Antoinette Champion (d. 1796), the future wife of Denis Diderot, is born in La Ferté-Bernard.

1712
Jean-Jacques Rousseau (d. 1778) is born in Geneva.

1713
Denis Diderot is born in Langres on the place Chambeau. The same year, his family moves from number 6 to number 9 place Chambeau.

1715
Denise Diderot (d. 1797) is born. She is more like her older brother than her two younger siblings, but is nonetheless quite pious.

1715

Jean le Rond d'Alembert (d. 1783) is born and abandoned on the steps of a small church on the Île de la Cité. He is adopted and raised by a woman named Madame Rousseau. His education is nonetheless paid for, presumably by his biological father.

1716

Louise-Henriette Volland, known as Sophie, is born. She dies on February 22, 1784, five months before her former lover, Denis Diderot.

1720

Angélique Diderot is born and named after her mother. Very religious, she joins the Ursuline convent, where she dies c. 1748, within months of the death of her mother.

1722

Didier-Pierre Diderot (d. 1787) is born. He will go on to join the priesthood and become an archdeacon at the Saint-Mammès cathedral.

1723

The future courtier and editor of the *Literary Correspondence*, Friedrich Melchior Grimm (d. 1807), is born in Regensburg. By the early 1750s, Grimm replaces Rousseau as Diderot's most intimate friend.

1723–28

After learning to read and write Latin and French, Diderot is admitted to (and attends) the collège Jésuite de Langres.

1726

Diderot's future wife, the sixteen-year-old Anne-Antoinette Champion, leaves the Miramiones Convent and moves in with her mother. She works as a laundress and seamstress.

In March, Louise Florence Pétronille Tardieu d'Esclavelles Épinay, or Madame d'Épinay (d. 1783), is born.

c. 1728–32
After arriving in Paris at age fifteen, Diderot attends the collège d'Harcourt.

1732–35
Diderot attends the Sorbonne, the university's faculty of theology. By 1735, he has completed two years of philosophy and three years of theology, far more than most of the philosophes. He leaves the Sorbonne in 1735.

c. 1735–40
Diderot's so-called dilettante years, during which he works at a variety of odd jobs, but also learns Italian and English, the latter enabling him to become a translator.

1737
The future militant atheist, Jacques-André Naigeon (d. 1810), is born. He will go on to become Diderot's literary executor.

c. 1740
Diderot begins a very modest publishing career.

1741
Diderot meets Anne-Antoinette Champion on the rue de la Boutebrie. She is thirty-one-years old.

c. 1741–42
Diderot works in a solicitor's office.

1742
Diderot translates Temple Stanyon's *The Grecian History*. Sometime in the fall, he meets Jean-Jacques Rousseau.

1742–43

Diderot travels to Langres to ask permission to marry "Toinette." His parents reject this idea and ultimately lock their rebellious son up in the Carmelite monastery.

1743

Diderot and Anne-Antoinette Champion are married in the Church of Saint-Pierre-aux-Bœufs on the Île de la Cité.

1745

Diderot translates Shaftesbury's *An Inquiry Concerning Virtue and Merit* (*Essai sur le mérite et la vertu*).

1746

Diderot's first real work of freethinking, *Pensées philosophiques* (*Philosophical Thoughts*), appears.

c. 1746

Diderot writes *La promenade du sceptique* (*The Skeptic's Walk*), published in 1830.

1747

Diderot and d'Alembert are named the coeditors of the *Encyclopédie*. Diderot also writes on mathematics.

1748

Angélique Diderot, the writer's mother, dies.

Diderot's salacious novel *Les bijoux indiscrets* (*Indiscreet Jewels*) is published. Although he later adds some somewhat pornographic chapters in 1770, he claims to regret publishing this his entire life. The same year, his translation of James's *Medicinal Dictionary* appears.

1749

The *Lettre sur les aveugles* (*Letter on the Blind*) appears. In July, Diderot is arrested and taken to Vincennes prison, where he remains until November.

1750

The *Encyclopédie*'s "Prospectus" is published.

1751

Volume 1 of the *Encyclopédie*, containing "Preliminary Discourse" and a new version of the "System of Human Knowledge," is published.

1752

Volume 2 of the *Encyclopédie* is published.

First interdiction of the *Encyclopédie* in February. An agreement brokered at Versailles allows the project to resume in May.

1753

Volume 3 of the *Encyclopédie* is published.

Marie-Angélique Diderot, the future Madame de Vandeul (d. 1824), is born. During this same year, Grimm begins distributing his cultural newsletter, the *Correspondance littéraire* (*Literary Correspondence*).

1754

Volumes 1, 2, and 3 of the *Encyclopédie* are reprinted for a larger subscription base. Volume 4 appears in October.

De l'inteprétation de la nature (*Pensées sur l'interprétation de la nature* / *On the Interpretation of Nature*) is published.

c. 1755

Volume 5 of the *Encyclopédie* is published.

Diderot meets Louise-Henriette Volland—Sophie—the woman who would arguably become the most important person in his life.

1756

Volume 6 of the *Encyclopédie* is published.

Diderot publishes *Le fils naturel* (*The Natural Son*). The play is accompanied by a theoretical meditation on the genre, the *Entretiens sur le fils naturel* (*Conversations on the Natural Son*).

1757

Volume 7 of the *Encyclopédie* is published.

Robert-François Damiens attempts to kill or perhaps injure Louis XV at Versailles by stabbing him with a knife.

1758

Helvétius's *De l'esprit* (*On the Mind*) creates further problems for the *Encyclopédie*. Diderot's play *Le père de famille* (*The Father of the Family*) also appears along with *Sur la poésie dramatique* (*On Dramatic Poetry*).

Diderot and Rousseau become mortal enemies.

1759

In March, the *Encyclopédie* loses its privilege for a second time. In June, Didier Diderot dies. In September, a new privilege is issued for the plates volumes, which gives cover to Diderot and a much smaller group of contributors. Late that year, Diderot also writes his first Salon review for Grimm's *Literary Correspondence*. He will go on to provide reviews for eight more Salons, his last in 1781.

c. 1760

Diderot begins *La religieuse* (*The Nun*). He will finish this as an old man. It is one of the first of his "lost" works to appear in print in 1796. In May, Charles Palissot's satirical play, *Les philosophes*, is staged at the Comédie-Française.

c. 1761

Diderot begins writing *Le neveu de Rameau* (*Rameau's Nephew*), presumably to ridicule the scoundrels who are satirizing him, including Palissot. Over

the course of the next two decades, this dialogue becomes his masterpiece. The final, complete version of this text is published 130 years later.

1761

Writes *Éloge de Richardson* (*Praise of Richardson*) and his second Salon review.

1762

Plates volume 1 of the *Encyclopédie* is published.

1763

Plates volumes 2 and 3 (referred to as the second installment) are
published.
Writes the third Salon review.

1764

Discovery that Le Breton has censored articles in the *Encyclopédie*.

1765

Volumes 8–17 of the *Encyclopédie* are published. During the interdiction,
the remaining volumes are presumably printed in Trévoux.
Plates volume 4 is published.
Diderot begins one of his most famous Salon reviews, for the Salon of 1765,
as well as his *Notes on Painting*. In the spring of that same year, Diderot sells
his library to Catherine II for 15,000 livres, plus a yearly stipend of one
thousand livres. A year later, after someone neglected to pay this stipend,
Catherine pays him fifty years in advance.

1766

Early in the year, the final ten volumes of the *Encyclopédie* are distributed.

1767

Plates volume 5 of the *Encyclopédie* is published.
Writes his review of the Salon of 1767.

1768

Plates volume 6 is published.

1769

Plates volume 7 is published.

Diderot begins the three-part text of what will later be known as *D'Alembert's Dream*. This is finally published in 1830. He also writes the review of the Salon of 1769 and a short essay, "Regrets sur ma vieille robe de chambre" ("Regrets over My Old Dressing Gown").

c. 1770

Diderot begins writing *Jacques le fataliste*. He will work on it throughout the 1770s. It appears in the *Literary Correspondence* in 1778. He begins an affair with Jeanne-Catherine de Maux, the eye-catching wife of a Paris lawyer. Travel to Langres and Bourbonne.

1771

Plates volumes 8 and 9 of the *Encyclopédie* are published.

On behalf of Catherine II, Diderot helps negotiate the purchase of an enormous collection of art belonging to the late Louis-Antoine Crozat, the baron of Thiers, who had died in December 1770. This collection will become one of the foundations of the Hermitage Museum. Writes review of the Salon of 1771.

1772

Plates volumes 10 and 11 of the *Encyclopédie* are published

As part of a threesome of three short works, Diderot writes his *Supplément au voyage de Bougainville* (*Supplement to Bougainville's Voyage*). In March, Diderot pens his "Les éleuthéromanes" ("The Maniacs for Liberty"), a Pindaric ode. In August, the final volume of plates appears. In September, Angélique Diderot marries Abel François Nicolas Caroillon de Vandeul at Saint-Sulpice. Throughout this same year, Diderot is ghostwriting significant portions of the second edition of the abbé Raynal's *Histoire philosophique et politique des deux Indes* (*Philosophical and Political History of the Two Indies*).

1773

Diderot leaves for Saint Petersburg in June, but spends two months in The Hague en route. Arriving in the Russian capital in October, he reads his so-called *Mémoires pour Catherine II* to the empress, short essays on a variety of subjects.

1774

On his return trip from Russia, Diderot dashes off his *Principes de politique des souverains* (*Political Principles of Sovereigns*), a satirical guidebook for autocrats. In May, the young Louis XVI, grandson of Louis XV, becomes king of France. At some point that same year, Diderot also finishes his *Observations sur le "Nakaz,"* a pointed critique of Catherine II's best-selling book of legal and political philosophy.

1775

He writes *Plan d'une université pour le gouvernement de Russie* (*Plan of a University for the Government of Russia*).

c. 1775

Diderot writes *Est-il bon? Est-il méchant?* (*Is He Good? Is He Wicked?*). Composes his review of the Salon of 1775.

1777

Contemplates complete edition of his works.

1778

Diderot publishes his *Essai sur Sénèque* (*Essay on the Life of Seneca*). During the spring, Diderot pays a visit to Voltaire not long before the elder philosophe dies. Rousseau dies in July. Throughout this time, Diderot continues to work on the third edition of Raynal's *History of the Two Indies*.

1780

Third and final version of the *History of the Two Indies*. Diderot's *Father of the Family* continues to be played throughout Europe, and at the Comédie-Française. It is Diderot's most successful stand-alone literary work during his lifetime.

1781

Diderot writes his last Salon review.

1782

Diderot publishes his *Essai sur les règnes de Claude et de Néron* (*Essay on the Reigns of Claudius and Nero*), a revised and expanded edition of his *Essai sur Sénèque*.

c. 1782

Diderot ends work on his fragmentary *Éléments de physiologie* (*Elements of Physiology*), a primer of materialism. He also completes final versions of *Est-il bon? Est-il méchant?* (*Is He Good? Is He Wicked?*), *Jacques the Fatalist*, *Rameau's Nephew*, and *D'Alembert's Dream*.

1783–84

Diderot's health declines. In February 1784, he has something of a stroke. Sophie Volland dies almost at the same time.

1784

Diderot dies on July 31 1784, at 39 rue de Richelieu, in an apartment that Catherine II rented for him.

NOTE: This timeline has benefited significantly from Raymond Trousson's *Diderot jour après jour: Chronologie* (Paris: Honoré Champion, 2006).

Cast of Characters

VOLTAIRE

(1694–1778)

JEAN-JACQUES ROUSSEAU

(1712–1778)

JEAN LE ROND
D'ALEMBERT

(1715–1783)

FRIEDRICH
MELCHIOR GRIMM

(1723–1807)

DIDIER DIDEROT

(1685–1759)

LOUIS DE JAUCOURT

(1704–1779)

MADAME D'ÉPINAY

(1726–1783)

CATHERINE THE GREAT

(1729–1796)

GUILLAUME-THOMAS
(ABBÉ) RAYNAL
(1713–1796)

PAUL-HENRI THIRY,
BARON D'HOLBACH
(1723–1789)

LOUIS XV
(1715–1774)

LOUIS XVI
(1754–1793)

JEANNE ANTOINETTE
POISSON, MARQUISE
DE POMPADOUR
(1721–1764)

MARIE-ANGÉLIQUE
CAROILLON DE VANDEUL
(1753–1824)

NICOLAS-RENÉ BERRYER, LIEU-
TENANT-GÉNÉRAL
DE POLICE
(1703–1762)

GUILLAUME-CHRÉTIEN
DE LAMOIGNON
DE MALESHERBES
(1721–1794)

Not pictured

ANNE-ANTOINETTE CHAMPION

(1710 – 1796)

LOUIS-HENRIETTE (SOPHIE) VOLLAND

(1716 – 1784)

DIDIER-PIERRE DIDEROT

(1722 – 1787)

Notes

In the notes below, frequently cited works have been identified by the following abbreviations:

Corr. *Denis Diderot, Correspondance.* Edited by Georges Roth and Jean Varloot. Paris: Les Éditions de Minuit, 1955–1970.

DPV Denis Diderot, *Œuvres complètes.* Paris: Hermann, 1975–. The initials refer to the three original editors, Herman Dieckmann, Jacques Proust, and Jean Varloot.

Enc. *Encyclopédie, ou, dictionnaire raisonné des sciences, des arts, et des métiers.* Edited by Diderot and d'Alembert. Paris, 1751–72.

HDI Guillaume Thomas Raynal. *Histoire philosophique et politique des établissements et du commerce des Européens dans les deux Indes.* Commonly abbreviated as *Histoire des deux Indes.* 4 vols., Amsterdam, 1770. 8 vols., The Hague, 1774. 10 vols., Geneva, 1780.

RDE *Recherches sur Diderot et sur l'Encyclopédie.* Multiple publishers.

Bearing in mind that this book was written for an Anglo-phone audience, I have often cited English-language editions of Diderot's works so as to encourage the public to read him in translation. Unless otherwise noted, all translations of French editions are my own. I have also modernized French and English in both text and notes, although actual titles have been given in their original forms.

PROLOGUE:

UNBURYING DIDEROT

1. Dominique Lecourt, *Diderot: passions, sexe, raison* (Paris: Presses Universitaires de France, 2013), 96.

2. Denis Diderot, *Rameau's Nephew. Le Neveu de Rameau: A Multi-Media Bilingual Edition*, ed. Marian Hobson, trans. Kate E. Tunstall and Caroline Warman (Cambridge, UK: Open Book Publishers, 2016), 32.

3. *Corr.*, 6:67.

4. The idea is projected onto his own character in *Rameau's Nephew*. See DPV, 4:74.

5. "Mort de M. Diderot," *Année Littéraire* 6 (1784): 282.

6. Jacques-Henri Meister, "Aux Mânes de Diderot," in *Œuvres Complètes de Diderot*, ed. Jules Assézat and Maurice Tourneux (Paris: Garnier Frères, 1875), xii–xix.

7. This pithy citation appears with no proof of its authenticity in Hippolyte Taine, *Les origines de la France contemporaine* (Paris: Hachette, 1887), 348.

8. See Martin Turnell, *The Rise of the French Novel* (New York: New Directions, 1978), 20–21.

9. Karl Marx, *The Portable Karl Marx*, trans. Eugene Kamenka (New York: Penguin, 1983), 53.

10. Christopher Cordess, "Criminality and Psychoanalysis," in *The Freud Encyclopedia: Theory, Therapy, and Culture*, ed. Edward Erwin (London: Routledge, 2002), 113.

11. An insightful remark made to me by Catherine Chiabaut.

12. DPV, 10:422. Diderot is here speaking about himself in the third person.

13. *Enc.*, 5:270.

14. Madame (Anne-Louise-Germaine) de Staël, *De L'Allemagne* (Paris: Firmin, 1845), 128.

15. Jean-Jacques Rousseau, *Œuvres complètes* (Paris: Gallimard, 1959), 1:1115.

16. Friedrich Melchior Grimm, Denis Diderot, Jacques-Henri Meister, Maurice Tourneux, and Abbé Raynal, *Correspondance littéraire, philosophique, et critique par Grimm, Diderot, Raynal, Meister, etc.* (Paris: Garnier Frères, 1878), 5:395.

17. Meister, "Aux Mânes de Diderot," 18–19.

18. See Maurice Tourneux, *Diderot et Catherine II* (Paris: Calmann Lévy, 1899), 76, for the origin of this apocryphal story.

19. Diderot, *Essais sur la peinture: Salons de 1759, 1761, 1763* (Paris: Hermann, 1984), 194.

20. Jeanette Geffriaud Rosso, *Diderot et le portrait* (Pise: Editrice Libreria Goliardica, 1998), 14.

21. Ibid., 20.

22. See Kate Tunstall, "Paradoxe sur le portrait: autoportrait de Diderot en Montaigne," *Diderot Studies* 30 (2007): 195–207, for a complete survey of Diderot's meditations on his portraits.

23. Diderot, *Diderot on Art II: The Salon of 1767*, ed. John Goodman (New Haven: Yale University Press, 1995), 2:20.

24. *Corr.*, 2:207.

25. The standard English biography of Diderot's life remains Arthur McCandless Wilson's exhaustive chronicle of the philosophe's life, his *Diderot* (New York: Oxford University Press, 1957). P. N. Furbank, who is far more critical about Diderot's life and actions, provided a second biography in the 1990s: *Diderot* (New York: Knopf, 1992). There are a number of French

biographies as well, many of which celebrate the radical, atheistic precursor and advocate of the secular French state. The most recent is by Gerhardt Stenger, *Diderot: le combattant de la liberté* (Lonrai, France: Perrin, 2013).

I.

THE ABBOT FROM LANGRES

1. Georges Viard, *Langres au XVIIIe siècle: tradition et Lumières au pays de Diderot* (Langres: Dominique Guénot, 1985), 53.

2. "Célébration du centenaire de Diderot," *La Revue occidentale philosophique, sociale et politique* 4 (1884): 263.

3. "Faits Divers," *Courrier de l'Art* 32 (1884): 383.

4. Francisco Lafarga, *Diderot* (Barcelona: University of Barcelona Publications, 1987), 66. The municipal council even received money from Czar Nicholas II of Russia in memory of Catherine II to help finance the event.

5. Viard, *Langres au XVIIIe siècle*, 12–13.

6. Madame de Vandeul, *Diderot, mon père* (Strasbourg: Circe, 1992), 7.

7. Ibid., 11.

8. Antoine-Augustin Bruzen de la Martinière, *Le Grand Dictionnaire géographique et critique* (Venice: Jean-Baptiste Pasquali, 1737), 6:44.

9. According to contemporary estimates, the Saint-Mammès Cathedral's lands, rents, and various enterprises generated annual revenues of approximately 100,000 livres in 1728. Of this sum, the duke-bishop of Langres, Pierre de Pardaillan de Gondrin, received the colossal salary of approximately 22,000 livres. This income reached 58,000 livres by the time of the Revolution. Other well-compensated ecclesiastics included the cathedral's treasurer, who received 10,000 livres a year. See Robert de Hesseln, *Dictionnaire universel de la France* (Paris: chez Desaint, 1771), 3:515.

10. John McManners, *Church and Society in Eighteenth-Century France*, vol. 2: *The Religion of the People and the Politics of Religion* (London: Oxford University Press, 1999), 2:8.

11. Ibid., 2:246.

12. In their first "mission statement," issued in the mid-sixteenth century, the Jesuits declared the primary objective of a Jesuit education to be the "progress of souls in Christian life and doctrine, and the propagation of the faith." John O'Malley, Introduction, *The Jesuits II: Cultures, Sciences and the Arts, 1540–1773* (Buffalo: University of Toronto Press, 2006), xxiv.

13. Bernard Picart, *Cérémonies et coutumes religieuses de tous les peuples du monde...* (Amsterdam: chez J. F. Bernard, 1723), 2:125, 2:127.

14. Abbé Charles Roussel, *Le Diocèse de Langres: histoire et statistique* (Langres: Librairie de Jules Dallet, 1879), 4:114.

15. Albert Collignon, *Diderot: sa vie, ses œuvres, sa correspondance* (Paris: Felix Alcan Éditeur, 1895), 8.

16. Vandeul, *Diderot, mon père*, 8.

17. Could it be that the young abbot and his father chose this Jansenist-leaning school because of an affinity? See Blake T. Hanna, "Denis Diderot: Formation traditionnelle et moderne," *RDE* 5, no. 1 (1988): 3–18.

18. Ibid., 382.

19. Henri Louis Alfred Bouquet, *L'Ancien collège d'Harcourt et le lycée Saint-Louis* (Paris: Delalain frères, 1891), 370.

20. *Enc.*, 8:516.

21. A. M. Wilson, *Diderot* (New York: Oxford University Press, 1957), 26–27. Wilson also posits that Diderot may have switched between the Jansenist collège d'Harcourt and the Jesuit Louis-le-Grand, another collège; this might explain certain acquaintances made during his life, as well as his knowledge of both Jansenist and Jesuit teachings. However, most sources seem to pass over the possibility of a switch. See also Gerhardt Stenger, *Diderot: le combattant de la liberté* (Lonrai, France: Perrin, 2013), 43–46.

22. Blake T. Hanna, "Diderot théologien," *Revue d'Histoire littéraire de la France* 1 (1978): 24.

23. This comes from Voltaire's epic poem, *La Henriade*. See *Œeuvres complètes de Voltaire* (Oxford: Voltaire Foundation, 1968), 2:613.

24. Noël Chomel, *Supplément au Dictionnaire œconomique* (Paris: chez la Veuve Éstienne, 1740), 1:1227.

25. See Stenger, *Diderot*, 26–27.

26. Vandeul, *Diderot, mon père*, 11–12.

27. Ibid., 11–12.

28. Ibid., 15.

29. Wilson, *Diderot*, 30–32.

30. Ibid., 15.

31. Ibid., 16.

32. Ibid., 18.

33. Ibid., 36.

34. Jean-Jacques Rousseau, *The Confessions*, trans. J. M. Cohen (London: Penguin, 1953), 19.

35. Vandeul, *Diderot, mon père*, 20.

36. See Samuel Huntington, *The Soldier and the State* (Cambridge, MA: Harvard University Press, 1985), 22. His family name was Maleville.

37. See Stenger, *Diderot*, 37.

38. Vandeul, *Diderot, mon père*, 22.

39. Wilson, *Diderot*, 39.

40. Ibid., 18.

41. P. N. Furbank, *Diderot* (New York: Knopf, 1992), 19.

42. *Corr.*, 1:42.

43. Ibid., 1:43.

44. Ibid., 1:44.

45. Ibid.

46. Diderot, *Diderot on Art II: The Salon of 1767*, 229.

II.

LEAVING GOD

1. *Corr.*, 1:94.

2. The satire of convent, monastery, and religious life in general had been an integral part of European literature for five hundred years, well before Diderot took up the pen. Petrarch lambasted clerical abuse of worldly power in his sonnets. Erasmus lashed out at the inconsistencies and senselessness of monastic life. And François Rabelais produced a memorable cast of anticlerical characters that became a part of French popular culture.

3. See William Doyle, *Jansenism: Catholic Resistance to Authority from the Reformation to the French Revolution* (New York: Saint Martin's, 2000), for a good summary of this conflict.

4. DPV, 2:51.

5. Ibid., 1:290.

6. Thinkers like Diderot also familiarized themselves with Epicurean philosophy by reading Diogenes Laertius's *Lives and Opinions of Eminent Philosophers.* See Lynn S. Joy, "Interpreting Nature: Gassendi Versus Diderot on the Unity of Knowledge," in Donald R. Kelley and Richard H. Popkin, eds., *The Shapes of Knowledge from the Renaissance to the Enlightenment* (Dordrecht: Kluwer, 1991), 123–34.

7. This has also been translated more poetically by A. E. Stallings: "So potent was Religion in persuading to do wrong." See *The Nature of Things*, trans. A. E. Stallings (London: Penguin Classics, 2007), 6.

8. For a comprehensive history of the text's rediscovery and consequent effect upon the progression of human thought, see Stephen Greenblatt, *The Swerve: How the World Became Modern* (New York: Norton, 2011).

9. In the decades after the *Tractatus* was first published, the term "Spinozist," which was applied somewhat haphazardly, became synonymous with unbeliever or atheist. Spinoza's *Ethics* had a great influence on Diderot. For an analysis of three of Diderot's later texts in relation to Spinoza's philosophy of ethics, see Louise Crowther, "Diderot, Spinoza, and the Question of Virtue," in *MHRA Working Papers in the Humanities* (Cambridge, UK: Modern Humanites Research Association, 2007), 2:11–18.

10. Jonathan I. Israel, *Radical Enlightenment: Philosophy and the Making of Modernity 1650–1750* (Oxford: Oxford University Press, 2001), 213.

11. Johann Franz Buddeus, *Traité de l'athéisme et de la superstition*, trans. Louis Philon (Amsterdam: chez Schreuder and Mortier, 1756), 78.

12. The *Testament* was only recently translated into its first English edition; see Jean Meslier, *Testament: Memoir of the Thoughts and Sentiments of Jean Meslier*, trans. Michael Shreve (Amherst, NY: Prometheus Books, 2009).

13. Bacon, Voltaire explains, first proposed this type of experimental philosophy. Newton became its champion. See J. B. Shank, *The Newton Wars and the Beginning of the French Enlightenment* (Chicago: University of Chicago Press, 2008), 309.

14. Nicholas Cronk, *Voltaire: A Very Short Introduction* (Oxford: Oxford University Press, 2017), 4.

15. Stenger, *Diderot*, 52.

16. To a large degree, Voltaire's *Lettres* sought to encourage shifts that were already taking place in France, chief among them the collapse of Cartesian philosophy. See *The Philosophical Writings of Descartes*, trans. John Cottingham, Robert Stoothoff, and Dugald Murdoch (Cambridge, UK: Cambridge University Press, 1984), 2:45.

17. He also annotated Silhouette's translation of Alexander Pope's *Essay on Man* sometime after 1736. See Jean Varloot's introduction in DPV, 1:167–89.

18. Isaac Newton, *Principia, The Motion of Bodies*, trans. Andrew Motte and Florian Cajori (Berkeley: University of California Press, 1934), 1:xviii.

19. Ibid.

20. See *The Cambridge History of Eighteenth-Century Philosophy*, ed. Knud Haakonsenn, (Cambridge, UK: Cambridge University Press, 2006), 2:647.

21. Similarly, Locke did not exclude God from the workings of nature—far from it. Although Locke's philosophical method certainly prompted skeptically minded thinkers to question what they could actually know about the deity, Locke continued to accord Holy Scripture a

status that seemingly escaped his own stringent restrictions. Humans were, as he put it, "sent into the world by [God's] order," and continue to be "his property." See his *Second Treatise of Government*, ed. C. B. Macpherson (Indianapolis: Hackett, 1980), 2:9.

22. Isaac Newton, *Newton: Philosophical Writings*, ed. Andrew Janiak (Cambridge, UK: Cambridge University Press, 2004), 111.

23. This is expressed in Romans 1:20.

24. There were earlier thinkers in this line, too, for example Edward, Lord Herbert of Cherbury (1583–1648), whose *De veritate* is the first early-modern book to put forward a deist understanding of religion. See *Deism: An Anthology*, ed. Peter Gay (Princeton: Van Nostrand, 1969), 30.

25. Ibid., 52.

26. Matthew Tindal, *Christianity as Old as the Creation* (Stuttgart-Bad Cannstatt: Frommann-Holzboog, 1967), 1:68.

27. See *The Portable Atheist: Essential Readings for the Nonbeliever*, ed. Christopher Hitchens (Philadelphia: Da Capo, 2007), xxiii.

28. This is a paraphrase of the well-known slogan of the World Union of Deists.

29. To protect himself, Diderot distinguished between deism and theism. In his view, deism was a somewhat indifferent understanding of God, whereas theism admits the existence of the revelation. He treated Shaftesbury as a theist. DPV, 1:297.

30. See, for example, the letter sent by Didier-Pierre to his older brother in January 1763, where he speaks about Diderot's many failings. *Corr.*, 4:241–45.

31. *Corr.*, 1:52.

32. See Roland Mortier, "Didier Diderot lecteur de Denis: ses *Réflexions sur l'Essai sur le mérite et la vertu*," RDE 10, no. 1 (1991): 21–39.

33. DPV, 1:306. Leibniz approached the problem of evil with similar optimism in his book *Theodicy*. See Gottfried Wilhelm Freiherr von Leibniz,

Theodicy, ed. Austin Farrer, trans. E. M. Huggard (New Haven: Yale University Press, 1952).

34. See Mortier, "Didier Diderot lecteur de Denis," 30.

35. Pierre Bayle, the famous author of the *Dictionnaire historique et critique* (*Critical and Historical Dictionary*, 1697) had famously refuted this idea in his *Pensées diverses sur la comète* (*Various Thoughts on the Occasion of a Comet*, 1682). See Pierre Bayle, *Pensées diverses sur la comète*, ed. Joyce and Hubert Bost (Paris: Garnier-Flammarion, 2007).

36. In the absence of any correspondence or telltale manuscripts, scholars continue to hesitate about the authorship of the orientalist short story "Oiseau blanc." See Nadine Berenguier for an excellent discussion of the reception of Puisieux's career, *Conduct Books for Girls in Enlightenment France* (New York: Routledge, 2016).

37. Pascal was, indeed, a favorite of authors including Voltaire, not only for his ironic tone, but for his evisceration of the hypocrisy of the Church and the Jesuits. See Robert Niklaus, "*Les Pensées philosophiques* de Diderot et les *Pensées* de Pascal," *Diderot Studies* 20 (1981): 201–17.

38. In this apology of Saint Augustine's Christianity, Pascal contemplates the God-shaped vacuum in one's heart, the space that "can only be filled by an infinite and immutable object, that is to say, only by God Himself." Blaise Pascal, *Pensées* (New York: Dutton, 1958), 113.

39. Ibid., 107.

40. Baron Anne-Robert-Jacques Turgot, *Œuvres de Turgot et documents le concernant, avec biographie et notes* (Paris: F. Alcan, 1913–23), 1:87.

41. DPV, 2:19.

42. Paul Valet, *Le Diacre Paris et les convulsionnaires de St.-Médard: le jansénisme et Port-Royal. Le masque de Pascal* (Paris: Champion, 1900), 22.

43. Brian E. Strayer, *Suffering Saints: Jansenists and Convulsionnaires in France, 1640–1799* (Brighton, UK: Sussex Academic Press, 2008), 243.

44. Louis-Basile Carré de Montgeron, *La vérité des miracles opérés à l'intercession de M. de Paris* (1737).

45. Strayer, *Suffering Saints*, 251.

46. Ibid., 243.

47. Ibid., 256.

48. Ibid., 257.

49. According to one of Diderot's critics, Jean Henri Samuel Formey, *Philosophical Thoughts* gives a highly exaggerated account of the *convulsionnaires* and of other religious sects. *Pensées raisonnables opposées aux pensées philosophiques* (Berlin: Chrét. Fréd. Voss., 1749), 24.

50. DPV, 2:19–20.

51. Ibid., 2:20.

52. *Matérialistes français du XVIIIème siècle: La Mettrie, Helvétius, d'Holbach*, ed. Sophie Audidière, Fondements de la politique (Paris: PUF, 2006), vii.

53. DPV., 2:49.

54. Ibid., 2:31.

55. Ibid., 2:51.

56. Ibid., 2:35.

57. Ibid.

58. Ibid., 2:34.

59. Ibid., 2:9–12.

III.

A PHILOSOPHE IN PRISON

1. Guillotte served as an *exempt* (military officer) for the provost of Île de France, technically under the authority of the man who would later arrest Diderot, the lieutenant-général de police, Berryer.

2. Wilson, *Diderot*, 61.

3. Charles Manneville, *Une vieille église de Paris: Saint-Médard* (Paris: H. Champignon, 1906), 48.

4. The role was established in 1667, according to the *Encyclopédie*, 9:509.

5. This also included arresting Jansenists, who often went to prison for longer terms than other "offenders."

6. *Corr.*, 1:54.

7. Paul Bonnefon, "Diderot prisonnier à Vincennes," *Revue d'histoire littéraire de la France* 2 (1899): 203.

8. Berryer also received two letters in 1748 from Jean-Louis Bonin, a printer, who identified Diderot as the author of *Les bijoux indiscrets* and Durand as his printer. See Wilson, *Diderot*, 86.

9. Anne Elisabeth Sejten, *Diderot ou Le défi esthétique. Les écrits de jeunesse, 1746–1751.* "Essais d'art et de philosophie" (Paris: Vrin, 1999), 79.

10. Diderot also wrote another unpublished work, *De la suffisance de la religion naturelle* (*On the Sufficiency of Natural Religion*), which finally appeared in 1770. This short text urged humankind to free itself from the bigotry and fanaticism created by revealed religion. See Jonathan I. Israel, *Enlightenment Contested: Philosophy, Modernity, and the Emancipation of Man, 1670–1752* (Oxford: Oxford University Press, 2006), 789.

11. He also dispatched two other copies. The first was sent to the Marquis d'Argens, who had belittled his translation of Shaftesbury as well as his *Philosophical Thoughts.* The second went to the famous mathematician and philosopher Pierre Louis Moreau de Maupertuis, who was then president of the Berlin Academy of Sciences (of which Diderot would soon be a member). See Anne-Marie Chouillet, "Trois lettres inédites de Diderot," *RDE* 11, no. 1 (1991): 8–18.

12. *Corr.*, 1:74.

13. Ibid.

14. According to actual reports, Saunderson became delirious before receiving (or allowing himself to receive) last rites. The Royal Society in England, of which Saunderson was a member, never forgave Diderot for his account. The Encyclopedist was voted down for membership because of this fabricated tale. See Anthony Strugnell, "La candidature de Diderot à la Société Royale de Londres," *RDE* 4, no. 1 (1988): 37–41.

15. Kate E. Tunstall has cautioned critics of Diderot from conflating Saunderson with the author himself and assuming that the blind man's

speech indicates Diderot's materialism in 1749. See her *Blindness and Enlightenment: An Essay* (New York: Continuum, 2011), 18–19. To avoid confusion, I will cite this book as Diderot, *Letter on the Blind*, trans. Tunstall, when referring to Tunstall's translation.

16. Ibid., 199–200.

17. Ibid., 200.

18. Ibid., 203.

19. Diderot was profoundly affected by Julien Offray de La Mettrie's radically materialist *The Natural History of the Soul*, the first in a series of books to ridicule Christianity.

20. See Edward G. Andrew, *Patrons of Enlightenment* (Toronto: University of Toronto Press, 2006), 137.

21. The peace treaty of Aix-la-Chapelle was signed in 1748 and ended the war of succession that had divided Austria.

22. The events of 1749 are admirably recounted by Robert Darnton in *Poetry and the Police* (Cambridge, MA: Harvard University Press, 2010).

23. Ibid., 50.

24. Bonnefon, "Diderot prisonnier à Vincennes," 204.

25. See François Moureau, *La plume et le plomb: espaces de l'imprimé et du manuscrit au siècle des Lumières* (Paris: PUPS, 2006), 610–11.

26. See Darnton, *Poetry and the Police*, 7-14.

27. Ibid., 14.

28. Some of this treatment also stemmed from the fact that he escaped three times. See his *Mémoires de Henri Masers de Latude* (Gand: Dullé, 1841).

29. Ronchères was really Fleurs de Rouvroy. He spent thirty-two years in the prison. Boyer arrived there in 1739 and had been there for ten years when Diderot came. See François de Fossa, *Le château historique de Vincennes à travers les âges* (Paris: H. Daragon, 1909), 2:116.

30. That Diderot numbered among those deemed worthy of decent treatment also shows up in a letter that the governor of the château, Marquis du Châtelet, dispatched to Berryer; remarkably enough, the prison

warden took the time to indicate that someone was coming to drop off linens and a "night cap" for the writer's stay. See Bonnefon, "Diderot prisonnier à Vincennes," 203.

31. Fossa, *Le château*, 2:50.

32. Diderot, *Œuvres complètes. Correspondance. Appendices*, ed. Jules Assézat
and Maurice Tourneux (Paris: Garnier Frères, 1877), 20:122–24.

33. Madame de Vandeul, *Diderot, mon père*, 30–31.

34. *Enc.*, 1:np. The irony of the inscription—honoring the man who
countersigned the lettre de cachet that imprisoned Diderot—would not
be lost on the philosophe. Decades later, Diderot fantasized about creating a new and better *Encyclopédie* that, unlike the first one, would honor the
great monarch of Russia, Catherine II, and not a "second-rate minister who
deprived me of my liberty in order to wring from me a tribute to which he
could not lay claim by merit." Wilson, *Diderot*, 116.

35. Reflected in Diderot's "engagement." See *Corr.*, 1:96.

36. Both of these letters are lost. We can infer their existence from the
letters that his father sent in response to them.

37. *Corr.*, 1:92.

38. The priest was presumably the *trésorier*, the keeper of the treasure
and relics, of the prison's Sainte-Chapelle, the nearby medieval chapel.

39. Jean-Jacques Rousseau, *The Confessions*, trans. J. M. Cohen (London:
Penguin, 1953), 327.

40. *Mercure de France, dédié au Roi* (Paris: Cailleau, 1749), 154–55.

41. Rousseau, *Confessions*, 327–28.

42. For a contemporary translation, see Rousseau, *Discourse on the Origin
of Inequality*, trans. Donald A. Cress (Indianapolis: Hackett), 1992.

43. Diderot, *Œuvres complètes de Diderot* (Paris: Garnier Frères, 1875),
2:285. Jean-François Marmontel and Diderot's daughter must have heard
a different story: according to their accounts, it was Diderot himself who

incited Rousseau to recast humankind as a depraved, miserable, and artificial species who left its best days behind in the state of nature. Madame de Vandeul relates that "my father gave Rousseau the idea for his *Discourse on the Sciences and the Arts*, [a work] that [my father] perhaps reread and maybe even corrected." *Diderot, mon père*, 56.

44. *Correspondance littéraire, philosophique, et critique par Grimm, Diderot, Raynal, Meister, etc.*, 5:134.

IV.

THE ENLIGHTENMENT BIBLE

1. René Louis de Voyer de Paulmy d'Argenson, *Mémoires et journal inédit du Marquis d'Argenson* (Paris: P. Jannet, 1857), 3:282.

2. According to the contract, the entire project was to be completed three years later, by 1748.

3. Jacques Proust, *Diderot et l'Encyclopédie* (Paris: Armand Colin, 1962), 47.

4. *Mémoires pour l'histoire des sciences et des beaux-arts* 177 (1745): 937.

5. Wilson, *Diderot*, 76.

6. This unseemly and very public skirmish prompted one of the most powerful men in France, Henri-François d'Aguesseau who held the posts of chancellor and overseer of the book trade—to lash out at both parties. D'Aguesseau rapped Le Breton on the knuckles for circumventing various publishing regulations, and withdrew the printer's privilege to publish the *Encyclopédie*. But the real loser in this decision was Mills. By declaring the contract null and void, d'Aguesseau effectively absolved Le Breton of any financial or contractual obligation vis-à-vis his English associate.

7. Gua's contract stipulated that he was to be paid 18,000 livres. From this significant sum, he contracted to pay Diderot and d'Alembert 1,200 livres each for their work. See Wilson, *Diderot*, 79.

8. See ibid., 78–79; and Frank A. Kafker, "Gua de Malves and the *Ency-clopédie*," *Diderot Studies* 19 (1978): 94.

9. During this grace period, the geometer lay the foundation for a refer-ence work that was much more ambitious than what Sellius and Mills had envisioned.

10. Kafker, "Gua de Malves and the *Encyclopédie*," 94–96.

11. Laurent Durand, one of the four partners, had published Diderot's unsanctioned translation of Shaftesbury, and had financed the publication of his *Philosophical Thoughts*. See Frank A. Kafker and Jeff Loveland, "Diderot et Laurent Durand, son éditeur principal," *RDE* 39 (2005): 29–40.

12. Le Breton was an *imprimeur ordinaire du roi*, which meant that he did not print specific types of books, e.g., on music or Greek. He printed various documents.

13. Well before Le Breton had taken on the infamous *Encyclopédie* project, the *Almanach* had been by far the publishing house's best-known production (and its largest print run at over seven thousand copies). Louis-Sébastien Mercier, *Tableau de Paris* (Amsterdam, 1782), 4:5–8.

14. See Richard Yeo, *Encyclopaedic Visions: Scientific Dictionaries and Enlight-enment Culture* (Cambridge, UK: Cambridge University Press, 2001), 14.

15. Ibid., 14. The definitive study on this question is Marie Leca-Tsiomis's *Écrire l'Encyclopédie: Diderot: de l'usage des dictionnaires à la grammaire philosophique* (Oxford: Voltaire Foundation, 1999).

16. John Millard and Philip Playstowe, *The Gentleman's Guide in His Tour through France* (London: G. Kearsly, 1770), 226.

17. Rousseau, *The Confessions*, 324.

18. Diderot was so taken by this lucid adaptation and revision of Locke's theory of cognition that he recommended the manuscript to his editor, Lau-rent Durand, who printed the essay that same year.

19. Lorne Falkenstein and Giovanni Grandi, "Étienne Bonnot de Con-dillac," *The Stanford Encyclopedia of Philosophy*, ed. Edward N. Zalta (Stanford: Metaphysics Research Lab, Stanford University, 2017).

20. Condillac was, however, far from an atheist or a materialist. He also added to Locke's understanding of mind by asserting that language itself is the via media between sensation and thought. See John Coffee O'Neal, *Changing Minds: The Shifting Perception of Culture in Eighteenth-Century France* (Newark: University of Delaware Press, 2002), 16; and Pierre Morère, "Signes et langage chez Locke et Condillac," *Société d'études anglo-américaines des 17e et 18e siècles* 23 (1986), 16.

21. *Enc.*, "Prospectus," 1.

22. Ibid., 2.

23. Proust, *Diderot et l'Encyclopédie*, 30–32.

24. By comparison, d'Alembert's contributions were limited to only two hundred articles on subjects generally having to do with mathematics or physics.

25. The actual order is from Memory to Imagination to Reason, and is developed in Part II of the "Discourse."

26. *Enc.*, "Prospectus," 4.

27. Chambers had offered a similar breakdown, but did not contaminate religion with various other superstitious ideas. Instead, Chambers's prefatory diagram followed the tradition of many other "commonplace" works that attempted to guide and simplify the reader's experience. See Richard Yeo, "A Solution to the Multitude of Books: Ephraim Chambers's *Cyclopaedia* (1728) as 'the Best Book in the Universe,'" *Journal of the History of Ideas* 64, no. 1 (January 2003): 66–68.

28. In the "Preliminary Discourse," d'Alembert mentioned that he and his partner had briefly considered abandoning this method of organization for a more thematic structure. This is precisely what the editors of the (more than two hundred) volumes of the *Encyclopédie méthodique* chose to do later in the century (1782–1832). For a history of the use of alphabetical ordering in reference works, see Annie Becq, "L'Encyclopédie: le choix de l'ordre alphabétique," *RDE* 18, no. 1 (1995): 133–37. Choosing alphabetical order for a dictionary was far from an innovation, of course. All of the *Encyclopédie*'s

predecessors had made the same choice: Antoine Furetière, *Dictionnaire universel*, 1690; Pierre Bayle, *Dictionnaire historique et critique*, 1697; John Harris, *Lexicon Technicum*, 1704; and Ephraim Chambers, *Cyclopaedia*, 1728.

29. Yeo, *Encyclopaedic Visions*, 25.

30. Ibid. The model for this facet of the *Encyclopédie* was Pierre Bayle's *Dictionnaire historique et critique*. In addition to using cross-referencing in much the same way that Diderot and d'Alembert would use it sixty years later, Bayle was also adept at criticizing the Church without overtly insulting it.

31. See Gilles Blanchard and Mark Olsen, "Le système de renvois dans l'*Encyclopédie*: une cartographie des structures de connaissances au XVIIIe siècle," *RDE* 31–32 (2002): 45–70.

32. *Enc.*, 5:642.

33. Ibid., 5:643

34. Ibid., 5:642.

35. Ibid., 2:640.

36. Ibid., 1:180.

37. See *Diderot: Choix d'articles de l'Encyclopédie*, ed. Marie Leca-Tsiomis (Paris: Éditions du C.T.H.S., 2001), 48–50; and Michèle Crampe-Casnabet, "Les articles 'âme' dans l'*Encyclopédie*," *RDE* 25 (1998): 91–99.

38. Crampe-Casnabet, "Les articles 'âme,'" 94.

39. *Enc.*, 1:342.

40. Diderot could never have added a cross-reference to make this point explicit. Yet a logical one would have been to his entry "*Spinosiste*," where he maintained that spinosists believe that "matter is sensitive," that it composes the entire universe, and it is all we need to explain "the whole process" of life. (*Enc.*, 15:474).

41. Some of this is vulgarization of both Hobbes and Locke. The idea that no man can give absolute power over himself to another—because he doesn't have absolute power over himself—is classic social contract theory.

So, too, is the idea that no man is born with the right to rule over another. As Hobbes and Locke point out, in an idealized "state of nature," the strong could dominate the weak—but this would be tyrannical domination that would only benefit the strong. See Thomas Hobbes, *Leviathan* (London: Penguin Classics, 1985); and John Locke, *Two Treatises of Government*, ed. Peter Laslett (Cambridge, UK: Cambridge University Press, 1988). The novelty of Diderot's article comes from the fact that he was espousing these views under the most absolute of European monarchies.

42. *Enc.*, 1:898.

43. Although Chambers had a small collection of images, such a massive collection of illustrations generally did not appear in dictionaries. See Stephen Werner, *Blueprint: A Study of Diderot and the Encyclopédie Plates* (Birmingham, AL: Summa, 1993), 2. See also Wilson, *Diderot*, 241–43.

44. D'Alembert promised six hundred plates of illustrations over two volumes in the "Preliminary Discourse."

45. *Enc.*, "Discours Préliminaire des Editeurs," 1:xxxix

46. Werner, *Blueprint*, 14. Goussier may have even produced more of the plates than indicated, but some were left unsigned. He also wrote about sixty-five articles.

47. Madeleine Pinault, "Diderot et les illustrateurs de l'*Encyclopédie*," *Revue de l'art* 66, no. 10 (1984): 32. See also Madeleine Pinault, "Sur les planches de l'*Encyclopédie* de Diderot et d'Alembert, in *L'Encyclopédisme—Actes du Colloque de Caen 12–16 janvier 1987*, ed. Annie Becq (Paris: Éditions aux Amateurs de Livres, 1991), 355–62.

48. The engraving process is detailed in the *Encyclopédie*'s fourth installment of plates (published in 1767). See *Enc.* 22:7:1. For a contemporary account of the engraving process, see Antoine-Joseph Pernety, *Dictionnaire portatif de peinture, sculpture, et gravure* (Paris: chez Bauche, 1757), 53.

49. See John Bender and Michael Marrinan, *The Culture of Diagram* (Stanford: Stanford University Press, 2010), 10.

50. Jaucourt's incendiary article *"Traite des nègres"* ("Slave Trade") was much more upfront about its intention. After declaring that African chattel slavery in French colonies violates "religion, morality, natural laws, and all the rights of human nature" (*Enc.*, 16:532), Jaucourt proclaims that he would prefer that the colonies "be destroyed" rather than causing so much suffering in the Caribbean (ibid., 16:553).

v.

THE *ENCYCLOPÉDIE* HAIR SHIRT

1. *Corr.*, 9:30.

2. Berryer was certainly involved, issuing a note of permission to publish the "Prospectus." See Wilson, *Diderot* (New York: Oxford University Press, 1957), 120.

3. James M. Byrne, *Religion and the Enlightenment: From Descartes to Kant* (Louisville, KY: Westminster John Knox, 1996), 35.

4. Some scholars even identify the development of humanism under the Jesuit order as a kind of "Catholic enlightenment." *See Medicine and Religion in Enlightenment Europe*, ed. Ole Peter Grell and Andrew Cunningham (Hampshire, UK: Ashgate, 2007), 118.

5. The full title was *Mémoires pour l'histoire des sciences et des beaux-arts, plus connus sous le nom de Journal de Trévoux ou Mémoires de Trévoux* (1701–67).

6. *Enc.*, 3:635.

7. Jean-François Marmontel, *Memoirs of Marmontel*, 2 vols. (New York: Merrill and Baker, 1903), 1:217

8. Madame de Pompadour also encouraged Diderot and d'Alembert to pursue their work in spite of political pressures, and especially while avoiding topics having to do with religion. Later in life, her opinions on Diderot's enterprise would change: despairing at France's instability and perceived decay, she expressed her dismay at a work that undermined religion, the monarchy, and the very foundation of the society and state. See Évelyne Lever, *Madame de Pompadour* (Paris: Éditions académiques Perrin, 2000); and

Christine Pevitt-Algrant, *Madame de Pompadour: Mistress of France* (New York: Grove, 2002).

9. This was actually a new post. The responsibility of supervising the publishing industry had previously been part of the chancellor's position. Malesherbes's father was Guillaume de Lamoignon de Blancmesnil.

10. The question itself is a rewording from Genesis 2:7, seemingly suggesting a contemplation of the status of Adam or perhaps a meditation on the intentions of God: "And God formed the man of the dust of the earth and breathed upon his face the breath of life."

11. Wilson, *Diderot*, 154.

12. Ibid., 154.

13. Ibid.

14. Parlement de Paris, *Recueil de pièces concernant la thèse de M. l'abbé de Prades, soutenue en Sorbonne le 18 Novembre 1751, censurée par la Faculté de Théologie le 27 janvier 1752, & par M. l'Archevêque de Paris le 29 du même mois, divisé en trois parties* (1753), 32.

15. Ibid.

16. Ibid.

17. Ibid.

18. In 1752, Prades published an apology that was everything but. Though he defended his positions one by one by pointing to their orthodoxy, he also took the time to praise Bayle and other anti-institution writers, and to dismiss Christian champions like Descartes and Malebranche. He remained in Berlin until his death. See John Stephenson Spink, "The abbé de Prades and the Encyclopaedists: Was There a Plot?," *French Studies* 24, no. 3 (July 1970): 225–36.

19. Diderot did, in fact, leave Paris on May 20 to visit Langres—the first time he had visited home in ten years. Diderot returned home on June 17 to continue work. See Raymond Trousson, *Denis Diderot, ou Le vrai Prométhée* (Paris: Tallandier, 2005), 185.

20. Marquis d'Argenson, *Mémoires et Journal inédit*, 4:77.

21. Diderot also published the *Suite de l'Apologie de M. l'abbé de Prades* (*The Supplement to the Apology of Monsieur abbé de Prades*), which he did in the exiled abbot's name. This was published in October and laid out a case both for the *Encyclopédie* and against religious intolerance.

22. Jacques Matter, *Lettres et pièces rares et inédites* (Paris: Librairie d'Amyot, 1846), 386.

23. Wilson, *Diderot*, 166.

24. See ibid. 164; and Margaret Bald, *Banned Books: Literature Suppressed on Religious Grounds* (New York: Facts On File, 2006), 92.

25. *Enc.*, 4: iii.

26. The naturalist supplanted Jean-Joseph Languet de Gergy, the late archbishop of Sens, while d'Alembert took over the seat previously held by the late Jean-Baptiste Surian, bishop of Vence. D'Alembert praised the bishop in his acceptance speech. See Jean-Baptiste-Louis Gresset, *Discours prononcés dans l'Académie françoise, le jeudi 19 décembre M. DCC. LIV à la réception de M. d'Alembert* (Paris: chez Brunet, 1754).

27. *Corr.*, 1:186. Perhaps most significantly, the document solidified Diderot's position as "editor of all the parts of the *Encyclopédie*." See *Corr.*, 1:185; and Wilson, *Diderot*, 219–20. Diderot's earnings from the entire project reached 80,000 livres.

28. The Jesuit priest Father Tholomas disparaged d'Alembert personally, insulting the bastard mathematician with a pithy, loose translation of Horace, turning "*cui nec pater est, nec res*" into "he who has no father, is nothing." Pierre Grosclaude, *Un audacieux message: l'Encyclopédie* (Paris: Nouvelles Éditions Latines, 1951), 80.

29. The first article of the first issue lambasted Diderot for his 1753 *Pensées sur l'interprétation de la nature* (*On the Interpretation of Nature*). See Jean Haechler, *L'Encyclopédie: les combats et les hommes* (Paris: Les Belles Lettres, 1998), 191–205.

30. See Berthe Thelliez, *L'homme qui poignarda Louis XV, Robert François*

Damiens (Paris: Tallandier, 2002); Dale K. Van Kley, *The Damiens Affair and the Unraveling of the Ancien Régime* (Princeton: Princeton University Press, 1984); and Pierre Rétat, *L'Attentat de Damiens: discours sur l'événement au XVIIIᵉ siècle, sous la direction de Pierre Rétat* (Paris: Éditions du C.N.R.S / Lyon: Presses universitaires de Lyon, 1979).

31. Authors who wrote for journals including the relatively moderate *Mercure de France* fell in line with the long-standing critics who had lambasted the *Encyclopédie* in the Jesuit *Mémoires de Trévoux* or the Jansenist *Nouvelles écclésiastiques.*

32. Wilson, *Diderot*, 277.

33. Jacob-Nicolas Moreau, *Nouveau mémoire pour servir à l'histoire des Cacouacs* (Amsterdam, 1757), 92. See Gerhardt Stenger, *L'affaire des Cacouacs: trois pamphlets contre les philosophes des Lumières, présentation et notes de Gerhardt Stenger* (Saint-Étienne, France: Publications de l'Université de Saint-Étienne-Jean Monnet, 2004).

34. Palissot followed up on his *Lettres* three years later with a much more successful broadside against the Encyclopedists, a play entitled *Les philosophes*, which the king's chief minister, Choiseul, forced upon the Comédie-Française. This play, to which we will return, ultimately had a tremendous effect on Diderot.

35. *Déclaration du roi* (Versailles, 1757).

36. D'Alembert was not the only person to make a strategic mistake at this time. Although much more careful about expressing his own opinions in the *Encyclopédie*, Diderot translated two Goldoni plays and made a flippant remark in the dedication that cost him one of his last remaining supporters at court, the Duc de Choiseul.

37. *Enc.*, 7:578.

38. Wilson, *Diderot*, 284.

39. See Yves Laissus, "Une lettre inédite de d'Alembert," *Revue d'histoire des sciences et de leurs applications* 7, no. 1 (1954): 1–5.

40. Rousseau, *The Confessions*, 355.

41. This had also been the case in 1754, when Rousseau chafed at the way Diderot and his friends had mocked an unsuspecting abbé who had had the audacity to submit an entire tragedy in prose to them for their approval.

42. See Leo Damrosch, *Jean-Jacques Rousseau: Restless Genius* (New York: Houghton Mifflin, 2007), 264, for an excellent summary of this debate.

43. Louise Florence Pétronille Tardieu d'Esclavelles Épinay, *Mémoires et correspondance de Madame d'Épinay* (Paris: Volland le jeune, 1818), 2:280.

44. Ibid.

45. Ibid.

46. Rousseau, *Confessions*, 329. They would both play a very public role, in fact, in the quarrel between partisans of Italian and French opera.

47. This was a pun on "Tirant lo Blanch," the principal character of the Renaissance-era poem from Catalonia. See Wilson, *Diderot*, 119.

48. Rousseau, *Confessions*, 436.

49. DPV, 10:62.

50. *Corr.*, 1:233.

51. Jean-Jacques Rousseau, *Œuvres complètes de Jean-Jacques Rousseau* (Paris: Hachette, 1945), 10:23.

52. It was perhaps with this in mind that, about this time, Diderot indelicately delegated the article "Geneva" to d'Alembert, despite the fact that Rousseau had been born and raised in this city-state.

53. *Corr.*, 1:256.

54. Jean-Jacques Rousseau, *Lettre à M. d'Alembert sur les spectacles* (Lille: Droz, 1948), 9.

55. Denis Diderot, *Œuvres philosophiques*, ed. Michel Delon (Paris: Bibliothèque de la Pléiade, 2010), 1023.

56. This letter was sent from Voltaire to the Count de Tressan on February 13, 1758. See *Corr.*, 2:36.

57. *Corr.*, 2:123.

58. Diderot in particular did not take well to these ideas. In the August 15, 1758, edition of the *Correspondance littéraire*, he wrote a critical summary of Helvétius's book, pinpointing four of the treatise's central propositions as untenable paradoxes. See Gerhardt Stenger, *Diderot: le combattant de la liberté*, 586; D. W. Smith, *Helvétius: A Study in Persecution* (Oxford: Clarendon, 1965), 157–58, 162; and Claude-Adrien Helvétius, *Œuvres complètes d'Helvétius*, vol. 1, eds. Gerhardt Stenger and Jonas Steffen (Paris: Honoré Champion, 2016).

59. A frequently retold anecdote. See Bernard Hours, *La vertu et le secret. Le dauphin, fils de Louis XV* (Paris: Honoré Champion, 2006), 359.

60. Abraham-Joseph de Chaumeix, *Préjugés légitimes contre l'Encyclopédie, et essai de réfutation de ce dictionnaire* (Paris: Herissant, 1758), xviii.

61. *Arrests de la Cour de Parlement, portant condamnation de plusieurs livres & autres ouvrages imprimés* (1759), 2.

62. Ibid., 26.

63. *Corr.*, 2:122. The infamous *Mémoires pour Abraham Chaumeix contre les prétendus philosophes Diderot et d'Alembert* has, since then, been attributed to André Morellet, clergyman, writer, and Encylopedist—he had, among other things, written the article "Faith" for Diderot. See Sylviane Albertan-Coppola, "Les Préjugés légitimes de Chaumeix ou l'*Encyclopédie* sous la loupe d'un apologiste," *RDE* 20, no. 1 (1996): 149–58.

64. *Corr.*, 2:119.

65. For a good summary of Jaucourt's life, see *Le Chevalier de Jaucourt: L'homme aux dix-sept mille articles*, ed. Gilles Barroux and François Pépin (Paris: Société Diderot, 2015).

66. *Enc.*, 8:i.

67. Andrew S. Curran, *Anatomy of Blackness: Science and Slavery in an Age of Enlightenment* (Baltimore: Johns Hopkins University Press, 2011), 62.

68. Ibid., 63.

69. Ibid., 64.

70. *Corr.*, 2: 126.

71. Wilson, *Diderot*, 311, 359.

72. See the remarkable research undertaken by Françoise Weil: "L'impression des tomes VIII à XVII de l'*Encyclopédie*," *RDE* 1, no. 1 (1986): 85–93.

73. The *Dictionnaire de Trévoux* was printed here in 1704 and 1721, and Bayle's dictionary was reprinted here in 1734.

74. Le Breton could not have known that the Dombes principality would be definitively annexed by France in 1762. Weil speculates that, while this was now a part of France during the printing, bribes would have easily silenced officials here. See Weil, "L'impression des tomes VIII à XVII."

75. The "Associates" group dwindled in the 1760s. Durand died in 1763, David in 1765.

76. The Jesuits' expulsion from France fits into the broader history of their banishment and disbandment throughout Europe over the course of a decade and a half, culminating, in 1773, in the dissolution of the Society of Jesus by the pope. See Jean Lacouture, *Jésuites: une multibiographie*, vol. 1, *Les conquérants* (Paris: Seuil, 1991).

77. Despite Diderot's anguish, Le Breton's attempts at tampering with the *Encyclopédie*'s subversive content must be put in perspective: oftentimes, his meddling did nothing to erase the overall message of an unorthodox article and, in whole, the so-called eighteenth volume contains only 3 percent of the gargantuan *Encyclopédie*. As Douglas Gordon and Norman Torrey put it, "the censored passages do not loom very large. They represent at best only the peaks lopped off the heights of Diderot's audacity" Douglas Gordon and Norman L. Torrey, *The Censoring of Diderot's Encyclopédie and the Re-established Text* (New York: Columbia University Press, 1947), 41.

78. *Enc.*, 18:664. This "eighteenth" volume was never published. The best place to peruse these articles is in the "ARTFL" project database. Page numbers refer to this volume.

79. *Enc.*, 18:771.

80. *Enc.*, 18:893.

81. *Enc.*, 18:621.

82. *Corr.*, 4:304.

83. *Corr.*, 4:172.

84. The man who most benefited from this enterprise was the French editor and writer Charles-Joseph Panckoucke. This entrepreneurial genius published edition after edition of the *Encyclopédie*, adding tables of contents, publishing the book in portable, thinner (i.e., truncated) formats, and eventually setting off in 1781 to rewrite, complete, and improve on Diderot's project by publishing his *Encyclopédie méthodique*. See Daniel Roche, "Encyclopedias and the Diffusion of Knowledge," in *The Cambridge History of Eighteenth-Century Political Thought*, ed. Mark Goldie and Robert Wolker (New York: Cambridge University Press, 2006), 172–94.

VI.

ON VIRTUE AND VICE

1. See DPV, 4:111–22.

2. Ibid., 4:43.

3. He had, however, authored the important article "Encyclopédie." In 1755, his only stand-alone publication was a small treatise explaining the ancient art of painting in wax.

4. See Paul Kuritz, *The Making of Theater History* (Upper Saddle River, NJ: Prentice Hall, 1988), 172.

5. See DPV, 10:144.

6. Ibid., 10:112. One of the sources for this domestic tragedy is George Lillo's *The London Merchant* (1731). In 1759, Diderot began work on, but never finished, a domestic tragedy of this type, called *Le shérif* (*The Sheriff*).

7. *Corr.*, 3:280. In several letters from the era, Diderot predicted that these plays—and the theoretical writings that he published with them—would herald a revolution in theatrical aesthetics and practice. In many ways, he

was not wrong. Beaumarchais's hugely successful *Barber of Seville* and *Marriage of Figaro* (both main characters of which are working class) drew heavily from Diderot's writings.

8. DPV, 10:373.

9. Caroline Warman has compellingly argued, perhaps in contrast to what I am writing here, that *The Natural Son* and its theoretical dialogues are also part of an eighteenth-century pre-Romantic movement. See "Pre-Romantic French Thought," in *The Oxford Handbook of European Romanticism*, ed., Paul Hamilton (Oxford: Oxford University Press, 2016), 17–32.

10. Technically, this was his father's brother-in-law.

11. Jacques Chouillet, *Diderot* (Paris: SEDES, 1977), 154.

12. Goldoni, who ultimately saw Diderot's play, refuted this belief in his memoirs. See Jean Balcou, *Fréron contre les philosophes* (Geneva: Droz, 1975), 257.

13. For an account of the play's seven performances, see Jean-François Edmond Barbier, *Chronique de la Régence et du règne de Louis XV (1718–1763), ou Journal de Barbier* (Paris: Charpentier, 1857), 7:248–50.

14. Henry Carrington Lancaster, *The Comédie Française, 1701–1774: Plays, Actors, Spectators, Finances* (Philadelphia: American Philosophical Society, 1951), 797.

15. The play was based more than loosely on one of Molière's first plays, *Les femmes savantes* (1672).

16. English Showalter, "'Madame a fait un livre': Madame de Graffigny, Palissot et *Les Philosophes*," RDE 23 (1997): 109–25.

17. Charles Palissot de Montenoy, *Les philosophes, comédie en trois actes, en vers* (Paris: Duchesne, 1760), 54. To add insult to injury, the philosophe found himself accused of writing a violent retort against Palissot and two of his patrons, the very powerful Princess de Robecq and the Countess de La Marck, who was the mistress of the Duc de Choiseul, the head of the government. It was later revealed that it had actually been his friend and fellow

Encyclopédie collaborator, the abbé Morellet, who authored the fraudulent *Preface to the Comedy of* Les Philosophes, *or the Vision of Charles Palissot*, which sent him (Morellet) to the Bastille.

18. Palissot de Montenoy, *Les Philosophes*, 74.

19. *Corr.*, 3:190.

20. Ibid., 3:292.

21. Robert Darnton, *The Great Cat Massacre and Other Episodes in French Cultural History* (New York: Basic Books, 1984), 242.

22. The following year, Rousseau followed up on this stunning achievement with his most important work of political theory, *Du contrat social* (*The Social Contract*, 1762). That same year, he published his treatise on education, *Émile*. By the mid-1760s, the increasingly hermitlike Rousseau had begun not only to have a cult following, but to displace Voltaire as the era's greatest living literary figurehead.

23. Diderot, *Rameau's Nephew — Le Neveu de Rameau: A Multi-Media Bilingual Edition*, trans. Kate E. Tunstall and Caroline Warman (Cambridge, UK: Open Book Publishers, 2016), 85.

24. Ibid., 15.

25. This association had begun in 1753, when Rameau helped write a musical vaudeville for the Comédie-Française that targeted Diderot and the Encyclopedists. This was entitled "Les philosophes du siècle," a so-called "vaudeville antiphilosophique" written by Bertin de Blagny, Palissot, and Rameau. See *Rameau le neveu: Textes et documents*, ed. André Magnan (Paris: CNRS, 1993), 60–66.

26. Ibid., 43.

27. Ibid., 12.

28. Louis-Sébastien Mercier, *Tableau de Paris*, ed. Jean-Claude Bonnet (Paris: Mercure de France, 1994), 2:1447.

29. *Rameau le Neveu*, 109.

30. Ibid., 10.

31. Diderot, *Rameau's Nephew — Le neveu de Rameau*, 15–16.

32. Ibid., 16.

33. Ibid.

34. As he wrote in the *Encyclopédie* article on "Natural Law," Diderot believed until his last breath that "Virtue is so beautiful that even thieves respect its image, even in the darkest parts of their caves" (*Enc.*, 5:131–34).

35. Diderot, *Rameau's Nephew — Le neveu de Rameau*, 43.

36. Ibid., 115.

37. Ibid., 95.

38. Ibid, 74.

39. Ibid., 82.

40. Ibid., 42.

41. Ibid., 66.

42. Johann Wolfgang von Goethe, *The Autobiography of Goethe: Truth and Poetry: From My Own Life*, trans. John Oxenford (London: G. Bell, 1894), 301.

43. Petr Lom provides an interesting analysis of *Rameau's Nephew* in relation to the philosophies of Goethe and, more importantly, Hegel. Petr Lom, *The Limits of Doubt: The Moral and Political Implications of Skepticism* (Albany: State University of New York Press, 2001), 65–66.

44. Friedrich Schiller and Johann Wolfgang von Goethe, *Correspondence Between Schiller and Goethe, from 1794 to 1805*, vol. 2,, trans. L. Dora Schmitz (London: G. Bell, 1879), 493.

45. Ibid., 493.

VII.

ON ART: DIDEROT AT THE LOUVRE

1. See Annie Becq, *Genèse de l'esthétique française moderne. De la raison classique à l'imagination créatrice: 1680–1814* (Paris: Albin Michel, 1994).

2. After 1773, however, Jacques-Henri Meister, Grimm's secretary, took over as editor of the *Correspondence*.

3. The Tuileries Palace became the seat of power until it burned in a fire

during the Paris Commune in 1871.

4. "Lettres sur l'Académie Royale de Sculpture et de Peinture et sur le Salon de 1777," reprinted in *Revue universelle des arts* 19 (Paris: veuve Jules Renouard, 1864): 185–86, cited in Thomas E. Crow, *Painters and Public Life in Eighteenth-Century Paris* (New Haven: Yale University Press, 1985), 4.

5. Jacqueline Lichtenstein, *The Blind Spot: An Essay on the Relations between Painting and Sculpture in the Modern Age*, trans. Chris Miller (Los Angeles: Getty Research Institute Publications Program, 2008), 11.

6. A notable exception to this would be that women were denied admission to the Academy itself.

7. The *Encyclopédie* article "Connoisseur" echoed this. *Enc.*, 3:898.

8. Crow, *Painters and Public Life*, 10.

9. Ibid., 8.

10. Diderot, *Diderot on Art I: The Salon of 1765 and Notes on Painting*, trans. John Goodman (New Haven: Yale University Press, 1995), 1.

11. Ibid., 238.

12. Diderot, *Essais sur la peinture: Salons de 1759, 1761, 1763* (Paris: Hermann, 1984), 112.

13. For a discussion of this trajectory, see Jacques Proust, "L'initiation artistique de Diderot," *Gazette des beaux-arts* 55 (1960): 225–32.

14. Interestingly enough, he asserts here that beauty is a profoundly relative concept that depends on the perception of *rapports* or links that take place in a given individual's mind. See Colas Duflo, *Diderot philosophe* (Paris: Champion, 2013), 103.

15. Diderot, *Diderot on Art I*, 1.

16. Diderot, *Essais sur la peinture*, 181. The first comprehensive history of art, Winckelmann's *Geschichte der Kunst des Alterthums* (*The History of Art in Antiquity*), actually appeared the following year, in 1764.

17. Michael Hatt and Charlotte Klonk, *Art History: A Critical Introduction to Its Methods* (Manchester, UK: Manchester University Press, 2006), 3.

18. Diderot, *Essais sur la peinture*, 181.

19. Diderot, *Diderot on Art I*, 158.

20. Diderot, *Essais sur la peinture*, 212.

21. Ibid., 213.

22. Diderot, *Diderot on Art II: The Salon of 1767*, trans. John Goodman (New Haven: Yale University Press, 1995), 1:86.

23. Diderot, *Essais sur la peinture*, 97.

24. Ibid., 220.

25. Ibid.

26. In 1765, after praising the rendering of a "painted and covered china tureen, a lemon, a napkin that's been unfolded and carelessly flung down, a pâté on a rounded board, and a glass half filled with wine," he realizes "there are scarcely any objects in nature that are unrewarding [as artistic subjects] and that it's only a question of rendering them properly." See *Diderot on Art I*, 62.

27. Ibid., 97.

28. Diderot, *Notes on Painting*, ibid., 222.

29. In fact, he is probably alluding to the landscapist Claude-Joseph Vernet, and his remarkable ability to conjure up horrific shipwrecks and storms that threatened the lives of the helpless humans on his canvases.

30. Diderot, *Diderot on Art I*, 225.

31. Peter Gay, *The Enlightenment: The Science of Freedom* (New York: Norton, 1996), 240.

32. Engraver, ceramicist, and designer of prized tapestries, Boucher had also been designated rector and Professor of History Painting at the Academy, the highest rank.

33. Diderot, *Essais sur la peinture*, 195.

34. Gay, *The Enlightenment*, 240.

35. Diderot, *Essais sur la peinture*, 197.

36. Diderot, *Diderot on Art II*, 224.

37. See René Démoris, "Le langage du corps et l'expression des passions

de Félibien à Diderot," *Des mots et des couleurs*, vol. 2 (Lille: Presses Universitaire de Lille, 1987), 64.

38. Diderot, *Pensées détachées sur la peinture, la sculpture, l'architecture et la poésie pour servir de suite aux Salons* (Paris: Ligaran, 2015), 10.

39. John Hope Mason makes a similar point in *The Irresistible Diderot* (London: Quartet Books, 1982), 171.

40. In his review of the Salon of 1781, Diderot would say of Jacques-Louis David, "this man shows great style in his work, he has spirit, the faces of his figures are expressive without affectation, their poses are natural and noble." Diderot, *Héros et martyrs, Salons de 1769, 1771, 1775, 1781* (Paris: Hermann, 1995), 350.

41. An uncommon subject since the Le Nain brothers. See Emma Barker, *Greuze and the Painting of Sentiment* (Cambridge, UK: Cambridge University Press, 2005).

42. *Année littéraire*, 1761, Lettre 9, 209.

43. Diderot, *Essais sur la peinture*, 234.

44. Diderot, *Diderot on Art I*, 97.

45. Ibid., 98.

46. Ibid., 98–99.

47. Ibid., 97–98.

48. Ibid., 99.

49. Ibid., 94.

50. Diderot, *Diderot on Art II*, 88.

51. Ibid., 88–89.

52. See Eik Kahng, "L'Affaire Greuze and the Sublime of History Painting," *Art Bulletin* 86, no. 1 (March 2004): 96–113. Kahng points out that this painting was the "exception and not the rule." Fragonard went on to paint a series of "unclassifiable" paintings, including scenes of domestic life, fantasy pieces, and erotic boudoir scenes.

53. Ibid., 145–46.

54. See Tom Baldwin for a summary of this idea, "Ekphrasis and Related Issues in Diderot's *Salons*," in *New Essays on Diderot*, ed. James Fowler (Cambridge, UK: Cambridge University Press, 2011), 236.

55. Ibid., 146.

56. Norman Bryson, *Word and Image: French Painting and the Ancien Régime* (Cambridge, UK: Cambridge University Press, 1981), 155.

57. See Wilda Anderson, *Diderot's Dream* (Baltimore: Johns Hopkins Univeristy Press, 1990). See also Andrew Herrick Clark, *Diderot's Part: Aesthetics and Physiology* (Hampshire, UK: Ashgate, 2008).

58. Theresa M. Kelly, *Reinventing Allegory* (Cambridge, UK: Cambridge University Press, 1997), 88.

59. Scholar Michael Fried has extensively explored the dizzying levels of critical fictionality in Diderot's art criticism. See Michael Fried, *Absorption and Theatricality: Painting and Beholder in the Age of Diderot* (Berkeley: University of California Press), 1980.

60. Diderot, *Diderot on Art I*, 141.

61. Plato's message is that people do not understand the forms of what we call Platonic reality. See Theresa M. Kelley, *Reinventing Allegory*, 90.

62. Diderot, *Diderot on Art I*, 141–42.

63. Carol Sherman, *Diderot and the Art of Dialogue* (Geneva: Droz, 1976), 41.

VIII.

ON THE ORIGIN OF SPECIES

1. Diderot, *Héros et martyrs, Salons de 1769, 1771, 1775, 1781* (Paris: Hermann, 1995), 100–01.

2. Thursday was the day of the "Synagogue." Sunday was the day where different guests came. Diderot had come to know d'Holbach shortly after he had been released from Vincennes prison, perhaps as early as November 1749. D'Holbach bought the rue Royale building in 1759. See A. C. Kors, *D'Holbach's Coterie: An Enlightenment in Paris* (Princeton: Princeton University Press, 1976), 12.

3. Diderot affectionately described the rue Royale as an intellectual sanctuary filled with the "finest and sharpest people" in Paris: "Titles and erudition aren't enough to guarantee entry there; one must also be good. There one can count on an exchange of ideas; there history, politics, finance, literature, and philosophy are discussed; there one is held in sufficiently high regard to be contradicted; there one finds the true cosmopolitan." Diderot, *Diderot on Art I: The Salon of 1765 and Notes on Painting*, trans. John Goodman (New Haven: Yale University Press, 1995), 128–29. The guest list was generally limited to fifteen after 1765. *Corr.*, 5:212. See also Antoine Lilti, *The World of the Salons: Sociability and Worldliness in Eighteenth-Century France*, trans. Lydia G. Cochrane (New York: Oxford University Press, 2005), 22.

4. To publish such works without suffering the wrath of the director of the book trade, d'Holbach sent his manuscripts to faraway publishers in either Amsterdam or Nancy. To further avoid censure, he also attributed his books to recently deceased authors. By 1770, this ploy had transformed the baron into the most prolific author of blasphemous books of the eighteenth century. See Mladen Kozul, *Les Lumières imaginaires: Holbach et la traduction* (Oxford: Oxford University Studies in the Enlightenment, 2016).

5. *Corr.*, 9:94–96.

6. Ibid., 9:125.

7. Ibid., 9:126.

8. Diderot, *Rameau's Nephew and D'Alembert's Dream*, trans. Leonard Tancock (London: Penguin, 1966), 149.

9. Descartes had first explored the issue in his *Meditations on First Philosophy* (1641), in which he hoped to demonstrate that the human soul was distinct from the body and did not die with its perishing. He would later assert that the body and the mind are connected in the pineal gland, that ideas represent the outside world without bearing a resemblance to them, and that humans have innate ideas that exist outside of the material world. For a discussion of Descartes's influence on Diderot, see Aram Vartanian,

Descartes and Diderot: A Study of Scientific Naturalism in the Enlightenment (Princeton: Princeton University Press, 1953), 3.

10. Diderot, *Rameau's Nephew and D'Alembert's Dream*, 149.

11. The statue was commissioned in 1763 for Madame de Pompadour, after which Diderot glowingly reviewed it for the Salon of 1763. It now resides on the ground floor of the Richelieu gallery at the Louvre.

12. See Mary D. Sheriff, *Moved by Love: Inspired Artists and Deviant Women in Eighteenth-Century France* (Chicago: University of Chicago Press, 2004), 183. See also Marc Buffat, "Diderot, Falconet, et l'amour de la postérité," *RDE* 43 (2008), 9–20.

13. Sheriff, *Moved by Love*, 183.

14. Diderot, *Rameau's Nephew and D'Alembert's Dream*, 151.

15. Ibid., 151–52.

16. Ibid., 152.

17. *Bibliothèque raisonnée des ouvrages des savants de l'Europe. Pour les mois de janvier, février et mars 1730* (Amsterdam: chez les Wetsteins et Smith, 1730), 4:377–91.

18. Diderot, *Rameau's Nephew and D'Alembert's Dream*, 152–53.

19. Rachel Ginnis Fuchs, "Crimes against Children in Nineteenth-Century France: Child Abuse," *Law and Human Behavior* 6, nos. 3–4 (1982): 240.

20. Diderot, *Rameau's Nephew and D'Alembert's Dream*, 153.

21. Ibid.

22. Ibid., 166.

23. Ibid., 167.

24. Ibid., 169. Elsewhere in the book, communication among body parts and the brain is compared to a harpsichord with memory and sensation playing itself, or a spider that is connected to a living web, feeling the world through its imperceptible threads.

25. Ibid., 170.

26. Ibid., 171.

27. In the first part of the dream, when the characters Diderot and d'Alembert are discussing d'Alembert's life, both men agree that preformationism is absurd. Bordeu will also later debunk de l'Espinasse's version of the same theory. For a discussion of Diderot's understanding of generation in relation to various theories of the era, e.g. Haller, Bonnet, and Buffon, see Andrew Herrick Clark, *Diderot's Part: Aesthetics and Physiology* (Hampshire, UK: Ashgate, 2008), 67–75.

28. Diderot, *Rameau's Nephew and D'Alembert's Dream*, 172.

29. Ibid.

30. Ibid., 173.

31. Ibid.

32. See W. G. Moore, "Lucretius and Montaigne," *Yale French Studies*, no. 38 (1967): 109–14; William B. Jensen, "Newton and Lucretius: Some Overlooked Parallels," in *Lucretius: His Continuing Influence and Contemporary Relevance*, ed. David B. Suits and Timothy J. Madigan (Rochester: RIT Press, 2011), 2.

33. Diderot, *Rameau's Nephew and D'Alembert's Dream*, 173–74.

34. Ibid., 174.

35. Ibid., 174–75.

36. See Ronald L. Numbers, *The Creationists: From Scientific Creationism to Intelligent Design* (Cambridge, MA: Harvard University Press, 2006).

37. Arthur O. Lovejoy explains this as a general interest in the great chain of being. See *The Great Chain of Being: A Study of the History of an Idea* (New Brunswick, NJ: Transaction Publishers, 2009), 183–84.

38. During antiquity, humans had been very much part of the natural chain of beings. Aristotle had classed animals into genera and species and conceived of a ladder with man at the summit.

39. See Thierry Hoquet, *Buffon/Linné: eternels rivaux de la biologie?* (Paris: Dunod, 2007), 97. For a much larger discussion of the theory of human degeneration and, in particular, its link to slavery and Africans, see Andrew

S. Curran, *The Anatomy of Blackness: Science and Slavery in an Age of Enlightenment* (Baltimore: Johns Hopkins University Press, 2011), especially chapter 3.

40. Diderot, *Rameau's Nephew and D'Alembert's Dream*, 175–76.

41. See Andrew Curran, *Sublime Disorder: Physical Monstrosity in Diderot's Universe* (Oxford: Studies on Voltaire and the Eighteenth Century, 2001).

42. Ibid., 190.

43. Diderot, *Rameau's Nephew and D'Alembert's Dream*, 225.

44. See Patrick Graille, "Portrait scientifique et littéraire de l'hybride au siècle des Lumières," in *Eighteenth-Century Life: Faces of Monstrosity in Eighteenth-Century Thought*, ed. Andrew Curran, Robert P. Maccubbin, and David F. Morill (Baltimore: Johns Hopkins University Press, 1997), 21: 2, 70–88.

45. Diderot, *Rameau's Nephew and d'Alembert's Dream*, 232. When she heard from d'Alembert that Monsieur Diderot had written a series of dialogues with her as one of the characters, she was livid and instructed d'Alembert to insist that Diderot burn the manuscript. Diderot falsely claimed that he had.

46. DPV, 17:27.

IX.

THE SEXOLOGIST

1. *Corr.*, 4:120.

2. *Corr.*, 16:64. He even believed that it was linked to childhood experiences that imprint on us. In a letter that he sent to an unknown recipient, Diderot confessed that one of his most formative erotic experiences occurred when he was but a small boy in Langres. "A young girl who was as pretty as a heart bit my hand. Her father, to whom I complained, pulled up her jacket [to spank her] in front of me. That little butt stuck with me and will remain with me for the rest of my life. Who knows what its influence is on my morals?"

3. *Corr.*, 3:216.

4. Adriann Beverland, *État de l'homme dans le péché originel* (Imprimé dans le monde, 1714), 37–38.

5. See *Opuscules divers, contenants un recueil de quelques lettres très instructives pour la conduite des curés et jeunes ecclésiastiques* (Langres: Claude Personne, 1719), 60.

6. Ibid., 58.

7. Ibid., 61 and 63.

8. Madame de Vandeul, *Diderot, mon père* (Strasbourg: Circe, 1992), 56.

9. DPV, 2:18.

10. DPV, 3:233.

11. André-Joseph Panckoucke, *L'art de désoppiler* [sic] *la rate* (Gallipoli, 175886 [Paris, 1758]), 148.

12. Jacques-André Naigeon, *Mémoires historiques et philosophiques sur la vie et les ouvrages de D. Diderot* (Paris: chez J.L.J. Brière, 1886), 37.

13. DPV, 17:412.

14. Diderot, *Sur les femmes* (Paris: Pichon, 1919), 11.

15. Ibid., 21.

16. Ibid.

17. Diderot, *Jacques the Fatalist*, trans. David Coward (Oxford: Oxford University Press, 1999), 97.

18. For an analysis of Rivette's film in relation to Diderot's philosophy of theater, as well as a history of the film's ban (and subsequent release and success), see Mary M. Wiles, *Jacques Rivette* (Urbana: University of Illinois Press, 2012), 22–40. Guillaume Nicloux also filmed another version of *La religieuse* in 2012.

19. This was the preface-annex, the portion of the text that closes the story and reveals its genesis.

20. DPV, 11:70.

21. Ibid., 11:30.

22. Ibid., 11:31.

23. Diderot, *The Nun*, trans. Russell Goulbourne (Oxford: Oxford University Press, 2005), 105.

24. Ibid., 26.

25. See Pierre Saint-Amand, *The Libertine's Progress: Seduction in the Eighteenth-Century French Novel*, trans. Jennifer Curtiss Gage (Hanover, NH: University Press of New England, 1994), 53.

26. Ibid., 35.

27. Ibid., 58.

28. Ibid., 123.

29. Ibid., 103.

30. Ibid., 136.

31. DPV, 11:31. See Jean de Booy and Alan Freer, *"Jacques le Fataliste" et "La Religieuse" devant la critique révolutionnaire* in *Studies on Voltaire and the Eighteenth Century* (Geneva: Institut et Musée Voltaire, 1965), 33, 157.

32. The review was never published.

33. Louis-Antoine de Bougainville, *Voyage autour du monde, par la frégate du roi La Boudeuse, et la flûte L'Étoile* (Paris: chez Saillant & Nyon, 1772).

34. Ibid., 3:74.

35. Ibid., 3:74–75.

36. Ibid., 3:78–79.

37. Ibid., 3:65.

38. Ibid., 2:44.

39. Ibid., 3:87.

40. Diderot, *Rameau's Nephew and Other Works* [inc. *Supplement to Bougainville's Voyage*] (Indianapolis: Hackett, 2001) 187.

41. Ibid., 194.

42. Ibid., 196.

43. Ibid., 198–99.

44. Ibid., 206.

45. Ibid., 204.

46. Ibid., 208.

47. See, for example, the semimonthly Catholic magazine *Revue pratique d'apologétique* (Paris: G. Beauchesne, 1796), 17:231.

48. *Code Pénal, ou Recueil des principales ordonnances, édits et déclarations* (Paris: chez Desaint et Saillant, 1752), 2: 256.

49. Ibid. See Maurice Lever, *Les Bûchers de Sodome* (Paris: Fayard, 1985).

50. *Enc.*, 16:617.

51. Diderot, *Rameau's Nephew and D'Alembert's Dream*, trans. Tancock, 170.

52. Ibid., 172.

53. Ibid., 175.

54. *Corr.*, 4:39.

55. Louis Crompton, *Homosexuality and Civilization* (Cambridge, MA: Harvard University Press, 2003), 522.

56. Diderot, *Diderot on Art I*, 217.

57. Diderot, *Rameau's Nephew and D'Alembert's Dream*, 135.

58. *Corr.*, 7:96.

59. *Corr.*, 8:118.

60. *Corr.*, 2:269.

X.

ON LOVE

1. *Corr.*, 2:97.

2. Ibid.

3. Friedrich Nietzsche, *On the Genealogy of Morals and Ecce Homo* (New York: Vintage, 1989), 107.

4. Ibid.

5. Ibid.

6. *Corr.*, 1:27–28.

7. Ibid., 1:32.

8. Alice Laborde, *Diderot et Madame de Puisieux* (Saratoga, CA: Anma Libri, 1984), 18.

9. DPV, 1:392.

10. The report is shown in Émile Campardon, *Les Prodigalités d'un fermier général: complément aux mémoires de Madame d'Épinay* (Paris: Charavay, 1882), 119–20.

11. *Denis Diderot*, ed. Raymond Trousson (Paris: PUPS, 2005), 60.

12. Ibid., 61.

13. *Corr.*, 1:141.

14. Ibid., 2:124–25.

15. Ibid., 5:69.

16. Meghan K. Roberts, *Sentimental Savants: Philosophical Families in Enlightenment France* (Chicago: University of Chicago Press, 2016), 125.

17. Sigmund Freud, *Civilization and Its Discontents*, ed. Todd Dufresne, trans. Gregory C. Richter (Peterborough, Ontario: Broadview), 2015.

18. Diderot, *Rameau's Nephew and d'Alembert's Dream*, trans. Tancock, 5–46.

19. Wilson, *Diderot*, 229. For a summary of the various places where the Vollands lived, see Laurent Versini, "Diderot piéton de Paris," in *Travaux de littérature* 13 (Geneva: Droz, 2000), 177–94.

20. Now the quai de la Tournelle.

21. *Corr.*, 2:168–69.

22. Ibid., 3:68.

23. Ibid., 2:136–37.

24. Ibid., 3:74.

25. Ibid.

26. Ibid.

27. See Stenger, *Diderot*, 185; and Michel Delon, *Diderot cul par-dessus tête* (Paris: Albin Michel, 2013), 259.

28. *Corr.*, 2:193.

29. Ibid., 3:63.

30. Ibid., 3:69.

31. Ibid., 5:35.

32. Ibid., 2:145.

33. Ibid., 7:68.

34. Ibid., 6:155–60.

35. Ibid., 4:52.

36. Auguste Rey, *Le Château de la Chevrette et Madame d'Épinay* (Paris: Plon, 1904), 121.

37. Ibid.

38. See Versini, "Diderot piéton de Paris," 185.

39. *Corr.*, 10:97. This is taken from his *Voyage à Bourbonne*.

40. *Corr.*, 10:142.

41. *Corr.*, 10:154.

42. *Corr.*, 10:155.

43. *Corr.*, 15:77.

44. *Corr.*, 15:254.

45. Lydia Claude Hartman, "Esquisse d'un portrait de Sophie Volland: quelques notes sur la vie privée, les amitiés du philosophe," *Diderot Studies* 16 (Geneva: Droz, 1973), 69–89, 71.

46. *Corr.*, 2:284.

47. Ibid.

XI.

A VOYAGE TO RUSSIA: POLITICS, PHILOSOPHY,
AND CATHERINE THE GREAT

1. Robert K. Massie, *Catherine the Great: Portrait of a Woman* (New York: Random House, 2012), 7

2. Ibid.

3. Ibid.

4. Catherine the Great, *The Memoires of Catherine the Great*, trans. Mark Cruse and Hilde Hoogenboom (New York: Modern Library, 2006), xxvi.

5. Ibid., xxx.

6. Stenger, *Diderot*, 306.

7. See Inna Gorbatov, *Catherine the Great and the French Philosophers of the Enlightenment: Montesquieu, Voltaire, Rousseau, Diderot, and Grimm* (Bethesda, MD: Academic Press, 2006), 77.

8. Catherine the Great, *The Memoirs of Catherine the Great*, xxvi.

9. Cited in *Corr.*, 7: 354.

10. Ibid., 7:355.

11. Ibid., 7:101.

12. Ibid., 7:67.

13. The paintings had been purchased by his uncle, the wealthy financier and art collector Antoine Crozat, during the late seventeenth and early eighteenth century. Diderot was helped in this by François Tronchin, who had the idea to purchase the collection, and by Robert Tronchin, who examined its contents.

14. See Joanna Pitman, *The Dragon's Trail: The Biography of Raphael's Masterpiece* (New York: Touchstone, 2007), for a discussion of the Crozat family. See also Alden Gordon's inventory of the collection, *The Houses and Collections of the Marquis de Marigny, Documents for the History of Collecting: French Inventories*, vol. 1 (Los Angeles: Getty, 2003).

15. Henry Tronchin, *Le Conseiller François Tronchin et ses amis: Voltaire, Grimm, Diderot, etc.* (Paris: Plon, 1895), 307.

16. *Corr.*, 12:49.

17. J. F. Bosher, "The French Crisis of 1770," *History: Journal of the Historical Association* 57, no. 189 (1972): 18.

18. This is the context for Abbé Galiani's *Dialogues sur le commerce des blés*, which was heavily edited and prepared for publication by Diderot in 1770. The debate on grain was also the source for Diderot's *Apologie de l'abbé Galiani*

(*Apology of Abbé Galiani*), which was composed in 1770 and 1771. This letter was never published and was discovered in the Fonds Vandeul.

19. Bosher, "The French Crisis of 1770," 24.

20. *Corr.*, 12:49.

21. Anthony Strugnell, *Diderot's Politics: A Study of the Evolution of Diderot's Political Thought After the Encyclopédie, International Archives of the History of Ideas* 62 (Heidelberg: Springer Netherlands, 1973), 134. A former president of the Parlement of Paris himself, René Nicolas Charles Augustin de Maupeou, who became chancellor of France in 1768, ultimately oversaw the suspension of the Parlement's functions.

22. *Corr.*, 12:49. He was speaking specifically of the fact that papal bulls no longer needed to be registered before being disseminated in France.

23. Strugnell, *Diderot's Politics*, 108.

24. *Corr.*, 12:49

25. Ibid., 12.64.

26. Ibid.

27. Diderot had begun making tentative arrangements to marry his daughter into this distinguished family of Langrois industrialists seventeen years prior. See ibid., 1:191. While he veered away from this unofficial arrangement in the mid-1760s—at one point he even briefly considered Grimm as a possible "son-in-law" – Diderot returned to his original idea by 1767. He had also considered the engineer Viallet as her husband. See ibid., 7:181.

28. Ibid., 10:40–41.

29. Ibid., 12:113.

30. Ibid., 12:135.

31. Ibid., 12:136.

32. In a similar note to his sister, he admitted grimly, "I no longer have a child, I am alone, and my solitude is unbearable" (ibid., 12:139). To Grimm, to whom he confessed his doubts about the marriage itself, he

angrily complained that Abel wanted to "dress [Angélique] like a doll" and seemingly had no interest in her continuing to play the harpsichord (ibid., 12:179–80).

33. Ibid., 12:126.

34. Diderot, *Mémoires pour Catherine II* (Paris: Garnier frères, 1966), 266.

35. *Corr.*, 12:232.

36. Ibid.

37. A. V. Naryshkin (1742–1800) had the official court rank of Kammerherr, or chamberlain.

38. The North Sea.

39. *Corr.*, 13:15.

40. *Corr.*, 13:31.

41. Diderot also found time to annotate Helvétius's *De l'homme* and Hemsterhuis's *Lettre sur l'homme et ses rapports.* He also added new material to *Rameau's Nephew* and *Jacques the Fatalist.*

42. Stenger, *Diderot*, 617.

43. Laurent Versini, "Note sur le voyage de Diderot en Russie," in *L'influence française en Russie au XVIIIème siècle*, ed. Jean-Pierre Poussou, Anne Mézin, and Yves Perret-Gentil (Paris: Institut d'études slaves, 2004), 227.

44.　And for an *écu* … for an *écu*?

　　What do I do? Well, I see her *cul* [butt].

　　For two *écus*? What do I do?

　　I grab her c●●●; and I f●●● her too.

　　And for my three *écus*, deux *testons*, and one *obole*,

　　I had a breast, a butt, the c●●●, as well as the *vérole* [pox or syphilis]

Herbert Dieckmann, *Inventaire du fonds Vandeul et inédits de Diderot* (Geneva: Droz, 1951), 288.

45. *Corr.*, 13:64.

46. Herbert Dieckmann, "An Unpublished Notice of Diderot on Falconet," *Journal of the Warburg and Courtauld Institutes* 15 (1952): 257–58.

47. *Corr.*, 12:228.

48. Wilson, *Diderot*, 631. Diderot must have thought about staying with his only other real friend in Saint Petersburg, Melchior Grimm. Grimm, however, was thoroughly occupied with the wedding of the grand duke, the son of the empress, which was taking place the next day.

49. Inna Gorbatov, "Le voyage de Diderot en Russie," *Études littéraires* 38, nos. 2–3 (2007): 215–29.

50. When Diderot was still in Russia (in February 1774), Catherine began the most important relationship of her life with Grigory Potemkin, who possibly became her secret husband and who most certainly became her most trusted deputy and adviser.

51. Massie, *Catherine the Great*, 524.

52. Ibid., 338.

53. Voltaire, *Œuvres complètes de Voltaire*, éd. Louis Moland (Paris: Garnier, 1877–85), 26:551.

54. *Corr.*, 13:81.

55. Indeed, under pressure Diderot was forced to recant in the "Errata" to volume 3. See the excellent introduction to Diderot, *Diderot, Political Writings*, ed. John Hope Mason and Robert Wokler (Cambridge, UK: Cambridge University Press, 1992), xii.

56. David Williams, ed., *The Enlightenment: Cambridge Readings in the History of Political Thought* (Cambridge, UK: Cambridge University Press, 1999), 33.

57. Diderot, *Mémoires pour Catherine II*, 178.

58. Virginia Cowles, *The Romanovs* (London: William Collins, 1979), 90. Jacques Necker proposed this in 1789, but the idea was rejected by the nobility.

59. Louis-Philippe, comte de Ségur, *Mémoires ou Souvenirs et anecdotes* (Paris: Henri Colburn, 1827), 3:35.

60. State Papers Foreign 91 [Russia], vol. 94, fol. 136, Public Records Office, British Museum.

61. He had also offered d'Alembert a significant pension and the presidency of the Royal Academy of Sciences in Berlin.

62. D'Holbach's *Essay* was published under the name of the late Encyclopedist César Chesneau Dumarsais. See Strugnell, *Diderot's Politics*, 132.

63. Diderot, "Introduction" [to *Pages contre un tyran*], *Œuvres politiques* (Paris: Garnier, 1963), 129.

64. Ibid., 148.

65. The occasion of the review was the publication of an unauthorized edition of Diderot's collected works that had recently appeared in Amsterdam; it included mediocre books and essays written by other authors. See Adrienne Hytier, "Le Philosophe et le despote," *Diderot Studies* 9 (1964): 74.

66. V. A. Bilbassov, *Diderot à Pétersbourg* (Saint Petersburg: Skorokhodov, 1884), 173. Grimm indicates that Frederick was behind this plot in a letter sent on February 7, 1774, to Nesselrode. *Corr.*, 13:192.

67. Ibid., 13:208.

68. Ibid., 13:203.

69. Ibid., 13:234.

XII.
LAST WORDS: SPEAKING TO DESPOTS
AND AMERICAN INSURGENTS

1. *Corr.*, 14:48.

2. Ibid., 13:223. Riga is twenty-five kilometers from "Mittau," where Diderot describes being thrown into a boat.

3. *Corr.*, 13:238.

4. He does not specify where they lost the carriage that Catherine had given him.

5. The author was Ivan Ivanovich Betskoy. See *Plans et statuts des différents établissements ordonnés par Sa Majesté Impériale Catherine II pour l'éducation de la jeunesse et l'utilité générale de son empire* (Amsterdam: M.M. Rey, 1775).

6. *Corr.*, 13:231.

7. According to Jean-Baptiste-Antoine Suard, who reported that Diderot came back "drunk with admiration" for this woman. See *Corr.*, 14:106–08.

8. Diderot, "Introduction" [to *Pages contre un tyran*], *Œuvres politiques* (Paris: Garnier, 1963), 179.

9. Ibid., 163.

10. See *Corr.*, 14:73. In December Diderot wrote to ask her to call back her Legislative Commission to forge a new code of laws that would be the foundation for a new Russia.

11. Diderot, "Introduction," 343.

12. Ibid., 344.

13. Ibid., 345.

14. Florence Boulerie, "Diderot a-t-il inventé une université pour le gouvernement de Russie?" in François Cadilhon, Jean Mondot, and Jacques Verger, eds., *Universités et institutions universitaires européennes au XVIIIe siècle: entre modernisation et tradition* (Bordeaux: Presses universitaires de Bordeaux, 1999), 131.

15. Diderot, *Œuvres complètes* (Paris: Le club français du livre, 1971), 11:745.

16. Ibid., 11:745–46. See Michèle Chabanon "Le *Plan d'une université*: une ouverture à demi-mot," *RDE* 35 (2003): 41–60, for a discussion of the link between civilization and the mission to civilize "savages" and education.

17. See Béatrice Didier, "Quand Diderot faisait le plan d'une université," *RDE* 18 (1995): 81–91.

18. Diderot, *Œuvres complètes* (1971), 11:750.

19. The Parlement registered an "Édit de tolerance" on November 29, 1787, that forbid Protestants from being persecuted and allowed them to gain positions in both the government and in the military. As for France's Jews, their own rehabilitation came with the Revolution, in September 1791.

20. Stenger, *Diderot*, 653.

21. *Corr.*, 14:218.

22. Ibid., 14:150.

23. Ibid., 14:218.

24. This started as the *Plan d'un divertissement domestique (Plan for a Domestic Entertainment)*, which appeared in the *Literary Correspondence*.

25. James Fowler, ed., "Introduction," in *New Essays on Diderot* (Cambridge, UK: Cambridge University Press, 2011), 7.

26. Pierre Frantz, *Est-il bon? Est-il méchant?* (Paris: Folio, 2012).

27. See *Corr.*, 14:169. See also Thierry Belleguic (dir.), *Le Dernier Diderot: autour de l'*Essai sur les règnes de Claude et de Néron, *Diderot Studies*, no. 32 (2012). D'Holbach and Naigeon completed this translation after the original translator, abbé La Grange, died before completing it.

28. The eighteenth century believed that he was not a dramatist.

29. DPV, 1:425.

30. Diderot, *Essai sur la vie de Sénèque le philosophe, sur ses écrits et sur les règnes de Claude et de Néron* (Paris: chez les frères De Bure, 1779), 7:11. See also Joanna Stalnaker, "Diderot's Literary Testament," *Diderot Studies* 31 (2009): 45–56.

31. See Elena Russo, "Slander and Glory in the Republic of Letters: Diderot and Seneca Confront Rousseau," *Republics of Letters*, no. 1 (May 2009), http://rofl.stanford.edu/node/40.

32. Diderot, *Essai sur la vie de Sénèque*, 7:11.

33. DPV 15:126–27.

34. Unlike Diderot's two books on Seneca, the *Confessions* immediately sold eight thousand copies. See Dorthea E. von Mücke, *The Practices of the Enlightenment: Aesthetics, Authorship, and the Public* (New York: Columbia University Press, 2015), 265.

35. *Nouvelles de la république des lettres et des arts* 11, March 13, 1782 (Paris: Ruault, 1782), 82.

36. See Michèle Duchet, *Diderot et l'Histoire des deux Indes* (Paris: A.G. Nizet, 1978), 31.

37. This was entitled *École militaire*. See Hans-Jürgen Lüsebrink and Manfred Tietz, "Introduction," in Hans-Jürgen Lüsebrink and Manfred Tietz, eds., *Lectures de Raynal: l'"Histoire des deux Indes" en Europe et en Amérique au XVIIIe siècle. Studies on Voltaire and the Eighteenth Century* 286 (Oxford: Voltaire Foundation, 1991), 2.

38. Girolamo Imbruglia, "Civilisation and Colonisation: Enlightenment

Theories in the Debate between Diderot and Raynal," *History of European Ideas* 41, no. 7 (2015): 859. A plantation holder himself on Saint-Domingue, Choiseul probably numbered among the more forward-thinking people calling for a so-called enlightened form of slavery.

39. Lüsebrink and Tietz, eds., *Lectures de Raynal*, 3.

40. Goggi, "Quelques remarques sur la collaboration de Diderot à la première édition de l'*Histoire des deux Indes*," ibid., 17.

41. Diderot, *Diderot, Political Writings*, ed. John Hope Mason and Robert Wokler (Cambridge, UK: Cambridge University Press, 1992), 171.

42. Ibid., 172.

43. Ibid., 182.

44. Andrew S. Curran, *Anatomy of Blackness: Science and Slavery in an Age of Enlightenment* (Baltimore: Johns Hopkins University Press, 2011), 229, n. 41.

45. *HDI*, 1770, 4:167–68.

46. Diderot, *Political Writings*, 212.

47. *HDI*, 1780, 3:280.

48. Ibid., 1780, 4:418.

49. See Guillaume Ansart, "Variations on Montesquieu: Raynal and Diderot's *Histoire des deux Indes* and the American Revolution," *Journal of the History of Ideas* 70 (3): 399–420.

50. Jonathan Israel, *The Expanding Blaze: How the American Revolution Ignited the World, 1775–1848* (Princeton: Princeton University Press, 2017), 117.

51. Though Diderot's correspondence from the last years of his life once again leaves big gaps, it is quite probable that he had at least some contact with Franklin. One snippet of proof comes in a letter from A. C. G. Deudon to Benjamin Franklin written on August 10, 1783, where he reminds Franklin that Diderot had arranged for Deudon to see his famous "glass armonica," which he had invented some twenty years earlier. The letter implies that Diderot had seen the instrument and, presumably, Franklin himself. See Benjamin Franklin, *The Papers of Benjamin Franklin* (New Haven: Yale University Press, 2011), 40:453.

52. Ibid., 20: 447–48.

53. C. P. Courtney, "Burke, Franklin et Raynal: à propos de deux lettres inédites," in *Revue d'histoire littéraire de la France* 62, no. 1 (1962): 81.

54. This honor was conferred despite the book's ridiculous assertions that the "new" continent suffered from endemic degeneration.

55. *HDI*, 1774, 7:182.

56. This is nicely summed up by Strugnell, *Diderot's Politics*, 208–09.

57. *HDI*, 1780, 4:417.

58. Ibid., 1780, 4:456.

59. Ibid., 1780, 1:398.

60. *Correspondance littéraire, philosophique et critique par Grimm, Diderot, Raynal, Meister, etc.*, 14:465. See *Corr.*, 14:225.

61. In theory this quote was dedicated to Elisa Drapper, but the title became associated with Raynal himself.

62. *Corr.*, 15:211.

63. Though we do not know for sure, it seems more than likely that Diderot never sent this letter.

64. *Corr.*, 15:213 and 15:226.

65. Ibid., 15:227.

66. Diderot, *Political Writings*, 214.

EPILOGUE:

WALKING BETWEEN TWO ETERNITIES

1. *Corr.*, 15:19. The two men exchanged twenty-six letters.

2. Ibid., 15:91.

3. Ibid., 15:38. I am quoting the actual analogy he had used while speaking to François Tronchin.

4. Ibid., 15:90.

5. Ibid.

6. Ibid.

7. Rousseau's death is admirably recounted by Leo Damrosch, *Jean-Jacques Rousseau: Restless Genius* (New York: Houghton Mifflin, 2007), 488.

8. *Corr.*, 15:132.

9. Ibid., 15:247. See Eric Hazan, *The Invention of Paris: A History in Footsteps*, trans. David Fernbach (London: Verso, 2010), 20. Louis-Sebastien Mercier described the typical flavors in *Tableau de Paris* (Amsterdam, 1789), 12:180.

10. DPV, 17:516.

11. I borrow this expression from Charles Wolfe. See *Materialism: A Historico-Philosophical Introduction* (Ghent: Springer, 2016), 62.

12. The fatalism evoked in the title of this book is quite different from what is evoked by the term "fatalism" today. In contemporary usage, fatalists bow down before providence or destiny, maintaining that they have no control over the future or themselves. In stark contrast, a fatalist from Diderot's point of view is someone who believes that one's entire life is not preordained by fate, but is certainly determined by one's biological and psychological essence.

13. Diderot, *Jacques the Fatalist*, trans. David Coward (Oxford: Oxford University Press, 1999), 3.

14. Fatalism and determinism are quite different, philosophically speaking, but they are essentially conflated in Diderot's system. See Anthony Strugnell, *Diderot's Politics: A Study of the Evolution of Diderot's Political Thought After the Encyclopédie*, International Archives of the History of Ideas 62 (Heidelberg: Springer Netherlands, 1973), 45.

15. In 1756, in a letter that he sent to the playwright Paul-Louis Landois, Diderot asserts quite brutally that in a world where all things are determined, human behavior was nothing more than what corresponds to "the general order, our organization [physiology], our education, and the chain of events." See DPV 9:257.

16. Colas Duflos, *Les aventures de Sophie: la philosophie dans le roman au XVIIIème siècle* (Paris: CNRS editions, 2013), 253.

17. Socrates had famously written that it was absurd to fear what we do not know. See Plato, *Apologie de Socrate, Criton, Phédon*, trans. Léon Robin and Joseph Moreau (Paris: Gallimard, 1968), 43.

18. Diderot, *Jacques the Fatalist*, 63.

19. *Corr.*, 15:321.

20. Madame de Vandeul, *Diderot, mon père* (Strasbourg: Circe, 1992), 48.

21. Ibid.

22. Ibid., 56.

23. *Corr.*, 15:320.

24. Ibid., 15:335.

25. Diderot, *Voyage à Bourbonne, à Langres et autres récits* (Paris: Aux Amateurs des livres, 1989), 27. Along with his friend, the celebrated Dr. Tronchin, Diderot had long believed that the most effective way to get over a malady was to exercise and avoid purges and bloodletting. This was a radical idea at the time.

26. Vandeul, *Diderot, mon père*, 48.

27. Ibid., 49.

28. See Roger Pearson's account of this death in *Voltaire Almighty* (New York: Bloomsbury, 2005), 385–91.

29. Absent his heart and brain, which had been removed, Voltaire's body remained in Romilly-sur-Seine until its pantheonization in 1791. D'Alembert, who died in 1783, was also threatened with the ignominy of the *voirie* as well. In his case, however, he received a decent burial thanks to a technicality: as secretary of the Académie française, he was accorded special protected status and granted a resting place within the common grave of the Porcherons cemetery. (See Wilson, *Diderot*, 711.)

30. L. Petit de Bachaumont et al., *Mémoires secrets pour servir à l'histoire de la République des Lettres en France* (London: chez John Adamson, 1784), 23:241.

31. Diderot's son-in-law, Caroillon de Vandeul, reported that the priest "captivated the esteem of both Monsieur and Madame [Diderot]." *Corr.*, 15:331.

32. Vandeul, *Diderot, mon père*, 50.

33. Ibid., 51.

34. Ibid.

35. Ibid., 51–52.

36. Ibid., 52.

37. Ibid.

38. *Enc.*, 8:576.

39. *Corr.*, 6:66.

40. Philippe Blom makes a similar point. See *A Wicked Company: The Forgotten Radicalism of the European Enlightenment* (Basic Books, 2010), 308.

41. René Tarin, *Diderot et la Révolution française: controverses et polémiques autour d'un philosophe* (Paris: Champion, 2001), 51–52.

42. Louis-Sébastien Mercier had actually attributed it to Diderot as early as 1791, claiming he heard Diderot say it in the café Procope. The quote is actually a paraphrase from Voltaire's version of Meslier's famous *Testament*, which Diderot knew well. See Pascal Pellerin, "Diderot, Voltaire et le curé Meslier: un sujet tabou," *Diderot Studies* 29 (2003), 54.

43. Henceforth, Diderot would be seen as a bloodthirsty proto-sansculottist associated with the proto-communist rabble rouser François-Noël Babeuf, who was guillotined in 1796. This image was also disseminated by abbé Barruel in his *Mémoires pour servir à l'histoire du Jacobinisme*, which treated Diderot as an extremist involved in an anti-Christian conspiracy.

44. F. G. de La Rochefoucauld, *Esprit des écrivains du 18ème siècle* (Paris: chez Giguet et Michaud, 1809), 29.

45. This is a famous quote from Auguste Comte, *Le Livre: revue mensuelle* (Paris: A. Quantin, 1884), 114.

46. Raymond Trousson, ed., *Denis Diderot*, 30.

47. *Célébration du centenaire de Diderot au Palais du Trocadéro le dimanche 27 juillet 1884: discours de M. Pierre Laffitte* (Paris: au dépôt de la *Revue occidentale*, 1884), 5.

48. Part of a much larger project that sought to inscribe the Republic's values onto the city's topography, Diderot's image was supposed to join a number of other statues that paid tribute to a series of eighteenth-century heroes, among them Jean-Paul Marat, Camille Desmoulins, Georges Danton, and the Marquis de Condorcet. The city of Paris commissioned another statue in 1884. Realized by Leon Aimé Joachim Lecointe, it was erected in the square d'Anvers. It was melted down in 1942.

49. Daniel Brewer, *The Enlightenment Past: Reconstructing Eighteenth-Century French Thought* (Cambridge, UK: Cambridge University Press, 2008), 151.

50. Ibid.

51. Gautherin had not been able to cast the statue in time for the dedication. Instead, he supplied a ghostlike plaster model of the philosophe that ultimately sat out in the elements for almost two years. See *Le Correspondant* (Paris: bureaux du *Correspondant*, 1884) 100: 910.

52. Colas Duflo, "Et pourquoi des dialogues en des temps de systèmes?," *Diderot Studies* 28 (2000): 95–109, p. 96.

53. Elisabeth de Fontenay, *Diderot ou le matérialisme enchanté* (Paris: Grasset et Fasquelle, 1981), 14. See also Andrew Curran, *Sublime Disorder: Physical Monstrosity in Diderot's Universe.*

54. Duflo, "Et pourquoi des dialogues?," 96.

Works Cited

Albertan-Coppola, Sylviane. "Les Préjugés légitimes de Chaumeix ou l'En-cyclopédie sous la loupe d'un apologiste." *Recherches sur Diderot et sur l'En-cyclopédie*, no. 20 (1996): 149–58. Paris: Aux Amateurs de Livres.

Alembert, Jean le Rond d'. *Discours prononcés dans l'Académie françoise, le jeudi 19 décembre MDCCLIV, à la réception de M. d'Alembert. Suivi de Réponse de M. Gresset* [Jean-Baptiste-Louis], *Directeur de l'Académie françoise, au Discours prononcé par M. d'Alembert*. Paris: Brunet, 1754.

——. *Preliminary Discourse to the Encyclopedia of Diderot*. Translated and introduced by Richard N. Schwab. Chicago: University of Chicago Press, 1995.

Algrant, Christine Pevitt. *Madame de Pompadour: Mistress of France*. New York: Grove, 2003.

Anderson, Wilda. *Diderot's Dream*. Baltimore: Johns Hopkins University Press, 1990.

Andrew, Edward G. *Patrons of Enlightenment*. Toronto: University of Toronto Press, 2006.

Ansart, Guillaume. "Variations on Montesquieu: Raynal and Diderot's *Histoire des deux Indes* and the American Revolution." *Journal of the History of Ideas* 3, no. 70 (2009): 399–420. Philadelphia: University of Pennsylvania Press.

Argenson, René-Louis de Voyer de Paulmy d'. *Mémoires et journal inédit du marquis d'Argenson*. Paris: P. Jannet, 1857.

Arrests de la Cour de Parlement, portant condamnation de plusieurs livres et autres ouvrages imprimés. Paris: P.G. Simon, 1759.

Bachaumont, Louis Petit de. *Mémoires secrets pour servir à l'histoire de la République des Lettres en France,* vol. 23. London: John Adamson, 1784.

Bacon, Francis. *The Advancement of Learning.* Edited by Stephen Jay Gould. New York: Random House and Modern Library, 2001.

Balcou, Jean. *Fréron contre les philosophes.* Geneva: Droz, 1975.

Bald, Margaret. *Literature Suppressed on Religious Grounds.* New York: Infobase Publishing, 2006.

Baldwin, Tom. "Ekphrasis and Related Issues in Diderot's *Salons.*" In James Fowler, ed., *New Essays on Diderot,* 234–47. Cambridge, UK: Cambridge University Press, 2011.

Barbier, Edmond Jean François. *Chronique de la Régence et du règne de Louis XV (1718–1763), ou Journal de Barbier,* Série 7. Paris: Charpentier, 1866.

Barker, Emma. *Greuze and the Painting of Sentiment.* Cambridge, UK: Cambridge University Press, 2005.

Barruel, abbé Augustin. *Mémoires pour servir à l'histoire du jacobinisme.* 5 vols. Ausburg: les libraires associés, 1797.

Bayle, Pierre. *Pensées diverses sur la comète.* Edited by Joyce Bost and Hubert Bost. Paris: Flammarion, 2007.

Becq, Annie. *Genèse de l'esthétique française moderne. De la Raison classique à l'Imagination créatrice, 1680–1814.* Paris: Albin Michel, coll. "Bibliothèque de l'évolution de l'humanité," [1984], 1994.

———. "L'*Encyclopédie*· le choix de l'ordre alphabétique." *Recherches sur Diderot et sur l'Encyclopédie* 18 (1995): 133–37. Paris: Aux Amateurs de Livres.

Belleguic, Thierry. "La matière de l'art: Diderot et l'expérience esthétique dans les premiers *Salons.*" *Diderot Studies,* no. 30 (2007): 3–10. Geneva: Droz.

Bender, John B., and Michael Marrinan. *The Culture of Diagram.* Stanford: Stanford University Press, 2010.

Berenguier, Nadine. *Conduct Books for Girls in Enlightenment France.* London: Routledge, 2016.

Betskoy, Ivanovich. *Plans et statuts des différents établissements ordonnés par Sa Majesté Impériale Catherine II pour l'éducation de la jeunesse et l'utilité générale de son empire.* Amsterdam: M. M. Rey, 1775.

Beverland, Adriaen. *État de l'homme dans le péché originel.* Amsterdam: Imprimé dans le monde, 1714.

Bibliothèque raisonnée des ouvrages des savants de l'Europe. Pour les mois de janvier, février et mars 1730, 4:377–91. Amsterdam: J. Wetstein and G. Smith, 1730.

Bilbassov, V. A. *Diderot à Pétersbourg.* Saint Petersburg: Skorokhodov, 1884.

Blanchard, Gilles, and Mark Olsen. "Le système de renvois dans l'*Encyclopédie*: une cartographie des structures de connaissances au XVIIIe siècle." *Recherches sur Diderot et sur l'Encyclopédie* 31–32 (April 2002): 45–70. Paris: Aux Amateurs de Livres.

Blom, Philippe. *Enlightening the World. Encyclopédie, The Book that Changed the World.* New York: Palgrave Macmillan, 2005.

———. *A Wicked Company: The Forgotten Radicalism of the European Enlightenment.* New York: Basic Books, 2010.

Bonnefon, Paul. "Diderot prisonnier à Vincennes." *Revue d'histoire littéraire de la France.*, no. 6 (1899): 200–24. Geneva: Droz.

Booy, Jean de, and Alan Freer. "*Jacques le Fataliste*" *et* "*La Religieuse*" *devant la critique révolutionnaire (1796–1800).* Geneva: Institut et Musée Voltaire, SVEC, 1965, no. 33.

Bosher, John Francis. "The French Crisis of 1770." *History: The Journal of the Historical Association* 57, no. 189 (1972). London: Historical Association.

Bougainville, Louis-Antoine de. *Voyage autour du monde, par la frégate du roi La Boudeuse et la flûte L'Étoile; en 1766, 1767, 1768 et 1769.* Paris: Saillant et Nyon, 1772.

Boulerie, Florence. "Diderot a-t-il inventé une université pour le gouvernement de Russie?" In François Cadilhon, Jean Mondot, and Jacques Verger, eds., *Universités et institutions universitaires européennes au XVIIIe siècle: entre modernisation et tradition*, 131–47. Bordeaux: Presses universitaires de Bordeaux, 1999.

Bouquet, Henri Louis. *L'Ancien collège d'Harcourt et le lycée Saint-Louis. Notes et documents.* Avec un dessin de George Antoine Rochegrosse. Paris: Delalain frères, 1891.

Brewer, Daniel. *The Discourse of Enlightenment in Eighteenth-Century France.* Cambridge, UK: Cambridge University Press, 1993.

———. *The Enlightenment Past: Reconstructing Eighteenth-Century French Thought.* Cambridge, UK: Cambridge University Press, 2008.

Brillon, Pierre-Jacques. *Dictionnaire de jurisprudence et des arrests,* vol. 6. Paris: Cavelier, Brunet, Gosselin et Cavelier, 1727.

British Museum, Public Records Office. *State Papers Foreign 91* [Russia], vol. 94, fol. 136.

Bruzen de la Martinière, Antoine Augustin. *Le Grand Dictionnaire géographique et critique.* 10 vols. Venice: Jean Baptiste Pasquali, 1726–39.

Bryson, Norman. *Word and Image: French Painting of the Ancien Régime.* Cambridge, UK: Cambridge University Press, 1981.

Buddeus, Johann Franz, Louis Philon, and Jean Chretien Fischer. *Traité de l'athéisme et de la superstition.* Translated by Louis Philon. Amsterdam: J. Schreuder et P. Mortier le jeune, 1756.

Buffat, Marc. "Diderot, Falconet et l'amour de la postérité." *Recherches sur Diderot et sur l'Encyclopédie,* no. 43 (2008): 9–20. Paris: Aux Amateurs de Livres.

Byrne, James M. *Religion and the Enlightenment: From Descartes to Kant.* Louisville: John Knox Press, 1996.

Cambridge History of Eighteenth Century Philosophy. Vol. 2. Cambridge, UK: Cambridge University Press, 2006.

Campardon, Émile. *Les Prodigalités d'un fermier général: complément aux mémoires de madame d'Épinay.* Paris: Charavay frères, 1882.

Catherine the Great. *The Memoirs of Catherine the Great.* Translated by Mark Cruise and Hilde Hoogenboom. New York: Modern Library Paperback, 2006.

"Célébration du centenaire de Diderot au Palais du Trocadéro le dimanche

27 juillet 1884: Discours de M. Pierre Laffitte." *La Revue occidentale philosophique, sociale et politique*, no. 4 (1884): 263. Paris: Au bureau de la *Revue*.

Censorship: A World Encyclopedia. Edited by Derek Jones. London: Routledge, 2001.

Chabanon, Michèle. "Le *Plan d'une université*: une ouverture à demi-mot." *Recherches sur Diderot et sur l'Encyclopédie*, no. 35 (2003): 41-60. Paris: Aux Amateurs de Livres.

Chaumeix, Abraham-Joseph de. *Préjugés légitimes contre* l'Encyclopédie *et essai de réfutation de ce dictionnaire*. 2 vols. Brussels: Herissant, 1758–59.

Le Chevalier de Jaucourt: l'homme aux dix-sept mille articles. Edited by Gilles Barroux and François Pépin. Paris: Société Diderot, 2015.

Chomel, Noël, and Pierre Roger. *Supplément au Dictionnaire œconomique* [sic] *contenant divers moyens d'augmenter son bien, et de conserver sa santé*. Amsterdam: J. Covens et C. Mortier, 1740.

Choudhury, Mita. *The Wanton Jesuit and the Wayward Saint: A Tale of Sex, Religion, and Politics in Eighteenth-Century France*. University Park: Pennsylvania State University Press, 2015.

Chouillet, Anne-Marie. "Trois lettres inédites de Diderot." *Recherches sur Diderot et sur l'Encyclopédie*. no. 11 (1991): 8–18. Paris: Aux Amateurs de Livres.

Chouillet, Jacques, et Anne-Marie Chouillet. *Diderot*. Paris: CDU-SEDES, 1977.

Clark, Andrew Herrick. *Diderot's Part*. Hampshire, UK: Ashgate, 2008.

Code Pénal, ou Recueil des principales ordonnances, édits et déclarations. 2 vols. Paris: Desaint et Saillant, 1752.

Collignon, Albert. *Diderot: sa vie, ses œuvres, sa correspondance*. Paris: F. Alcan, 1895.

Comte, Auguste. *Le Livre: revue mensuelle des lettres, des sciences et des arts* 114 (1884). Paris: A. Quantin.

Cordess, Christopher. "Criminality and Psychoanalysis." In *The Freud Encyclopedia: Theory, Therapy, and Culture*, ed. Edward Erwin. London: Routledge, 2002.

Le Correspondant, recueil périodique. Vol. 100. Paris: Bureaux du *Correspondant*, 1884.

Courtney, C. P. "Burke, Franklin et Raynal: à propos de deux lettres inédites." *Revue d'histoire littéraire de la France* 62, no. 1 (1962): 78–86. Geneva: Droz.

Cowles, Virginia. *The Romanovs.* London: Collins, Smith, 1979.

Crampe-Casnabet, Michèle. "Les articles 'Âme' dans l'*Encyclopédie.*" *Recherches sur Diderot et sur l'Encyclopédie*, no. 25 (1998): 91–99. Paris: Aux Amateurs de Livres.

Crompton, Louis. *Homosexuality and Civilization.* Cambridge, MA: Harvard University Press, 2003.

Cronk, Nicholas. *Voltaire: A Very Short Introduction.* Oxford: Oxford University Press, 2017.

Crow, Thomas E. *Painters and Public Life in Eighteenth-Century Paris.* New Haven: Yale University Press, 1985.

Crowther, Louise. "Diderot, Spinoza, and the Question of Virtue." *MHRA Working Papers in the Humanities* 2 (2007): 11–18. Cambridge, UK: Modern Humanities Research Association.

Cunningham, Andrew, and Ole Peter Grell. *Medicine and Religion in Enlightenment Europe.* Hampshire, UK: Ashgate, 2007.

Curran, Andrew S. *Sublime Disorder: Physical Monstrosity in Diderot's Universe.* Oxford: Studies on Voltaire and the Eighteenth Century, 2001.

———. *The Anatomy of Blackness: Science and Slavery in an Age of Enlightenment.* Baltimore: Johns Hopkins University Press, 2011.

Damrosch, Leopold. *Jean-Jacques Rousseau: Restless Genius.* Boston: Houghton Mifflin, 2007.

Darnton, Robert. *The Business of Enlightenment: A Publishing History of the* Encyclopédie, *1775–1800.* Cambridge, MA: Harvard University Press, 1779.

———. *The Great Cat Massacre and Other Episodes in French Cultural History.* New York: Basic Books, 1984.

——. *Poetry and the Police: Communication Networks in Eighteenth-Century Paris.* Cambridge, MA: Belknap Press, 2010.

Delon, Michel. *Diderot cul par-dessus tête.* Paris: Albin Michel, 2013.

*Le Dernier Diderot: autour de l'*Essai sur les règnes de Claude et de Néron. Edited by Thierry Belleguic. *Diderot Studies*, no. 32 (2012). Geneva: Droz.

Descartes, René. *The Philosophical Writings of Descartes.* Vol. 2. Translated by John Cottingham, Robert Stoothoff, and Dugald Murdoch. New York: Cambridge University Press, 2008.

Diderot, Denis. *Essai sur la vie de Sénèque le philosophe, sur ses écrits et sur les règnes de Claude et de Néron.* 2 vols. La Haye, France: Detune, 1779.

——. *Œuvres complètes de Diderot.* 20 vols. Edited by Jules Assézat. Paris: Garnier Frères, 1875–77.

——. *Sur les femmes.* Paris: L. Pichon, 1919.

——. *Correspondance.* Edited by Georges Roth and Jean Varloot. Paris: Éditions de Minuit, 1955.

——. "Introduction" [to *Pages contre un tyran*], *Œuvres politiques.* Paris: Garnier, 1963.

——. *Mémoires pour Catherine II.* Paris: Garnier, 1966.

——. *Rameau's Nephew and D'Alembert's Dream.* Translated by Leonard Tancock. London: Penguin, 1966.

——. *Œuvres complètes.* 15 vols. Edited by Roger Lewinter. Paris: Le Club français du livre, 1969–73.

——. *Œuvres complètes.* 34 vols. expected. Edited by Herbert Dieckmann, Jean Varloot, Jacques Proust, and Jean Fabre. Paris: Hermann, 1975–.

——. *Essais sur la peinture: Salons de 1759, 1761, 1763.* Edited by Jacques Chouillet and Gita May. Paris: Hermann, 1984.

——. *Voyage à Bourbonne, à Langres et autres récits.* Paris: Aux Amateurs de Livres, 1989.

——. *Political Writings.* Edited by John Hope Mason and Robert Wokler. Cambridge, UK: Cambridge University Press, 1992.

———. *Diderot on Art I*. Translated by John Goodman, introduced by Thomas E. Crow. New Haven: Yale University Press, 1995.

———. *Diderot on Art II*. Translated by John Goodman, introduced by Thomas E. Crow. New Haven: Yale University Press, 1995.

———. *Jacques the Fatalist and His Master*. Edited by David Coward. Oxford: Oxford University Press, 1999.

———. *Rameau's Nephew and Other Works*. Edited by Ralph Henry Bowen, translated by Jacques Barzun. Indianapolis: Hackett, 2001.

———. *The Nun*. Translated by Russell Goulbourne. Oxford: Oxford University Press, 2005.

———. *Diderot, Rameau's Nephew and First Satire*. Translated by Margaret Mauldon. New York: Oxford University Press, 2006.

———. *Œuvres philosophiques*. Edited by Michel Delon with Barbara De Negroni. Paris: Gallimard, 2010.

———. *Pensées détachées sur la peinture, la sculpture, l'architecture et la poésie pour servir de suite aux Salons*. Chalon-sur-Saône: Éditions Ligaran, 2015.

———. *De la poésie dramatique: réponse à la lettre de Mme Riccoboni*. Chalon-sur-Saône: Éditions Ligaran, 2015.

———. *Rameau's Nephew. Le neveu de Rameau: A Multi-Media Bilingual Edition*. Edited by Marian Hobson, Kate E. Tunstall, and Caroline Warman. Cambridge, UK: Open Book, 2016.

Diderot, Denis, and Jean le Rond d'Alembert. *Encyclopédie, ou Dictionnaire raisonné des sciences, des arts et des métiers*. 17 vols. of text, 11 vols. of illustrations. Paris: Briasson, David l'aîné, Le Breton, Durand, 1751–72.

Didier, Béatrice. "Quand Diderot faisait le plan d'une université." *Recherches sur Diderot et sur l'Encyclopédie*. no. 18 (1995): 81–91. Paris: Aux Amateurs de Livres.

Dieckman, Herbert. *Inventaire du fonds Vandeul et inédits de Diderot*. Geneva: Droz, 1951.

———. "An Unpublished Notice of Diderot on Falconet." *Journal of the Warburg and Courtauld Institutes*, no. 15 (1952): 257–58. London: Warburg Institute.

Doyle, William. *Jansenism: Catholic Resistance to Authority from the Reformation to the French Revolution*. New York: Saint Martin's, 2000.

Duchet, Michèle. *Diderot et l'Histoire des deux Indes*. Paris: Éditions A.G. Nizet, 1978.

Duflo, Colas. "Et pourquoi des dialogues en des temps de systèmes?" *Diderot Studies*, no. 28 (2000): 95–109. Geneva: Droz.

——. *Les aventures de Sophie: la philosophie dans le roman au XVIIIème siècle*. Paris: CNRS Éditions, 2013.

——. *Diderot philosophe*. Paris: Champion, 2013.

Encyclopedia of the Enlightenment. Edited by Michel Delon. Chicago: Fitzroy Dearborn, 2001.

The Enlightenment: Cambridge Readings in the History of Political Thought. Edited by David Williams. Cambridge, UK: Cambridge University Press, 1999.

Epinay, Louise Tardieu d'Esclavelles, marquise d'. *Mémoires et correspondance de Madame d'Épinay, où elle donne des détails sur ses liaisons avec Duclos, J.-J. Rousseau, Grimm, Diderot, le baron d'Holbach, Saint-Lambert, Mme d'Houdetot, et autres personnages célèbres du dix-huitième siècle*. Paris: Volland le jeune, 1818.

Erwin, Edward. *The Freud Encyclopedia: Theory, Therapy, and Culture*. New York: Routledge, 2002.

Falkenstein, Lorne, and Giovanni Grandi. "Étienne Bonnot de Condillac." In *The Stanford Encyclopedia of Philosophy*, ed. Edward N. Zalta. Stanford: Metaphysics Research Lab, Stanford University, 2017.

Fontenay, Élisabeth de. *Diderot ou le matérialisme enchanté*. Paris: Grasset et Fasquelle, 1981.

Formey, Jean-Henri-Samuel. *Pensées raisonnables opposées aux "Pensées philosophiques"; avec un essai de critique sur le livre intitulé "Les Mœurs"* [de François-Vincent Toussaint]. Berlin: Chretien Frederic Voss, 1769.

Fossa, François de. *Le Château historique de Vincennes à travers les âges*. 2 vols. Paris: H. Daragon, 1908.

Fowler, James. *New Essays on Diderot.* Cambridge, UK: Cambridge University Press, 2011.

François, L. *Lettres à M. Bizot de Fonteny à propos de l'érection de la statue de Diderot.* Langres, France: Rallet-Bideau, 1884.

Franklin, Benjamin. *The Papers of Benjamin Franklin.* New Haven: Yale University Press, 2011.

Frantz, Pierre, and Élisabeth Lavezzi. *Les Salons de Diderot: théorie et écriture.* Paris: Presses de l'Université de Paris-Sorbonne, 2008.

Freud, Sigmund. *Civilization and Its Discontents.* Edited by Todd Dufresne, translated by Gregory C. Richter. Peterborough, Ontario: Broadview Press, 2016.

Fried, Michael. *Absorption and Theatricality: Painting and Beholder in the Age of Diderot.* Berkeley: University of California Press, 1980.

Fuchs, Rachel Ginnis. "Crimes against Children in Nineteenth-Century France: Child Abuse." *Law and Human Behavior* (American Psychological Association) 6, nos. 3–4 (1982): 237–59.

Furbank, Philip Nicholas. *Diderot: A Critical Biography.* New York: Knopf, 1992.

Gay, Peter. *Deism: An Anthology.* Princeton: Van Nostrand, 1969.

Geffriaud Rosso, Jeannette. *Diderot et le portrait.* Pisa, Italy: Libreria Goliardica, 1998.

Giffart, Pierre-François, and Raphaël Trichet du Fresne. *Traité de la peinture, par Léonard de Vinci.* Paris: Pierre-François Giffart, 1716.

Goethe, Johann Wolfgang von. *The Autobiography of Goethe: Truth and Poetry: From My Own Life.* Translated by John Oxenford. London: G. Bell, 1894.

Goggi, Gianluigi. "Quelques remarques sur la collaboration de Diderot à la première édition de l'*Histoire des deux Indes.*" *Studies on Voltaire and the Eighteenth Century,* no. 286 (1991): 17–52. Oxford: Voltaire Foundation.

Gorbatov, Inna. *Catherine the Great and the French Philosophers of the Enlightenment: Montesquieu, Voltaire, Rousseau, Diderot, and Grimm.* Bethesda, MD: Academic Press, 2006.

———. "Le voyage de Diderot en Russie." *Études littéraires* 38, nos. 2–3 (2007): 215–29.

Gordon, Alden. *The Houses and Collections of the Marquis de Marigny.* In *Documents for the History of Collecting: French Inventories*, vol, 1. Los Angeles: Getty, 2003.

Gordon, Douglas H., and Norman L. Torrey. *The Censoring of Diderot's Encyclopédie and the Re-established Text.* New York: Columbia University Press, 1947.

Graille, Patrick. "Portrait scientifique et littéraire de l'hybride au siècle des Lumières." In Andrew Curran, Robert P. Maccubbin, and David F. Morill, eds., *Faces of Monstrosity in Eighteenth-Century Thought.* Special issue of *Eighteenth-Century Life*, no. 21 (May 1997): 70–88. Baltimore: Johns Hopkins University Press.

Greenblatt, Stephen. *The Swerve: How the World Became Modern.* New York: Norton, 2011.

Grimm, Friedrich-Melchior, Denis Diderot, Jacques-Henri Meister, and Guillaume-Thomas Raynal. *Correspondance littéraire, philosophique et critique par Grimm, Diderot, Raynal, Meister, etc.* 16 vols. Paris: Garnier Frères, 1877–82.

Grosclaude, Pierre. *L'Encyclopédie: un audacieux message.* Paris: Nouvelles Éditions Latines, 1951.

Haechler, Jean. *L'Encyclopédie: les combats et les hommes.* Paris: Belles Lettres, 1998.

Hanna, Blake T. "Diderot théologien." *Revue d'histoire littéraire de la France*, no. 78 (January–February 1978): 19–35. Paris: Armand Colin.

———. "Denis Diderot: formation traditionnelle et moderne." *Recherches sur Diderot et sur l'Encyclopédie*, no. 5 (1988): 3–18. Paris: Aux Amateurs de Livres.

Hartman, Lydia Claude. "Esquisse d'un portrait de Sophie Volland: quelques notes sur la vie privée, les amitiés du philosophe." *Diderot Studies*, no. 16 (1973): 69–89. Geneva: Droz.

Hatt, Michael, and Charlotte Klonk. *Art History: A Critical Introduction to Its Methods.* Manchester: Manchester University Press, 2006.

Hazan, Éric. *The Invention of Paris: A History in Footsteps.* Translated by David Fernbach. London: Verso, 2010.

Helvétius, Claude-Adrien. *Œuvres complètes d'Helvétius.* Vol. 1. Edited by Gerhardt Stenger and Jonas Steffen. Paris: Honoré Champion, 2016.

Hesseln, Mathias Robert de. *Dictionnaire universel de la France.* 6 vols. Paris: Dessaint, 1771.

Hitchens, Christopher. *The Portable Atheist: Essential Readings for the Nonbeliever.* Philadelphia: Da Capo, 2007.

Hobbes, Thomas. *Leviathan.* Edited by C. B. Macpherson. London: Penguin Classics, 1985.

Hoquet, Thierry. *Buffon-Linné: éternels rivaux de la biologie.* Paris: Dunod, 2007.

Hours, Bernard. *La vertu et le secret. Le dauphin, fils de Louis XV.* Paris: Champion, 2006.

Huntington, Samuel P. *The Soldier and the State: The Theory and Politics of Civil-Military Relations.* Cambridge, MA: Belknap Press, 1985.

Hytier, Adrienne. "Le Philosophe et le despote: histoire d'une inimitié, Diderot et Frédéric II." *Diderot Studies* 6 (1964): 55–87. Geneva: Droz.

Imbruglia, Girolamo. "Civilisation and Colonisation: Enlightenment Theories in the Debate between Diderot and Raynal." *History of European Ideas* 41, no. 7 (2015): 858–82.

Israel, Jonathan Irvine. *Radical Enlightenment: Philosophy and the Making of Modernity 1650–1750.* Oxford: Oxford University Press, 2001.

——. *Enlightenment Contested: Philosophy, Modernity, and the Emancipation of Man, 1670–1752.* Oxford: Oxford University Press, 2006.

——. *The Expanding Blaze: How the American Revolution Ignited the World, 1775–1848.* Princeton: Princeton University Press, 2017.

Jensen, William B. "Newton and Lucretius: Some Overlooked Parallels." In David B. Suits and Timothy J. Madigan, eds. *Lucretius: His Continuing Influence and Contemporary Relevance,* 13–27. Rochester: RIT Press, 2011.

Joy, Lynn S. "Interpreting Nature: Gassendi Versus Diderot on the Unity of Knowledge." In Donald R. Kelley and Richard H. Popkin, eds. *The Shapes of Knowledge from the Renaissance to the Enlightenment*, 123–34. Dordrecht: Kluwer, 1991.

Kafker, Frank A. "Gua de Malves and the *Encyclopédie*." *Diderot Studies*, no. 19 (1978): 93–102. Geneva: Droz.

——, and Jeff Loveland. "Diderot et Laurent Durand, son éditeur principal." In *Recherches sur Diderot et sur l'Encyclopédie*, 29–40. Paris: Aux Amateurs de Livres, 2005.

Kahng, Eik. "L'Affaire Greuze and the Sublime of History Painting." *Art Bulletin*, no. 86, issue 1 (March 2004): 96–113.

Kelly, Theresa M. *Reinventing Allegory*. Cambridge, UK: Cambridge University Press, 1997.

Kors, Alan Charles. *D'Holbach's Coterie. An Enlightenment in Paris*. Princeton: Princeton University Press, 1976.

Kozul, Mladen. *Les Lumières imaginaires: Holbach et la traduction*. Oxford: Oxford University Studies in the Enlightenment, 2016.

Kuritz, Paul. *The Making of Theatre History*. Upper Saddle River, NJ: Prentice Hall, 1988.

Laborde, Alice M. *Diderot et Madame de Puisieux*. Saratoga, CA: Anma libri, 1984.

Lacouture, Jean. *Jésuites: une multibiographie*. Vol. 1. Paris: Seuil, 1995.

Lafarga, Francisco. *Diderot*. Barcelona: Publicacions Edicions Universitat de Barcelona, 1987.

Laffitte, Pierre. *Célébration du centenaire de Diderot au Palais du Trocadéro le dimanche 27 juillet 1884. Discours de M. Pierre Laffitte*. Paris: au dépôt de la *Revue occidentale*, 1884.

Laissus, Yves. "Une lettre inédite de d'Alembert." *Revue d'histoire des sciences et de leurs applications*, no. 7 (1954): 1–5. Paris: Presses universitaires de France.

Lancaster, Henry Carrington. *The Comédie Française, 1701–1774: Plays, Actors, Spectators, Finances*. Philadelphia: American Philosophical Society, 1951.

La Rochefoucauld-Liancourt, Frédéric Gaëtan de. *Esprit des écrivains du 18ème siècle*. Paris: Giguet et Michaud, 1809.

Latude, Jean Henri. *Mémoires de Henri Masers de Latude, prisonnier pendant trente-cinq ans à la Bastille, à Vincennes, à Charenton et à Bicêtre*. Gand: Dullé, 1841.

Le Breton, André-François. "Brevet exclusif qui permet aux sieurs Guerin, Testard, et autres artificiers, de faire et exécuter, pendant 12 ans, un feu d'artifice sur la rivière de Seine, la veille de la fête de S. Louis, du dix-neuf mai 1741." Paris: Le Breton, 1741.

Leca-Tsiomis, Marie. *Écrire l'Encyclopédie: Diderot: de l'usage des dictionnaires à la grammaire philosophique*. Oxford: Voltaire Foundation, 1999.

——. *Diderot, choix d'articles de l'Encyclopédie*. Paris: Éditions du CTHS, 2001.

Lecourt, Dominique. *Diderot: passions, sexe, raison*. Paris: Presses Universitaires de France, 2013.

Lectures de Raynal: l'"Histoire des deux Indes" en Europe et en Amérique au XVIIIe siècle. Edited by Hans-Jürgen Lüsebrink and Manfred Tietz. *Studies on Voltaire and the Eighteenth Century*, no. 286 (1991). Oxford: Voltaire Foundation.

Leibniz, Gottfried Wilhelm. *Theodicy: Essays on the Goodness of God, the Freedom of Man, and the Origin of Evil*. Edited by Austin Farrer, translated by E. M. Huggard. New Haven: Yale University Press, 1952.

Lever, Évelyne. *Madame de Pompadour*. Paris: Éditions académiques Perrin, 2000.

Lever, Maurice. *Les Bûchers de Sodome*. Paris: Fayard, 1985.

Lichtenstein, Jacqueline. *The Blind Spot: An Essay on the Relations between Painting and Sculpture in the Modern Age*. Translated by Chris Miller. Los Angeles: Getty Research Institute, 2008.

Lilti, Antoine. *The World of the Salons: Sociability and Worldliness in Eighteenth-Century France*. Translated by Lydia G. Cochrane. New York: Oxford University Press, 2005.

Locke, John. *The Second Treatise of Government*. Edited by C. B. Macpherson. Indianapolis: Hackett, 1980.

———. *Two Treatises of Government.* Edited by Peter Laslett. Cambridge, UK: Cambridge University Press, 1988.

Lom, Petr. *The Limits of Doubt: The Moral and Political Implications of Skepticism.* Albany: State University Press, 2001.

Lovejoy, Arthur O. *The Great Chain of Being: A Study of the History of an Idea.* New Brunswick, NJ: Transaction, 2009.

Magnan, André. *Rameau le neveu. Textes et documents.* Paris: CNRS, and Saint-Étienne: Éditions de l'Université de Saint-Étienne, 1993.

Manneville, Charles. *Une vieille église de Paris: Saint-Médard.* Paris: Champion, 1906.

Marmontel, Jean-François. *Memoirs of Marmontel.* 2 vols. Paris: Société des bibliophiles, Merrill & Baker, 1903.

Marx, Karl. "Confessions." Translated by Andy Blunden. *International Review of Social History* 1 (1956). Cambridge, UK: Cambridge University Press.

Mason, John Hope. *The Irresistible Diderot.* London: Quartet Books, 1982.

Massie, Robert K. *Catherine the Great: Portrait of a Woman.* New York: Random House, 2012.

Matérialistes français du XVIIIe siècle: La Mettrie, Helvétius, d'Holbach. Edited by Sophie Audidière, Jean Claude Bourdin, Jean-Marie Lardic, Francine Markovits, and Charles Zarka. Paris: Presses universitaires de France, 2006.

Matter, Jacques. *Lettres et pièces rares ou inédites publiées et accompagnées d'introductions et de notes.* Paris: Librairie D'Amyot, 1846.

McCracken, Grant David. *Culture and Consumption: New Approaches to the Symbolic Character of Consumer Goods and Activities.* Bloomington: Indiana University Press, 1988.

McManners, John. *Church and Society in Eighteenth-Century France.* Vol. 2: *The Religion of the People and the Politics of Religion.* Oxford: Oxford University Press, 1999.

Medicine and Religion in Enlightenment Europe. Edited by Ole Peter Grell and Andrew Cunningham. Hampshire, UK: Ashgate, 2007.

Meister, Jacques-Henri. "Aux Mânes de Diderot." In Jules Assézat and Maurice Tourneux, eds., *Œuvres complètes de Diderot*, xii–xix. Paris: Garnier Frères, 1875.

Mémoires pour l'histoire des sciences et des beaux-arts. Vol. 177. Paris: Jean Boudot, 1745.

Mercier, Louis Sébastien. *Tableau de Paris.* Vol. 4. Amsterdam, 1782.

——. *Tableau de Paris.* 2 vols. Edited by Jean-Claude Bonnet. Paris: Mercure de France, 1994.

Mercure de France, dédié au Roi. Paris: Cailleau, October 1749.

Meslier, Jean. *Testament: Memoir of the Thoughts and Sentiments of Jean Meslier.* Edited by Mike Shreve. Amherst, NY: Prometheus Books, 2009.

Millard, John, and Philip Playstowe. *The Gentleman's Guide in His Tour through France.* London: G. Kearsly, 1770.

Montgeron, Louis-Basile Carré de. *La vérité des miracles opérés à l'intercession de M. de Pâris.* 1737.

Moore, W. G. "Lucretius and Montaigne." *Yale French Studies*, no. 38 (1967): 109–14. New Haven: Yale University Press.

Moreau, Jacob-Nicolas. *Nouveau mémoire pour servir à l'histoire des Cacouacs.* Amsterdam, 1757.

Morère, Pierre. "Signes et langage chez Locke et Condillac." *Bulletin de la société d'études anglo-américaines des XVIIe et XVIIIe siècles*, no. 23 (1986): 16–29. Reims: Presses Universitaires de Reims.

"Mort de M. Diderot." *Année littéraire* 6 (1784): 282. Paris: Mérigot le jeune.

Mortier, Roland. "Didier Diderot lecteur de Denis: ses *Réflexions sur l'Essai sur le mérite et la vertu.*" *Recherches sur Diderot et sur l'Encyclopédie*, no. 10 (1991): 21–39. Paris: Aux Amateurs de Livres.

Moureau, François. *La plume et le plomb: espaces de l'imprimé et du manuscrit au siècle des Lumières.* Paris: PUPS, 2006.

Mücke, Dorthea E. von. *The Practices of the Enlightenment: Aesthetics, Authorship, and the Public.* New York: Columbia University Press, 2015.

Naigeon, Jacques-André. *Mémoires historiques et philosophiques sur la vie et les ouvrages de D. Diderot.* Paris: J. L. J. Brière, 1886.

Newton, Isaac. *Sir Isaac Newton's Mathematical Principles of Natural Philosophy and His System of the World.* Edited by Florian Cajori. Berkeley: University of California Press, 1934.

———. *Philosophical Writings.* Edited by Andrew Janiak. Cambridge Texts in the History of Philosophy. Cambridge: Cambridge University Press, 2004.

Nietzsche, Friedrich Wilhelm, *On the Genealogy of Morals: Ecce Homo.* Edited by Walter Kaufmann and R. J. Hollingdale. New York: Vintage, 1989.

Niklaus, Robert. "Les *Pensées philosophiques* de Diderot et les *Pensées* de Pascal." *Diderot Studies,* no. 20 (1981): 201–17. Geneva: Droz.

Nouvelles de la République des lettres et des arts. Vol. 11. Paris: Ruault, March 1782.

Numbers, Ronald L. *The Creationists: From Scientific Creationism to Intelligent Design.* Cambridge, MA: Harvard University Press, 2006.

O'Malley, John W., ed. *The Jesuits II: Cultures, Sciences, and the Arts, 1540–1773.* Toronto: University of Toronto Press, 2006.

O'Neal, John C. *Changing Minds: The Shifting Perception of Culture in Eighteenth-Century France.* Newark: University of Delaware Press, 2002.

Opuscules divers, contenants un recueil de quelques lettres très instructives pour la conduite des curés et des jeunes ecclésiastiques; avec un faux raisonnement des gens du monde sur leur conduite, détruit par les principes du bon sens et de la religion. Langres, France: Claude Personne, 1719.

Palissot de Montenoy, Charles. *Les philosophes, comédie en trois actes, en vers.* Paris: Duchesne, 1760.

Panckoucke, André Joseph. *L'Art de désoppiler* [sic] *la rate, Sive de modo C. prudenter: en prenant chaque Feuillet pour se T. Le D. Entremêlé de quelques bonnes choses.* Gallipoli, 175886 [Paris, 1758].

Parlement de Paris. *Recueil de pièces concernant la thèse de M. l'abbé de Prades, soutenue en Sorbonne le 18 Novembre 1751, censurée par la Faculté de Théologie le 27 janvier 1752, & par M. l'Archevêque de Paris le 29 du même mois, divisée en trois parties.* 1753.

———. *Arrests de la Cour de Parlement, portant condamnation de plusieurs livres & autres ouvrages imprimés.* 1759.

Pascal, Blaise. *Pascal's Pensées.* Introduction by T. S. Eliot. New York: Dutton, 1958.

Pearson, Roger. *Voltaire Almighty.* New York: Bloomsbury, 2005.

Pellerin, Pascal. "Diderot, Voltaire et le curé Meslier: un sujet tabou." *Diderot Studies,* no. 29 (2003): 53–63. Geneva: Droz.

Pernety, Dom Antoine-Joseph. *Dictionnaire portatif de peinture, sculpture et gravure; avec un Traité pratique des différentes manières de peindre, dont la théorie est développée dans les articles qui en sont susceptibles.* Paris: Bauche, 1757.

Picart, Bernard, and Jean Frédéric Bernard. *Cérémonies et coutumes religieuses de tous les peuples du monde.* Vol. 1. Amsterdam: Bernard, 1723.

Pinault, Madeleine. "Diderot et les illustrateurs de l'*Encyclopédie.*" *Revue de l'art,* no. 66 (1984): 17–38. Paris: Éditions du CNRS.

———. "Sur les planches de l'*Encyclopédie* de Diderot et d'Alembert." *L'Encyclopédisme.* Actes du colloque de Caen. 12–16 janvier 1987, Paris: Klincksieck, 1991: 355–62.

Pitman, Joanna. *The Dragon's Trail: The Biography of Raphael's Masterpiece.* New York: Touchstone, 2007.

Platon. *Apologie de Socrate, Criton, Phédon.* Translated by Léon Robin and Joseph Moreau. Paris: Gallimard, 1968.

Proust, Jacques. "L'initiation artistique de Diderot." *Gazette des beaux-arts,* no. 55 (April 1960): 225–32. Paris: Presses Universitaires de France.

———. *Diderot et l'Encyclopédie.* Paris: Albin Michel, 1962.

Rétat, Pierre. *L'Attentat de Damiens: discours sur l'événement au XVIIIe siècle.* Lyon: Éditions du C.N.R.S/Presses universitaires de Lyon, Centre d'études du XVIIIe siècle, Université Lyon II, 1979.

Rey, Auguste. *Le Château de la Chevrette et Madame d'Épinay*. Paris: Plon, 1904.

Roberts, Meghan K. *Sentimental Savants: Philosophical Families in Enlightenment France*. Chicago: University of Chicago Press, 2016.

Roche, Daniel. "Encyclopedias and the Diffusion of Knowledge." In *Cambridge History of Eighteenth-Century Political Thought*, 172–94, ed. Mark Goldie and Robert Wolker. New York: Cambridge University Press, 2006.

Rousseau, Jean-Jacques. *Discourse on the Origin of Inequality*. Indianapolis: Hackett, 1992.

——. *Confessions*. Translated by Angela Scholar. Oxford: Oxford University Press, 2000.

——. *Œuvres complètes*. Vol. 1. Edited by Bernard Gagnebin, Marcel Raymond, and Robert Osmont. Paris: Gallimard, 2001.

——. *The Confessions of Jean-Jacques Rousseau*. Edited by J. M. Cohen. London: Penguin, 2007.

Roussel, Charles François. *Le Diocèse de Langres: histoire et statistique*. Vol. 4. Langres, France: Librairie de Jules Dalet, 1879.

Russo, Elena. "Slander and Glory in the Republic of Letters: Diderot and Seneca Confront Rousseau." *Republics of Letters. A Journal for the Study of Knowledge, Politics, and the Arts*, no. 1 (May 2009), http://rofl.stanford.edu/node/40. Stanford: Stanford University Press.

Saint-Amand, Pierre. *The Libertine's Progress: Seduction in the Eighteenth-Century French Novel*. Translated by Jennifer Curtiss Gage. Hanover, NH: University Press of New England, 1994.

Schiller, Friedrich, and Johann Wolfgang von Goethe. *Correspondence between Schiller and Goethe from 1794 to 1805*. 2 vols. Edited by L. Dora Schmitz. London: G. Bell, 1877.

Ségur, Louis-Philippe, comte de. *Mémoires ou Souvenirs et anecdotes*. Paris: Henri Colburn, 1827.

Sejten, Anne Elisabeth. *Diderot ou Le défi esthétique. Les écrits de jeunesse, 1746–1751*. Paris: Jean Vrin, coll. "Essais d'art et de philosophie," 1999.

Shank, John Bennett. *The Newton Wars and the Beginning of the French Enlighten-ment.* Chicago: University of Chicago Press, 2008.

Sheriff, Mary D. *Moved by Love: Inspired Artists and Deviant Women in Eighteenth-Century France.* Chicago: University of Chicago Press, 2004.

Sherman, Carol. *Diderot and the Art of Dialogue.* Geneva: Droz, 1976.

Showalter, English. "'Madame a fait un livre': Madame de Graffigny, Palis-sot et *Les Philosophes.*" *Recherches sur Diderot et sur l'Encyclopédie,* no. 23 (1997): 109–25. Paris: Aux Amateurs de Livres,

Smith, David Warner. *Helvetius: A Study in Persecution.* Oxford: Clarendon Press, 1965.

Spink, John Stephenson. "The Abbé de Prades and the Encyclopaedists: Was There a Plot?" *French Studies* 24, no. 3 (July 1970): 225–36. New Haven: Yale University Press.

Stallings, Alicia Elsbeth. "So Potent was Religion in Persuading to do Wrong." In *The Nature of Things,* 6–15, trans. A. E. Stallings. London, 2007.

Stalnaker, Joanna. "Diderot's Literary Testament." *Diderot Studies,* no. 31 (2009): 45–56. Geneva: Droz.

———.*The Unfinished Enlightenment: Description in the Age of the Encyclopedia.* Ithaca: Cornell University Press, 2010.

Stenger, Gerhardt. *L'affaire des Cacouacs: trois pamphlets contre les philo-sophes des Lumières.* Saint-Étienne, France: Éditions de l'Université de Saint-Étienne, coll. "Lire le dix-huitième siècle," 2004.

———. *Diderot: le combattant de la liberté.* Paris: Perrin, 2013.

Strayer, Brian Eugene. *Suffering Saints: Jansenists and Convulsionnaires in France, 1640–1799.* Brighton: Sussex Academic Press, 2012.

Strugnell, Anthony. *Diderot's Politics: A Study of the Evolution of Diderot's Polit-ical Thought After the Encyclopédie.* International Archives of the History of Ideas. Vol. 62. Netherlands: Springer, 1973.

———. "La candidature de Diderot à la Société Royale de Londres." *Recherches sur Diderot et sur l'Encyclopédie,* no. 4 (1988): 37–41. Paris: Aux Amateurs de Livres.

Taine, Hippolyte. *Les Origines de la France contemporaine.* Paris: Librairie Hachette, 1885.

Tarin, René. *Diderot et la Révolution française.* Paris: Champion, 2001.

Thelliez, Berthe. *L'Homme qui poignarda Louis XV: Robert-François Damien, 1715–1757.* Paris: Tallandier, 2002.

Tindal, Matthew. *Christianity as Old as the Creation.* Vol. 1. Stuttgart-Bad Cannstatt: Frommann-Holzboog, 1967.

Tronchin, Henry. *Le conseiller François Tronchin et ses amis Voltaire, Grimm, Diderot, etc.* Paris: Plon, 1895.

Trousson, Raymond. *Denis Diderot,* textes réunis et présentés par Raymond Trousson. Paris: Presses de l'Université de Paris-Sorbonne, coll. "Mémoire de la critique," 2005.

——. *Denis Diderot ou Le vrai Prométhée.* Paris: Tallandier, 2005.

Tunstall, Kate E. "Paradoxe sur le portrait: autoportrait de Diderot en Montaigne." *Diderot Studies,* no. 30 (2007): 195–207. Geneva: Droz.

——. *Blindness and Enlightenment: An Essay.* New York: Continuum, 2011.

Turgot, Anne-Robert-Jacques. *Œuvres de Turgot et documents le concernant, avec biographie et notes.* Paris: F. Alcan, 1913.

Turnell, Martin. *The Rise of the French Novel: Marivaux, Crébillon fils, Rousseau, Stendhal, Flaubert, Alain-Fournier, Raymond Radiguet.* London: H. Hamilton, 1979.

Valet, Paul. *Le Diacre Paris et les convulsionnaires de St. Médard. Le jansénisme et Port-Royal. Le masque de Pascal.* Paris: Champion, 1900.

Vandeul, Marie-Angélique de. *Diderot, mon père.* Strasbourg: Circé, 1992.

Van Kley, Dale K. *The Damiens Affair and the Unraveling of the Ancien Regime, 1750–1770.* Princeton: Princeton University Press, 1984.

——. *The Religious Origins of the French Revolution: From Calvin to the Civil Constitution, 1560–1791.* New Haven: Yale University Press, 1996.

Vartanian, Aram. *Diderot and Descartes: A Study of Scientific Naturalism in the Enlightenment.* Princeton: Princeton University Press, 1953.

Versini, Laurent. "Diderot piéton de Paris." *Travaux de littérature,* no. 13 (2000): 177–94. Geneva: Droz.

———. "Note sur le voyage de Diderot en Russie." In Jean-Pierre Poussou, Anne Mézin, and Yves Perret-Gentil, eds. *L'Influence française en Russie au XVIIIème siècle*, 223–34. Paris: Presses de l'Université de Paris-Sorbonne, collection historique de l'Institut d'études slaves, 2004.

Viard, Georges. *Langres au XVIIIe siècle: tradition et lumières au pays de Diderot*. Langres, France: Dominique Guéniot, 1985.

Voltaire. *Œuvres complètes de Voltaire*. 52 vols. Edited by Louis Moland. Paris: Garnier, 1877–85.

———. *The Complete Works of Voltaire. Les Œuvres Complètes de Voltaire*. Oxford: Voltaire Foundation, 1996.

———. *Letters on England*. Translated by Leonard Tancock. New York: Penguin, 2005.

Weil, Françoise. "L'impression des tomes VIII à XVII de l'*Encyclopédie*." *Recherches sur Diderot et sur l'Encyclopédie*, no. 1 (1986): 85–93. Paris: Aux Amateurs de Livres.

Werner, Stephen. *Blueprint: A Study of Diderot and the Encyclopédie Plates*. Birmingham, AL: Summa, 1993.

Wiles, Mary M. *Jacques Rivette*. Urbana: University of Illinois Press, 2012.

Wilson, Arthur McCandless. *Diderot*. New York: Oxford University Press, 1957.

Wolfe, Charles. *Materialism: A Historico-Philosophical Introduction*. Ghent: Springer, 2016.

Yeo, Richard R. "A Solution to the Multitude of Books: Ephraim Chambers's *Cyclopaedia* (1728) as 'the Best Book in the Universe.'" *Journal of the History of Ideas*, no. 64 (2003): 61–72. Philadelphia: University of Pennsylvania Press.

———. *Encyclopaedic Visions: Scientific Dictionaries and Enlightenment Culture*. Cambridge, UK: Cambridge University Press, 2010.

Illustrations

Index